The CPM Silver Yearbook 2010

CPM Group

MetalBulletin

Copyright © 2010 by CPM Group. All rights reserved.

Published by Euromoney Books.

No part of this publication may be reproduced, stored in a retrieval system, or transmitted in any form or by any means, electronic, mechanical, photocopying, recording, scanning, or otherwise, except as permitted under Section 107 or 108 of the 1976 United States Copyright Act, without the prior written permission of CPM Group. Requests to CPM Group for permission should be addressed to Adam J. Crown, CPM Group, 30 Broad Street 37th Floor, New York, NY 10004, (212) 785-8320, fax (212) 785-8315, or email info@cpmgroup.com.

Limit of Liability/Disclaimer of Warranty: While the publisher and author have used their best efforts in preparing this book, they make no representations or warranties with respect to the accuracy or completeness of the contents of this book and specifically disclaim any implied warranties of merchantability or fitness for a particular purpose. No warranty may be created or extended by sales representatives or written sales materials. The advice and strategies contained herein may not be suitable for your situation. You should consult with a professional where appropriate. Neither the publisher nor author shall be liable for any loss of profit or any other commercial damages, including but not limited to special, incidental, consequential, or other damages.

For general information on our other products and services or for technical support, please contact Adam J. Crown or visit our website at www.cpmgroup.com.

Printed in the United States of America.

ISBN-978-0-9826741-1-6

CPM Group's Silver Yearbook 2010
May 2010
Volume 24, Number 1

CPM Group
30 Broad Street
37th Floor
New York, NY 10004
USA

Telephone: 212-785-8320
Telefax: 212-785-8325
E-mail: info@cpmgroup.com
Website: www.cpmgroup.com

Jeffrey M. Christian, Managing Director
Adam J. Crown, Executive Vice President
Doug Sherrod, Managing Director, Investment Banking
Alec Kushnir, Director, Investment Banking
Mark Hansen, Director of Price Risk Management
Jenee Peele, Administrator

Carlos Sanchez, Associate Director, Research
Catherine Virga, Senior Research Analyst
Rohit Savant, Senior Research Analyst
Chintan Parikh, Research Analyst
Doug Horn, Research Analyst
Madhusudan Daga, Consultant
Bhargava Vaidya, Consultant

CPM Group   **Silver Yearbook 2010**

CPM Group provides a range of research and consulting services related to precious metals and commodities. These range from research studies on individual markets and market segments to materials management services. In addition to publishing precious metals and commodities research, CPM Group produces special reports. CPM Group produces special reports on topics which have piqued investor interests, such as molybdenum, uranium, vanadium, chromium, cobalt, and other specialty metals.

The core of CPM Group's product is its consulting services. These include specific projects related to the special needs of individual producers, refiners, fabricators, institutional investors, financial institutions, governments, central banks, and others. CPM Group provides advisory services related to hedging production and raw materials requirements, and manages positions for producers, consumers, and accredited investors. CPM Group's financial engineering includes impartial advice, structuring, placements, and management of hedging and investment positions.

CPM Group provides investment banking advisory programs for commodities-oriented corporations, and metals, materials and asset management services for producers, consumers and institutional investors.

Annual Research Reports
 The CPM Gold Yearbook
 The CPM Silver Yearbook
 The CPM Platinum Group Metals Yearbook
 The CPM Gold Long-Term Outlook: Ten Year Projections
 The CPM Silver Long-Term Outlook: Ten Year Projections
 The CPM Platinum Group Metals Long-Term Outlook: Ten Year Projections

Monthly Research Reports
 Precious Metals Advisory
 Base Metals Advisory

Weekly Research Report
 CPM Commodities Views

Specialized Reports
 The Molybdenum Market Outlook
 The Vanadium Industry Outlook
 The Chromium Market Outlook

Visit www.cpmgroup.com for additional information.

Preface

Last year was the fourth consecutive year in which strong investment demand for physical silver had a dramatic impact on silver prices. As the global economic recession, which began in late 2007, gripped the world financial markets, investors around the world turned to silver as a safe haven. Silver is viewed as one of the key financial assets during economic downturn and is also a form of savings in many countries and regions, including China, India, the Middle East, and North America. On a net basis investors are estimated to have bought 209.7 million ounces of silver in 2009, surpassing the 207.2 million ounces of silver bought in 1980.

As long as economic, financial, and political issues continue to generate investor ill-ease, investors are expected to continue purchasing high volumes of silver. This year investors are forecast to remain net buyers, purchasing close to 213.9 million ounces of silver. Investor activity always has and continues to be one of the key drivers of silver prices. Silver prices broke above $20 in the first quarter of 2008, as investor poured money into the silver market out of various due to growing economic and financial problems around the world. Silver prices have come off since then but remain high on a historical basis. Last year silver prices averaged $14.67, down slightly from $14.97 in 2008.

The **CPM Silver Yearbook 2010** reviews and analyzes the silver market over the past year, and lays out projections for supply, fabrication demand, and investment demand trends in 2010.

As always CPM Group is thankful to the corporate sponsors of this report, who help underwrite this annual report. The sponsors of this year's **Silver Yearbook** include Bear Creek Mining Corp., CME Group, Commodities Now, Endeavour Silver Corp., First Majestic Silver Corp., Fortuna Silver Mines Inc., Great Panther Resources Ltd., Hecla Mining Company, Kitco Inc., Mines Management, Inc., Oremex Resources Inc., Orko Silver Corp., Silver Standard Resources Inc., the Silver Users Association, Silver Wheaton Corp., Silvercorp Metals Inc., South American Silver Corp., the Institute of Scrap Recycling Industries, Inc., and the Prospector Exploration & Investment Newspaper.

CPM Group has shifted publishers this year for the series of gold, silver, and platinum group metals Yearbooks. We are pleased to have Euromoney Books and Metal Bulletin as the new publisher of these reports.

The Following Organizations Assisted in the Preparation of the Silver Yearbook

Bear Creek Mining Corp.
TSX-V: BCM

Bear Creek Mining Corporation's focus is on the discovery of high quality economic gold and silver deposits in Peru. Our flagship project is the Corani deposit which represents an emerging exploration discovery of potentially bulk-mineable, silver-lead-zinc (and gold) mineralization. Based upon drilling results from June 2005 through November 2007, the latest resource estimate contained over 362 million ounces silver, 4.4 billion pounds lead, and 2.7 billion pounds zinc, making Corani a world class silver discovery within a very small population of bulk-tonnage silver deposits worldwide. A recently released scoping study and preliminary economic assessment demonstrated that Corani has the capacity to become a large robust silver and base metals producer.

The property portfolio also includes five additional prospects with high quality silver, gold or copper-gold targets, including Bear Creek's Santa Ana project, a newly emerging near-surface, bulk-tonnage deposit amenable to low-cost heap-leaching and open-pit mining. Bear Creek also maintains an active and aggressive exploration and property acquisition program.

Bear Creek's management share an unparalleled instinct for successful mineral projects. Our Chairman, Catherine McLeod-Seltzer, co-founded Arequipa Resources which was acquired by Barrick in mid-1996. Numerous deposit discoveries are also attributed to Andrew Swarthout, President, and David Volkert, Vice-President of Exploration. Bear Creek's board is comprised of experienced mining executives who have had distinguished careers throughout the world with major mining companies.

Bear Creek Mining Corporation is committed to achieving a highly professional exploration and project development process that is sensitive to local economic and environmental concerns. Our extensive experience in Peru has allowed us to develop the strong relationships within communities which are crucial for successful exploration projects.

Contact Details: Patrick De Witt
Investor Relations
pdewitt@bearcreekmining.com
www.bearcreekmining.com

CME Group

As the world's largest and most diverse derivatives marketplace, CME Group is where the world comes to manage risk. CME Group exchanges offer the widest range of global benchmark products across all major asset classes, including futures and options based on interest rates, equity indexes, foreign exchange, energy, agricultural commodities, metals, weather and real estate. CME Group brings buyers and sellers together through its CME Globex electronic trading platform and its trading facilities in New York and Chicago. CME Group also operates CME Clearing, one of the largest central counterparty clearing services in the world, which provides clearing and settlement services for exchange-traded contracts, as well as for over-the-counter derivatives transactions through CME ClearPort. These products and services ensure that businesses everywhere can substantially mitigate counterparty credit risk in both listed and over-the-counter derivatives markets.

NYMEX and COMEX are now a part of CME Group, the world's largest and most diverse derivatives marketplace. Our metals futures markets include full-size contracts on gold, silver, platinum, palladium, copper and steel; as well as smaller-sized contracts for gold, silver and copper. These metal markets combine a unique volatility trading opportunity with an effective means for risk management. And with average daily volume of approximately 225,000 futures and options contracts traded, our metals markets are the most liquid in the world for these products. In addition, we have recently launched a new clearing service - Cleared OTC London Gold Forwards.

For more information visit www.cmegroup.com/metals or contact a member of our metals team.

Contact Details:

NEW YORK
Patricia Cauley   patricia.cauley@cmegroup.com   + 1 212 299 2424
Bruce Gilbert   bruce.gilbert@cmegroup.com   + 1 212 299 2346

CHICAGO
Angie DiCarlo   angie.dicarlo@cmegroup.com   +1 312 930 4515

LONDON
James Oliver   james.oliver@cmegroup.com   + 44 20 7796 7116

SINGAPORE
Lawrence Leong   lawrence.leong@cmegroup.com   + 65 6593 5564

Commodities Now

Commodities Now is the quarterly magazine and associated website for the globally traded commodities markets. The primary focus is on the base and precious metals, power and energy, and agricultural and soft commodities markets. It is the trends and developments within these sectors that are addressed, such as supply and demand, trading and risk management, and technology through to regulation. Read by professional commodity market participants around the world, Commodities Now has regular updates on the bullion and precious metals markets with contributions and special reports from leading metal market and mining specialists such as CPM Group, TheBullionDesk, Dow Jones Newswires and many more. Commodities Now also produces an annual LME Week Supplement looking at base and precious metals and mining.

The associated website: www.commodities-now.com provides daily news and research of interest to players throughout the commodity complex with prices and charts from leading precious metals exchanges included.

Contact Details: Guy Isherwood
                   gish@commodities-now.com
                   www.commodities-now.com

Endeavour Silver Corp.
NYSE-Amex:EXK, TSX: EDR, DBFrankfurt:EJD

Endeavour Silver Corp. is a Canadian based silver mining company focused on the growth of its silver production, reserves and resources from its Mexican operations. Expansion plans are ongoing at the Guanacevi Mine in the State of Durango and the Guanajuato Mine in the State of Guanajuato. Additionally, the company has three exploration projects, also in Mexico, and an aggressive exploration campaign is underway at all five properties. Through its expansion and acquisition programs, Endeavour's goal is to become the world's premier mid-tier primary silver producer.

The company's growth strategy is focused on acquiring, exploring and developing accretive, district scale silver mining properties in Mexico and other jurisdictions. Endeavour is currently pursuing several opportunities, both production and exploration, in order to fuel its growth in 2010 and beyond.

Key Highlights:
2009 Production - 2.6 million oz. silver plus 13,300 oz. gold
2010 Targets - 3.1 million oz. silver plus 15,000 oz. gold
Reserves and resources as at 12/31/09 - 75 million oz. silver equivalents
Cash costs reduced to the low $5.00 range
Shares Issued as at 12/31/09 - 61 million
Working Capital as at 12/31/09 - US$ 37 million

Contact Details:	Hugh Clarke
V-P Corporate Communications
hugh@edrsilver.com
Toll Free 1-877-685-9775
www.edrsilver.com

First Majestic Silver Corp.
TSX: FR, OTC PNK: FRMSF

First Majestic Silver Corp. is a pure silver producing mining company focused in Mexico. The Company presently owns three silver mines and continues to strive through a proven strategy of growth through acquisition and development of advanced staged silver projects. In 2010, First Majestic continued its strategy by not only completing the expansion at the La Encantada Silver Mine, but also completed another acquisition, the purchase of Normabec Mining and the Real de Catorce Silver Project.

This past year the Company's primary focus was to complete the expansion of the La Encantada operations from 1,000 tpd to 3,500 tpd. The construction was completed in November, which will result in full production in Q2 2010. The La Encantada is now First Majestic's largest operation and at full production will contribute over 4 million ounces annually to the Company's production.

The other significant event was the acquisition of the Real de Catorce Silver Project through the purchase of Normabec Mining Co. This exciting and interesting project added over 47 million ounces of silver to First Majestic's asset base and at the same time has given the Company ownership of a 6,000 hectare prolific silver district.

First Majestic's total silver equivalent resource (all categories) now sits at over 340,000,000 ounces.

First Majestic is led by President and CEO Keith Neumeyer, founder of First Quantum Minerals, and COO Ramon Davila, who has over 30 years of mining experience in Mexico, most recently with Pan American Silver and who presently sits on the board of the Chamber of Mines in Mexico. This management team has led the Company to incredible growth over the last 5 years, growing from 85 to almost 1,800 employees corporate wide

The flagship La Parrilla Silver Mine continues its positive growth, now with a land package of over 53,000 hectares which is operating with a mill capacity of 850 tpd. First Majestic's third producing mine, San Martin Silver Mine, is operating with a mill capacity of 950 tpd. The San Martin currently produces 100% of its production in the form of silver doré bars.

First Majestic's largest and newest operation, the La Encantada Silver Mine, has undergone a US$32 million facelift with the addition of a 3,500 tpd cyanidation plant. This plant, when fully operational in Q2 2010, will result in 100% of the La Encantada's production being in the form of silver doré bars.

2010 is expected to be a big year for First Majestic. Its three producing silver mines are expected to produce over 6 million ounces this year and grow even further in 2011. This compares to production of 4.35 million ounces of silver equivalent in 2009.

Contact Details: Dan McIntyre, Investor Relations
Jill Anne Arias, Corporate Relations
info@firstmajestic.com

Fortuna Silver Mines Inc.
TSX-V: FVI, Lima Exchange: FVI

Investing in Silver. Investing in Growth
One of North America's fastest-growing silver producers, Fortuna Silver Mines has increased its annual production by more than 250% in the past three years. The Company's Caylloma Mine in Peru produced more than 1.68 million ounces of silver in 2009. The larger San Jose Project, located in southern Mexico, is scheduled to start production in 2011 and boost Fortuna's annual silver equivalent production to over 5 million ounces.

Caylloma Mine - Steady Sustainable Growth
The Caylloma silver-lead-zinc-copper Mine has operated profitably since opening in 2006. In its first full year of production in 2007, the mine produced 480,000 ounces of silver. Production increased by 80% in 2008, to 860,000 ounces and by a further 95% in 2009 to 1,685,000 ounces. Silver production in 2009 accounted for approximately 50% of revenues.

Fortuna expects to sustain production at around 1.7 million ounces in 2010 and increase throughput from 1,200 tpd to 1,300 tpd. A new exploration program is underway to test other high-grade silver targets within the 9,000 hectare land package.

San Jose Project - Second Mine in the Making
With Indicated Resources of 37.6 million ounces of silver equivalent and Inferred Resources of 30.4 million ounces silver equivalent, Fortuna's San Jose Project is expected to triple the Company's annual silver production in 2012. Mine construction begins in 2010 with first production by mid 2011. The mine is forecast to produce over 3 million ounces of silver equivalent per year.

Management - Latin American Expertise
Fortuna's key strength is industry expertise in Latin America. Management's knowledge of regional mining, finance, exploration, geology and regulatory environments has allowed the Company to identify, seize and materialize accretive opportunities within the region. We are committed to profitability, sustainable growth, high standards and best practices while maintaining the well being of workers, neighboring communities and the environment. We are aggressively pursuing and evaluating further acquisition opportunities throughout the Americas.

Contact Details:

Corporate Office:
Suite 840-355 Burrard St.
Vancouver, BC, Canada V6C 2G8
Telephone: 1 (604) 484-4085

Perú Office:
Piso 17
Av. Pardo y Aliaga # 640
San Isidro, Lima - Perú
Teléfono: +511-616-6060

Contact Details:
Carlos Baca
Investor Relations
info@fortunasilver.com
www.fortunasilver.com

Great Panther Resources Ltd.
TSX: GPR

Great Panther Silver Limited, headquartered in Vancouver, Canada, is one of the fastest growing primary silver producers in Mexico with strong leverage to future rises in the price of silver. Since commencing production in Q1 2006, the Company has seen 13 out of 16 successive increases in quarterly production.

The centerpiece of the Company's operations is the Guanajuato Silver-Gold Mine Complex, in the State of Guanajuato. Metal production for the year 2009 at the Guanajuato Mine Complex was 1,541,220 silver equivalent ounces (Ag eq oz), which represented a 37% increase over 2008 and the fourth consecutive year of production growth for Great Panther. At Great Panther's second producing mine, the Topia Silver-Lead-Zinc Mine in Durango State, production totalled 661,236 Ag eq oz in 2009.

Great Panther's new 3-year growth strategy is focused on an immediate and aggressive increase in production and resources while maintaining profitability. It is anticipated that the new strategy should see the Company's annual production increase to approximately 3.8 million Ag eq oz by 2012 from its two existing mines in Mexico.

In addition, Great Panther intends to build its resource base at the Guanajuato and Topia operations to support a minimum 10-year mine life at the planned rate - a minimum of 40 million Ag eq oz. Consequently, a major deep drilling program has commenced at the Rayas area of the Guanajuato Mine Complex. This initial phase of approximately 12,000 metres of underground drilling in the Rayas area at Guanajuato is part of an ongoing program of approximately 20,000 metres at Guanajuato, and 8,000 metres at Topia planned for 2010. Recent discoveries such as the gold-rich Santa Margarita and high grade Los Pozos zones highlight the potential for both increased production and resources.

Great Panther Silver is confident that the targets outlined in its new strategy will be achieved or exceeded.

Contact Details: Robert A. Archer, P.GEO
                   President and CEO
                   info@greatpanther.com
                   www.greatpanther.com

Hecla Mining Company
NYSE: HL

Established in 1891 in northern Idaho's Silver Valley, Hecla Mining Company's rich history of mining has distinguished it as a respected precious metals producer. Hecla is the oldest U.S.-based precious metals mining company in North America and the largest producer of silver in the U.S. Headquartered in Coeur d'Alene, Idaho, this international, publicly traded company is 118 years old.

In April 2008, Hecla acquired 100% ownership of the sixth largest silver mine in the world - the Greens Creek joint venture in Alaska. This transaction has dramatically increased Hecla's annual silver production in 2009, while maintaining a low cash cost per ounce of silver, relative to its peers.

In 2008, Hecla was one of the lowest-cost primary silver producers in North America, producing 8.7 million ounces of silver at an average total cash cost of $4.20 per ounce. The company has exploration properties and operating mines in the U.S. and Mexico. Hecla has proven operating expertise and highly prospective exploration opportunities.

Hecla mines, processes or explores for silver and gold in the U.S. and Mexico. Hecla currently produces silver from two silver mines, Greens Creek and Lucky Friday. In 2008, the Greens Creek mine in Alaska produced 5.8 million ounces of silver for Hecla's account (Hecla's 100% share as of April 16, 2008, and its 29.73% interest prior to that date), and the Lucky Friday mine in northern Idaho produced 2.9 million ounces.

Hecla has long been well known in the United States as a quality producer of silver and gold. The name "Hecla" is commonly associated with precious metals by investors. Hecla's common stock has been traded on the New York Stock Exchange for over 40 years under the symbol "HL."

Contact Details:	Don Poirier
Vice President - Investor & Public Relations
dpoirier@hecla-mining.com
www.hecla-mining.com

Kitco Inc.

Since 1977, Kitco Metals of Montreal has earned the reputation of being the world's premier online retailer of precious metals. Kitco offers a complete line of high-quality pure gold, silver, platinum, and palladium bullion coins, bars, and precious metals buying as well as a range of highly secure storage programs to individual investors and corporate partners worldwide.

Most individuals are familiar with Kitco by virtue of its extremely popular internet website. Kitco's precious metals website has the distinction of being the most frequently accessed precious metals news and price information website on the internet, as well as frequently being ranked in the top 2,000 most popular websites worldwide. About 5 million individual page views are recorded each week on Kitco's homepage, www.kitco.com. Out of one million Internet users online at any given moment, close to 1,000 are visiting Kitco's website.

Whether it is for purchasing gold coins or bars, checking live, 24/7 precious metals prices, researching detailed price charts, or reading up-to-the-minute news and gold market commentaries, investors from all over the world know they can rely on Kitco's unsurpassed information quality and competitive online and telephone gold buying services. In addition, the Kitco site covers the base metals and silver markets, and also offers discussion forums to its users.

Contact Details:	Jon Nadler
			Senior Analyst, Head of PR
			JNadler@kitco.com
			www.kitco.com

Mines Management, Inc.
Amex: MGN, TSX: MGT

Mines Management, Inc., founded in 1947, is a US-based mineral exploration and development company engaged in the acquisition, exploration, and development of silver-dominant mineral projects. The Company's current focus is advancement and development of the Montanore Silver-Copper Deposit, one of the largest silver-copper deposits in the world.

Originally discovered in the early 1980's, the Montanore underwent extensive exploration by previous operators. More than 70,000 ft. of diamond core drilling outlined a deposit containing more than 100 million tons of material grading approximately 2.0 ounces Silver per ton plus 0.75% Copper, making it the largest undeveloped Silver-Copper project in the United States, and one of the largest in the world. The thickness and nature of mineralization may make the deposit amenable to bulk mining methods.

The deposit is located in northwestern Montana, about forty miles north of the famed Silver Valley of Idaho, within one of the world's most prolific silver districts. Mines Management acquired the Montanore deposit in 2002 when its partner and operator, Noranda Minerals of Canada, withdrew due to low metals prices at the time.

Currently the project is undergoing advanced stage engineering and project permitting. The project is currently designed to produce approximately 8 million ounces of silver and 60 million pounds of copper per year at its base case operating capacity.

The Company's skilled management team and board reflect the unique challenges of advancing such a large project toward development. With a world class project and highly experienced management team in operations and finance, the company considers the Montanore as an excellent foundation from which to build a new mid-tier mining company.

Contact Details:	Doug Dobbs
Vice President, Corporate Development
info@minesmanagement.com
www.minesmanagement.com

Oremex Resources Inc.
TSX-V: ORM, Frankfurt Exchange: OSI

With a 50.8 million ounce silver resource at its Tejamen Property and an experienced mine development team, Oremex Resources Inc. is an up and coming silver producer in Mexico. The Company is exploring and developing projects along the highly productive mineralized belt that has made Mexico one of the largest silver producers in the world. In addition to the Company's flagship Tejamen Silver Property, Oremex's portfolio of additional properties offers an opportunity for potential growth. Oremex Resources Inc. is a Canadian-based silver resource company listed on the TSX Venture Exchange (ORM) and the Frankfurt Exchange (OSI).

Contact Details: John Carlesso
                         jcarlesso@cervellocapital.com
                         http://www.oremex.com

Orko Silver Corp.
TSX-V: OK

Orko Silver Corp. is developing one of the world's largest primary silver deposits, La Preciosa, located near the city of Durango, in Durango State, Mexico. The La Preciosa silver project and adjacent mineral concessions cover 32,400 hectares (80,000 acres) of contiguous mining claims.

On February 18, 2009, the Company released its 6th NI 43-101 compliant Resource Estimate. The La Preciosa deposit now comprises 47% Indicated Resources and 53% Inferred Resources. Current Indicated Resources are 10.64 million tonnes grading 0.27 g/t Au and 185 g/t Ag for a Silver-Equivalent grade of 201 g/t. at a cut off grade of 100 g/t. The contained metal equals 63.2 million ounces of Silver and 94,000 ounces of Gold for a Silver Equivalent of 68.9 Million Ounces. Current Inferred Resources are 12.0 million tonnes grading 0.25 g/t Au and 185 g/t Ag for a Silver-Equivalent grade of 200 g/t. at a cut off grade of 100 g/t. The contained metal equals 71.8 million ounces of Silver and 97,000 ounces of Gold for a Silver Equivalent of 77.6 Million Ounces.*

*Estimated at a 60 to 1 Silver/Gold ratio with metallurgical recoveries and net smelter returns assumed to be 100%.

On April 14th, 2009 Pan American Silver Corp. and Orko Silver announced that they have agreed to form a joint venture to develop the La Preciosa project. Pan American will contribute its demonstrated mine development expertise, as well as 100% of the funds necessary to develop and construct an operating mine, in consideration for a 55% interest in the joint venture. Orko Silver retains a 45% interest fully carried to production.

Key aspects to the joint venture and the development strategy for La Preciosa include:

* Pan American currently operates 7 primary silver mines
* Pan American has completed 3 successful mining projects in the past 4 years
* Pan American will fast track the deposit to production
* Orko Silver retains a 45% fully carried interest to production
* No financing risk or further dilution for Orko Silver shareholders

Pan American has budgeted $10 million for the planned 2010 exploration and development and is working towards completing a full feasibility study towards the end of the year; more than a year ahead of the timing contemplated in the April 2009 joint venture agreement.

Contact Details: Mike Devji
                   Executive Vice-President
                   Mike.Devji@orkosilver.com
                   www.orkosilver.com

Silver Standard Resources Inc.
NASDAQ: SSRI, TSX: SSO

Silver Standard Resources Inc. is a silver producer with the new Pirquitas Mine in Argentina and development and exploration projects in Argentina, Peru, Mexico, Canada, the United States, Chile and Australia. At full production, Pirquitas's nameplate production is expected to be 8.0 million ounces to 10 million ounces of silver in 2011, placing it among the largest primary silver mines in the world.

The company controls the largest in-ground silver resources of any publicly traded silver company. At December 31, 2009, the company has proven and probable silver reserves of 287 million ounces, measured and indicated silver resources exceeding 1.1 billion ounces plus inferred resources totaling 519 million ounces.

In addition, Silver Standard has significant gold resources: measured and indicated gold total 26.3 million ounces, and inferred gold resources total 16.2 million ounces.

At February 29, 2010, the company had 78.7 million shares issued and outstanding.

In addition to the achievement of commercial production at Pirquitas in 2009, Silver Standard expects to report a feasibility study for the San Luis gold-silver project in Peru in Q2 2010 and a feasibility study for the Pitarrilla project in Mexico in Q4. The company will also have significant drill programs, the basis for its success in building shareholder value, at the Snowfield gold-copper-molybdenum project and Brucejack gold-silver project in Canada, and at Berenguela, Peru, Challacollo, Chile and San Agustin, Mexico, all three of which have bulk tonnage target potential at depth.

Contact Details: Paul LaFontaine
                   Director, Investor Relations
                   (604) 484-8212
                   invest@silverstandard.com
                   www.silverstandard.com

Silver Users Association

Founded in 1947, the Silver Users Association is a non-profit organization that represents the interests of companies that make, sell, and distribute products and services in which silver is an essential part.

SUA Members include representatives from photographic, electronic, silverware, mirror and jewelry industries, producers of semi-fabricated and industrial products, and trading and service organizations responding to member needs.

The SUA is active in providing timely research on industry issues for its members, the government, and the public. The Association is actively engaged on the legislative and regulatory fronts in Washington. Also, the SUA meets semiannually to provide members cost effective networking opportunities, to promote the Association's mission, and to hear from industry experts about issues affecting their business. The SUA is the premiere industry association that every company in the silver industry should belong to.

The members, which account for the bulk of silver used in the U.S., include the following:

Ablestik Laboratories
Dow Chemical Company
FideliTrade Incorporated
GFMS
International Commodities, Inc.
Mitsui & Company (USA)
Precision Engineered Products, Inc.
Pyromet
Reed & Barton Corporation
Technic, Inc.
Wolverine

Ames Goldsmith
Eastman Kodak Company
Gannon & Scott, Inc.
Heraeus Precious Metal Management
James Avery Craftsman
Ohio Precious Metals, Inc.
Prudential Bache Commodities, LLC
QML Metals & Logistics
ScotiaMocatta
Umicore Technical Materials NA

Contact Details: Paul Miller
Executive Director
(703) 934-0219
pmiller@mwcapitol.com
www.silverusersassociation.org

Silver Wheaton Corp.
TSX: SLW, NYSE: SLW

Established in 2004, Silver Wheaton has quickly positioned itself as the largest silver streaming company in the world. The company has entered into a number of agreements where, in exchange for an upfront payment, it has the right to purchase all or a portion of the silver production, at a low fixed cost, from high-quality mines located in politically stable regions. Silver Wheaton currently has agreements for 14 operating mines and 5 development stage projects. The company's industry-leading growth profile is driven by a portfolio of world-class assets, including silver streams on Goldcorp's Peñasquito mine in Mexico and Barrick's Pascua-Lama project straddling the border of Chile and Argentina. Silver Wheaton's unique business model creates significant shareholder value by providing considerable leverage to increases in the silver price, while reducing the downside risks faced by traditional mining companies. The company has an experienced management team with a strong track record of success and is well positioned for further growth.

Contact Details:	Brad Kopp
	Director, Investor Relations
	bkopp@silverwheaton.com
	www.silverwheaton.com

Silvercorp Metals Inc.
TSX: SVM, NYSE-Alternext: SVM

Silvercorp Metals Inc. is a Canadian-based primary silver producer with mining operations and development projects located in China and Canada. Since commencing commercial production in 2006, Silvercorp has enjoyed industry-leading profitability and returns due to the exceptionally high-grade nature of its Ying silver-lead-zinc deposit and the incredibly efficient and low-cost jurisdiction in which it operates. Today, Silvercorp is China's largest primary silver producer and has achieved an enviable three-year track record of being the lowest cost producer of silver among its global industry peers.

In the quarter that ended December 31, 2009, the company produced 1.22 million ounces of silver at a cash cost of negative $7.73 per ounce and achieved gross profit margins of 77%. Due to the company's high profitability, it is one of only a handful of producers to pay shareholders a dividend of C$0.02 per share per quarter.

Silvercorp has established itself as a preferred mining company in Henan Province, China, where it operates in the Ying Mining District. Having built a solid reputation for upholding high safety and environmental standards and supporting local community initiatives, Silvercorp has grown its camp from one mine to four mines from 2006 - 2008. At the same time, the company is applying for a mining permit at its GC development property in Guangdong Province to establish a second base of production in China.

With US$87.8-million in cash and short-term investments, no long-term debt, strong operations and the lowest production costs in the industry, Silvercorp is also growing its resource base through continuous exploration of existing projects as well as seeking to acquire new projects in multiple jurisdictions. The company's latest acquisition of the Silvertip project in northern British Columbia, Canada, represents its ability to make acquisitions beyond China's borders and its pursuit of new platforms for growth plus geographic diversification. The company remains committed to growing shareholder value for the long run.

The company is publicly traded on the Toronto Stock Exchange and New York Stock Exchange under the ticker symbol "SVM" and is a component of the S&P/TSX Composite and S&P/TSX Global Mining Indexes.

Contact Details: Shirley Zhou
                    Corporate Communications Manager
                    shirleyzhou@silvercorp.ca
                    www.silvercorp.ca

South American Silver Corp.
TSX: SAC

South American Silver Corporation is a mineral exploration company that primarily explores for silver in South America. The flagship project is the Malku Khota project in Bolivia where a silver-indium resource has been developed and the economics described in a National Instrument 43-101 compliant Preliminary Economic Assessment Study ("PEA") prepared by Pincock Allen & Holt Inc.("PAH") and that was announced in late February 2009. The silver-indium mineralization was initially identified within a surface area of 448,000 square metres and to a drilled depth of up to 400 metres below the surface. Eighty-eight diamond drill holes have been completed on the property comprising 30,365 metres. PAH had also previously prepared an updated resource at Malku Khota.

Results of the resource and PEA studies are summarized in the following:

Key Resource Facts:
Indicated Resource - Silver (Troy Ounces)	144.6 million
Indicated Resource - Indium (Kilograms)	845,000
Inferred Resource - Silver (Troy Ounces)	177.8 million
Inferred Resource - Indium (Kilograms)	968,000

Key Economic Indicators:
Pre-tax NPV (at 0% discount rate)	US$1,233 million
Pre-tax NPV (at 10% discount rate)	US$ 326 million
Initial capex	US$104.7 million
Cash cost (net of credits)	US$3.75/oz. silver
Pre-tax IRR	50.7%
First ten years silver grade	38.6 grams per tonne
First ten years indium grade	8.1 grams per tonne
Years to payback from start of production	1.4 years
Mining cost	US$ 1.14 per tonne
Processing cost	US$ 2.60 per tonne

The Company is listed on the senior Canadian stock exchange, the Toronto Stock Exchange, under the trading symbol "SAC". The Company has initiated a prefeasibility engineering study on the Malku Khota project that is expected to be completed by the end of 2010. At that time the bankable feasibility study will begin leading to the mine development and expected production to commence in the 2012-2014 period.

Contact Details:	Richard Doran
	rdoran@soamsilver.com
	www.soamsilver.com

The Institute of Scrap Recycling Industries, Inc.

The Institute of Scrap Recycling Industries, Inc. (ISRI) is the "Voice of the Recycling Industry." ISRI represents over 1,600 companies in 21 chapters nationwide that process, broker, and consume scrap commodities, including metals, paper, plastics, glass, rubber, electronics, and textiles. With headquarters in Washington, D.C., the Institute provides education, advocacy, and compliance training, and promotes public awareness of the vital role recycling plays in the U.S. economy, global trade and environment. For more information about ISRI, please visit www.ISRI.org.

Contact Details: Bob Garino
                    Director of Commodities
                    bobgarino@isri.org
                    www.isri.org

The Prospector Exploration & Investment Newspaper

The Prospector News is North America's leading source of in-depth information about news-making junior mining companies. Published in Vancouver, the bimonthly journal includes company profiles, area play analysis, commodities studies, and investment advice from leading stock analysts. The Prospector also produces an online Daily News, the only daily source of mining news coverage of its kind.

Contact Details: Editorial / New Releases
Kevin Dale McKeown
Managing Editor
editor@theprospectornews.com
604.345.3548

Advertising / Distribution
Michael Fox
sales@theprospectornews.com
604.639.5495

The CPM Silver Yearbook, 2010

Table of Contents

I. Review and Outlook
Chart:	The Price of Silver	3
Chart:	Silver Market Surplus/Deficit	5
Table:	Silver Statistical Position	6-7
Chart:	Supply and Demand Balance	9
Chart:	Annual Total Supply	11
Chart:	Annual Total Demand	12
Chart:	The Silver Market	15
Chart:	Precious Metals Bullion Stocks	16
Chart:	Estimated Silver Inventories in London and Zurich	16
Chart:	Deficits' Effects on Prices Depend on Inventories	
	Annual Surpluses and Deficits	17
	Estimated Total Silver Bullion Inventories, Year-End	17
	Silver Bullion Inventories as Months of Demand, Year-End	17
Table:	The Economy	18
Chart:	Cumulative World Silver Production and Distribution	19
Table:	World Silver Supply and Fabrication Demand	20
Table:	Real and Nominal Silver Prices	21

II. Supply
Chart:	Annual Total Supply	25
Chart:	Mine Output in Major Silver Producing Countries, 1990-2010p	26
Chart:	Estimated Silver Production Additions	27
Table:	Near-termMine Development Projects	28
Chart:	Mine Production in China, Mexico, Peru, and Australia	29
Table:	Mine Production of Silver	30
Table:	Silver Mine Production by Major Silver Producing Countries	33
Chart:	Primary Silver Producer's Cash Cost	36
Chart:	Primary Silver Mines Cash Cost and Average Silver Price	37
Chart:	Silver Reserves and Reserves Base	38
Chart:	Transitional Economy Mine Production	39
Table:	Capacity Additions in China and Russia	40
Chart:	Annual Secondary Supply	42
Chart:	Other Supply	43
Table:	World Silver Mine Production	44-45
Table:	Mine Production by Country	46-49
Table:	Secondary and Other Supplies	50
Table:	Indian Silver Supply	51
Chart:	South Asian Silver Trade	52

III. Fabrication Demand

Chart:	Annual Total Demand	55
Chart:	Fabrication Demand for Silver in 2009	56
Chart:	Jewelry and Silverware Demand for Silver	57
Chart:	Silver in Photography in 2009	58
Chart:	Photographic Demand	59
Chart:	Electronics and Batteries	61
Chart:	Other Uses	63
Table:	Annual Silver Use	64-65
Chart:	U.S. Fabrication Demand	66
Chart:	Indian Silver Fabrication Demand	67
Chart:	Italian Fabrication Demand	68
Chart:	Japanese Fabrication Demand	69
Chart:	European Fabrication Demand	69
Table:	Fabrication Demand by Country, 1960-2010p	70-71
Table:	European Silver Fabrication Demand	72
Table:	Italian Silver Fabrication Demand	73
Chart:	German Silver Fabrication Demand	74
Table:	German Silver Fabrication Demand	75
Chart:	U.K. Silver Fabrication Demand	76
Table:	United Kingdom Silver Fabrication Demand	77
Chart:	Belgian Silver Fabrication Demand	78
Table:	Belgian Silver Fabrication Demand	79
Chart:	French Silver Fabrication Demand	80
Table:	French Silver Fabrication Demand	81
Chart:	Austrian Silver Fabrication Demand	82
Table:	Austrian Silver Fabrication Demand	83
Chart:	Netherlands Silver Fabrication Demand	84
Table:	Netherlands Silver Fabrication Demand	85
Table:	Annual U.S. Silver Fabrication Demand, 1986-1997	86
Table:	Annual U.S. Silver Fabrication Demand, 1998-2010p	87
Table:	Japanese Silver Fabrication Demand, 1973-1990	88
Table:	Japanese Silver Fabrication Demand, 1991-2010p	89
Chart:	Thai Silver Fabrication Demand	90
Table:	Thai Silver Fabrication Demand	91
Chart:	South Korean Silver Fabrication Demand	92
Table:	South Korean Silver Fabrication Demand	93
Chart:	Taiwan Silver Fabrication Demand	94
Table:	Taiwan Silver Fabrication Demand	95

Chart:	Hong Kong Silver Fabrication Demand	96
Table:	Hong Kong Silver Fabrication Demand	97
Chart:	Indian Silver Fabrication Demand	98
Table:	Indian Silver Fabrication Demand	99
Chart:	Pakistan Silver Fabrication Demand	100
Table:	Pakistan Silver Fabrication Demand	101
Chart:	Bangladesh Silver Fabrication Demand	102
Table:	Bangladesh Silver Fabrication Demand	103
Chart:	Mexican Silver Fabrication Demand	104
Table:	Mexican Silver Fabrication Demand	105
Chart:	Brazilian Silver Fabrication Demand	106
Table:	Brazilian Silver Fabrication Demand	107
Chart:	Peruvian Silver Fabrication Demand	108
Table:	Peruvian Silver Fabrication Demand	109
Chart:	Canadian Silver Fabrication Demand	110
Table:	Canadian Silver Fabrication Demand	111
Chart:	Australian Silver Fabrication Demand	112
Table:	Australian Silver Fabrication Demand	113

IV. Investment Demand

Chart:	Annual Net Investment Demand and Prices	117
Chart:	Exchange Traded Funds' Physical Silver Holdings	119
Chart:	Silver Price and Total ETF Holdings	120
Chart:	Monthly Change in Silver ETF Holdings & Percent Change in Price	121
Table:	Exchange Traded Funds' Physical Silver Holdings	122
Chart:	Recent Trends in U.S. Eagle Sales	124
Chart:	One Month Implied Lease Rate	124
Chart:	Comex Disaggragated Non-Commercial Positions	125
Chart:	Large Non-Commercial Comex Silver Positions	126
Table:	Silver Coinage	128-129
Table:	U.S. Mint Silver Coin Sales	130-131
Chart:	Silver and U.S. Inflation	132
Chart:	Interest Rates and Silver Prices	132
Chart:	Silver and the U.S. Dollar	133
Chart:	Silver and the 30-year U.S. Treasury Bond	133
Table:	Comparative Investments	134

Silver Yearbook 2010   CPM Group

V. Inventories

Chart:	Market and Reported Inventories and Prices	137
Table:	Reported and Estimated Silver Inventories	139
Chart:	Government Silver Inventories	141
Chart:	Comex Stocks	141
Table:	Government Silver Inventories	142
Table:	Silver in Comex Approved Depositories	143
Table:	Ratio Between Silver Demand and Reported Stocks	144-145
Table:	Market Silver Inventories	146-149
Chart:	Reported Market Inventories	150
Chart:	Market Stocks	150
Table:	Reported and Unreported Silver Holdings	151
Table:	Comex Inventories	152-156

VI. Markets

Chart:	The Silver Market	159
Table:	The Silver Market 1997 - 2009	160
Chart:	London Bullion Market Association Average Transaction Size	162
Chart:	Trading Volumes on Major Silver Exchanges	163
Table:	London Bullion Market Clearing Turnover	166
Chart:	London Bullion Market Association	
	Ounces of Silver Transferred	167
	Value of Silver Transferred	167
	Number of Transfers	167
Chart:	Trading Volume in the Futures Market	168
Chart:	Open Interest in the Futures Market	168
Chart:	Trading Volume in the Options Market - Puts and Calls	169
Chart:	Open Interest in the Options Market - Puts and Calls	169
Table:	Silver Futures Exchange Activity	170-171
Chart:	Comex Trading Volume	172
Chart:	Comex Open Interest	172
Chart:	Tocom Trading Volume	173
Chart:	Tocom Open Interest	173
Table:	Comex Trading Volume	174-175
Table:	Comex Open Interest	176-177
Table:	Tocom Trading Volume	178
Table:	Tocom Open Interest	179
Table:	Multi Commodity Exchange Silver Trading Volume	180
Table:	Multi Commodity Exchange Silver Open Interest	181

xxxiv

Chart:	Trading Volume on Comex and Tocom	182
Chart:	Open Interest on Comex and Tocom	182
Chart:	Trading Volume in Comex Silver Options	183
Chart:	Open Interest in Comex Silver Options	183
Table:	Annual Silver Options Activity	184-185
Table:	Comex Options Trading Volume	186
Table:	Comex Options Open Interest	187
Chart:	Comex Options Put/Call Ratio	188

VII. Prices

Chart:	Weekly Average Silver Prices	191
Chart:	High, Low, and Average Silver Prices	192
Chart:	High, Low, and Settlement Prices in 2005-2010	192
Chart:	Monthly Silver Price Volatility	193
Chart:	Silver Contango and Backwardation	194
Chart:	Monthly Silver Price Seasonality	195
Chart:	Quarterly Real and Nominal Silver Prices	196
Chart:	Daily Gold and Silver Prices	197
Chart:	The Gold/Silver Price Ratio	197
Chart:	Silver Prices in Rupees	198
Chart:	Quarterly Silver Price Volatility	199
Chart:	Annual Silver Price Volatility	199
Table:	Monthly Average Silver Prices	200-201

Review and Outlook

Review and Outlook

Silver prices averaged $14.67 last year, down 2.0% from the average price of $14.97 in 2008. Despite the decline in the average silver price last year, it was the third highest annual average silver price. The highest annual average price was $20.65 in 1980, the year in which prices spiked toward $50.

While silver prices seemed to move sideways on an annual average basis in 2009, in fact they were quite volatile, extending a period of high volatility that had characterized 2008. Silver traded between $10.44 and $19.33 in 2009. This was narrower than the $12 range in which silver moved during 2008, from $8.79 to $20.79. To understand the price and fundamental developments in silver last year, the events of 2009 must be viewed in the context of what had transpired the year before.

Silver prices had risen to a 27-year high of $20.79 on 5 March 2008, as the financial storm that was soon to engulf the global economy gained force. This was less than two weeks before the forced marriage of Bear Stearns into JP Morgan, organized by the U.S. Treasury. After the shock of the Bear Stearns tragedy had been absorbed by the markets, silver prices subsided to trade largely between $16 and $19 from late March into August 2008. Silver then fell sharply during September and October, hitting a low of $8.79 on 28 October 2008. (Unless otherwise noted, prices in

The Price of Silver

Monthly Average Comex, Through February 2010.

this report are Comex nearby active futures contract settlement prices.)

Even as prices were falling, investors were pouring into the physical silver market. There was a shortage of small-sized (1, 10, and 100-ounce) silver bars, medallions, and coins - favored by retail and other investors - as people around the world rushed to build up cash and precious metals holdings in the face of what many feared to be the imminent collapse of the global financial system. Prices fell, however, for two primary reasons. The first was that there were massive leveraged trades in silver (and other precious metals) issued by banks and brokerage companies and held by institutional and high net worth individual investors. As the financial markets froze around the world, the credit allocated to both the issuers and the buyers of these silver-backed securities plummeted. Many had to liquidate their positions, built on credit. Additionally, other investors were selling their silver, along with gold, in a race to raise cash to cover other financial obligations. Thus, even as investors were flooding into the silver market as buyers, the price dropped roughly by half. In fact, of course, the sharp decline in silver and gold prices helped stimulate additional demand for physical metals from investors who had both the cash and the foresight to view silver prices at the low levels of October and November as a tremendous buying opportunity.

Silver remained low for much of the rest of 2008, ending the year at $11.30. The metal continued to trade between $10.32 and $11.77 in early 2009, breaking out of this range in the final week of January. From that point forward prices moved higher, albeit in a choppy, volatile fashion. Prices rose through the year, reaching a high for 2009 of $19.33 on 2 December. Prices came off after that, ending 2009 at $16.85. this was a 49.1% increase from $11.30 at the end of 2008 and 91.6% from the $8.79 low in October 2008. Thus, while the average silver price in 2009 was 30 cents lower than that of 2008, the price rose strongly throughout 2009.

Prices picked up in early 2010, reaching $18.80 on 19 January before declining into the first half of February. Prices fell to $14.83 on 5 February, but strong investor interest and increased buying from fabricators helped push prices back above $15 the next day. By 16 March silver had risen to close at $17.44, demonstrating a great deal of upward price pressure.

Investor Demand

These wild vacillations in the silver price reflect trends in investment demand for silver. Investors have been stocking up on this metal at near-record highs. The only other times in history in which investors loaded up on silver with the intensity seen in 2009 were in the 1960s, when they bought so much silver that the U.S. Treasury had to remove silver from coinage and as backing for Silver Certificates, and in 1980. In 1980 investors bought 207.2 million ounces of silver. In 1968 investors bought 226.0 million ounces of silver bullion. They also were buying hundreds of millions of ounces of additional silver both in bullion and coin form from the U.S. Treasury between 1960 and 1970. (The U.S. Treasury sold 905.0 million ounces of silver bullion from 1964 through 1970, much of which wound up in the hands of investors, while the Treasury used another 969.0 million ounces of silver in coins between 1960 and 1970, much of which was quickly either bought in coin form by investors or melted down into bullion bars. A total of 2.2 billion ounces is estimated to have been taken up by investors during the 11 years from 1960 through 1970.)

For the third time in history, investors are buying more than 200 million ounces per year on a net basis for addition to their inventories. Investors bought an estimated 209.7 million ounces of bullion in 2009, surpassing net purchases in 1980 and approaching the 1968 peak. Investors are projected to purchase another 213.9 million ounces in 2010. Investor buying has remained high in the early part of 2010, and is expected to stay strong through the year.

Not only are investors buying historically high volumes of silver, but they also are buying significantly more silver than in recent years: The rate of change in investor net buying patterns for silver has been very dramatic, in a pattern reminiscent of the 1960s and 1979 - 1980. Investors were heavy net sellers of silver for 16 years, from 1990 through 2005. They shifted to net buyers in 2006, buy-

Silver Market Surplus/Deficit
Projected Through 2010. Average Annual Price.

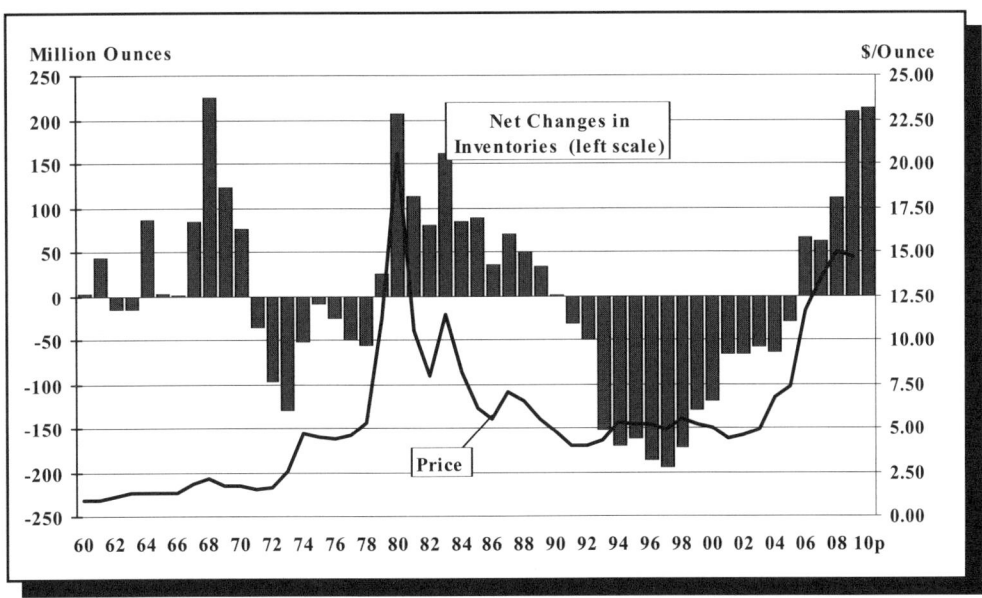

Silver Yearbook 2010 - Review and Outlook — CPM Group

Silver Statistical Position
Million Troy Ounces

	1977	1978	1979	1980	1981	1982	1983	1984	1985	1986	1987	1988	1989	1990	1991	1992	1993
Mine Production																	
Mexico	47.0	50.8	49.4	47.3	53.2	49.8	55.0	63.9	69.2	69.4	69.8	70.0	70.0	69.0	70.0	65.0	61.0
United States	38.2	39.4	37.9	32.3	40.7	40.2	43.4	44.6	39.4	34.2	39.8	53.4	60.8	66.5	61.0	61.0	55.7
Peru	39.1	37.0	41.9	44.8	42.6	54.4	55.6	53.3	54.9	59.9	63.6	47.7	56.8	55.5	56.9	48.0	47.0
Canada	42.2	40.7	36.9	34.4	36.3	42.2	38.7	42.0	38.5	35.0	38.1	44.1	41.3	44.4	40.6	36.3	28.3
Australia	27.5	26.1	26.7	25.0	23.9	29.2	33.2	31.3	34.9	32.9	35.9	35.8	37.3	37.8	38.0	40.1	39.1
Other	93.2	98.0	104.7	110.1	109.7	105.9	112.1	116.0	122.4	119.7	121.4	132.6	132.0	129.9	134.0	142.8	136.3
Total	287.2	292.0	297.6	293.9	306.4	321.7	338.0	351.0	359.3	351.1	368.6	383.6	398.2	403.1	400.4	393.1	367.3
% Change Year Ago	—	1.7%	1.9%	-1.2%	4.3%	5.0%	5.1%	3.9%	2.4%	-2.3%	5.0%	4.1%	3.8%	1.2%	-0.7%	-1.8%	-6.6%
Secondary Supply																	
Old Scrap	93.0	82.0	130.0	164.0	125.0	111.0	133.4	123.5	101.5	103.4	113.3	121.9	125.0	120.0	117.6	130.5	137.1
Coin Melt	33.0	21.0	45.0	94.0	18.0	7.0	20.1	20.1	18.4	9.9	10.1	8.8	6.4	6.0	4.0	3.0	2.0
Indian Scrap	43.0	49.0	41.0	44.0	41.0	37.0	44.0	22.0	21.0	16.0	14.5	13.2	4.8	—	9.6	7.2	3.8
Total	169.0	152.0	216.0	302.0	184.0	155.0	197.5	165.6	140.9	129.3	137.9	143.9	136.2	126.0	131.2	140.7	142.9
% Change Year Ago	—	-10.1%	42.1%	39.8%	-39.1%	-15.8%	27.4%	-16.2%	-14.9%	-8.2%	6.6%	4.4%	-5.3%	-7.5%	4.2%	7.2%	1.5%
Other Supply																	
Government Disposals	5	9	3	5	4	1	19	16	13	14	20	8.3	10.7	11	11.5	8.1	11.2
Net Exports from Transitional Economies	—	—	—	—	—	—	—	—	—	—	—	—	—	—	—	—	—
	5	9	3	5	4	1	19	16	13	14	20	8.3	10.7	11	11.5	8.1	11.2
% Change Year Ago	—	80.0%	-66.7%	66.7%	-20.0%	-75.0%	NM	-15.8%	-18.8%	7.7%	42.9%	-58.5%	28.9%	2.8%	4.5%	-29.6%	38.3%
Total Supply	461.2	453.0	516.6	600.9	494.4	477.7	554.5	532.6	513.2	494.4	526.5	535.8	545.1	540.1	543.2	542.0	521.4
% Change Year Ago	—	-1.8%	14.0%	16.3%	-17.7%	-3.4%	16.1%	-3.9%	-3.6%	-3.7%	6.5%	1.8%	1.7%	-0.9%	0.6%	-0.2%	-3.8%
Fabrication Demand																	
Photography	129.6	142.9	146.1	123.8	128.1	136.5	140.3	147.3	152.7	157.8	172.1	185.1	189.2	196.5	196.2	198.6	201.0
Jewelry & Silverware	91.0	91.9	82.8	52.3	47.8	56.4	47.6	47.4	55.5	75.3	87.2	91.2	114.2	128.3	155.3	172.0	234.5
Electronics and Batteries	78.7	79.3	80.4	71.2	62.2	62.6	60.9	63.1	67.8	69.4	69.4	74.6	80.3	84.3	83.7	81.3	83.6
Other Uses	87.5	84.0	86.2	71.0	66.1	62.6	61.9	69.3	68.0	66.2	78.5	77.8	94.2	102.0	109.7	112.5	120.1
Other Countries	73.1	54.3	52.8	46.1	51.3	43.4	45.8	49.6	37.2	41.3	23.5	24.7	0.2	3.1	3.4	0.4	5.0
Net Imports into the Transitional Economies	15.9	18.2	11.5	14.5	15.3	23.8	25.4	56.6	30.4	49.2	24.9	32.9	32.6	25.0	27.2	27.5	30.0
Total	475.8	470.6	459.7	378.8	370.7	385.2	381.8	433.3	411.6	459.2	455.5	486.2	510.6	539.1	575.6	591.5	674.3
% Change Year Ago	—	-1.1%	-2.3%	-17.6%	-2.1%	3.9%	-0.9%	13.5%	-5.0%	11.6%	-0.8%	6.7%	5.0%	5.6%	6.8%	2.8%	14.0%
Net Surplus or Deficit in the Bullion Market	-14.6	-17.6	56.9	222.2	123.8	92.6	172.7	99.4	101.6	35.2	71.0	49.6	34.6	1.0	-32.5	-49.5	-152.9
Addenda																	
Coinage	34.5	39.5	31.0	15.0	9.5	12.0	10.2	13.7	13.4	26.8	30.4	25.3	26.3	29.8	27.7	29.4	38.0
Changes in Inventories																	
Unreported	-60.9	-39.6	32.7	190.5	143.6	66.5	114.3	86.2	45.6	50.9	41.3	6.9	-49.2	-59.4	-71.6	-150.5	-194.6
Reported	11.8	-17.5	-6.8	16.7	-29.3	14.0	48.2	-0.5	42.6	-42.5	-0.6	17.4	57.5	30.5	11.4	70.7	5.6
Total	-49.1	-57.1	25.9	207.2	114.3	80.5	162.5	85.7	88.2	8.4	40.7	24.3	8.3	-28.9	-60.2	-79.7	-189.0
% Change Year Ago	—	16.3%	NM	701.3%	-44.8%	-29.5%	101.7%	-47.3%	2.9%	-90.4%	382.3%	-40.2%	-66.1%	NM	108.5%	32.5%	137.0%
Price Per Ounce																	
High	$4.98	$6.32	$34.45	$48.70	$16.29	$11.21	$14.72	$10.06	$6.84	$6.29	$9.66	$7.83	$6.19	$5.33	$4.55	$4.32	$5.44
Low	4.31	4.81	5.92	10.80	7.99	4.98	8.40	6.30	5.53	4.85	5.38	6.00	5.03	3.94	3.51	3.64	3.52
Average	4.63	5.34	11.20	20.65	10.53	7.93	11.46	8.15	6.15	5.47	6.99	6.53	5.50	4.82	4.03	3.93	4.30
% Change Year Ago	—	15.3%	109.7%	84.4%	-49.0%	-24.7%	44.5%	-28.9%	-24.5%	-11.1%	27.8%	-6.6%	-15.8%	-12.3%	-19.6%	0.1%	-5.8%

Notes: Totals may not equal the sum of categories due to rounding. Mine production in Poland, Bulgaria, Romania, Hungary, the Czech Republic, and Slovakia is included in "other" mine production. Photography, jewelry and silverware, electronics, and 'other' industrial use reflects demand in Europe, the United States, and Japan. These sectors include Canada from 1979, Mexico from 1982, Hong Kong from 1985, Thailand from 1986, India from 1987, Australia, Brazil, Peru, Colombia, Argentina, Chile, Korea, Pakistan, and Bangladesh from 1989, and Taiwan from 1990. Demand excludes the transitional economies, except for imports. The price is the Comex nearby active settlement, percent change from year earlier period. 2010 through February. There may be discrepancies due to rounding. p - projections.
NM - Not meaningful.
Source: CPM Group.
March 16, 2010

	1994	1995	1996	1997	1998	1999	2000	2001	2002	2003	2004	2005	2006	2007	2008	2009	2010p	
																		Mine Production
	65.0	67.3	75.0	83.0	88.0	79.0	88.5	89.0	88.5	83.0	83.0	93.0	96.1	99.5	104.1	104.7	120.0	Mexico
	54.0	49.5	50.0	59.0	62.4	65.3	65.6	55.9	43.4	39.9	40.2	39.5	36.7	39.0	39.5	39.5	39.9	United States
	48.0	51.0	55.0	63.0	61.4	67.1	78.4	83.0	92.3	93.9	98.4	102.7	111.6	112.3	118.5	123.9	125.1	Peru
	23.6	41.3	42.0	39.4	37.9	39.6	39.0	42.4	45.3	42.1	43.0	36.1	32.0	27.7	23.4	20.2	21.5	Canada
	36.8	32.0	35.0	38.7	50.8	57.7	68.5	63.3	66.6	60.1	71.0	77.0	56.0	60.5	61.9	53.0	56.5	Australia
	133.9	142.7	142.2	144.8	154.9	159.7	159.0	167.5	161.5	164.7	168.7	169.2	180.6	195.4	205.0	212.6	218.2	Other
	361.2	383.9	399.2	427.8	455.5	468.4	498.9	501.2	497.5	483.7	504.3	517.5	512.8	534.4	552.4	553.9	581.2	Total
	-1.7%	6.3%	4.0%	7.2%	6.5%	2.9%	6.5%	0.5%	-0.8%	-2.8%	4.3%	2.6%	-0.9%	4.2%	3.4%	0.3%	4.9%	% Change Year Ago
																		Secondary Supply
	138.4	148.1	155.5	163.3	171.5	176.5	187.1	192.0	190.0	196.0	202.0	205.0	215.0	222.0	233.0	236.0	238.4	Old Scrap
	1.3	1.5	1.7	1.7	2.5	18.5	6.0	2.0	3.0	5.0	5.0	5.0	7.0	5.0	4.0	4.0	3.0	Coin Melt
	6.5	9.6	6.4	10.0	13.5	12.9	6.4	9.6	4.8	16.1	9.7	16.1	22.5	16.1	17.5	32.2	22.5	Indian Scrap
	146.2	159.2	163.6	175.0	187.5	207.9	199.5	203.6	197.8	217.1	216.7	226.1	244.5	243.1	254.5	272.2	263.9	Total
	2.3%	8.9%	2.7%	7.0%	7.1%	10.9%	-4.0%	2.0%	-2.8%	9.8%	-0.2%	4.4%	8.2%	-0.6%	4.7%	7.0%	-3.1%	% Change Year Ago
																		Other Supply
	15.8	19	8.1	5.3	6	10	20	25	15	15	10	35	26	8	—	—	—	Government Disposals
																		Net Exports from
	—	—	—	—	—	—	15	15	15	15	5	—	—	—	—	—	—	Transitional Economies
	15.8	19	8.1	5.3	6	10	35	40	30	30	15	35	26	8	—	—	—	
	41.1%	20.3%	-57.4%	-34.6%	13.2%	66.7%	250.0%	14.3%	-25.0%	0.0%	-50.0%	133.3%	-25.7%	-69.2%	-100.0%	—	—	% Change Year Ago
	523.2	562.1	570.9	608.1	649.0	686.3	733.5	744.8	725.3	730.8	736.0	778.6	783.4	785.5	806.9	826.1	845.1	Total Supply
	0.3%	7.4%	1.6%	6.5%	6.7%	5.8%	6.9%	1.6%	-2.6%	0.8%	0.7%	5.8%	0.6%	0.3%	2.7%	2.4%	2.3%	% Change Year Ago
																		Fabrication Demand
	215.5	221.2	230.9	242.2	257.1	267.2	261.7	256.7	255.5	249.2	242.7	207.6	180.9	169.5	134.4	112.3	105.3	Photography
	234.5	245.2	262.2	283.1	293.5	291.7	285.5	287.6	270.9	264.9	242.8	288.8	241.9	261.6	261.0	242.1	246.3	Jewelry & Silverware
	83.2	88.6	88.7	96.9	96.2	99.1	115.3	102.4	106.0	104.4	106.6	101.9	112.2	119.5	123.2	119.5	125.2	Electronics and Batteries
	129.2	137.0	142.5	145.2	137.3	139.8	183.4	157.6	151.4	162.7	201.3	195.0	171.3	162.1	166.3	134.9	146.0	Other Uses
	3.9	3.4	6.0	6.5	6.4	6.9	6.4	6.2	7.0	7.2	7.5	3.9	1.4	1.3	1.8	1.6	2.4	Other Countries
																		Net Imports into the
	28.0	29.3	27.9	29.6	31.2	11.0	—	—	—	—	—	10.0	10.0	10.0	8.0	6.0	6.0	Transitional Economies
	694.3	724.7	758.2	803.6	821.7	815.8	852.3	810.5	790.8	788.4	800.9	807.2	717.7	724.0	694.7	616.4	631.2	Total
	3.0%	4.4%	4.6%	6.0%	2.3%	-0.7%	4.5%	-4.9%	-2.4%	-0.3%	1.6%	0.8%	-11.1%	0.9%	-4.0%	-11.3%	2.4%	% Change Year Ago
																		Net Surplus or Deficit
	-171.1	-162.6	-187.3	-195.5	-172.8	-129.4	-118.8	-65.7	-65.5	-57.6	-64.9	-28.7	65.7	61.5	112.2	209.7	213.9	in the Bullion Market
																		Addenda
	33.5	22.0	18.1	18.9	25.0	29.5	25.2	17.6	20.5	17.7	18.2	16.5	17.8	17.4	28.2	38.3	25.0	Coinage
																		Changes in Inventories
	-174.7	-63.5	-179.1	-108.3	-160.7	-169.5	-164.5	-89.9	-93.7	-83.1	-76.6	-66.1	-70.4	-51.4	5.4	36.5	—	Unreported
	-29.9	-121.2	-26.3	-106.0	-37.0	10.6	20.5	6.7	7.7	7.8	-6.6	21.0	118.2	95.5	78.6	135.0	—	Reported
	-204.6	-184.7	-205.4	-214.3	-197.8	-158.9	-144.1	-83.3	-86.0	-75.3	-83.2	-45.1	47.9	44.1	84.0	171.5	188.9	Total
	8.3%	-9.7%	11.2%	4.4%	-7.7%	-19.7%	-9.3%	-42.2%	3.3%	-12.4%	10.4%	-45.7%	NM	-7.9%	90.5%	104.2%	10.2%	% Change Year Ago
																		YTD Price Per Ounce
	$5.78	$6.16	$5.84	$6.38	$7.28	$5.77	$5.57	$4.83	$5.13	$5.99	$8.22	$9.10	$14.94	$15.55	$20.79	$19.33	$18.80	High
	4.61	4.42	4.71	4.19	4.62	4.86	4.62	4.03	4.22	4.35	5.52	6.45	8.87	11.50	8.79	10.44	14.83	Low
	5.28	5.20	5.21	4.91	5.53	5.23	5.00	4.38	4.60	4.90	6.70	7.35	11.61	13.45	14.97	14.67	17.67	Average
	12.7%	-5.3%	-4.5%	-5.8%	12.7%	-5.3%	-4.5%	-12.4%	5.2%	6.3%	36.8%	9.7%	58.0%	15.9%	11.3%	-2.0%	42.7%	% Change Year Ago

Apparent private investment demand from new supply is total supply for a given year less fabrication demand and coinage. Apparent bullion demand from market stocks reflects the change in market inventories; a negative figure here indicates that investors were net sellers of metal that entered market stocks, while a positive figure indicates that market stocks fell to meet demand from investors, and fabricators of industrial products and coins. Changes in market inventories are year-end; 1999 through end-December. Reported inventories between 1992 and 1996 are adjusted to reflect Wilmington Trust silver stocks that would have been eligible for Comex delivery. Wilmington Trust became a licensed Comex depository on January 1, 1997.

ing around 65.7 million ounces of silver on a net basis that year. They added another 61.5 million ounces of silver to their holdings in 2007.

In 2008 they bought 112.2 million ounces of silver. They would have bought more, but as mentioned above there was a shortage of silver investment products in small sizes, which limited the net buying during the second half of 2008. As those bottlenecks passed in early 2009, investors loaded up on metal. In fact, the experience of not being able to buy silver during the worst of the financial crisis and economic recession convinced investors of the wisdom and attractiveness of holding silver as an investment, accentuating and adding to the demand in 2009.

These levels of investment demand are projected to continue this year, as stated above. History has shown that investor buying and selling trends in silver, as in many other assets, tends to be auto-correlated, meaning that once investors start buying, or selling, they will tend to continue this practice for several years.

For example, investors shifted from being net sellers in 1978 to being net buyers in 1979. In 1980 they bought the historically enormous 207.2 million ounces of silver mentioned above. They continued to buy large volumes of silver until 1987, although in diminishing volumes compared to the 1980 level of demand. Annual net investor demand remained above 80 million ounces until 1985, and trailed off only slowly after that. It was not until 1990 that investors as a segment of the market shifted to net selling. During the 1980s, investors kept buying, in part due to expectations of a repeat of the tremendous increase in silver prices at the end of the previous decade, and in part because some of these investors assumed throughout the 1980s that the massive, roughly 10-fold increase in the U.S. federal budget and trade deficits in the 1980s would lead to the collapse of the U.S. Treasury during that decade. By 1990, attitudes toward prospects for U.S. and global financial markets instability, and silver's price potential, had shifted. It had taken a decade to effect that change, however.

The parallels of the 1980s and the current decade appear interesting, at least from the perspective allowed in 2010. The previous decade ended with the deepest recession since World War Two and the Great Depression. The double-dip recessions of 1980 - 1982 were the deepest postwar recessions at that time, surpassed only by the 2007 - 2009 recession. The world was plagued with a host of financial, economic, and political issues in 2008 and 2009, just as they were in 1979 - 1982. Major governments, including Mexico, Argentina, and Brazil, were close to defaulting on their sovereign debt at the bottom of the 1982 recession, just as Greece's government fiscal problems have caused great concerns in the first two months of 2010. There were many other parallels in the broader financial and political realms, all of which have led investors in early 2010 to be extremely concerned about future economic and financial stability - just as they were in 1980 - 1982.

The parallels extend to the silver market, and to broader precious metals and commodities markets. The key parallel was the surge in investor demand for silver, both in 1979 - 1980 and again now, since 2006. Given the severity of today's financial imbalances, and the fact that major governments have allowed them to compound over the ensuing three decades, it seems fair to assume that investors will remain concerned about their financial futures for years to come, and consequently remain interested in buying more silver to add to their portfolios. Thus, it is reasonable to assume that investors will continue to add large volumes of silver to their inventories in 2010 and for the next several years.

Supply and Demand Balance

Fabrication demand for silver rose sharply from the early 1980s until 2000. Supply of silver lagged fabrication demand growth for many years, however. From 1990 through 2005 fabrication demand for silver far exceeded the silver supply, which resulted in a deficit in those years. Net selling of silver by investors and bullion banks from historically high inventories at the outset of the 1990s kept the silver market well supplied, however. Investors were net sellers of the bulk of the silver sold during the 16 years from 1990 through 2005. This kept silver prices depressed during that time, mostly moving between $4.00 and $6.00.

The year of heaviest net selling by

Supply and Demand Balance
Projected Through 2010.

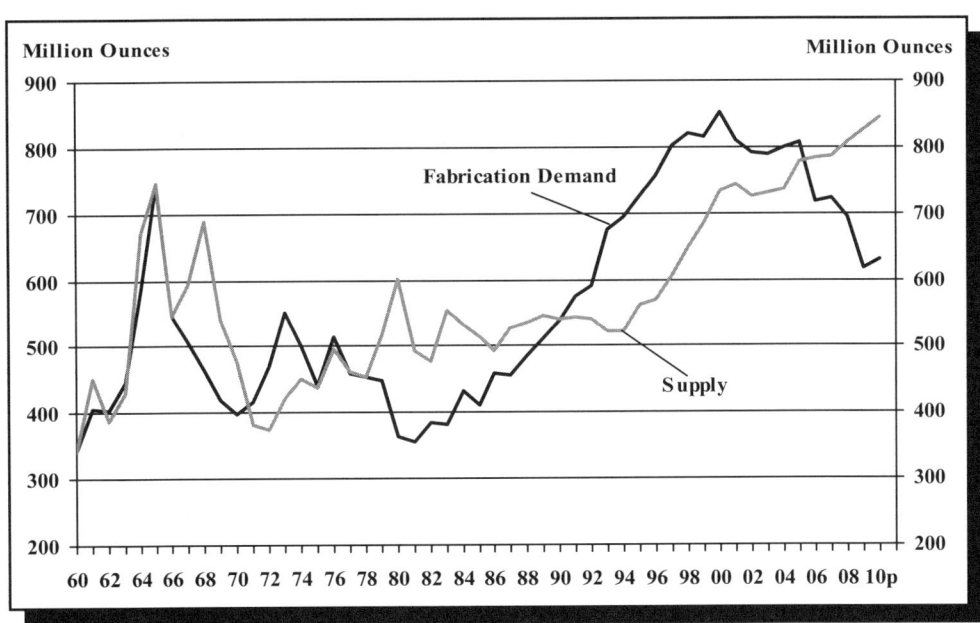

investors was 1997, the very year that Warren Buffet's Berkshire Hathaway was accumulating its 129.7 million ounces. While Berkshire Hathaway was buying, other investors were selling. A minimum estimated 325 million ounces of silver were sold by investors on a gross basis in that one year alone. Knowing that, no one should be surprised to learn that the silver price averaged $4.91 in 1997.

After 1997 the volumes of investor selling declined. Although investors remained net sellers through 2005, they were selling steadily less metal. Those long-term investors that were disenchanted appeared to be running low on metal to sell. Other, new investors were turning their attention to silver. After the stock market crash, tech bubble burst, recession, financial market scandals, and terrorist attacks in 2000 and 2001, investors began to become increasingly bullish toward silver and interested in buying silver.

The period of net selling by investors ended in 2006. Since then the silver market has been in what may be called a technical surplus, in which the flow of newly refined silver into the market has exceeded fabrication demand. It is not so much that there is a surplus of metal in the market, as it is that investors have been bidding up silver prices, adding metal to inventories rather than having manufacturers use the metal in fabricated products. Thus the surplus has been a function of investment demand. Strong investor interest has driven prices up, discouraging manufacturers from using metal. Recessionary economic conditions and the move away from silver-based photographic materials have added to the reduction in fabrication demand, while the higher prices resulting from the increased investor interest has encouraged further increases in supplies from both mines and secondary recovery.

Supply from both mine production and secondary supply has surged beginning in 2006. High silver prices have encouraged many mining companies to ramp up their silver production at existing mine. Also, several new mine projects, which were not economically mineable at low silver prices, have started production. Secondary supply also has been rising as recovery of silver from old scrap has picked up with increase in silver prices.

Since 2006 the pace of increase in supply silver has accelerated while fabrication demand for silver has dwindled. The use of silver is relatively inelastic in many industrial uses. Also, silver is a low cost substitute for gold, palladium and platinum in some applications. This has prevented fabrication demand for silver from falling more sharply. Several new uses of silver in batteries, solar panels, radio frequency identification (RFID) chips, and biocides have emerged in the past few years.

Total Silver Supply

Total silver supply includes mine production, secondary supply, government disposals, and net exports from transitional economies. Mine production is the largest component of total silver supply, accounting for approximately 70%.

Total silver supply reached 826.1 million ounces last year. This was up 2.4% from 806.9 million ounces in 2008 and a record volume of silver supply. A further 2.3% increase to 845.1 million ounces is projected for 2010.

The largest increase in total supply last year was from market economy mine production. Around 553.9 million ounces of silver was estimated to have been mined in the market economies in 2009. This was up 0.3% from 552.4 million ounces mined in 2008. Peru was the largest producer of silver last year, followed by Mexico. Mine production is projected to rise 4.9% to 581.2 million ounces in 2010, with large increases expected in Mexico, Australia, and some smaller producing nations.

Around 272.2 million ounces of silver are estimated to have been recovered from old scrapped jewelry, silverware, photographic materials, electronics, chemical catalysts, and batteries last year. This was up sharply from 2008 levels, reflecting heavy selling to take advantage of the high silver prices. High and rising silver prices over the past several years along with economic disloca-

Annual Total Supply
Projected Through 2010.

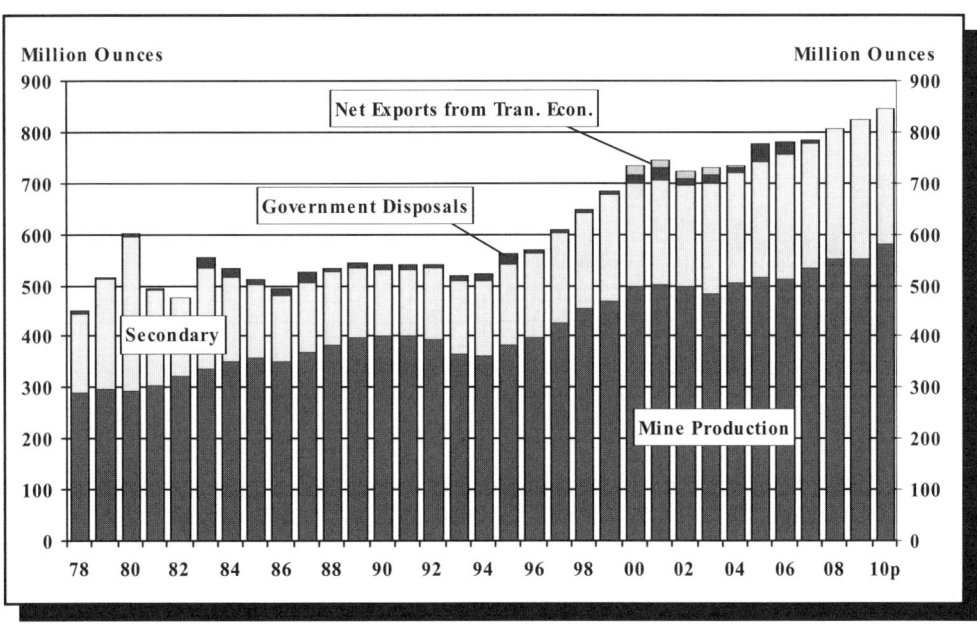

tions have spurred increased recovery of silver from old scrap. Consumers in India, the Middle East, and other Asian nations took advantage of high silver prices and sold old jewelry and silverware to scrap refiners.

The bulk of silver scrap traditionally has come from photographic materials. While the flow of silver recovery from photo products has been declining over the past several years, this has been offset by increases in silver recovery from old jewelry and decorative objects that are being sold for their metal content during a time of historically high silver prices.

Total Fabrication Demand

Total fabrication demand for silver is estimated to have fallen to 616.4 million ounces in 2009, a decline of 11.3% from 694.7 million ounces in 2008. The steepest decline of silver use was in photography. Silver is used in many industries: photography, jewelry and silverware, electronics and batteries, dental and medical, solar panels, chemical catalysts, and many other applications.

Demand for silver in jewelry and silverware, which is currently the largest use of silver, declined last year. High silver prices, reductions in consumer spend-

Annual Total Demand
Projected Through 2010.

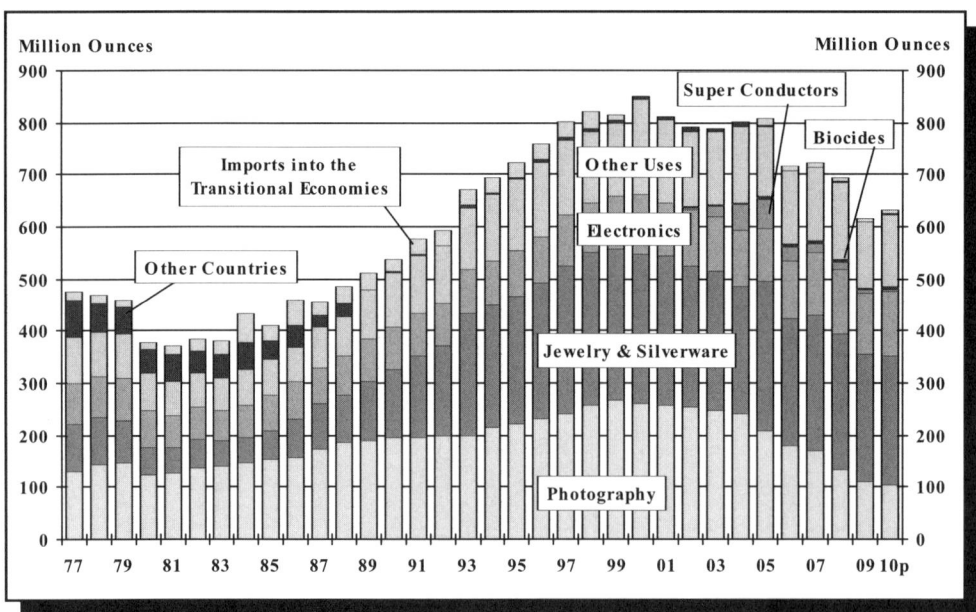

Note: Photography, jewelry and silverware, electronics, and "other" industrial uses includes Canada from 1979, Mexico from 1982, Hong Kong from 1985, Thailand from 1986, India from 1987, South Korea, Australia, Brazil, Chile, Argentina, Peru, Colombia, Pakistan, and Bangladesh from 1989, and Taiwan from 1990.

ing, and high unemployment amid the worldwide recession reduced demand for non-discretionary items. That said, demand for silver in jewelry held up fairly well compared to gold and platinum jewelry. While silver use in jewelry and silverware declined 7.2% in 2009, gold use in jewelry dropped 18.2%.

Photography was the largest use of silver until the early 1990s. However, with the advent of digital imaging use of silver in photography has declined sharply over the past several years. Other uses of silver, especially in electronics, batteries, solar panels, and chemical catalysts also declined in 2009, but the rate of decline was not too sharp.

Exchange Traded Funds and Coins

Investing in silver through exchange traded funds (ETFs) has gained increased popularity since the advent of these funds in 2006. Investors worldwide have been increasing their purchases of silver through ETFs. There are more than six silver ETFs around the world. ETFs provide investors with what many of them perceive to be a more convenient way to buy, hold, and sell physical silver. Silver ETFs are designed to track the price of silver as closely as possible. ETFs are traded on stock exchanges.

Last year investors added 151.0 million ounces of silver to ETF holdings on a global basis. Combined ETF silver holdings stood at 464.9 million ounces at the end of 2009, up 48.1% from 313.9 million ounces at the end of 2008. Combined ETF silver holdings further increased during early 2010. As silver prices fell below $16.00 in late January and early February many investors bought silver ETFs on dips. As of 26 February combined ETF silver holdings had reached a record 474.2 million ounces, an increase of 9.3 million ounces from the end of 2009. The total amount of silver held in the ETFs has been in an upward trend since their inception in 2006.

Individual investors also have been actively investing in physical silver through bullion coins and bars. Worldwide coin sales of silver in 2009 are estimated to have been 35.0 million ounces. Total Silver Eagle coin sales by the U.S. Mint during 2009 were a record 28.8 million ounces, up 47.4% from 19.5 million ounces in 2008.

Demand for one-ounce silver bullion coins continued to surge in the first two months of 2010. U.S. Mint Silver Eagle coin sales totaled 5.6 million ounces in January and February, up 40.2% from 4.0 million ounces sold in the first two months of 2009. Sales in January 2009 were constricted by supply shortages, which makes 2010's sales figures that much greater than the year-ago figures. January's Silver Eagle coin sales were the highest monthly coin sales since 1987. Given strong investor interest in silver, total coin sales this year could surpass 2009 levels.

Markets

Total trading activity in the silver market declined to 85.7 billion ounces in 2009 from 102.0 billion ounces in 2008. (This figure includes physical supply of newly refined silver, trading in futures and options on the largest international exchanges, and clearing volumes through the London interbank market.) Despite the decline in trading volumes, market activity was still very healthy. In terms of value in U.S. dollars, total trading activity in the silver market last year posted the second highest dollar value, at $1.26 trillion, down from a record $1.53 trillion in 2008.

Of this total, futures and options exchange volumes remained strong by historical standards, totaling 60.4 billion ounces last year, down 13.2% from 69.6 billion ounces in 2008. This trading volume includes activity on the New York Comex, now part of CME Group; NYSE Liffe, the Tokyo Commodity Exchange, and the Multi Commodity Exchange of India. Clearing activity through the London Bullion Market Association (LBMA) member banks fell to 24.5 billion ounces in 2009 from 31.5 billion ounces in 2008. Although clearing volume fell in the London market last year, it was still above 2002 and 2003 levels. Trading activity has been shifting to organized futures and options exchanges over the past decade.

Trading activity is projected to remain buoyed and possibly rebound from 2009 levels this year as investors are expected to continue to remain interested in silver on both concerns over economic conditions and on expectations that fabrication demand for silver rises.

The Silver Market
Through 2009

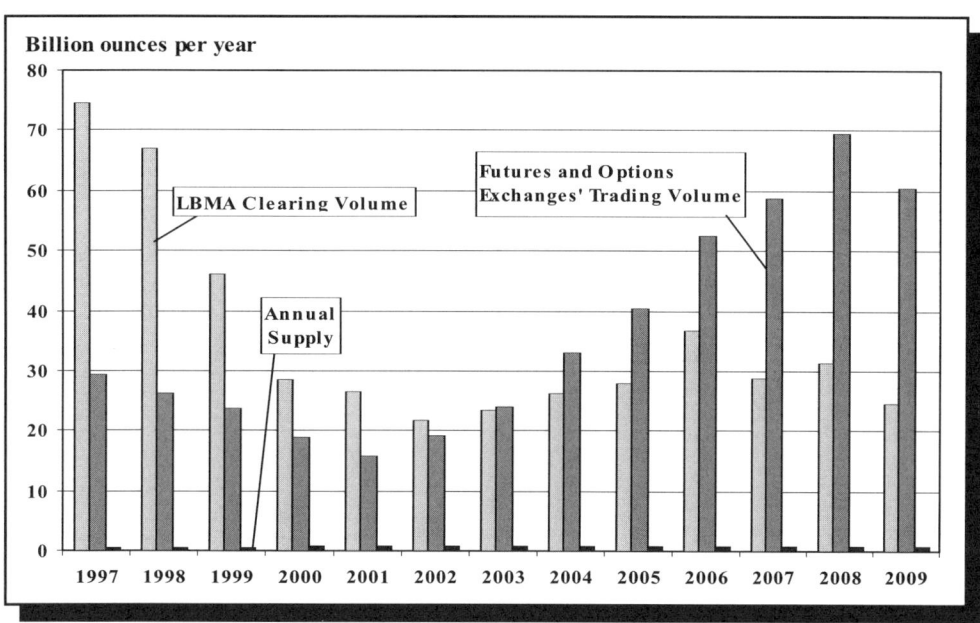

Silver Yearbook 2010 - Review and Outlook — CPM Group

Precious Metals Bullion Stocks

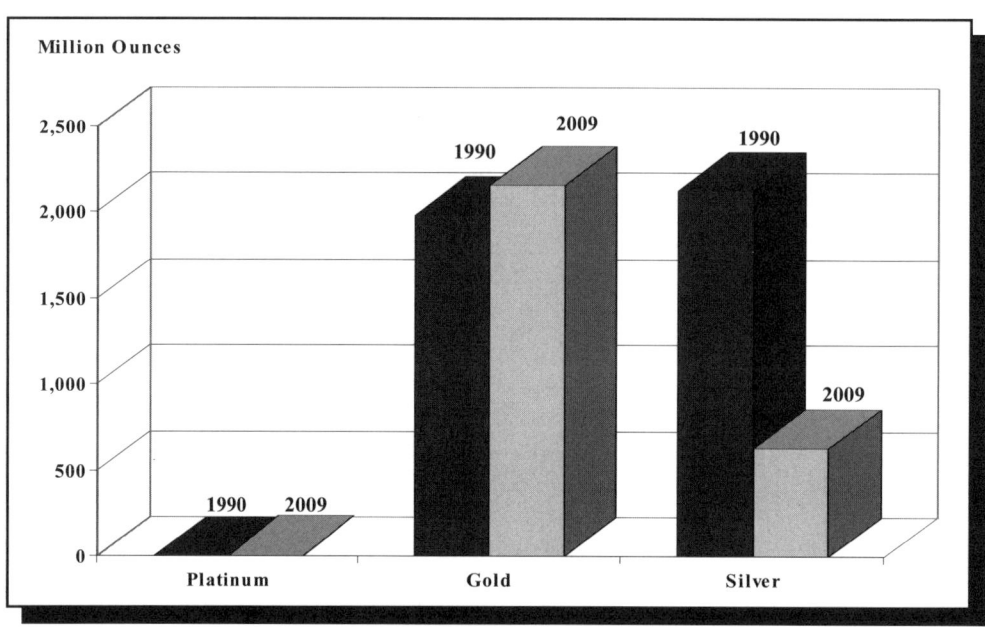

Estimated Silver Inventories in London and Zurich

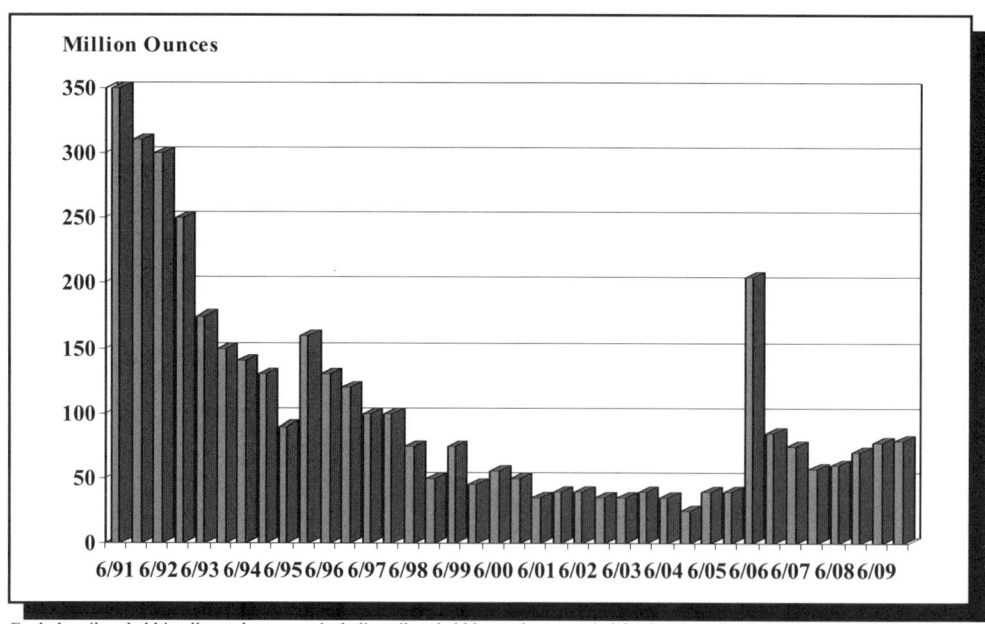

Excludes silver held in allocated accounts including silver held by exchange traded funds.

Deficits' Effects on Prices Depend On Inventories
Annual Surpluses and Deficits

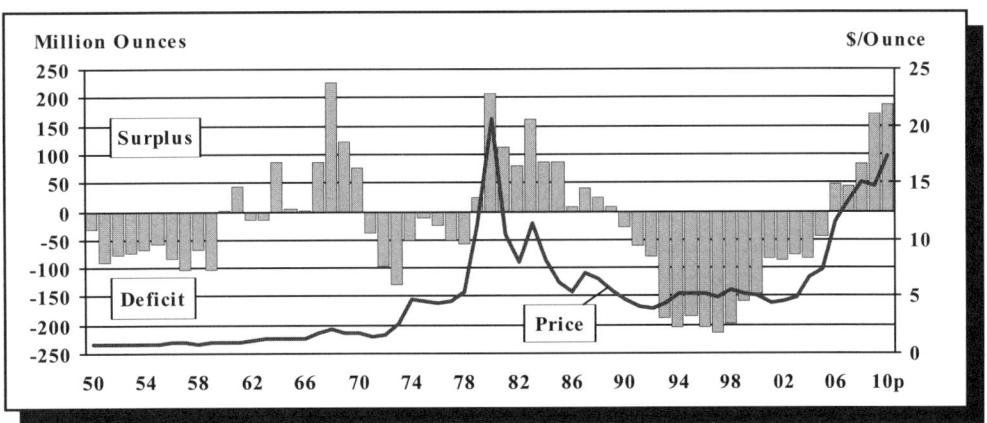

Estimated Total Silver Bullion Inventories, Year-End

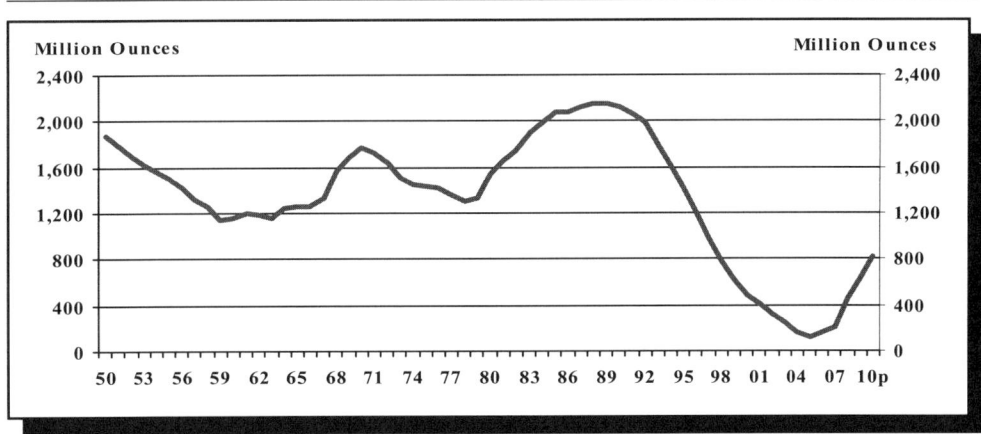

Silver Bullion Inventories as Months of Demand, Year-End

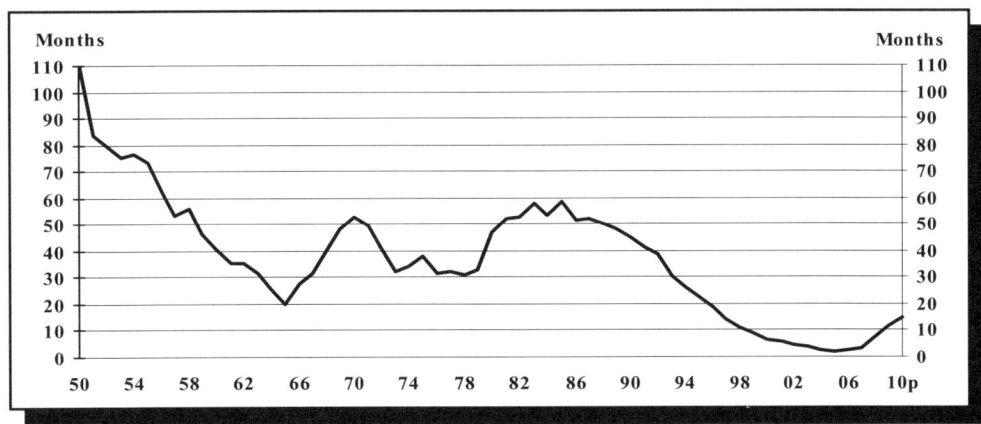

The Economy

	1994	1995	1996	1997	1998	1999	2000	2001	2002	2003	2004	2005	2006	2007	2008	2009	2010p
Real GDP (a)																	
(Percent Change)																	
United States	4.0	2.5	3.7	4.5	4.2	4.4	3.8	0.8	1.6	2.5	3.6	3.1	2.9	2.0	1.1	-2.5	2.8
Japan	0.6	1.5	5.0	1.6	-2.5	0.3	1.7	0.7	-0.7	0.5	4.0	2.4	2.8	1.9	-0.3	-5.4	1.5
Eurozone	2.5	2.6	1.5	2.6	2.8	3.0	3.9	1.9	0.9	0.8	2.0	1.4	2.6	2.3	1.0	-4.0	1.3
China	13.1	10.9	10	9.3	7.8	7.6	8.4	8.3	9.1	10.0	10.1	10.4	11.1	11.5	9.0	8.7	9.5
India	6.8	7.6	7.5	4.9	5.9	6.9	5.4	3.9	4.5	6.9	7.9	9.0	9.7	8.9	7.3	5.5	7.3
Total OECD	2.9	2.2	2.6	3.1	2.3	2.8	3.7	2.4	1.0	1.7	3.6	2.7	3.2	2.6	1.0	-3.4	1.6
Consumer Price																	
Inflation (a)																	
(Percent Change)																	
United States	2.6	2.8	2.9	2.3	1.6	2.2	3.4	2.8	1.6	2.3	2.7	3.4	2.7	2.5	1.0	0.0	1.9
Japan	0.7	-0.1	0.1	1.7	0.6	-0.3	-1.7	-0.7	-0.9	-0.7	-2.3	0.3	0.3	1.4	0.5	-1.7	-1.0
Eurozone	2.7	2.4	2.2	1.6	1.1	1.1	2.1	2.4	2.3	2.1	2.1	2.2	2.2	3.0	1.0	0.5	1.3
China	25.5	10.1	7.0	0.4	-1.0	-0.9	0.9	-0.1	-0.6	2.7	3.2	1.4	2.0	5.9	3.0	0.8	2.5
India	8.8	11.3	10.1	5.3	16.3	0.0	3.2	5.2	4.0	2.9	4.6	5.3	6.7	7.0	5.0	7.5	8.0
Total OECD	2.4	2.5	2.3	1.7	1.3	2.6	1.4	2.8	2.0	1.7	1.8	2.1	2.2	3.0	1.0	0.1	1.5
Industrial Output (a)																	
(Percent Change)																	
United States	5.3	3.3	3.2	5.0	4.9	3.5	5.6	-3.7	1.5	1.8	2.2	2.2	3.0	1.5	-8.9	-2.0	
Japan	0.8	3.5	2.6	4.4	0.1	1.7	6.3	-13.5	1.3	1.3	1.5	1.5	4.7	0.7	-20.7	5.3	
Eurozone	-	-	-	-	-	-	-	0.4	-0.5	0.3	1.8	1.8	3.9	1.3	-12.4	-6.8	
China	21.4	16.1	15.1	13.2	9.6	9.8	11.2	9.9	12.7	16.7	16.3	15.9	15.4	17.4	5.7	11.0	
India	-	12.6	8.6	5.4	3.3	7.6	7.4	2.1	5.1	6.4	8.3	7.9	10.3	7.6	-0.2	11.7	
Total OECD	3.9	3.0	2.8	4.3	3.5	2.1	5.7	-3.6	2.5	1.3	1.6	1.6	2.0	2.5	-1.7		
Interest Rates																	
(Percent)																	
United States	4.3	5.5	5.0	5.1	4.8	4.6	5.8	3.4	1.6	1.1	1.5	2.8	4.7	4.4	0.3	0.2	
Japan	3.7	2.5	2.2	1.7	1.1	1.8	1.7	1.3	1.3	1.0	1.5	1.4	1.7	1.7	0.6	0.3	
Eurozone	-	-	-	-	3.7	3.0	4.4	4.3	3.3	2.3	2.1	2.2	3.1	3.8	2.1	0.7	
China	10.1	10.4	9.0	8.6	4.6	3.2	3.2	3.2	2.7	2.7	3.3	3.3	3.3	3.3	1.4	1.8	
India	12.0	12.0	12.0	9.0	9.0	8.0	8.0	6.5	6.3	6.0	6.0	6.0	6.0	6.0	4.7	3.7	
United Kingdom	5.2	6.3	5.8	6.5	6.8	5.0	5.8	4.8	3.9	3.6	4.4	4.6	4.7	5.6	2.1	0.7	

Notes: (a) Seasonally adjusted annual rates of change from previous period. Projections are based on those of the OECD and IMF, modified by CPM Group. (b) U.S. interest rates are annual average rates on three-month Treasury bills. Japanese interest rates are annual average rates on government bonds. U.K. interest rates are average rates on treasury bills. China and India interest rates are bank rates. Projections are CPM Group's, based on OECD's. p -- projections. e -- estimates.
Sources: OECD, IMF, U.S. Dept. of Commerce, CPM Group.
March 10, 2010

Cumulative World Silver Production and Distribution
Estimated data as of end 2009

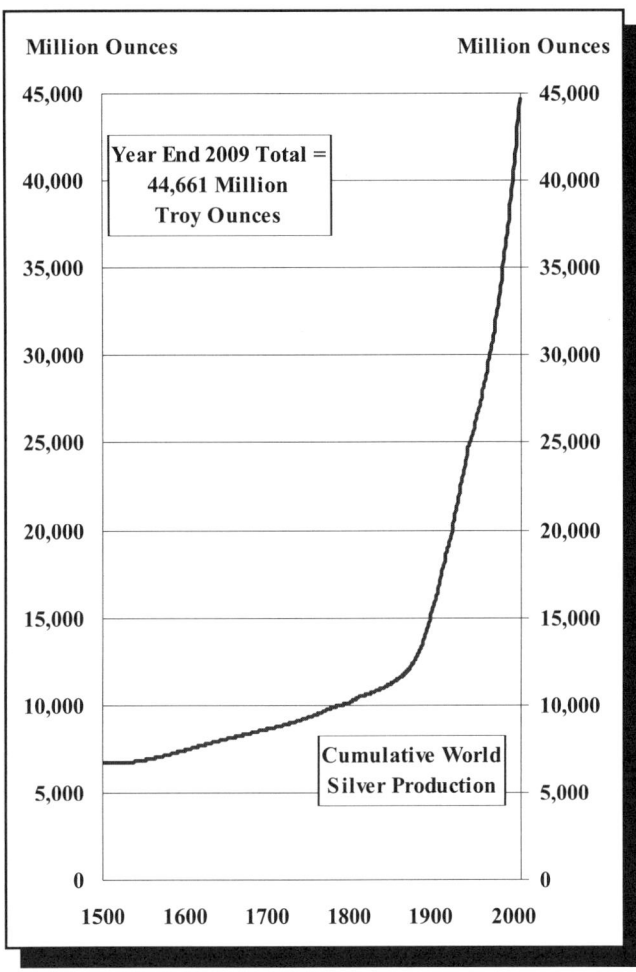

Estimated Disposition
(Million Troy Ounces)

Silver Bullion and Coins
Bullion: 806
Coins: 625
Subtotal: 1,431

Jewelry, Decorative,
and Religious
Objects: 20,926

Industrial Use,
Undetermined
or Lost: 22,303

Total: 44,661

Notes: Total disposition may not equal cumulative production due to rounding and other discrepancies in the historical data. The distribution of 6,681 million ounces of pre-1493 production is not able to be discerned. Silver in product form includes jewelry, art, sterlingware, religious objects, museum pieces, and other silver-bearing objects. Historical information on the production and consumption of silver over the past five millennia necessarily has a high degree of potential error. Some estimates of cumulative production vary by a couple of billion ounces from the sources used here. Sources: Australian Minerals Economics Pty. Ltd., Schmitz, Metschaft, United Nations, Handy and Harman, Ministry of Natural Resources Ontario, Dr. Adolph Soetbeer 1493-1850, USGS, and CPM Group since 1850

Silver Yearbook 2010 - Review and Outlook CPM Group

World Silver Supply and Fabrication Demand
Million Troy Ounces

Year	Supply				Demand			
	Mine Output	Secondary	Other	Total	Industrial	Coinage	Imports into the Transitional Economies	Total
1950	169.5	NA	NA	169.5	157.4	44.1	—	201.5
1951	165.5	NA	NA	165.5	164.6	90.5	—	255.1
1952	180.6	NA	NA	180.6	142.1	114.3	—	256.4
1953	184.7	NA	NA	184.7	168.3	90.8	—	259.1
1954	178.6	NA	NA	178.6	160.8	83.4	—	244.2
1955	187.7	NA	10.3	198.0	192.8	52.6	—	245.4
1956	189.8	30.5	3.7	224.0	215.9	56.6	—	272.5
1957	194.6	25.0	3.8	223.4	212.6	84.2	—	296.8
1958	202.3	17.0	1.3	220.6	190.5	79.5	—	270.0
1959	195.6	33.4	42.0	271.0	212.9	86.4	—	299.3
1960	201.8	52.0	90.0	343.8	237.8	103.9	—	341.7
1961	203.9	65.0	181.0	449.9	269.6	136.0	—	405.6
1962	210.8	69.0	107.0	386.8	275.5	127.6	—	403.1
1963	214.0	68.0	147.0	429.0	278.9	166.4	—	445.3
1964	211.5	86.0	374.0	671.5	318.2	267.1	—	585.3
1965	218.4	103.0	426.0	747.4	358.5	385.1	—	743.6
1966	225.2	105.0	217.0	547.2	417.1	129.5	—	546.6
1967	214.7	126.0	252.0	592.7	401.9	105.3	—	507.2
1968	230.2	227.0	232.0	689.2	373.9	89.3	—	463.2
1969	248.7	174.0	119.0	541.7	386.3	32.7	—	419.0
1970	260.6	127.0	88.9	476.5	376.0	23.4	—	399.4
1971	249.7	127.0	7.0	383.7	389.5	27.8	2.4	419.7
1972	255.1	112.0	12.0	379.1	431.4	38.1	6.2	475.7
1973	261.8	122.0	46.0	429.8	522.5	28.5	7.8	558.8
1974	245.7	192.0	21.0	458.7	470.0	31.6	9.1	510.7
1975	249.9	177.0	15.0	441.9	407.7	33.4	10.9	452.0
1976	264.1	235.0	11.0	510.1	484.7	30.0	21.1	535.8
1977	287.2	169.0	5.0	461.2	459.9	34.5	15.9	510.3
1978	292.0	152.0	9.0	453.0	452.4	39.5	18.2	510.1
1979	297.6	216.0	3.0	516.6	448.2	31.0	11.5	490.7
1980	293.9	302.0	5.0	600.9	364.3	15.0	14.5	393.8
1981	306.4	184.0	4.0	494.4	355.4	9.5	15.3	380.2
1982	321.7	155.0	1.0	477.7	361.4	12.0	23.8	397.2
1983	338.0	197.5	19.0	554.5	356.4	10.2	25.4	392.0
1984	351.0	165.6	16.0	532.6	376.7	13.7	56.6	447.0
1985	359.3	140.9	13.0	513.2	381.2	13.4	30.4	425.0
1986	351.1	129.3	14.0	494.4	410.0	26.8	49.2	486.0
1987	368.6	137.9	20.0	526.5	430.6	30.4	24.9	485.8
1988	383.6	143.9	8.3	535.8	453.3	25.3	32.9	511.5
1989	398.2	136.2	10.7	545.1	478.0	26.3	32.6	536.8
1990	403.1	126.0	11.0	540.1	514.2	29.8	25.0	569.0
1991	400.4	131.2	11.5	543.1	548.4	27.7	27.2	603.3
1992	393.1	140.7	8.1	542.0	564.8	29.4	27.5	621.7
1993	367.3	142.9	11.2	521.4	642.4	38.0	30.0	710.4
1994	361.2	146.2	15.8	523.2	666.3	33.5	28.0	727.8
1995	383.9	159.2	19.0	562.1	695.5	22.0	29.3	746.8
1996	399.2	163.6	8.1	570.9	730.3	18.1	27.9	776.3
1997	427.8	175.0	5.3	608.1	773.9	18.9	29.6	822.4
1998	455.5	187.5	6.0	649.0	790.5	25.0	31.2	846.7
1999	468.4	207.9	10.0	686.3	804.7	29.5	11.0	845.2
2000	498.9	199.5	35.0	733.5	852.3	25.2	0.0	877.5
2001	501.2	203.6	40.0	744.8	810.5	17.6	0.0	828.1
2002	497.5	197.8	30.0	725.3	790.8	20.5	0.0	811.3
2003	483.7	217.1	30.0	730.8	788.4	17.7	0.0	806.1
2004	504.3	216.7	15.0	736.0	800.9	18.2	0.0	819.1
2005	517.5	226.1	35.0	778.6	797.2	16.5	10.0	823.7
2006	512.8	244.6	26.0	783.4	707.7	17.8	10.0	735.5
2007	534.4	243.1	8.0	785.5	714.0	17.4	10.0	741.4
2008	552.4	254.5	0.0	806.9	686.7	28.2	8.0	722.9
2009	553.9	272.2	0.0	826.1	610.4	38.3	6.0	654.6
2010p	581.2	263.9	0.0	845.1	625.2	25.0	6.0	656.2

Note: p - projections. na - not available.
Sources: CPM Group, industry sources.
March 15, 2010

Real and Nominal Silver Prices

Year	Surplus or Deficit	Surplus or Deficit excl. Coin	Surplus or Deficit excl. Coin after 1985	Year	Prices, Base=2009 Real	% Change	Nominal	% Change	US CPI % Change
1950	-32.0	12.1	-32.0	1950	$6.92	--	$0.74	--	--
1951	-89.6	--	-89.6	1951	$7.80	12.6%	$0.89	20.5%	7.9%
1952	-75.8	--	-75.8	1952	$7.26	-6.9%	$0.85	-5.0%	1.9%
1953	-74.4	--	-74.4	1953	$7.23	-0.5%	$0.85	0.3%	0.8%
1954	-65.6	--	-65.6	1954	$7.18	-0.7%	$0.85	0.1%	0.7%
1955	-57.7	-5.1	-57.7	1955	$7.53	4.9%	$0.89	4.5%	-0.4%
1956	-82.7	-26.1	-82.7	1956	$7.56	0.4%	$0.91	1.9%	1.5%
1957	-102.2	-18.0	-102.2	1957	$7.31	-3.3%	$0.91	0.0%	3.3%
1958	-67.7	11.8	-67.7	1958	$6.96	-4.8%	$0.89	-2.0%	2.8%
1959	-103.7	-17.3	-103.7	1959	$7.08	1.7%	$0.91	2.4%	0.7%
1960	2.1	106.0	2.1	1960	$6.97	-1.5%	$0.91	0.2%	1.7%
1961	44.3	180.3	44.3	1961	$6.99	0.2%	$0.92	1.2%	1.0%
1962	-16.3	111.3	-16.3	1962	$8.12	16.2%	$1.08	17.2%	1.0%
1963	-16.3	150.1	-16.3	1963	$9.56	17.7%	$1.29	19.0%	1.3%
1964	86.2	353.3	86.2	1964	$9.45	-1.1%	$1.29	0.2%	1.3%
1965	3.8	388.9	3.8	1965	$9.30	-1.6%	$1.29	0.0%	1.6%
1966	0.6	130.1	0.6	1966	$9.03	-2.9%	$1.29	0.0%	2.9%
1967	85.5	190.8	85.5	1967	$12.44	37.7%	$1.82	40.8%	3.1%
1968	226.0	315.3	226.0	1968	$14.25	14.5%	$2.16	18.7%	4.1%
1969	122.7	155.4	122.7	1969	$10.96	-23.1%	$1.78	-17.6%	5.5%
1970	77.1	100.5	77.1	1970	$10.20	-7.0%	$1.76	-1.1%	5.8%
1971	-36.0	-8.2	-36.0	1971	$8.49	-16.8%	$1.54	-12.5%	4.3%
1972	-96.6	-58.5	-96.6	1972	$8.98	5.8%	$1.68	9.1%	3.3%
1973	-129.0	-100.5	-129.0	1973	$13.02	45.0%	$2.54	51.2%	6.2%
1974	-52.0	-20.4	-52.0	1974	$22.61	73.6%	$4.69	84.6%	11.1%
1975	-10.1	23.3	-10.1	1975	$19.82	-12.3%	$4.54	-3.2%	9.1%
1976	-25.7	4.3	-25.7	1976	$17.94	-9.5%	$4.37	-3.7%	5.7%
1977	-49.1	-14.6	-49.1	1977	$17.84	-0.6%	$4.63	5.9%	6.5%
1978	-57.1	-17.6	-57.1	1978	$19.21	7.7%	$5.34	15.3%	7.6%
1979	25.9	56.9	25.9	1979	$38.13	98.5%	$11.20	109.7%	11.3%
1980	207.2	222.2	207.2	1980	$65.14	70.8%	$20.65	84.4%	13.5%
1981	114.3	123.8	114.3	1981	$26.48	-59.3%	$10.53	-49.0%	10.3%
1982	80.5	92.5	80.5	1982	$18.32	-30.8%	$7.93	-24.7%	6.1%
1983	162.5	172.7	162.5	1983	$25.89	41.3%	$11.46	44.5%	3.2%
1984	85.7	99.4	85.7	1984	$17.30	-33.2%	$8.15	-28.9%	4.3%
1985	88.2	101.6	88.2	1985	$12.44	-28.1%	$6.15	-24.5%	3.5%
1986	8.4	35.2	35.2	1986	$10.83	-13.0%	$5.47	-11.1%	1.9%
1987	40.7	71.1	71.1	1987	$13.44	24.1%	$6.99	27.8%	3.7%
1988	24.3	49.6	49.6	1988	$12.01	-10.7%	$6.53	-6.6%	4.1%
1989	8.3	34.6	34.6	1989	$9.53	-20.6%	$5.50	-15.8%	4.8%
1990	-28.9	0.9	0.9	1990	$7.84	-17.8%	$4.82	-12.4%	5.4%
1991	-60.2	-32.5	-32.5	1991	$6.22	-20.6%	$4.03	-16.4%	4.2%
1992	-79.7	-50.3	-50.3	1992	$5.88	-5.5%	$3.93	-2.5%	3.0%
1993	-189.0	-151.0	-151.0	1993	$6.32	7.5%	$4.34	10.4%	3.0%
1994	-204.6	-171.1	-171.1	1994	$7.52	19.1%	$5.28	21.7%	2.6%
1995	-184.7	-162.7	-162.7	1995	$7.20	-4.3%	$5.20	-1.5%	2.8%
1996	-205.4	-187.3	-187.3	1996	$7.00	-2.7%	$5.21	0.2%	2.9%
1997	-214.3	-195.5	-195.5	1997	$6.43	-8.1%	$4.91	-5.8%	2.3%
1998	-197.8	-172.8	-172.8	1998	$7.15	11.1%	$5.53	12.7%	1.6%
1999	-158.9	-129.4	-129.4	1999	$6.61	-7.5%	$5.23	-5.3%	2.2%
2000	-144.1	-118.8	-118.8	2000	$6.09	-7.9%	$5.00	-4.5%	3.4%
2001	-83.3	-65.7	-65.7	2001	$5.16	-15.2%	$4.38	-12.4%	2.8%
2002	-86.0	-65.5	-65.5	2002	$5.35	3.6%	$4.60	5.2%	1.6%
2003	-75.3	-57.6	-57.6	2003	$5.56	4.0%	$4.90	6.3%	2.3%
2004	-83.2	-64.9	-64.9	2004	$7.46	34.1%	$6.70	36.8%	2.7%
2005	-45.1	-28.7	-28.7	2005	$7.93	6.3%	$7.35	9.7%	3.4%
2006	47.9	65.7	65.7	2006	$12.27	54.8%	$11.61	58.0%	3.2%
2007	44.1	61.5	61.5	2007	$13.88	13.1%	$13.45	15.9%	2.9%
2008	84.0	112.2	112.2	2008	$14.91	7.4%	$14.97	11.3%	3.8%
2009	171.5	209.7	209.7	2009	$14.67	-1.5%	$14.67	-2.0%	-0.4%
2010p	188.9	213.9	213.9						

Annual Averages
1950 - 2009	$11.98	$4.84
1960 - 2009	$12.92	$5.63
1977 - 2009	$13.58	$7.47
1990 - 2009	$8.07	$6.81

Supply

Supply

Total silver supply rose 2.4% to 826.1 million ounces last year from what had been a record 806.9 million ounces of total newly refined silver supply in 2008. Both mine production and secondary supply from scrap recycling rose last year, but the larger part of the increase came from secondary supply.

Mine production of silver in market economies rose to 553.9 million ounces last year, up slightly from 552.4 million ounces in 2008. Mine production of silver was mixed in major market economies in 2009: Silver output rose in Peru and Mexico, the two largest producers of silver in the world, but fell in Australia, Canada, and Chile. Silver production was unchanged in the United States. Silver production in other market economies rose last year. Mine output rose in Argentina and Bolivia, but fell slightly in Poland.

Secondary supply of silver rose to 272.2 million ounces last year, a 7.0% increase from 254.5 million ounces in 2008. The largest increase came from silver recovered from Indian silver scrap. Silver supply from this source is very price-sensitive. High silver prices encouraged many individuals, especially in rural areas of India, to sell their old silverware, jewelry, and decorative objects for the metal content. Indian silver scrap kept the domestic silver market well supplied and dealer inventories high, which reduced demand for imported silver in India last year.

Annual Total Supply
Projected Through 2010.

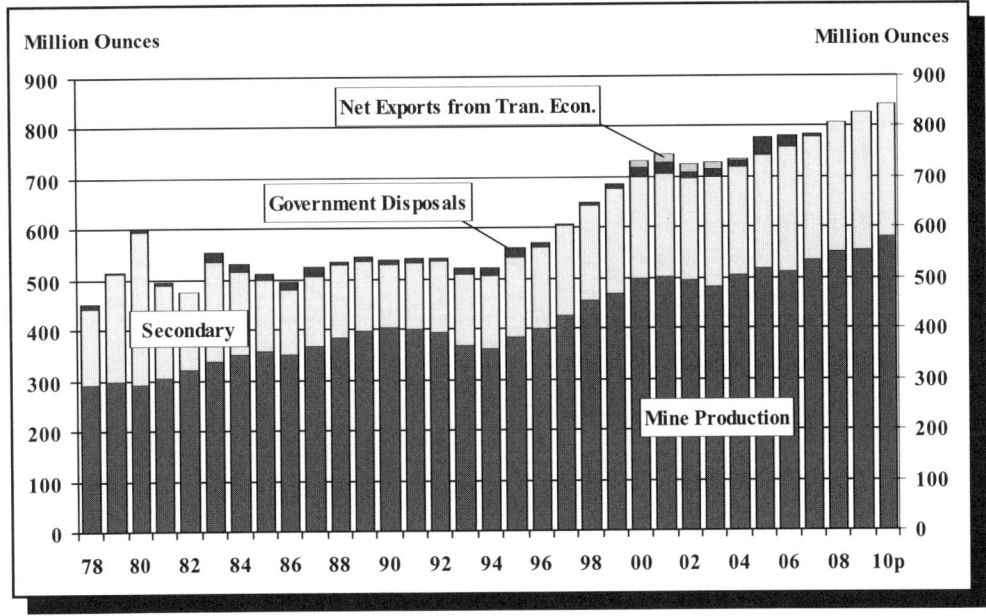

Silver Yearbook 2010 - Supply   CPM Group

Total silver supply is forecast to rise once again this year, to 845.1 million ounces. All of the increase in total supply is projected to come from increases in mine production. Mine production of silver is forecast to rise to 581.2 million ounces this year. Secondary supply of silver meanwhile is expected to decline to 263.9 million ounces.

There are several new mine projects which are likely to come into production this year. At present production of silver at new or expanding mining operations that are slated to come on stream this year is projected at 26.0 million ounces. Annual capacity increases slated to come on stream this year are greater, but since these projections will come onstream and build toward full operating capacity over the course of 2010 and into 2011, they will not and should not be expected to produce at their full capacity within calendar year 2010.

More projects are expected to begin production over the next five years, adding to this total. Silver production from new mine projects that already are scheduled, under development, and due within the next five years is projected to be at least 113.0 million ounces. Apart from these new mine projects, there are several existing mines in many countries that have plans to ramp up their silver output over the next couple of years. This should be expected to add further to total silver production.

Mine Output in Major Silver Producing Countries, 1990-2010p

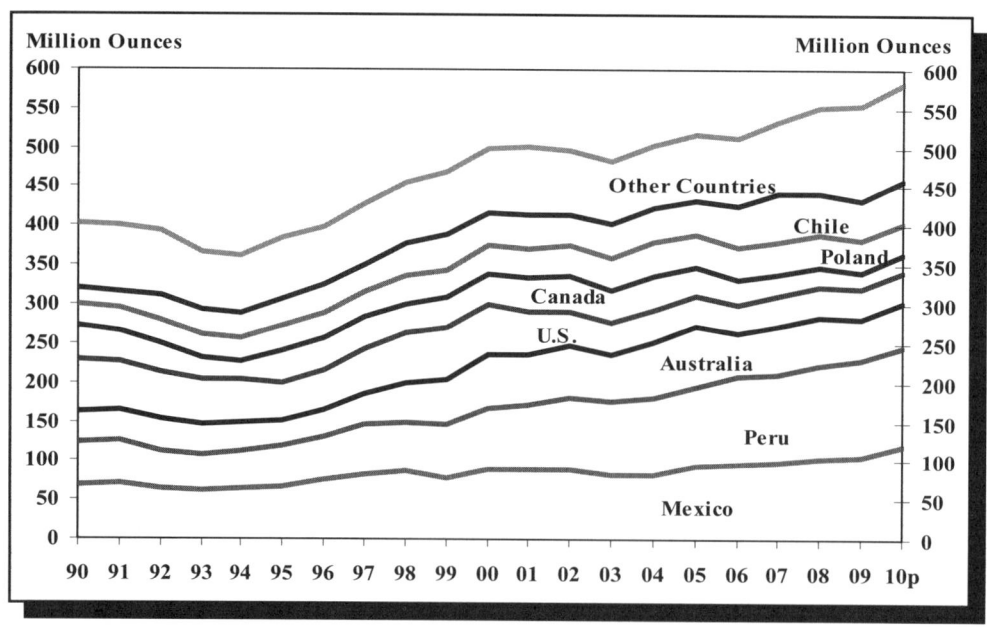

Mine Production

Peru was the largest producer of silver in the world in 2009. Last year silver mine output in Peru was 123.9 million ounces, up 4.6% from the record output of 118.5 million ounces in 2008. Mine output in Peru accounted for 22.4% of total market economy silver output in 2009. Peru has rapidly expanded its silver production since 1999, and has over taken Mexico as the largest silver producing nation. Peru holds around 13% of the world's entire silver reserves.

The Antamina mine, which is owned by BHP Billiton, Xstrata and others, was the largest producing silver mine in Peru in 2009. This mine produced 15.7 million ounces of silver last year, up 25.6% from 12.5 million ounces in 2008. In early 2010 a mine expansion was approved at the Antamina mine. This expansion is expected to be completed in late 2011, which could result in another sharp increase in annual metal production. Also, the known mine life of Antamina has been extended until 2029.

Hochschild's Arcata mine produced 9.5 million ounces of silver in 2009, an increase of 5.6% from 9.0 million ounces in 2008. Silver output at Hochchild's Pallancata mine rose sharply last year. Pallancata produced 8.4 million ounces of silver in 2009 double the 4.2 million ounces produced in 2008. Lower silver output was reported at Buenaventura's Uchucchacua and Colquijirca mines in 2009. Uchucchacua

Estimated Silver Production Additions

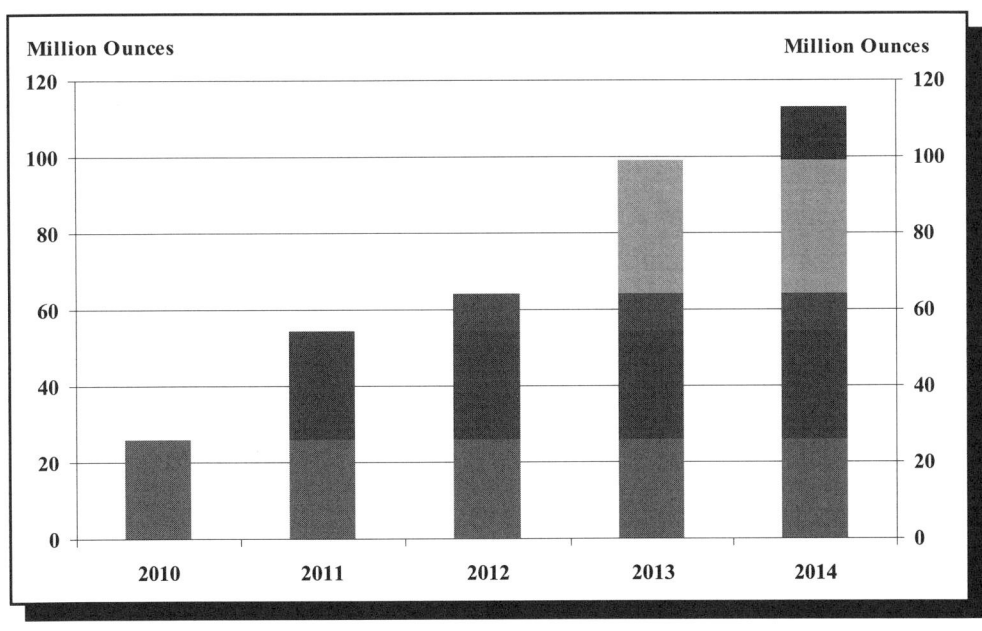

Silver Yearbook 2010 - Supply   CPM Group

Near-term Mine Development Projects, As of March 2010
Annual Production, Due within five years

Project	Company	Country	Production Mil. Oz.	Commencement
Penasquito	Goldcorp	Mexico	14.8	2010
Mirador	Corriente Resources Inc	Ecuador	0.4	2010
El Aguila	Gold Resource	Mexico	4.2	2010
Wolverine	Yukon Zinc Corp.	Canada	2.0	2010
Keno Hill	Alexco Resource Corp	Canada	3.3	2010
Casposo	Intrepid Mines	Argentina	1.1	2010
La Zanja	Buenaventura	Peru	0.2	2010
Santa Elena	SilverCrest Mines Inc	Mexico	0.6	2011
Martabe	Oxiana	Indonesia	2.0	2011
Kanmantoo	Hillgrove Res	Australia	0.1	2011
El Saucito	Fresnillo Plc	Mexico	4.7	2011
Santa Ana	Bear Creek Mg	Peru	4.6	2011
Salobo	Vale	Brazil	1.2	2011
Esperanza	Antofagasta plc	Chile	1.6	2011
Caracoles	Antofagasta plc	Chile	1.0	2011
Wonawinta	Cobar Consolidated Resources	Australia	1.0	2011
Hellyer	Bass Metals Ltd	Australia	0.9	2011
Ban Houayxai	Pan Australian	Laos	0.8	2011
Las Lagunas	EnviroGold	Dominican Rep	0.6	2011
Tantahuatay	Southern Copper/ Buenaventura	Peru	0.5	2011
Prairie Downs	Prairie Downs Metals Ltd	Australia	0.6	2011
Malartic	Osisko Mining Corp	Canada	0.8	2011
Magistral	Inca Pacific	Peru	0.4	2011
Cöpler	Anatolia Mineral	Turkey	0.1	2011
Mount Cannindah	Metallica Minerals Ltd	Australia	0.4	2011
San Jose	Fortuna Silver	Mexico	3.0	2011
Cerro Negro	Andean Resources	Argentina	3.5	2011
Quimsacocha	Iamgold	Ecuador	0.3	2012
Angostura	Greystar Resources Ltd	Colombia	1.1	2012
Galeno	Minmetals, Jiangxi Copper	Peru	2.0	2012
Rosemont	Augusta Resource Corp	U.S.	1.8	2012
Rosario	Silvermex Resources	Mexico	1.2	2012
Kutcho Creek	Capstone Mining Corp	Canada	0.5	2012
Rio Blanco	Intl Minerals	Ecuador	0.4	2012
Constancia	Norsemont Mining	Peru	1.0	2012
Kodu	State of Papua New Guinea	Papua New Guinea	0.9	2012
Marcona	Chariot Resources Ltd	Peru	1.0	2012
Pascua Lama	Barrick Gold Corp	Chile	25.0	2013
Navidad	Pan American Silver Corp	Argentina	5.0	2013
Hardshell	Wildcat Silver Corp	U.S.	2.8	2013
Schaft Creek	Copper Fox, Teck	Canada	1.4	2013
Mercedes	Yamana Gold Inc	Mexico	0.4	2013
Tulsequah Chief	Redcorp Ventures Ltd	Canada	0.1	2013
Dugald River	China Minmetals Corp	Australia	1.0	2014
Corani	Bear Creek Mining	Peru	10.0	2014
Bahuerachi	Jinchuan Group Ltd	Mexico	1.0	2014
Cerro Casale	Kinross/Barrick	Chile	0.3	2014
Rosia Montana	Gabriel Resources	Romania	1.8	2014
Total			113.0	

Notes: Some dates are approximate. These statistics were collected prior to March 2010.
Some project plans may have changed since that time. Some project figures are estimated.
Actual production could be lower than initial projections.
Sources: Company reports, RMD, MEG, CPM Group.
March 08, 2010

produced 10.4 million ounces of silver last year, down slightly from 10.6 million ounces in 2008. Colquijirca produced 3.8 million ounces of silver, a decline of 19.1% from 4.7 million ounces in 2008. Silver output was mixed at other mine operations, with increase at some mines more than offsetting declines in mine production at other operations. Peruvian silver output is projected at 125.1 million ounces this year, an increase of 1.0% from 123.9 million ounces in 2009.

In 2009 **Mexico** was the second largest producer of silver, contributing around 19% to market economy silver production. Mine output in Mexico last year was 104.7 million ounces, up 0.6% from 104.1 million ounces produced in 2008.

Silver output in Mexico has been increasing over the past several years, a trend that is expected to continue in 2010. Mine output in Mexico is forecast to jump sharply to 120.0 million ounces this year, an increase of 14.6% from 2009.

Fresnillo plc's Fresnillo mine remains the largest silver producing mine in Mexico. Silver output at this mine reached a record 35.4 million ounces in 2009, a 4.9% increase from 33.8 million ounces produced in 2008. Most of the increase in silver production at the Fresnillo mine was a result of higher ore grades. Grupo Mexico's Santa Barbara mine produced 4.7 million ounces of silver last year, up 4.4% from 4.5 million ounces in 2008 while Grupo Mexico's

Mine Production in China, Mexico, Peru, and Australia

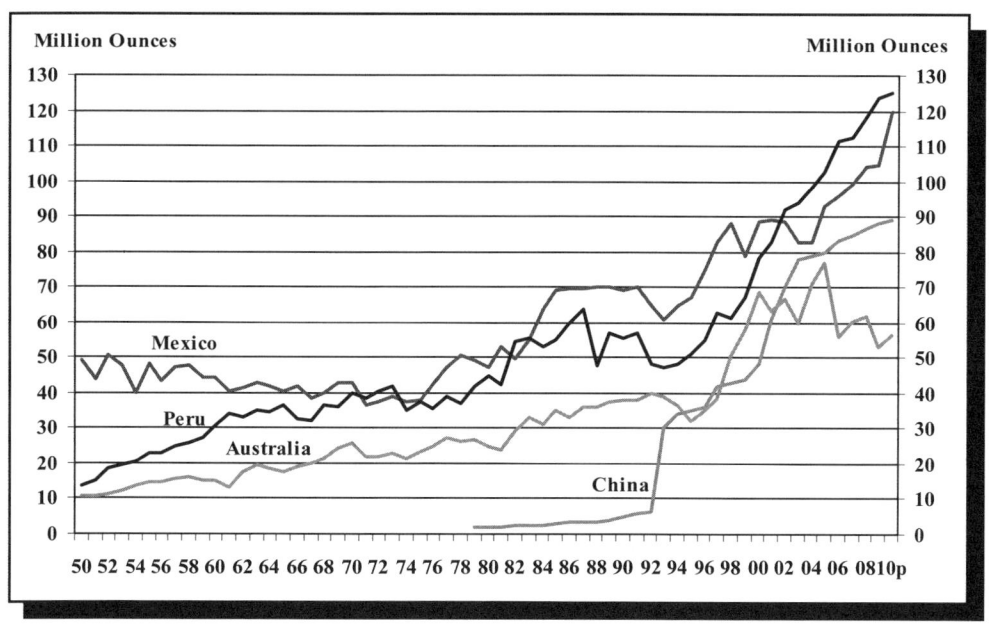

Silver Yearbook 2010 - Supply — CPM Group

Mine Production of Silver
Million Troy Ounces

Year	Australia	Canada	Mexico	Peru	United States	Other Market Economies	Total Market Economies	FSU	Other Transitional Economies	Total	Year
1960	15.2	34.0	44.5	30.8	30.8	46.5	201.8	25.0	8.5	235.3	1960
1961	13.1	31.4	40.3	34.2	34.8	50.1	203.9	25.0	8.0	236.9	1961
1962	17.6	30.7	41.2	33.1	36.8	51.4	210.8	27.0	8.0	245.8	1962
1963	19.6	29.8	42.8	35.2	35.2	51.4	214.0	28.0	8.0	250.0	1963
1964	18.4	29.9	41.7	34.4	36.3	50.8	211.5	29.0	8.0	248.5	1964
1965	17.3	32.3	40.3	36.5	39.8	52.2	218.4	31.0	8.0	257.4	1965
1966	18.9	32.8	42.0	32.8	43.7	55.0	225.2	33.0	8.5	266.7	1966
1967	19.8	37.2	38.3	32.1	32.3	55.0	214.7	35.0	8.5	258.2	1967
1968	21.3	45.0	40.0	36.4	32.7	54.8	230.2	35.0	9.5	274.7	1968
1969	24.5	43.5	42.9	35.9	41.9	60.0	248.7	37.0	10.0	295.7	1969
1970	26.0	44.3	42.8	39.8	45.0	62.7	260.6	41.8	10.0	312.4	1970
1971	21.8	46.0	36.7	38.4	41.6	65.2	249.7	43.3	10.7	303.7	1971
1972	21.9	44.8	37.5	40.2	37.2	73.5	255.1	44.8	10.1	310.0	1972
1973	22.7	47.5	38.8	42.0	37.8	73.0	261.8	46.4	9.4	317.6	1973
1974	21.5	42.8	37.5	34.9	33.8	75.2	245.7	48.0	10.0	303.7	1974
1975	23.3	39.7	38.0	37.5	34.9	76.5	249.9	49.8	10.2	309.9	1975
1976	25.0	41.2	42.6	35.6	34.3	85.4	264.1	49.8	4.1	318.0	1976
1977	27.5	42.2	47.0	39.1	38.2	93.2	287.2	49.8	4.1	341.1	1977
1978	26.1	40.7	50.8	37.0	39.4	98.0	292.0	49.8	6.2	348.0	1978
1979	26.7	36.9	49.4	41.9	37.9	104.7	297.6	49.8	5.0	352.4	1979
1980	25.0	34.4	47.3	44.8	32.3	110.1	293.9	49.8	4.9	348.6	1980
1981	23.9	36.3	53.2	42.6	40.7	109.8	306.4	50.5	4.8	361.8	1981
1982	29.2	42.2	49.8	54.4	40.2	105.8	321.7	52.0	4.7	378.4	1982
1983	33.2	38.7	55.0	55.6	43.4	112.1	338.0	55.0	4.8	397.9	1983
1984	31.3	42.0	63.9	53.3	44.6	116.0	351.0	57.0	5.5	413.5	1984
1985	34.9	38.5	69.2	54.9	39.4	122.5	359.3	63.0	5.7	428.0	1985
1986	32.9	35.0	69.4	59.9	34.2	119.7	351.1	64.0	6.1	421.2	1986
1987	35.9	38.1	69.8	63.6	39.8	121.4	368.6	64.4	6.1	439.1	1987
1988	35.8	44.1	70.0	47.7	53.4	132.6	383.6	64.5	6.4	454.5	1988
1989	37.3	41.3	70.0	56.8	60.8	132.0	398.2	64.7	6.9	469.9	1989
1990	37.8	44.4	69.0	55.5	66.5	129.9	403.1	64.4	6.6	474.0	1990
1991	38.0	40.6	70.0	56.9	61.0	134.0	400.4	64.5	7.6	472.5	1991
1992	40.1	36.3	65.0	48.0	61.0	142.8	393.1	63.4	8.0	464.5	1992
1993	39.1	28.3	61.0	47.0	55.7	136.3	367.3	55.4	31.6	454.3	1993
1994	36.8	23.6	65.0	48.0	54.0	133.9	361.2	49.5	35.6	446.3	1994
1995	32.0	41.3	67.3	51.0	49.5	142.7	383.9	46.2	36.6	466.7	1995
1996	35.0	42.0	75.0	55.0	50.0	142.2	399.2	42.6	37.6	479.5	1996
1997	38.7	39.4	83.0	63.0	59.0	144.8	427.8	37.9	43.6	509.3	1997
1998	50.8	37.9	88.0	61.4	62.4	154.9	455.5	39.0	44.6	539.1	1998
1999	57.7	39.6	79.0	67.1	65.3	159.7	468.4	40.3	45.6	554.3	1999
2000	68.5	39.0	88.5	78.4	65.6	159.0	498.9	44.3	49.6	592.8	2000
2001	63.3	42.4	89.0	83.0	55.9	167.5	501.2	46.3	62.4	609.9	2001
2002	66.6	45.3	88.5	92.3	43.4	161.5	497.5	43.8	71.5	612.8	2002
2003	60.1	42.1	83.0	93.9	39.9	164.7	483.7	51.8	79.4	614.9	2003
2004	71.0	43.0	83.0	98.4	40.2	168.7	504.3	67.3	80.1	651.7	2004
2005	77.0	36.1	93.0	102.7	39.5	169.2	517.5	73.7	81.4	672.6	2005
2006	56.0	32.0	96.1	111.6	36.7	180.6	512.8	73.3	84.9	671.1	2006
2007	60.5	27.7	99.5	112.3	39.0	195.4	534.4	70.3	85.9	690.6	2007
2008	61.9	23.4	104.1	118.5	39.5	205.0	552.4	69.5	87.9	709.8	2008
2009	53.0	20.2	104.7	123.9	39.5	212.6	553.9	70.1	89.7	713.7	2009
2010p	56.5	21.5	120.0	125.1	39.9	218.2	581.2	-	-	581.2	2010p

Notes: Totals may not equal the sums of countries due to rounding. 'Other Market Economies' figure includes Poland, Hungary, Romania, Czech Republic, and Slovakia from 1970, and Bulgaria from 1973. NA -- not available.
Sources: U.S. Bureau of Mines, American Bureau of Metals Statistics, Statistics Canada, Silver Institute, Andean Report, Consejo de Recursos Minerales Mexico, Australian Bureau of Mineral Resources, government agencies, trade sources, CPM Group.
March 11, 2010

La Caridad mine produced 2.1 million ounces of silver, a 16.7% increase from 1.8 million ounces in 2008.

Silver output at Pan American's Alamo Dorado and La Colorado mines fell in 2009. Alamo Dorado mine produced 5.3 million ounces of silver last year, a decline of 13.1% from 6.1 million ounces in 2008. La Colorado mine meanwhile produced 3.5 million ounces of silver, down 10.3% from 3.9 million ounces in 2009.

Minefinders's Dolores mine is a relatively new mine in Mexico, having begun production in the fourth quarter of 2008. This mine produced 1.3 million ounces of silver last year, up from 57,400 ounces in 2008. Dolores began its commercial production in May 2009 and is projected to produce around 2.3 million ounces of silver this year. The Palmarejo mine, owned by Couer d'Alene Mines Corporation, began its operations in the first quarter of 2009. This mine produced 3.0 million ounces of silver last year with a cash cost of $9.80. Couer d' Alene forecast silver output from Palmarejo to reach 7.9 million ounces this year.

There are several plausible mine projects in Mexico that could begin production in 2010. Goldcorp's Penasquito project is one of the potentially sizable byproduct silver projects in Mexico. This mine is expected to begin commercial production in 2010, producing between 14.5 million ounces and 22.5 million ounces of silver annually during the first two years. After that this mine could contribute up to 31.0 million ounces of silver annually over a 22-year initial mine life.

Gold Resources' El Aguila mine is expected to begin production in early 2010. This mine is currently in pre-production. Once in full production it is targeted to produce around 4.2 million ounces of silver per annum during the first three to four years. SilverCrest's Santa Elena mine is currently under construction and could ramp up to commercial production in the last quarter of 2010 or early 2011. This mine is expected to produce on average 500,000 ounces of silver per year over an estimated initial mine life of eight years.

Agnico-Eagle's Pinos Altos mine, which began production in the last quarter of 2009, produced 116,000 ounces of silver in 2009. This mine is scheduled to begin commercial production in late 2010. Pinos Altos could contribute around 1.6 million ounces of silver this year. Once in full production, Pinos Altos has a capacity to produce between 2.0 million ounces and 2.5 million ounces of silver annually.

In **Australia** silver output is estimated to have been 53.0 million ounces in 2009, a sharp decline of 14.4% from 61.9 million ounces in 2008. Weather-related issues during the first quarter of 2009 adversely affected silver output at some of the major silver producing mines in Australia. Several mines also experienced lower ore grades, reducing the amount of metal that could be recovered. All of these mines were base metals mines at which silver is a by-product. With extremely low base metals prices and very weak demand for these metals in early 2009, the weather problems exacerbated already tough conditions.

BHP Billiton's Cannington mine is the largest silver producing mine in Australia. It produced 33.8 million ounces last year, down 2.6% from 34.6 million ounces in 2008. This mine accounted for 64% of total silver production in Australia in 2009. Silver production at Xstrata's Mount Isa mine fell to 7.8 million ounces last year, a 23.5% decline from 10.2 million ounces in 2008. Mine production at the Century mine, which is owned by China Minmetal's, fell to 780,000 ounces last year. This was a sharp decline from 4.2 million ounces produced in 2008. There were several issues, from heavy rainfall to a broken pipeline, which resulted in lower silver output from Century mine. Also, metal production at this mine was placed on hold in early 2009 due to lower base metal prices. China Minmetal's Golden Grove mine produced 1.4 million ounces last year, less than half of the 3.2 million ounces it produced in 2008.

Silver production in Australia is project to recover to 56.5 million ounces this year, assuming there are no major production disruptions.

Silver output in **Chile** is estimated to have declined to 52.0 million ounces in 2009, down 3.7% from 54.0 million ounces in 2008. Yamana Gold's El Penon mine produced 10.0 million ounces of silver in 2009, down slightly from 10.1 million ounces in 2008. Mine production at BHP Billiton's Escondida mine was 5.4 million ounces last year, a decline of 12.9% from 6.2 million ounces in 2008. LaCoipa mine, controlled by Kinross gold, produced 5.3 million ounces of silver last year, down 7.0% from 5.7 million ounces in 2008. In 2009 there was no silver production from Couer d'Alene's Cerro Bayo mine due to suspension of mining activities. Cerro Bayo produced 1.2 million ounces of silver in 2008. This mine could resume production in 2010. Silver production in Chile may rise slightly to 53.5 million ounces this year.

Silver output in the **United States** is estimated to have been 39.5 million ounces in 2009, largely unchanged from 2008. Around 85% of the silver produced in the United States comes from base metal or gold mines. There are a handful of primary silver mines operating in the United States. Silver output from the United States actually has been in a declining trend over the past several years. Since 2003 silver mine production in the United States has hovered mostly between 35.0 million ounces and 40.0 million ounces.

Hecla's Green Creek mine is one of the largest silver mines in the United States, producing 7.5 million ounces of silver last year. This was up 29.3% from 5.8 million ounces in 2008. Green Creek accounted for approximately 20% of total silver output in the United States during 2009. Silver production at Hecla's Lucky Friday mine rose to 3.5 million ounces last year, an increase of 20.7% from 2.9 million ounces in 2008.

U.S. Silver's Galena silver mine produced 2.4 million ounces of silver in 2009, up 41.2% from 1.7 million ounces in 2008. Silver output at Couer d' Alene's Rochester mine fell to 2.1 million ounces last year, from 3.0 million ounces in 2008. Despite increases in silver production at some of these mines, silver output in the United States remained unchanged last year from 2008 levels. This was because increases at some of these mines were not large enough to offset declines at many other smaller mines. Great Basin Gold's Hollister mine began limited production in 2008, and is presently in the ramp-up stage. This mine could add around 300,000 to 400,000 ounces of byproduct silver this year. There may be a few other byproduct silver projects which could come on stream in the United States this year, but the total silver output from these mines is expected to be minimal. Silver output in the United States is forecast to increase slightly to 39.9 million ounces in 2010.

Silver output in **Canada** has been on a declining trend since 2002. One of the

Silver Mine Production By Major Silver Producing Countries
Thousand Troy Ounces

Company	2008	2009e	% Change	2010p	% Change
Peru	118,506	123,900	4.6%	125,100	1.0%
Mexico	104,050	104,692	0.6%	120,000	14.6%
China	86,500	88,300	2.1%	89,000	0.8%
Australia	61,922	53,000	-14.4%	56,500	6.6%
Chile	54,000	52,000	-3.7%	53,500	2.9%
Russia	41,700	42,000	0.7%	42,500	1.2%
Poland	41,000	40,000	-2.4%	40,500	1.3%
Bolivia	35,000	40,000	14.3%	41,000	2.5%
United States	39,500	39,500	0.0%	39,900	1.0%
Kazakhstan	24,500	24,800	1.2%	24,800	0.0%
Canada	23,382	20,238	-13.4%	21,500	6.2%
Sub-Total	630,060	628,430		654,300	
World Silver Mine Production	709,806	713,713		742,208	
Percentage of Production Accounted	88.8%	88.1%		88.2%	

Source: Raw Materiels Group, CPM Group.
March 10, 2010

primary reasons for the decline in silver output in Canada has been a significant decline in its base metals mining operations. Reserves of many base metals in Canada are near their lowest levels since the 1980's. Last year silver mine output in Canada fell to 20.2 million ounces, a 13.4% decline from 23.4 million ounces produced in 2008. In 2009 silver production in Canada fell to its lowest level since at least the 1950's.

A large part of decline in Canada is attributable to the closure of Barrick's Eskay Creek mine, which reached its end of life in early 2008. Xstrata's Brunswick mine is currently the largest silver mine in Canada. This mine produced 9.5 million ounces of silver last year, up 61.0% from 5.9 million ounces in 2008. However, increases in silver output at this mine were not enough to offset declines in other mining operations. LaRonde mine, which is controlled by Agnico-Eagle, produced 3.9 million ounces of silver last year, down slightly from 4.0 million ounces in 2008. Vale Inco's Manitoba mine produced 1.2 million ounces of silver last year, almost half of the 2.3 million ounces it produced in 2008. This year silver production in Canada may edge higher to around 21.5 million ounces. There are a couple of projects that could come on stream during the second half of 2010, which may increase silver output in Canada. For instance, Yukon Zinc Corporation's Wolverine mine is slated to begin production in the middle of 2010. This mine could produce around 2.0 million ounces of silver this year.

After that it is expected to produce between 4.0 million ounces and 4.5 million ounces of silver annually.

Several **other countries** around the world also mine silver, mostly as a byproduct or as a co-product of base metals or gold. Mine production of silver in other market economies is estimated to have totaled 212.6 million ounces in 2009, up 3.5% from 205.0 million ounces in 2008. This year mine output in other market economies is projected to rise further to 218.2 million ounces.

Silver production in **Argentina** has been rising sharply over the past several years. Last year silver output in Argentina is estimated to have been 15.5 million ounces, up 55% from 10.0 million ounces in 2008. Hochschild's San Jose mine produced 5.0 million ounces of silver last year, an increase of 13.6% from 4.4 million ounces in 2008. Couer d' Alene's Martha silver mine produced 3.9 million ounces of silver last year, up from 2.7 million ounces in 2008. Pan American's Manantial Espejo mine began commercial production in the first quarter of 2009. It produced 3.8 million ounces of silver last year. This year Manantial Espejo is forecast to produce 4.6 million ounces of silver. Silver Standard's Pirquitas mine began production in the second quarter of 2009, producing 1.1 million ounces of silver. Lower than anticipated initial production at Pirquitas mine in 2009 was largely due to delays in ramping up production and to adverse weather conditions.

In 2010 Pirquitas is expected to produce 7.0 million ounces of silver. Once in full production Pirquitas has the potential to produce 10.0 million ounces of silver each year over its 14 years of initial mine life. Silver output from Argentina is forecast to rise to 18.0 million ounces this year.

In 2009 mine production in **Poland** is estimated to be 40.0 million ounces, down slightly from 41.0 million ounces in 2008. Silver output at some of the KGHM Polska's copper mines: Rudna, Lubin, and Polkowice, was lower last year. These three mines account for more than 90% of silver production in Poland. This year mine output from Poland is forecast to be 40.5 million ounces.

Mine production of silver in **Bolivia** is estimated to have totaled 40.0 million ounces last year, a 14.3% increase from 35.0 million ounces in 2008. Sumitomo's San Cristobal mine and Couer d Alene's San Bartolome mine are the two largest silver mines in Bolivia. Combined silver production from these two mines accounted for more than 50% of silver output from Bolivia in 2009. San Cristobal mine, owned by Sumitomo Corporation, is estimated to have produced 18.0 million ounces of silver last year, up from 16.0 million ounces in 2008. Couer d' Alene's San Bartolome mine produced 7.5 million ounces of silver last year, more than double the 2.9 million ounces produced in 2008. This year San Bartolome could produce around 9.0 million ounces of silver. South American Silver's Malku Khota project is currently under reserves development. It is a large silver-indium project, which could come into production sometime between 2012 and 2014. Malku Khota project is expected to produce around 4.0 million ounces of silver each year. At present it is too early to gauge the annual silver production from this mine, however.

Cash Costs

Cash costs are comprised of direct mining expenses, smelting, refining and transport costs, labor costs, power and energy costs, as well as other direct costs. Cash costs have been rising over the past several years at most mines, following higher metal prices. Even so, they remain low compared to market prices.

Two sets of factors are driving production costs upward. First, there is real tightness in the supply of virtually every input in mining, from engineers and miners to heavy equipment, structural steel, concrete, and explosives. This is pushing prices higher. Also, with higher prices for silver and other metals, mining companies are mining higher cost portions of existing mines, reopening higher cost mines that had closed earlier, and developing new mines with higher costs. In this way, the rise in market prices for silver pull production costs higher along with them. It should be noted that some of the new mines being opened are extremely lost cost operations.

Silver Yearbook 2010 - Supply   CPM Group

Primary silver producers' average cash costs were $5.17 in 2009, down slightly from $5.30 in 2008 but up from $4.25 in 2007 and $3.81 in 2006. Cash costs of silver declined last year as the costs of many inputs such as energy and transportation fell from 2008 levels. This provides sufficient margins to silver mining companies. Furthermore, these are cash costs of primary silver producers. Since around 70% of silver is mined as a byproduct of base metals or gold, cash costs at other mining operations are much lower.

There are some mines with high costs, above $9 or $10, but the amount of total silver production they represent is rather small. Primary silver producers' cash costs last year were $5.17 while the average silver price was $14.67. This cash cost is calculated based on silver output at 21 mines accounting for approximately 65% of primary silver mine output.

Reserves and Resources

Most mining companies replace reserves on an on-going basis. Even in the face of the enormous expansion of worldwide silver mine production over the past three decades mine reserves have held steady in terms of the number of ounces of reserves while the reserve base of silver, a sub-set of resources, has more than tripled.

Primary Silver Producers' Cash Cost in 2009

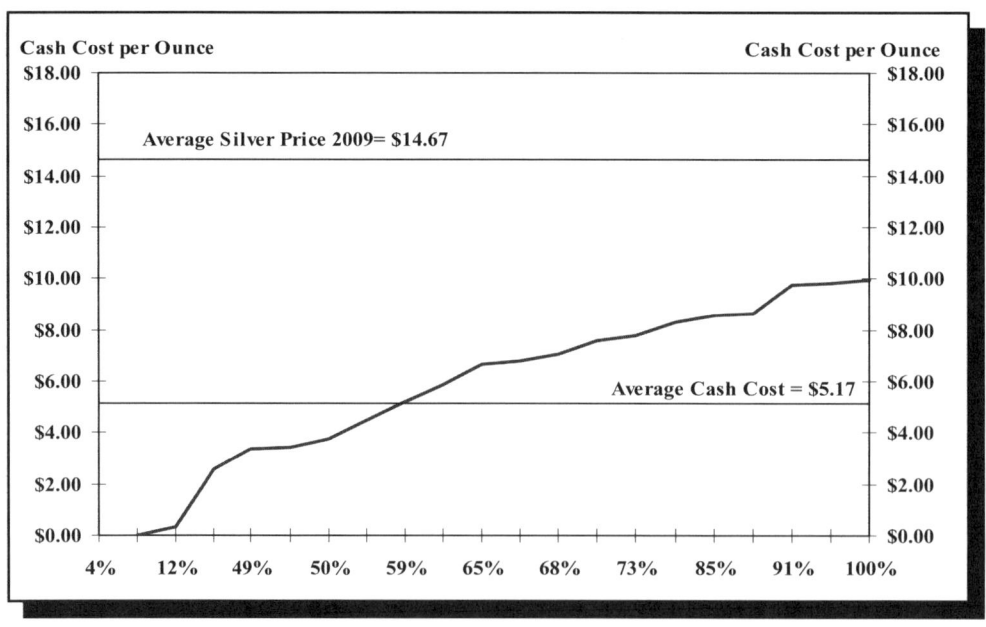

CPM Group　　　　　　　　　　　　　　　　Silver Yearbook 2010 - Supply

This is phenomenal considering that global silver mine production has doubled during this time. In 1980, mine production totaled around 348.6 million ounces. It more than doubled to 713.7 million ounces by 2009. Even with this tremendous increase in silver mine output, reserves have been maintained and the reserve base has tripled.

The reserve base is that portion of resources that are in-place and demonstrated resources from which reserves are estimated. It may encompass those parts of the resources that have a reasonable potential for becoming economically available within planning horizons beyond those that assume proven technology and current economics. The reserve base includes those resources that are currently economic reserves, marginally economic reserves, and some of those that are currently sub-economic resources. The reserve base includes reserves, and measured and indicated resources.

Reserves are that part of resources that could be economically extracted or produced at the time of determination. The term reserves need not signify that extraction facilities are in place and operative. In other words, reserves are proven and probable reserves.

Investors and lenders have to be assured that they can make a decent return on new mining investments. One of the

Primary Silver Mines Cash Cost and Average Silver Price
Annual, Through 2009.

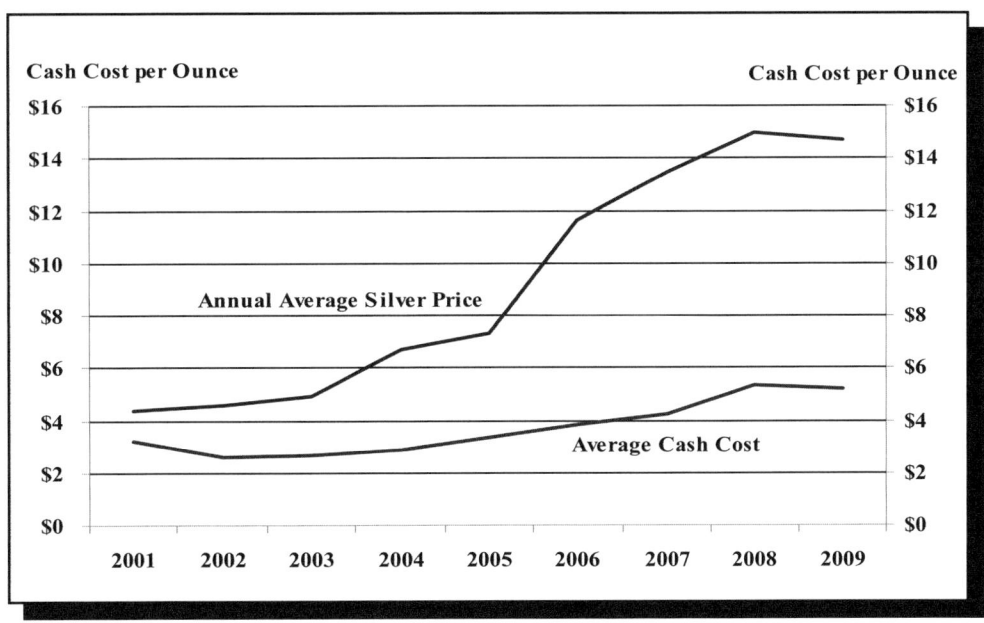

Silver Yearbook 2010 - Supply

main reasons why reserves are not increased to their full potential at the beginning of a mine's operation is because it does not make economic sense to do so. Proving reserves is an expensive proposition, even more so with underground mines than in open pit mines. It takes capital to increase the amount of reserve and resources in a mine. Because of the costs of proving reserves, most companies try to balance between the costs and the need to replace the reserves they mine out each year.

This report is using United States Geological Survey (USGS) data on reserves and reserve bases. There are other systems of measuring reserves, reserve bases and resources, and mining industry experts debate the efficacy of various systems. We leave that debate to the geologists and mining engineers for now, and are using the USGS data because it is available and historically more complete.

Transitional Economies

The Transitional Economies includes a range of countries at various stages of political development. Some are still Communist countries, such as North Korea and Cuba, and produce small amounts of silver. Others are at various stages of transformation from Communist or other Centrally Planned Economies to market economy nations. This latter category includes many countries, including major silver producers

Silver Reserves and Reserves Base

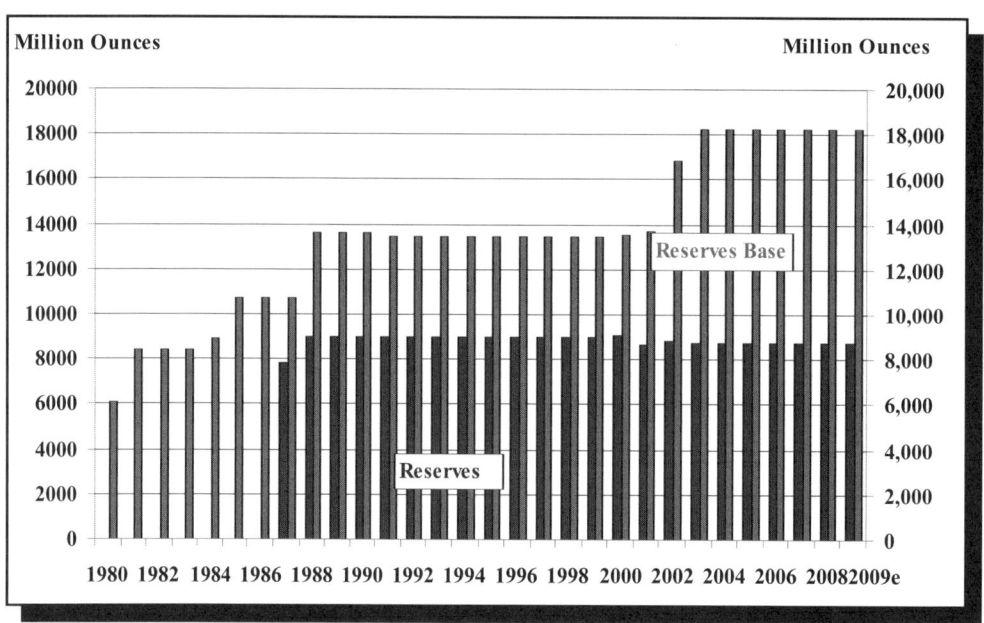

such as China, Russia, and Kazakhstan. These countries are at various stages of integrating their economies into the international or global economy. Mine production in transitional economies rose from 157.4 million ounces in 2008 to 159.8 million ounces in 2009. Silver production in transitional economies is projected to rise once again this year, to around 161.0 million ounces.

Silver mine production in **China** totaled only a few million ounces per year in the early 1990s, mostly as byproduct at base metals mines, and some small scale mining. By 2009 China was estimated to have been producing around 88.0 million ounces of silver per year, mostly derived from zinc and copper mines with some significant primary or co-product silver deposits. China is the third largest silver-producing country, after Peru and Mexico. The Shuikoushan mine, owned by Hunan Nonferrous Metals Corp Ltd, is one of China's largest silver producing mines. The Shuikoushan mine has annual silver production capacity of 16.0 million ounces. Baiyu Xinyuan Mining's Xiacun mine is a fairly large primary silver producing mine with annual output of 3.8 million ounces. Silvercorp mines silver, lead, and zinc at four mines in its Ying mining complex, recovering several million ounces of silver annually.

In response to higher silver prices and the general trend of increasing demand for precious metals, China has a few new silver projects that could come

Transitional Economy Mine Production
Annual, Through 2009.

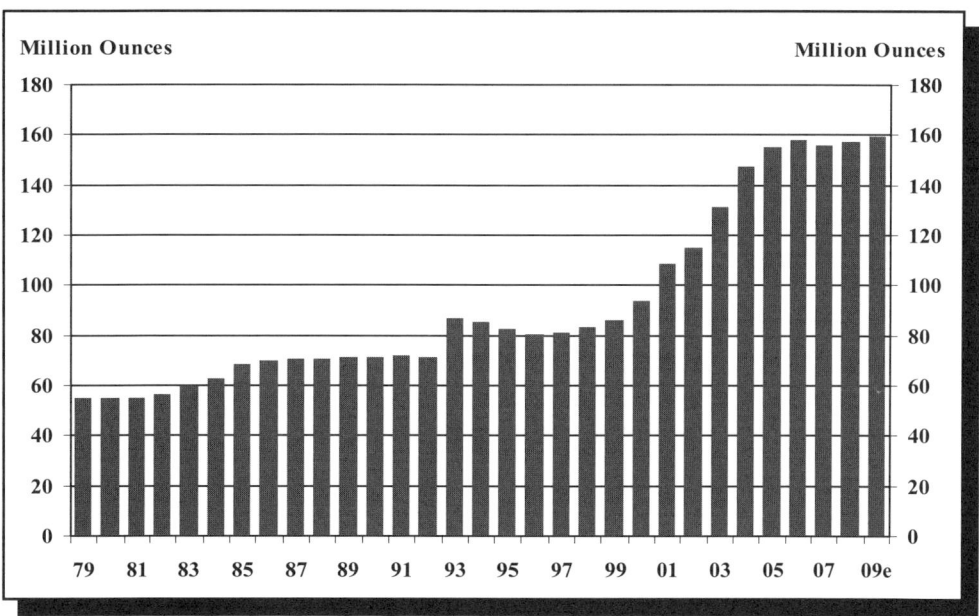

online within the next two to three years. China is expected to continue to increase exploration and development of its silver mines. This year silver output from China is forecast to rise to 89.0 million ounces.

In 2009 **Russia** was the sixth largest silver producer in the world, contributing 42.0 million ounces of the precious metal. In spite of the large resource base in Russia, for many years the Russian silver mining industry has been underdeveloped. Many investors and potential miners are reluctant to conduct mining business in Russia, in part reflecting questions about the legal and regulatory environment in which business has been conducted. The legal and regulatory environment is showing indications that it may be improving at present. While some investors and mining companies have avoided investing in Russia's extractive industries for these reasons, others have taken a more forceful positive approach.

The Dukat mine, owned by Polymetal MNPO, is Russia's largest silver producing mine. It produced 11.8 million ounces of silver last year, down from 12.5 million ounces in 2008. The Lunnoye mine, also owned by Polymetal, is another large silver producing mine in Russia. Lunnoye produced 3.7 million ounces of silver last year, an increase of 8.8% from 3.4 million ounces in 2008. Like China, Russia also is looking to increase its silver production in the next few years. Russia is projected to produce 42.5 million ounces of silver this year.

Over the last decade **Kazakhstan** supplied between 20.0 and 30.0 million ounces of silver per year to internation-

Capacity Additions in China and Russia
Annual Production Capacity. Million Ounces

Country/Projects	Company	2009	2010
Russia			
Lunnoye	Polymetal MNPO	3.40	3.40
Yubileinoye	Ooo Bashkirskaya Med	0.52	0.52
Chebachye	Russian Copper Co Ltd	-	0.85
Asacha	Trans-Siberian Gold plc	-	0.04
Goltsovoye Silver Deposit	Polymetal	-	3.20
Kyzyl-Tashytygsjkoe	Zijin Mining Group Co Ltd	-	2.70
Capacity Addition Subtotal		3.92	10.71
China			
WQ(SLB)	China National Resources Development Holding	0.28	0.28
Zheng Guang	Heilongjiang Heilong Mining	0.05	0.21
Ying	Silvercorp Metals Inc.	4.20	4.50
Xiangguang	Sinovus Mining Ltd	-	2.20
Capacity Addition Subtotal		4.53	7.19
Total Capacity Additions		8.45	17.90

Source: Metals Economics Group, CPM Group
March 16, 2010

al markets, with a majority of the country's output being sourced from Kazakhmys' by-product mines. Last year Kazakhstan is estimated to have produced 24.8 million ounces of silver, up slightly from 24.5 million ounces in 2008. Kazakhmys, which is the largest byproduct silver producer in Kazakhstan, produced 16.9 million ounces of silver last year, an increase of 1.2% from 16.7 million ounces in 2008. The Zhezkazgan mine, the Artemyevsky mine, and the Orlovsky mine are the three Kazakhmys-owned mines that produce significant amounts of silver. In 2009 these mines contributed 8.4 million ounces, 2.6 million ounces, and 1.9 million ounces of silver, respectively. In 2010 silver output in Kazakhstan is forecast to be maintained at last year's level.

There are a host of other smaller mines in Kyrgyzstan, Uzbekistan, and other countries in the transitional economies, but annual silver production statistics for these mines either is not publicly available or if it is available, it is a very small portion of total transitional economy mine production. There are large silver reserves known to exist in these countries, including Tajikistan. Laos also is known to host silver-bearing deposits, as are Cuba and Vietnam.

Secondary Supply

Secondary supply is the second largest source of silver after mine production. Secondary supply of silver rose sharply to 272.2 million ounces last year, up 7.0% from 254.5 million ounces in 2008. This year secondary supply is pro-

Annual Secondary Supply
Projected Through 2010.

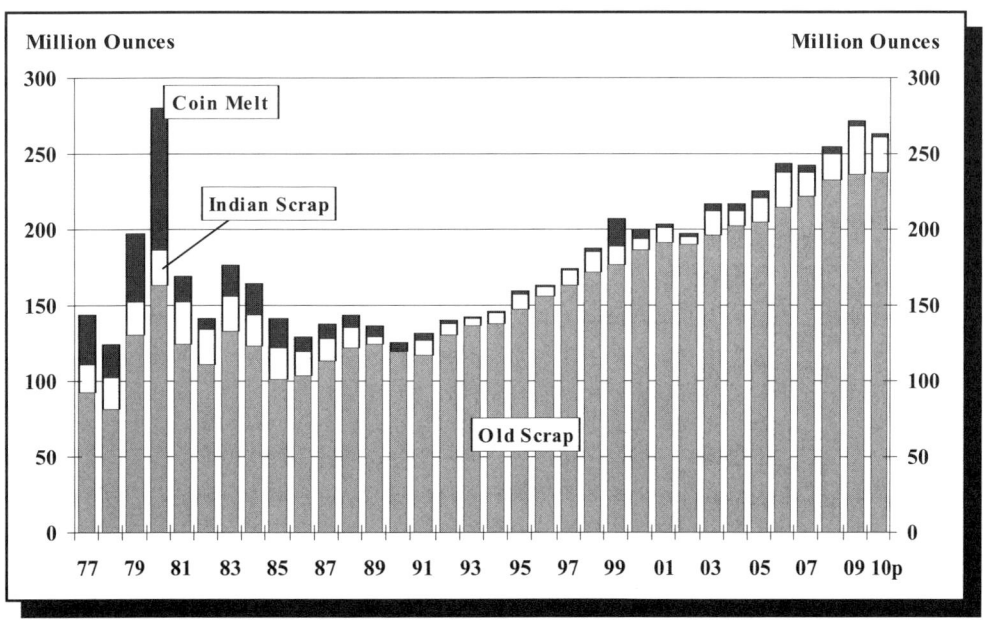

Silver Yearbook 2010 - Supply — CPM Group

jected to decline to 263.9 million ounces.

Secondary supply includes old scrap, Indian silver scrap and old coins. **Old scrap**-which primarily includes the recovery of silver from spent photographic papers, films and solutions, old jewelry and decorative objects, spent batteries, end-of-life electrical and electronic equipment, spent ethylene oxide catalysts, and a wide range of industrial waste-witnessed a 1.3% increase to 236.0 million ounces in 2009. In 2010 silver recovered from old scrap could rise to 238.0 million ounces.

Supply of silver from **Indian scrap** is highly price-sensitive. This is the silver that is recovered in India from old coins, jewelry, silverware, and decorative objects when silver prices rise sharply. Last year supply from silver from this source jumped sharply to 32.2 million ounces, an increase of 84% from 17.5 million ounces in 2008. Many individuals in India took advantage of high silver prices and sold their old silver scrap into domestic markets for profit. This year Indian silver scrap is forecast to decline to 22.5 million ounces. This is based on the assumption that many people who wanted to sell their old silver scrap at prices around $14 - $17, the current range of prices, already may have done so last year. That is not to say there would be no selling or limited selling of silver scrap this year. Should silver prices surge toward $19.00 or

Indian Silver Market

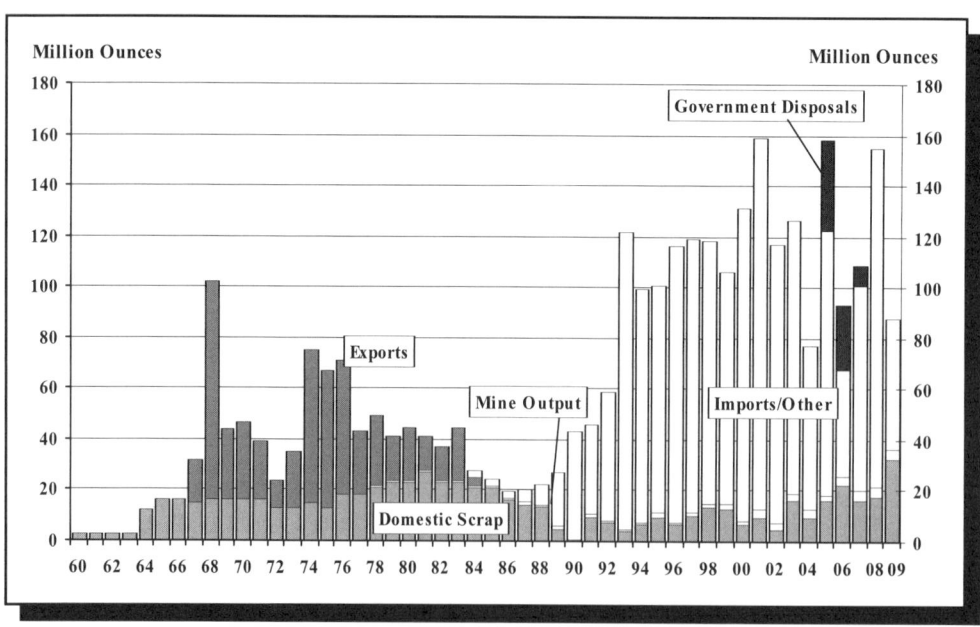

$20.00 this year, a sharp rise in silver recovery from old scrap could be triggered.

Silver recovered from melting **old coins** was estimated to be 4.0 million ounces last year, unchanged from 2008. Many longer term investors continue to hold on to old silver coins. This year silver recovered from coin melt is projected to decline to 3.0 million ounces.

Other Supply
Projected Through 2010.

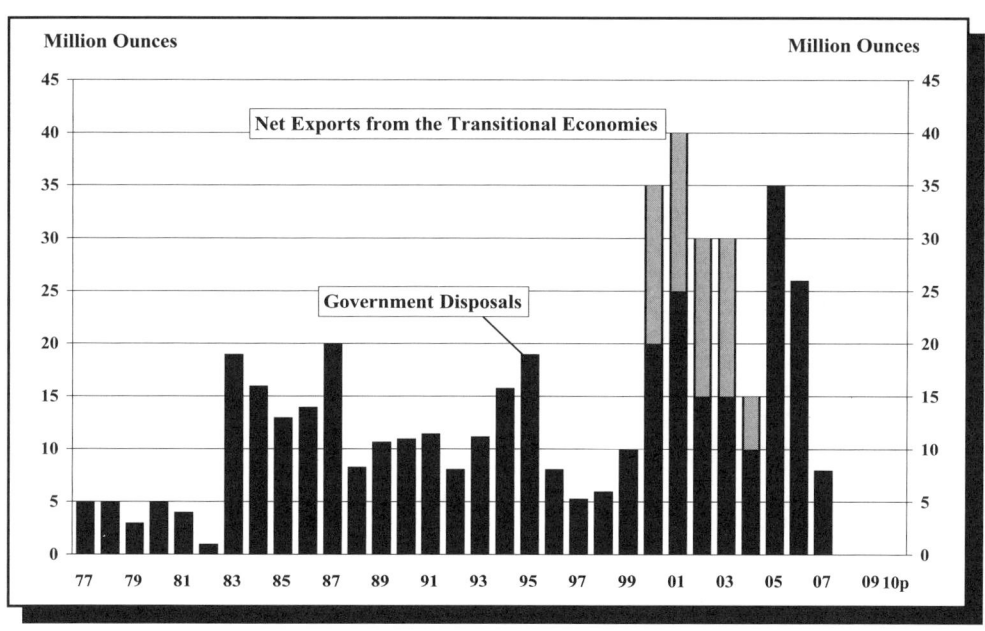

Silver Yearbook 2010 - Supply   CPM Group

World Silver Mine Production
Thousand Troy Ounces

Mine		2009
1 Fresnillo Silver Mine	Mexico	35,420
2 Cannington Silver Lead/Zinc Mine	Australia	33,758
3 San Cristobal Mine	Bolivia	18,000
4 Antamina Copper/Zinc Mine	Peru	15,722
5 Rudna Copper Mine	Poland	15,432
6 Lubin Copper Mine	Poland	12,217
7 Dukat Silver/Gold Mine	Russia	11,799
8 Uchucchacua Silver Mine	Peru	10,404
9 El Penon Gold Mine	Chile	9,967
10 Polkowice-Sieroszowice Copper Mine	Poland	9,645
11 Arcata Silver Mine	Peru	9,500
12 Brunswick (Bathurst) Lead/Zinc Mine	Canada	9,465
13 Pallancata Silver/Gold Deposit	Peru	8,400
14 Zhezkazgan Copper Mines	Kazakhstan	8,359
15 Kupol Gold Mine	Russia	8,205
16 Mount Isa Lead/Zinc Mine	Australia	7,793
17 San Bartolome Silver Mine	Bolivia	7,500
18 Greens Creek Polymetallic Mine	USA	7,459
19 Imiter Silver Mine	Morocco	6,269
20 Codelco Norte Copper Mines	Chile	6,109
21 Escondida Copper Mine	Chile	5,424
22 Alamo Dorado Silver Mine	Mexico	5,321
23 La Coipa Silver/Gold Mine	Chile	5,263
24 Cerro de Pasco Zinc Mine	Peru	5,188
25 San José Gold/Silver Mine (Arg.)	Argentina	4,999
26 Bingham Canyon Copper Mine	USA	4,871
27 Andaychagua Zinc Mine	Peru	4,787
28 Santa Barbara Polymetallic Mine	Mexico	4,662
29 Garpenberg Lead/Zinc Mines	Sweden	4,473
30 San Cristobal Zinc Mine	Peru	4,238
31 Chungar (Animon) Zinc Mine	Peru	4,036
32 LaRonde Gold Mine	Canada	3,919
33 Martha Silver Mine	Argentina	3,858
34 Tizapa Polymetallic Mine	Mexico	3,858
35 Colquijirca Lead/Zinc Mine	Peru	3,822
36 Manantial Espejo Gold/Silver Mine	Argentina	3,783
37 Grasberg Expansion Copper/Gold Mine	Indonesia	3,697
38 Lunnoye Silver/Gold Mine	Russia	3,697
39 Grasberg/Ertsberg Copper/Gold Mine	Indonesia	3,601
40 Lucky Friday Lead/Silver Mine	USA	3,531
41 Huaron Lead/Zinc/Silver Mine	Peru	3,476
42 La Colorada Silver Mine	Mexico	3,468
43 Casapalca (Yauliyacu) Polymetallic Mine	Peru	3,465
44 Palmarejo Gold Mine	Mexico	3,376
45 Sabinas Silver/Lead Mine	Mexico	3,215
46 Rosebery Base Metal Mine	Australia	3,089

World Silver Mine Production
Thousand Troy Ounces

Mine	Country	2009
47 Yanacocha Gold Mines	Peru	2,928
48 Ocampo UG Gold/Silver Mine	Mexico	2,701
49 San Vicente Zinc Mine	Bolivia	2,627
50 Cuajone (SPCC) Copper Mine	Peru	2,583
51 Andina Copper Mine	Chile	2,572
52 Artemyevsky Copper/Zinc Mine	Kazakhstan	2,572
53 Naica Silver/Lead/Zinc Mine	Mexico	2,572
54 Yauricocha Lead/Zinc Mine	Peru	2,435
55 Galena Silver Mine	USA	2,427
56 Casapalca (Americana) Polymetallic Mine	Peru	2,251
57 El Teniente Copper Mine	Chile	2,090
58 La Caridad Copper Mine	Mexico	2,090
59 Rochester Silver Mine	USA	2,058
60 Aruntani Gold Mine	Peru	2,012
61 Orlovsky Copper/Zinc Mine	Kazakhstan	1,929
62 Guanacevi Silver Mine	Mexico	1,870
63 Zinkgruvan Zinc/Lead Mine	Sweden	1,861
64 El Mochito Lead/Zinc Mine	Honduras	1,855
65 Broken Hill (North and South) Lead/Zinc Mines	Australia	1,817
66 Cerro Lindo Copper Mine	Peru	1,811
67 El Porvenir (Milpo) Polymetallic Mine	Peru	1,796
68 Toquepala (SPCC) Copper Mine	Peru	1,787
69 Julcani Silver Mine	Peru	1,776
70 Charcas Polymetallic Mine	Mexico	1,768
71 Khakanja Silver/Gold Mine	Russia	1,704
72 Caylloma Silver Mine	Peru	1,684
73 Morococha (Pan Am) Silver Mine	Peru	1,641
74 Francisco I Maderos (Zacatecas) Lead/Zinc Mine	Mexico	1,608
75 La Ciénega Gold Mine	Mexico	1,589
76 Boliden/Kristineberg Polymetallic Mines	Sweden	1,549
77 Maria Teresa Lead/Zinc Mine	Peru	1,523
78 Cerro San Pedro Gold/Silver Mine	Mexico	1,497
79 McArthur River Base Metal Mine	Australia	1,469
80 Cozamin Copper Mine	Mexico	1,462
81 Atacocha Lead/Zinc/Silver Mine	Peru	1,431
82 Quiruvilca Silver/Zinc Mine	Peru	1,422
83 Huanzala Zinc Mine	Peru	1,399
84 Golden Grove Base/Precious Metals Mine	Australia	1,381
Subtotal		432,087
Global Mine Production		713,713
Percentage of Production Accounted For:		60.5%

Note: Production total estimates for some mines.
Source: Raw Materials Group, company filings, CPM Group
March 10, 2010

Silver Yearbook 2010 - Supply — CPM Group

Mine Production By Country
Thousand Troy Ounces

	1979	1980	1981	1982	1983	1984	1985	1986	1987	1988	1989	1990	1991	1992	1993
Africa															
Algeria	100	100	110	110	120	120	120	120	120	120	120	100	100	100	100
Ghana	20	18	17	17	14	14	14	20	25	25	25	25	50	50	60
Morocco	3,283	3,154	2,120	2,640	2,850	2,409	2,733	1,566	4,300	7,273	8,300	12,100	12,000	7,500	6,500
Namibia	3,617	3,365	3,456	3,150	3,532	3,255	3,400	3,981	3,331	3,472	4,437	2,958	2,926	2,900	2,300
South Africa	3,238	7,458	7,569	6,943	6,485	6,980	6,700	7,144	6,691	6,424	5,781	5,176	5,517	5,874	6,186
Tunisia	231	233	85	117	90	85	26	30	30	30	30	30	25	25	32
Zaire	3,420	2,535	2,575	1,905	1,288	1,499	1,520	1,499	1,400	1,400	1,499	2,700	1,890	950	570
Zambia	914	764	715	887	933	794	625	842	962	942	890	633	547	465	400
Zimbabwe	978	948	858	919	938	892	800	843	817	895	774	682	623	561	550
Total	15,801	18,575	17,505	16,688	16,250	16,048	15,938	16,045	17,676	20,581	21,856	24,404	23,678	18,425	16,698
Asia															
India	370	366	556	466	508	933	822	1,135	1,221	1,318	1,286	868	900	1,109	1,250
Indonesia	793	700	828	1,032	1,047	1,122	1,175	1,371	1,531	1,986	2,012	1,700	2,000	2,300	2,200
Iran	—	—	—	—	—	—	—	—	—	—	—	—	—	1,608	1,929
Japan	8,932	8,195	9,279	9,042	9,877	10,403	10,914	11,307	9,032	8,102	5,008	4,819	5,488	5,733	4,401
Malaysia	433	437	473	522	481	470	522	452	497	641	641	410	500	550	600
Mongolia	—	—	—	—	—	—	—	—	—	—	—	—	—	—	—
Myanmar	340	430	450	526	558	575	569	443	400	378	321	230	230	250	100
Philippines	1,838	1,951	2,021	1,983	1,823	1,574	1,743	1,689	1,638	1,759	1,852	1,528	1,235	926	900
Saudi Arabia	—	—	—	—	—	—	—	—	—	—	—	—	—	926	579
South Korea	2,823	2,293	3,147	3,523	3,366	3,759	3,990	2,584	2,823	1,571	2,762	1,700	2,250	2,250	2,200
Taiwan	84	96	216	505	344	364	366	405	373	268	268	210	250	260	260
Turkey	250	200	200	220	219	219	224	286	283	513	513	640	600	2,100	2,000
Total	15,863	14,668	17,170	17,819	18,223	19,419	20,325	19,672	17,798	16,536	14,663	12,105	13,453	18,012	16,419
Europe															
Bulgaria	805	773	741	805	805	837	837	2,315	2,476	2,733	3,054	3,215	3,054	3,054	1,500
Czech Republic/Slovakia	1,126	1,126	1,126	1,062	964	1,029	1,030	1,062	1,100	1,126	1,100	600	580	550	600
Finland	1,028	1,430	1,215	1,190	980	1,123	1,566	1,193	1,415	997	997	932	964	874	830
France	2,409	2,374	1,706	986	688	769	866	825	831	678	627	710	739	750	430
Germany	1,042	1,213	1,263	1,286	1,167	1,225	1,102	884	994	642	700	260	129	65	50
Greece	1,752	1,671	1,945	1,581	1,797	1,799	1,630	1,726	1,668	1,977	1,668	1,700	1,700	1,700	1,700
Greenland	763	771	720	758	607	335	425	385	402	458	470	300	300	0	0
Hungary	34	34	31	30	30	25	25	25	25	25	25	25	24	24	24
Ireland	1,058	773	595	352	318	280	277	262	232	177	231	282	338	289	420
Italy	1,065	1,365	1,779	1,791	2,362	1,560	513	577	449	513	510	360	200	150	300
Macedonia	—	—	—	—	—	—	—	—	—	—	—	—	—	320	320
Poland	22,569	24,628	20,577	21,058	21,800	23,900	26,717	26,652	26,717	34,176	34,000	26,750	28,903	28,936	29,800
Portugal	35	29	23	23	32	29	108	175	120	120	120	620	650	700	700
Romania	965	901	805	805	805	773	805	741	642	691	671	386	450	500	650
Spain	3,168	5,711	6,186	3,789	5,938	5,000	6,405	5,562	6,880	7,298	7,088	7,400	7,500	7,500	5,000
Sweden	5,650	5,337	5,171	5,396	5,491	7,677	8,038	7,554	8,520	7,201	6,099	7,000	6,500	7,694	8,600
Yugoslavia	5,214	4,789	4,422	3,342	3,987	4,051	5,017	5,702	4,859	4,468	4,276	3,376	2,894	2,600	2,100
Total	48,683	52,925	48,305	44,254	47,771	50,412	55,361	55,640	57,330	63,280	61,636	53,916	54,925	55,706	53,024

Sources: U.S. Bureau of Mines; American Bureau of Metals Statistics; Statistics Canada; Chamber of Mines of South Africa; Silver Institute; Central Intelligence Agency; other government and industry sources; CPM Group.
March 11, 2010

CPM Group — Silver Yearbook 2010 - Supply

1994	1995	1996	1997	1998	1999	2000	2001	2002	2003	2004	2005	2006	2007	2008	2009	
																Africa
100	100	100	100	100	100	100	48	48	55	55	55	55	55	55	55	Algeria
60	60	60	60	65	67	121	110	90	100	100	100	100	100	100	100	Ghana
6,500	6,500	6,000	7,100	7,800	8,295	8,295	9,000	8,900	6,500	6,500	6,500	6,500	6,100	6,000	6,000	Morocco
2,100	2,000	1,875	1,400	800	342	518	1,400	1,400	1,400	900	800	800	800	750	750	Namibia
6,295	6,400	6,400	6,025	5,171	4,886	5,421	3,530	3,600	2,550	2,300	2,800	2,850	2,500	2,400	2,400	South Africa
30	20	20	20	20	25	32	113	96	96	100	100	100	100	100	100	Tunisia
520	490	440	100	100	100	100	32	50	1,150	2,250	1,500	2,200	2,500	950	0	Zaire
400	380	380	390	360	360	360	193	225	300	300	300	300	275	275	275	Zambia
540	354	354	212	200	200	100	57	64	24	50	25	20	20	20	20	Zimbabwe
16,545	16,304	15,629	15,408	14,615	14,374	15,046	14,483	14,474	12,175	12,555	12,180	12,925	12,450	10,650	9,700	Total
																Asia
1,150	1,617	1,145	1,616	1,640	2,198	1,640	2,926	2,926	2,950	2,926	2,251	3,472	4,310	4,310	4,480	India
2,200	5,800	7,684	9,370	10,560	9,768	10,000	11,000	9,300	9,000	8,500	9,000	9,000	9,300	9,000	9,000	Indonesia
1,929	2,315	2,083	1,994	1,894	1,966	1,988	1,929	1,929	1,929	1,929	1,929	1,900	1,900	1,900	1,900	Iran
4,299	3,525	2,600	2,742	2,660	2,633	2,912	2,588	2,604	2,600	3,000	2,000	500	0	0	0	Japan
600	640	365	389	389	212	164	164	164	164	164	100	100	100	100	100	Malaysia
—	—	621	627	633	640	640	643	800	800	800	800	800	800	800	800	Mongolia
100	120	184	253	329	332	332	200	100	100	100	100	100	100	100	100	Myanmar
940	1,000	804	745	659	622	746	1,000	290	300	300	600	800	850	850	825	Philippines
547	539	514	543	445	442	422	322	450	450	300	300	300	290	290	290	Saudi Arabia
2,200	2,200	2,100	1,800	1,800	1,962	1,962	1,962	1,922	1,922	1,922	1,900	1,900	1,900	1,900	1,900	South Korea
260	240	225	220	220	220	220	220	0	0	0	0	0	0	0	0	Taiwan
2,000	2,100	2,000	3,076	3,170	3,233	3,500	3,750	4,000	3,950	4,500	7,000	7,000	7,200	7,200	7,200	Turkey
16,225	20,096	20,325	23,375	24,400	24,228	24,525	26,704	24,485	24,165	24,441	25,980	25,872	26,750	26,450	26,595	Total
																Europe
1,200	1,000	1,125	1,020	989	1,100	1,300	1,600	2,000	2,000	2,100	2,100	2,100	2,100	2,100	2,100	Bulgaria
630	660	300	250	263	268	268	268	268	268	268	268	268	268	268	260	Czech Republic/Slovakia
803	868	900	900	900	900	900	739	900	950	1,100	1,500	1,500	1,500	1,500	1,450	Finland
430	400	64	0	0	0	0	32	32	32	32	32	32	32	32	32	France
50	50	0	0	0	0	0	0	0	0	0	0	0	0	0	0	Germany
1,700	1,700	965	900	972	991	1,400	2,005	2,411	2,411	2,500	2,500	3,000	3,300	3,000	2,800	Greece
0	0	0	0	0	0	0	0	0	0	0	0	0	0	0	0	Greenland
24	24	0	0	0	0	0	0	0	0	0	0	0	0	0	0	Hungary
390	450	514	466	461	492	537	643	161	450	643	643	650	625	675	625	Ireland
300	400	386	393	440	486	490	129	129	129	130	130	130	130	130	130	Italy
320	320	320	320	320	320	320	320	322	322	321	321	321	322	322	322	Macedonia
29,418	31,500	30,543	33,070	35,293	35,129	36,000	38,000	39,000	41,000	44,000	41,000	42,000	41,700	41,000	40,000	Poland
700	1,000	1,286	1,330	1,520	1,389	1,245	643	611	700	800	800	700	875	900	900	Portugal
700	700	700	700	700	700	700	579	579	625	1,000	1,000	1,000	800	800	800	Romania
5,300	3,125	3,070	1,812	1,376	1,175	2,265	2,411	1,500	500	100	150	200	200	200	200	Spain
7,877	8,616	9,000	8,836	9,000	11,000	10,200	9,650	10,300	11,000	10,200	10,000	9,400	9,400	8,500	8,600	Sweden
2,100	1,300	1,930	1,255	1,192	1,216	1,216	1,216	0	0	0	0	0	0	0	0	Yugoslavia
51,942	52,113	51,104	51,251	53,425	55,166	56,840	58,235	58,212	60,386	63,194	60,444	61,301	61,252	59,427	58,219	Total

Silver Yearbook 2010 - Supply — CPM Group

Mine Production By Country – Continued
Thousand Troy Ounces

	1979	1980	1981	1982	1983	1984	1985	1986	1987	1988	1989	1990	1991	1992	1993
North & Central America															
Canada	36,874	34,390	36,311	42,234	38,692	42,001	38,485	34,980	38,118	44,100	41,310	44,374	40,554	36,277	28,255
Costa Rica	2	2	2	2	2	2	2	2	2	2	2	2	2	2	2
Dominican Republic	2,268	1,642	2,062	2,112	1,270	1,222	1,609	1,318	1,149	1,400	700	700	700	750	200
El Salvador	152	146	137	86	23	22	20	17	17	17	17	17	17	17	20
Guatemala	10	10	8	8	3	0	0	0	0	0	0	0	0	0	0
Honduras	2,186	1,721	1,665	2,050	2,587	2,698	2,765	1,747	741	796	796	1,000	1,000	1,200	777
Mexico	49,408	47,344	53,204	49,841	55,000	63,900	69,200	69,400	69,800	70,000	70,000	69,000	70,000	65,000	61,000
Nicaragua	388	163	82	76	63	50	52	26	29	23	23	40	50	55	55
United States	37,896	32,329	40,683	40,248	43,431	44,592	39,357	34,221	39,790	53,402	60,797	66,488	60,984	60,957	55,655
Total	129,184	117,747	134,154	136,657	141,071	154,487	151,490	141,711	149,646	169,740	173,645	181,621	173,307	164,258	145,964
Oceania															
Australia	26,749	24,981	23,920	29,161	33,212	31,250	34,916	32,890	35,912	35,815	37,295	37,800	38,000	40,123	39,100
Fiji	9	9	9	19	12	13	15	15	0	0	34	25	16	20	20
New Zealand	2	1	1	1	0	0	41	41	0	59	156	275	355	400	460
Papua New Guinea	1,434	1,187	1,365	1,394	1,531	1,426	1,487	1,802	2,004	2,100	1,966	2,600	3,215	3,530	3,700
Total	28,194	26,178	25,295	30,575	34,755	32,689	36,459	34,748	37,916	37,974	39,451	40,700	41,586	44,073	43,280
South America															
Argentina	2,209	2,357	2,518	2,684	2,502	1,983	2,170	2,135	1,899	1,608	1,547	2,300	2,300	1,400	1,400
Bolivia	5,742	6,099	6,394	5,472	6,024	4,559	3,614	3,057	4,565	7,451	8,586	9,984	10,835	9,077	10,700
Brazil	1,065	737	765	748	750	2,275	2,301	1,913	1,966	2,252	2,056	1,800	1,500	1,200	1,200
Chile	8,740	9,596	11,608	12,288	14,955	15,776	16,642	16,080	16,068	16,301	17,701	20,500	21,750	33,000	31,200
Colombia	99	146	134	137	134	128	155	187	167	211	220	210	200	267	240
Ecuador	70	70	32	9	3	3	2	2	2	2	2	0	0	130	170
Peru	41,900	44,815	42,553	54,379	55,565	53,257	54,854	59,924	63,576	47,657	56,830	55,548	56,882	48,000	47,000
Total	59,825	63,820	64,004	75,717	79,933	77,981	79,738	83,298	88,243	75,482	86,942	90,342	93,467	93,074	91,910
Subtotal	297,550	293,913	306,433	321,710	338,003	351,036	359,311	351,114	368,608	383,593	398,193	403,088	400,416	393,547	367,295
Transitional Economies															
China	1,928	1,928	2,091	2,252	2,300	2,600	2,800	3,214	3,214	3,500	4,000	5,000	6,000	6,400	30,000
East Germany	1,543	1,511	1,447	1,447	1,382	1,286	1,318	1,318	1,318	1,286	1,298	—	—	—	—
North Korea	1,543	1,447	1,286	965	1,100	1,600	1,600	1,600	1,600	1,600	1,600	1,600	1,600	1,600	1,600
Russia	—	—	—	—	—	—	—	—	—	—	—	—	—	27,328	26,900
Kazakhstan	—	—	—	—	—	—	—	—	—	—	—	—	—	32,151	25,000
Tajikistan	—	—	—	—	—	—	—	—	—	—	—	—	—	200	200
Uzbekistan	—	—	—	—	—	—	—	—	—	—	—	—	—	2,894	2,500
Armenia	—	—	—	—	—	—	—	—	—	—	—	—	—	482	500
Kyrgyzstan	—	—	—	—	—	—	—	—	—	—	—	—	—	—	—
Other C.I.S.	—	—	—	—	—	—	—	—	—	—	—	—	—	322	300
Soviet Union	49,834	49,834	50,500	52,000	55,000	57,000	63,000	64,000	64,400	64,500	64,700	64,400	64,500	—	—
Total	54,848	54,720	55,324	56,664	59,782	62,486	68,718	70,132	70,532	70,886	71,598	71,000	72,100	71,376	87,000
WORLD TOTAL	352,398	348,633	361,757	378,374	397,785	413,522	428,029	421,246	439,141	454,479	469,791	474,088	472,516	464,924	454,295

1994	1995	1996	1997	1998	1999	2000	2001	2002	2003	2004	2005	2006	2007	2008	2009	
																North & Central America
23,613	41,306	42,041	39,351	37,892	39,587	38,979	42,440	45,254	42,122	43,001	36,132	31,991	27,664	23,382	20,238	Canada
2	2	2	2	25	17	9	16	16	16	16	16	16	16	16	16	Costa Rica
600	677	650	520	364	100	100	2	2	2	2	2	2	2	2	2	Dominican Republic
20	25	25	25	25	25	26	26	26	26	26	26	26	26	26	26	El Salvador
0	0	0	0	0	0	0	0	0	0	0	155	1,600	2,840	3,200	3,200	Guatemala
888	971	1,170	1,379	1,381	1,496	1,690	1,506	1,700	1,650	1,570	1,730	1,780	1,730	1,900	1,850	Honduras
65,000	67,300	75,000	83,000	87,980	79,000	88,500	89,000	88,500	83,000	83,000	93,000	96,058	99,500	104,050	104,692	Mexico
55	50	77	180	161	177	177	133	96	100	100	100	100	100	100	100	Nicaragua
54,001	49,500	50,000	59,000	62,422	65,293	65,620	55,942	43,404	39,867	40,189	39,545	36,652	39,000	39,500	39,500	United States
144,179	159,831	168,965	183,457	190,250	185,695	195,100	189,065	178,998	166,783	167,903	170,707	168,225	170,878	172,176	169,624	Total
																Oceania
36,750	32,000	35,000	38,700	50,810	57,700	68,450	63,300	66,550	60,100	71,000	77,000	56,000	60,500	61,922	53,000	Australia
20	67	63	83	73	88	80	68	68	50	50	40	40	40	40	40	Fiji
887	900	960	1,021	736	775	804	804	950	1,000	1,000	1,300	1,200	1,000	975	975	New Zealand
2,112	2,095	1,898	1,553	1,854	2,109	2,500	2,300	2,000	2,000	1,800	1,800	1,700	1,300	1,400	2,500	Papua New Guinea
39,769	35,062	37,921	41,357	53,474	60,672	71,834	66,472	69,568	63,150	73,850	80,140	58,940	62,840	64,337	56,515	Total
																South America
1,300	1,500	1,600	1,700	1,100	2,400	2,500	4,920	4,350	4,400	5,400	5,600	6,200	7,000	10,000	15,500	Argentina
11,300	13,600	11,000	12,500	13,000	13,600	14,000	13,100	14,700	15,000	13,200	13,500	15,000	18,000	35,000	40,000	Bolivia
500	400	400	400	400	400	350	1,450	1,050	1,000	1,150	1,150	1,250	1,300	1,300	1,300	Brazil
31,000	33,500	36,800	35,000	43,000	44,400	40,000	43,300	38,900	42,200	43,700	44,600	51,000	61,000	54,000	52,000	Chile
255	230	230	127	129	132	132	257	225	300	300	300	300	300	300	300	Colombia
200	220	240	228	233	235	235	235	235	235	235	250	250	250	250	250	Ecuador
48,000	51,000	55,000	63,000	61,425	67,138	78,370	83,000	92,260	93,910	98,375	102,662	111,587	112,332	118,506	123,900	Peru
92,555	100,450	105,270	112,955	119,287	128,304	135,586	146,262	151,720	157,045	162,360	168,062	185,587	200,182	219,356	233,250	Total
361,215	383,856	399,214	427,803	455,450	468,439	498,932	501,221	497,456	483,705	504,303	517,512	512,850	534,352	552,396	553,903	Subtotal
																Transitional Economies
34,000	35,000	36,000	42,000	43,000	44,000	48,000	61,000	70,100	78,000	78,700	80,000	83,500	84,500	86,500	88,300	China
—	—	—	—	—	—	—	—	—	—	—	—	—	—	—	—	East Germany
1,600	1,600	1,600	1,600	1,600	1,600	1,600	1,400	1,400	1,400	1,400	1,400	1,400	1,400	1,400	1,400	North Korea
25,000	23,500	24,636	20,900	19,000	16,000	13,000	13,000	13,000	22,500	41,000	43,400	42,000	40,500	41,700	42,000	Russia
21,500	20,000	15,000	14,000	17,000	21,000	28,000	30,000	27,500	26,000	23,000	27,000	28,000	26,500	24,500	24,800	Kazakhstan
200	200	200	200	200	200	200	200	200	200	200	200	200	200	200	200	Tajikistan
2,000	1,700	1,700	1,700	1,700	2,000	2,000	2,000	2,000	2,000	2,000	2,000	2,000	2,000	2,000	2,000	Uzbekistan
500	500	500	500	500	500	500	500	500	500	500	500	500	500	500	500	Armenia
—	—	300	300	300	300	300	300	300	300	300	300	300	300	300	300	Kyrgyzstan
300	300	310	310	310	310	310	310	310	310	310	310	310	310	310	310	Other C.I.S.
—	—	—	—	—	—	—	—	—	—	—	—	—	—	—	—	Soviet Union
85,100	82,800	80,246	81,510	83,610	85,910	93,910	108,710	115,310	131,210	147,410	155,110	158,210	156,210	157,410	159,810	Total
446,315	466,656	479,460	509,313	539,060	554,349	592,842	609,931	612,766	614,915	651,713	672,622	671,060	690,562	709,806	713,713	**WORLD TOTAL**

Silver Yearbook 2010 - Supply — CPM Group

Secondary and Other Supplies
Million Troy Ounces

Year	Old Scrap	Demonetized Coin	Secondary Indian Scrap used Domestically	South Asian Exports	Government Disposals	Net Exports from T.E.	Total Secondary and Other	U.S. Treasury Sales	U.S. Treasury Coinage	Total	Year
1960	40.0	10.0	2.0	—	12.0	10.0	74.0	22.0	46.0	142.0	1960
1961	43.0	20.0	2.0	—	7.0	55.0	127.0	63.0	56.0	246.0	1961
1962	47.0	20.0	2.0	—	4.0	25.0	98.0	1.0	77.0	176.0	1962
1963	50.0	15.0	3.0	—	10.0	—	78.0	25.0	112.0	215.0	1963
1964	54.0	20.0	12.0	—	20.0	—	106.0	151.0	203.0	460.0	1964
1965	57.0	30.0	16.0	—	17.0	9.0	129.0	80.0	320.0	529.0	1965
1966	61.0	28.0	16.0	—	10.0	10.0	125.0	143.0	54.0	322.0	1966
1967	59.0	35.0	15.0	17.0	5.0	8.0	139.0	195.0	44.0	378.0	1967
1968	75.0	50.0	16.0	86.0	15.0	—	242.0	180.0	37.0	459.0	1968
1969	80.0	50.0	16.0	28.0	—	11.0	185.0	89.0	19.0	293.0	1969
1970	55.0	25.0	16.0	31.0	10.0	10.9	147.9	67.0	1.0	215.9	1970
1971	68.0	20.0	16.0	23.0	7.0	—	134.0	—	—	134.0	1971
1972	73.0	15.0	13.0	11.0	12.0	—	124.0	—	—	124.0	1972
1973	72.0	15.0	13.0	22.0	46.0	—	168.0	—	—	168.0	1973
1974	82.0	35.0	15.0	60.0	21.0	—	213.0	—	—	213.0	1974
1975	90.0	20.0	13.0	54.0	15.0	—	192.0	—	—	192.0	1975
1976	92.0	72.0	18.0	53.0	11.0	—	246.0	—	—	246.0	1976
1977	93.0	33.0	18.0	25.0	5.0	—	174.0	—	—	174.0	1977
1978	82.0	21.0	21.0	28.0	9.0	—	161.0	—	—	161.0	1978
1979	130.0	45.0	23.0	18.0	3.0	—	219.0	—	—	219.0	1979
1980	164.0	94.0	23.0	21.0	5.0	—	307.0	—	—	307.0	1980
1981	125.0	18.0	27.0	14.0	4.0	—	188.0	—	—	188.0	1981
1982	111.0	7.0	23.0	14.0	1.0	—	156.0	—	—	156.0	1982
1983	133.4	20.1	23.0	21.0	19.0	—	216.5	—	—	216.5	1983
1984	123.5	20.1	21.0	1.0	16.0	—	181.6	—	—	181.6	1984
1985	101.5	18.4	21.0	—	13.0	—	153.9	—	—	153.9	1985
1986	103.4	9.9	16.0	—	14.0	—	143.3	—	—	143.3	1986
1987	113.3	10.1	14.5	—	20.0	—	157.9	—	—	157.9	1987
1988	121.9	8.8	13.2	—	8.3	—	152.2	—	—	152.2	1988
1989	125.0	6.4	4.8	—	10.7	—	146.9	—	—	146.9	1989
1990	120.0	6.0	0.0	—	11.0	—	137.0	—	—	137.0	1990
1991	117.6	4.0	9.6	—	11.5	—	142.7	—	—	142.7	1991
1992	130.5	3.0	7.2	—	8.1	—	148.8	—	—	148.8	1992
1993	137.1	2.0	3.8	—	11.2	—	154.1	—	—	154.1	1993
1994	138.4	1.3	6.5	—	15.8	—	162.0	—	—	162.0	1994
1995	148.1	1.5	9.6	—	19.0	—	178.2	—	—	178.2	1995
1996	155.5	1.7	6.4	—	8.1	—	171.7	—	—	171.7	1996
1997	163.3	1.7	10.0	—	5.3	—	180.3	—	—	180.3	1997
1998	171.5	2.5	13.5	—	6.0	—	193.5	—	—	193.5	1998
1999	176.5	18.5	12.9	—	10.0	—	217.9	—	—	217.9	1999
2000	187.1	6.0	6.4	—	20.0	15.0	234.5	—	—	234.5	2000
2001	192.0	2.0	9.6	—	25.0	15.0	243.6	—	—	243.6	2001
2002	190.0	3.0	4.8	—	15.0	15.0	227.8	—	—	227.8	2002
2003	196.0	5.0	16.1	—	15.0	15.0	247.1	—	—	247.1	2003
2004	202.0	5.0	9.7	—	10.0	5.0	231.7	—	—	231.7	2004
2005	205.0	5.0	16.1	—	35.0	—	261.1	—	—	261.1	2005
2006	215.0	7.0	22.5	—	26.0	—	270.5	—	—	270.5	2006
2007	222.0	5.0	16.1	—	8.0	—	251.1	—	—	251.1	2007
2008	233.0	4.0	17.5	—	0.0	—	254.5	—	—	254.5	2008
2009	236.0	4.0	32.2	—	0.0	—	272.2	—	—	272.2	2009
2010p	238.4	3.0	22.5	—	0.0	—	263.9	—	—	263.9	2010p

Note: "Government Disposals" includes silver used in coins from stocks and bullion sales from governments other than the United States for the years through 1970. The U.S. Treasury bullion sales and the use of silver from the U.S. Treasury Stocks in coins during the 1960s are separated. After 1970, U.S. government bullion sales and use of government stocks in coinage are included in the "Government Disposals" category.
T.E. -- Transitional Economies.
Sources: U.S. Bureau of Mines; Handy & Harman; Samuel Montagu; Silver Institute; trade sources; CPM Group
March 11, 2010

Indian Silver Supply
Troy Ounces

	1987	1988	1989	1990	1991
Mine Production	1,221,727	1,318,179	1,286,028	868,069	900,220
Secondary Supply	14,467,815	13,181,787	4,822,605	—	9,645,210
Imports	4,404,646	8,037,675	20,897,955	42,052,910	35,237,167
Total	20,094,188	22,537,641	27,006,588	42,920,979	45,782,597
% Change Year Ago	—	12.2%	19.8%	58.9%	6.7%

	1992	1993	1994	1995	1996
Mine Production	1,109,000	1,250,000	1,150,000	1,617,000	1,145,000
Secondary Supply	7,233,908	3,800,000	6,500,000	9,645,210	6,430,140
Imports	50,894,558	113,528,526	85,844,169	78,458,401	106,439,352
Other	—	3,210,116	7,295,890	11,206,577	2,305,610
Total	59,253,740	121,788,643	100,790,060	100,927,188	116,320,101
% Change Year Ago	29.4%	105.5%	-17.2%	0.1%	15.3%

	1997	1998	1999	2000	2001
Mine Production	1,616,000	1,640,000	2,198,000	1,639,686	2,925,714
Secondary Supply	9,966,717	13,503,336	12,860,280	6,430,140	9,645,210
Imports	106,258,875	102,776,845	90,455,994	122,976,428	146,665,937
Other	1,250,211	750,130	964,521	32,151	160,754
Total	119,091,803	118,670,310	106,478,795	131,078,405	159,397,615
% Change Year Ago	2.4%	-0.4%	-10.3%	23.1%	21.6%

	2002	2003	2004	2005	2006
Mine Production	2,925,714	2,950,000	2,926,000	2,250,549	3,472,276
Secondary Supply	4,800,000	16,100,000	9,650,000	16,075,350	22,505,490
Imports	109,137,801	107,704,845	64,301,600	104,489,775	41,795,910
Other	—	—	—	—	—
Government	—	—	—	35,365,770	25,720,560
Total	116,863,515	126,754,845	76,877,600	158,181,444	93,494,236
% Change Year Ago	-26.7%	8.5%	-39.3%	105.8%	-40.9%

	2007	2008	2009
Mine Production	4,310,000	4,310,000	4,480,000
Secondary Supply	16,100,000	17,500,000	32,200,000
Imports	80,377,000	133,425,820	51,441,280
Other	—	—	—
Government	8,000,000	—	—
Total	108,787,000	155,235,820	88,121,280
% Change Year Ago	16.4%	42.7%	-43.2%

Note: Other includes unofficial imports.
Source: CPM Group, Indian trade sources.
March 11, 2010

Silver Yearbook 2010 - Supply   CPM Group

South Asian Silver Trade

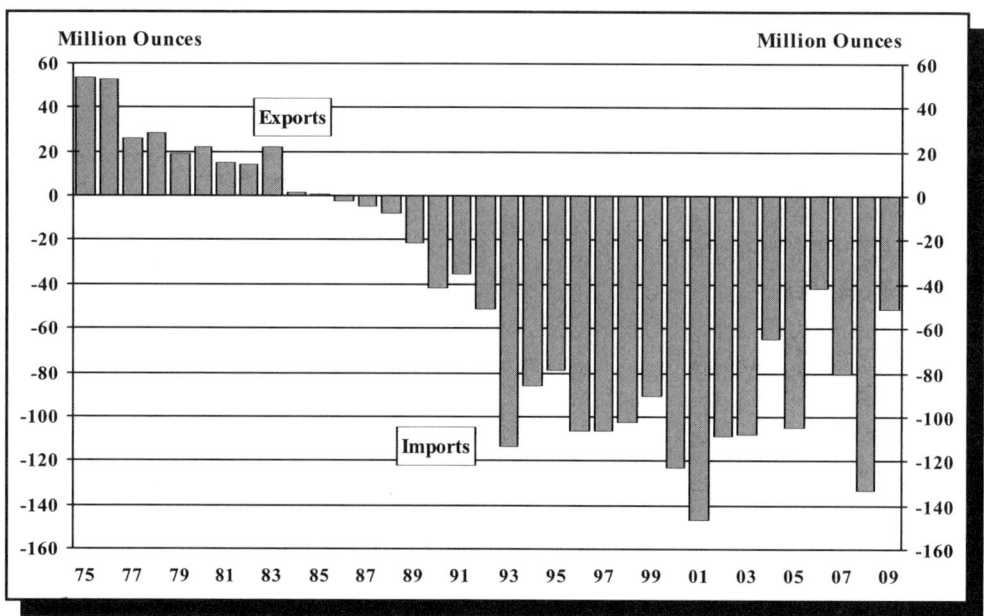

Fabrication Demand

Fabrication Demand

Fabrication demand for silver dropped a sharp 11.3% in 2009, as the global economic recession combined with on-going loss of photographic markets to reduce silver use to 616.4 million ounces last year. The decline in 2009 was greater than the 4.0% reduction in 2008. It was the seventh year of the past 11 years in which total silver fabrication demand declined, extending a period of generally contracting silver use that began in 1999. Demand was lower in most parts of the world.

In most markets, demand for silver fell sharply in the first three months of 2009. Industrial users slashed production of a wide range of manufactured products, including the myriad of products that use silver either as a component or in the equipment used to manufacture the product. This reversed relatively quickly in some silver-using industries, beginning in late March and April. By June of last year demand for silver was strong in some electronics applications, especially in the use of silver in solar panels, connectors, and flat screen display panels, and in catalysts used in some chemical applications.

Last year silver use declined in all of its major applications. Silver use in photographic applications continued its

Annual Total Demand
Projected Through 2010.

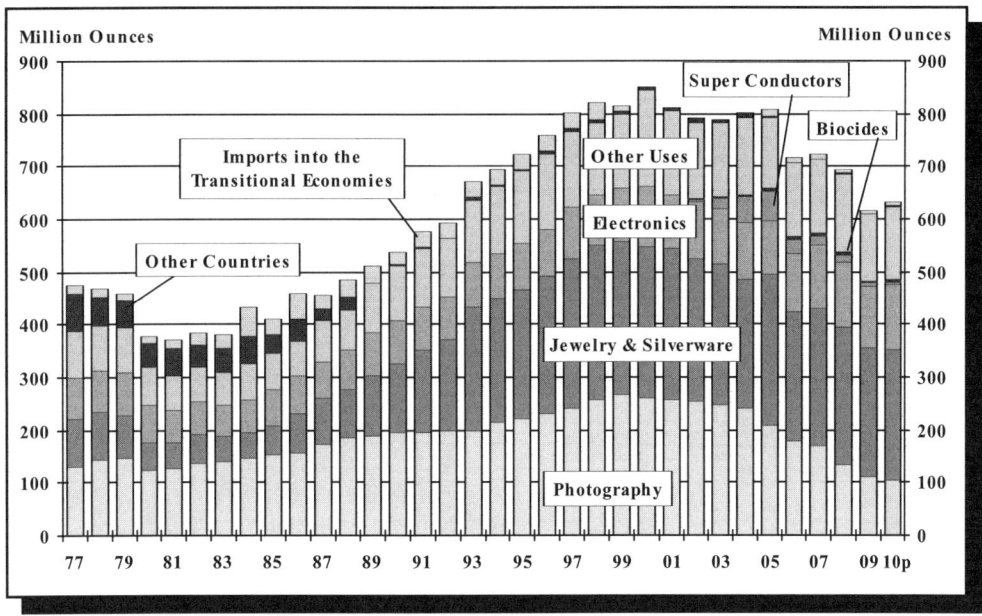

Note: Photography, jewelry and silverware, electronics, and "other" industrial uses includes Canada from 1979, Mexico from 1982, Hong Kong from 1985, Thailand from 1986, India from 1987, South Korea, Australia, Brazil, Chile, Argentina, Peru, Colombia, Pakistan, and Bangladesh from 1989, and Taiwan from 1990.

Silver Yearbook 2010 - Fabrication Demand — CPM Group

decade-long downward trend. Demand for silver in jewelry and silverware, the largest use of silver also declined, dropping 7.2% to 242.1 million ounces. In electronics, silver use fell 3.0% in 2009 to 119.5 million ounces. Fabrication demand in other uses fell to 134.9 million ounces in 2009, down 18.9% year-on-year.

In 2010 fabrication demand for silver is projected to reverse course, growing 2.4% to 631.2 million ounces. This positive outlook is largely based on the assumption that fabrication demand for silver in electrical connectors, electronic components, batteries, chemical catalysts, and a range of other manufactured products from brazing alloys to mirrors will surge as the global economic recovery gains momentum. Demand in the jewelry and silverware industries may grow only slightly, while photographic use of silver is projected to continue to lose market share to digital imaging. Fabrication demand for silver is relatively price inelastic in most applications, and silver remains a low-cost substitute for other metals in a wide number of industrial applications.

Jewelry and Silverware

Jewelry and silverware are among the oldest uses of silver. These uses of silver currently account for 40% of total fabrication demand. Jewelry and silverware includes all types of decorative objects, religious statues, and gift items. A large part of the demand from this sector

Fabrication Demand for Silver in 2009
Million ounces

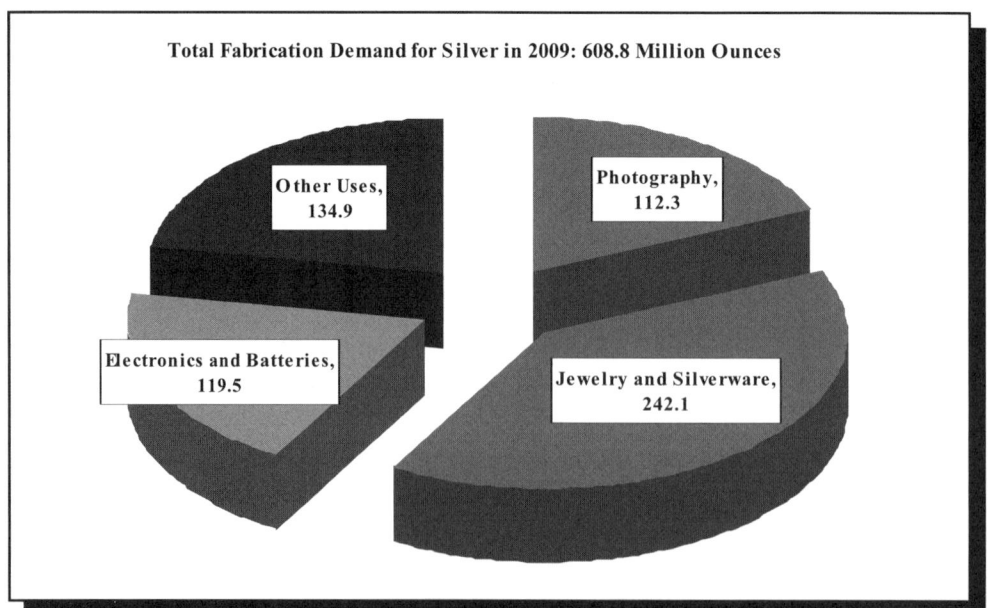

comes from India, the Middle East, and other Asian nations and is extremely price-sensitive.

The extended period of silver prices below $5 or $6 per ounce helped buoy demand for silver in jewelry and silverware during the late 1990s and early 2000s. Use of silver in jewelry and silverware peaked in 1998 at 293.5 million ounces. Healthy and steady growth in the U.S. economy coupled with a modest recovery from the Asian crisis of 1997 helped fuel demand for silver in this area in that year. Demand for silver in jewelry and silverware then fell sharply, almost entirely due to a sharp reduction in purchases of silver jewelry and decorative objects in India. In India silver jewelry and decorative objects are used as a form of savings and investment, as well as for decorative purposes. Starting in 1999, there was a pronounced shift on the part of some Indian investors and consumers away from using jewelry and decorative statues as silver investments, in favor of using silver kilo bars, smaller bars, coins, and medallions (known as fake coins in the Indian market). As a result of this shift, silver use in jewelry and silverware declined over the course of the 2000s, even as demand for silver in bars and coins rose as a partial offset. It must be noted that while some portions of Indian society shifted from jewelry as their preferred means for

Jewelry and Silverware Demand for Silver

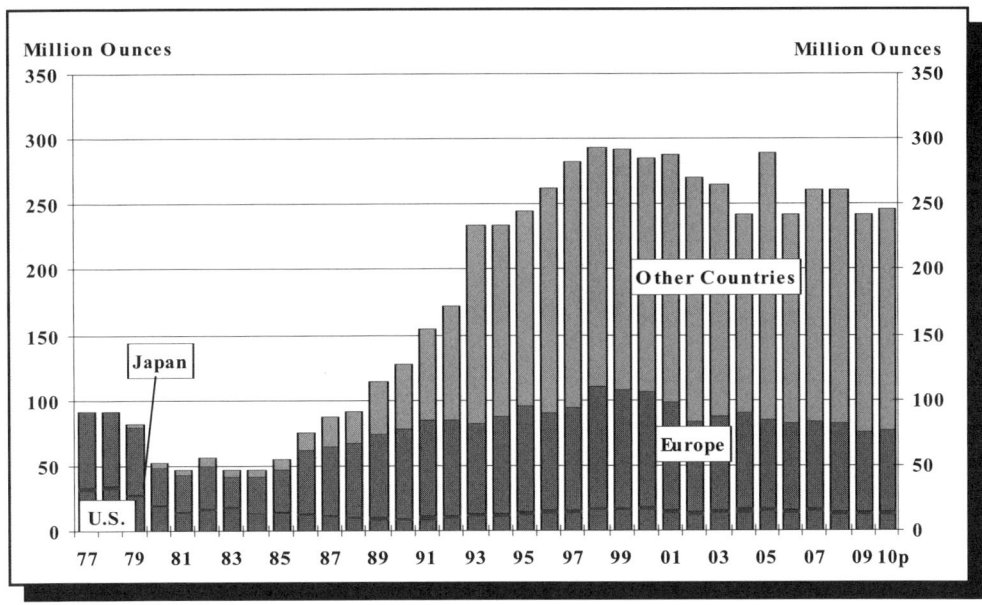

Note: Other Countries includes Mexico from 1982, Hong Kong from 1985, Thailand from 1986, India from 1987, Korea from 1989, and Taiwan from 1990.

Silver Yearbook 2010 - Fabrication Demand   CPM Group

investing in silver, and gold, other parts of Indian society have continued to use jewelry and silverware as investment vehicles.

Since 2004 silver use in jewelry and silverware was reduced further by jewelers' and consumers' reactions to higher silver prices. Jewelers started making lighter pieces of jewelry using less silver, to keep their products affordable or at attractive prices for consumers. Consumers meanwhile pulled back from buying so much jewelry.

The use of silver in jewelry and silverware rose in 2007 and 2008 as consumers grew accustomed to higher priced silver. While silver jewelry was more expensive than it had been just two to three years earlier, it remained far less expensive and more affordable than jewelry made with more expensive metals such as gold, platinum, and palladium. The fact that consumers could buy larger pieces of silver jewelry for lower prices made silver jewelry more attractive as gold and platinum prices rose sharply.

The global economic recession that began at the end of 2007 combined with even higher prices to result in the 7.2% decline in demand for silver in jewelry and silverware last year. Demand in this category is estimated to have totaled 242.1 million ounces in 2009. In 2010 use of silver in jewelry and silverware is projected to rise to 246.3 million ounces, a 1.7% increase from 2009.

Silver in Photography in 2009

Million ounces

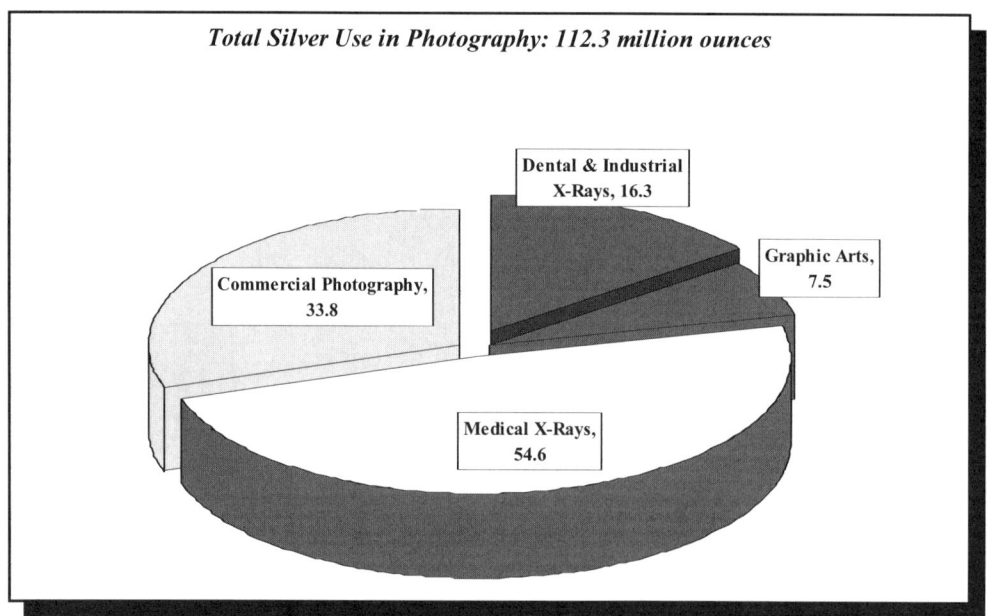

CPM Group — Silver Yearbook 2010 - Fabrication Demand

Photography

Since peaking in 1999, demand for silver in the photographic sector has been consistently declining. In 2009 the photographic industry used 112.3 million ounces of silver, down 16.5% from 134.4 million ounces in 2008. This is less than half of the 267.2 million ounces used a decade ago. This year silver use in photography is projected to decline 6.2% to 105.3 million ounces, as the rate of decline slows from the steep decreases over the past two years.

The sharp decline in silver use in the photographic industry over the past several years has been due to a surge in consumers moving away from conventional photography toward digital imaging. This trend is projected to continue for the foreseeable future, although perhaps not at the velocity of decline as has been seen over the past decade. The decline in demand for silver-bearing paper and film over the last couple of years was accelerated due to recessionary economic conditions in most parts of the world and reduced consumer discretionary spending in basic photography. Consumers also reduced their vacation travel, typically a period of increased picture taking.

Demand for silver in the x-ray sector of the photographic industry also declined, mostly due to weakness in the industrial uses of x-rays. The decline in manufacturing and industrial output over the past couple of years weighed on the use of x-

Photographic Demand

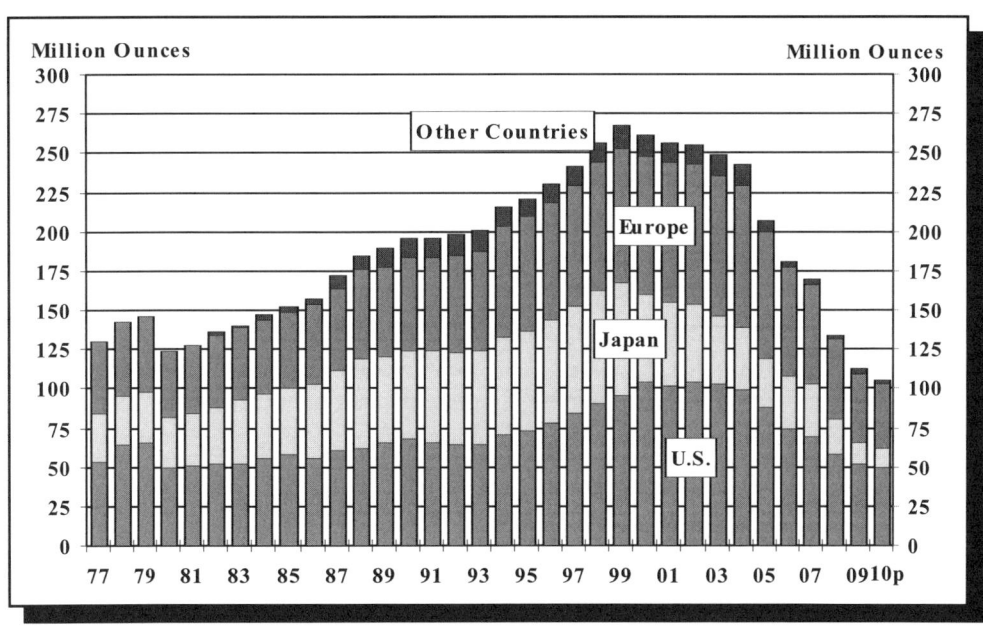

rays in these areas. The use of silver-bearing x-rays in medical and dental areas held up. Digital imaging has been slow to make inroads in this sector, given the medical and dental industry's preference still for silver-bearing x-ray film because of the ease of use. Digital imaging appears to be making greater inroads in the medical sector than in the dental segment of this market, although the relatively high cost of digital imaging readers and storage systems present obstacles to a more rapid introduction.

Silver use in the graphic arts sector, which is silver used in the printing of newspapers, magazines, advertising, and other specialty uses, declined in 2009. The internet, television, and other media outlets have been aiding in the reduction of silver use in print media outlets. This trend is projected to continue this year.

The United States, Japan, and Western Europe all saw sharp declines in silver use in photography in 2008 and 2009. Some of the particularly sharp declines in silver use in individual countries represented silver paper or film factories being closed in 2009. The decline in silver use in photography may not be as pronounced this year, given an emerging economic recovery and an already large shift from basic photography to digital imaging having taken place.

Fuji Film, which is the second largest producer of camera films, shut down one of its film-processing plants in the United States in July 2009. Many other large camera films manufacturers such as Kodak, Agfa Photo, and Konica-Minolta have been consolidating their factories, cutting jobs, and moving some of their operations to China as traditional photography is moving toward digital imaging.

Electrical and Electronics

The third largest use of silver is in electrical and electronics equipment. The many different applications for silver in these industries currently account for 19% of total fabrication demand for silver. Use of silver in electronics and electrical equipment has been in a rising trend over the past several years as production of these types of electrical and electronic components has risen sharply. Given that small quantities of silver per unit are used in manufacturing electronics and electrical products, rising silver prices have a less dramatic effect on the costs of the components and the profitability of manufacturing these components and using them in electronic consumer and industrial products. Some of the electrical and electronics components where silver is used include mobile phones, semiconductors, flat panel televisions, circuit boards, watches, calculators, and hearing aids. New uses of silver, in flat panel televisions, solar panels, and other electronic applications are helping to keep silver demand strong across the electronics industry.

In recent years there have been many new uses for silver developed in electronics. One new and substantial use of silver is in solar panels and photovoltaic cells. More important, problems with record high prices and supply disruptions in the palladium market led to moves to substitute silver or palladium-plated silver for palladium in some electronic applications, including some multilayered capacitors, and electronic and electrical connectors. In some computer circuitry, for example, palladium-plated silver now is used in place of solid palladium wiring. As a result of these types of applications, silver use in electronics has been rising sharply since 2005. Silver use in electronics peaked at 123.2 million ounces in 2008.

The 2009 recession hit demand for electronic goods very hard hit in the first quarter. After that demand for silver in this sector rose steadily through the rest of the year. Use of silver in electronics fell in the United States, Japan, and Western Europe, as well as in many other countries. Demand for silver in electrical and electronics sector fell to 119.5 million ounces last year, down 3.0% from 123.2 million ounces in 2008.

The weakness in demand for silver in electrical and electronics was relatively short-lived. The final four months or so of 2009 saw a relatively healthy demand. As the global economy continues to recover from the recession, demand for silver in electronics is expected to pick up sharply. This year

Electronics and Batteries

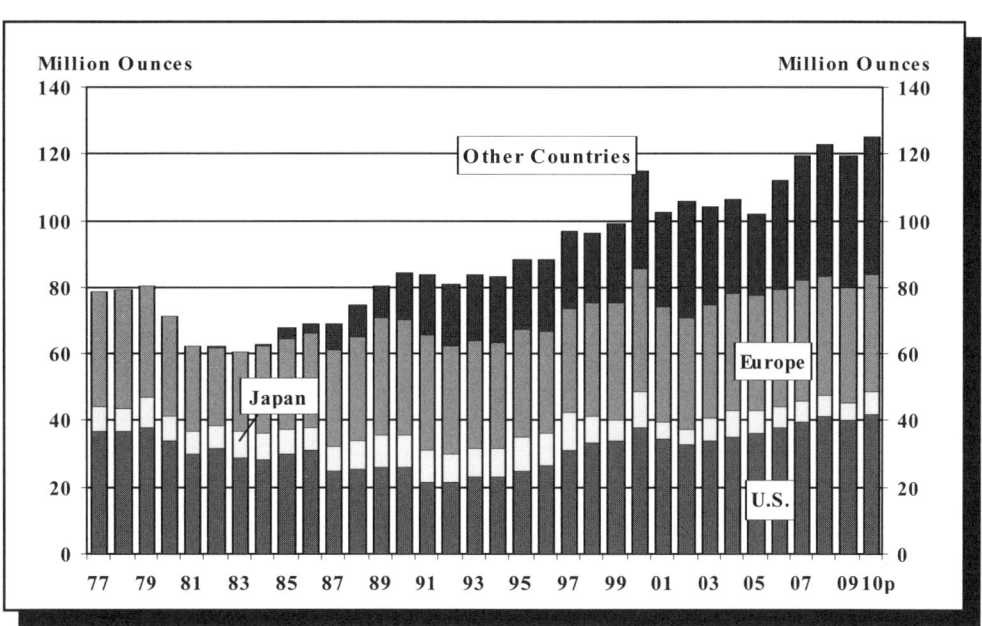

demand for silver in this sector is projected to be 125.2 million ounces, a 4.8% increase from 2009 levels.

Other Uses

Besides silver's major appearances in jewelry, photography, and electronics, silver also is used in a host of other applications, including superconductors, biocides, chemical catalysts, mirrors, brazing alloys and solders, medical devices, and dental fillings. Silver fabrication demand in these other uses peaked in 2004 at 201.3 million ounces.

Silver demand in these other uses is estimated to have plunged 18.9% from 166.3 million ounces in 2008 to 134.9 million ounces in 2009. Silver's "other uses" category accounted for 22% of annual silver demand in 2009. This year demand for silver in other uses is forecast to increase to 146.0 million ounces, 8.2% above last year's level.

Other Uses

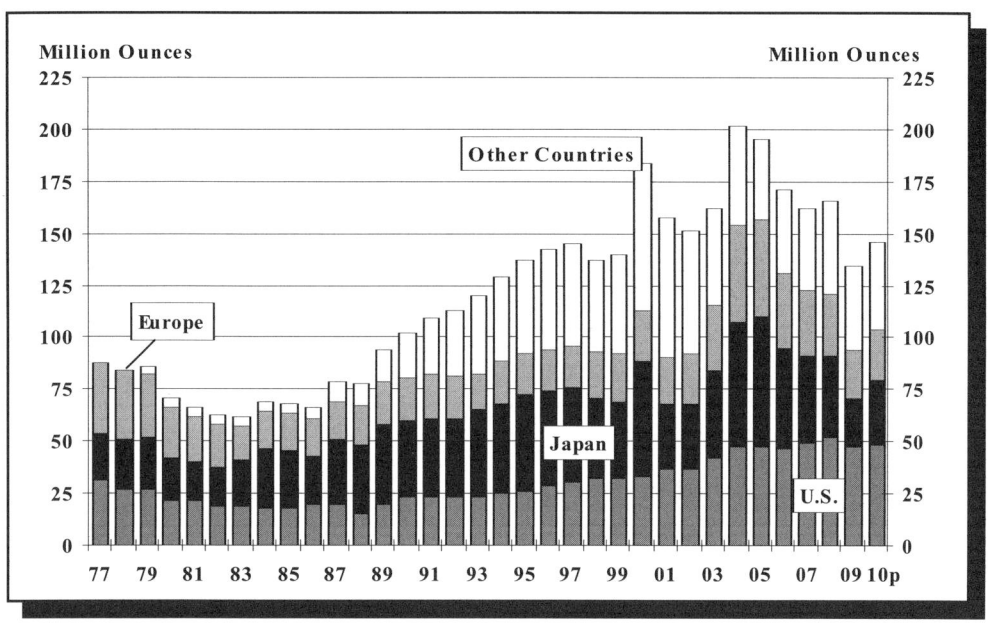

Silver Yearbook 2010 - Fabrication Demand — CPM Group

Annual Silver Use
Million Troy Ounces

	1977	1978	1979	1980	1981	1982	1983	1984	1985	1986	1987	1988	1989	1990	1991	1992	1993
Photography																	
United States	53.7	64.3	66.0	49.8	51.0	51.8	51.8	55.3	57.9	55.4	60.2	62.5	65.2	68.0	66.0	64.4	65.0
Japan	31.2	31.4	32.2	32.6	33.9	36.6	40.9	41.3	42.2	47.0	51.3	56.8	54.8	56.5	57.8	58.0	58.5
Western Europe	44.7	47.2	47.9	41.4	43.2	44.9	45.6	47.6	48.1	51.1	52.6	57.0	57.1	59.0	60.0	62.2	63.9
Other Countries	-	-	-	-	-	3.2	2.0	3.1	4.5	4.3	8.0	8.8	12.1	13.0	12.4	14.0	13.6
Subtotal	129.6	142.9	146.1	123.8	128.1	136.5	140.3	147.3	152.7	157.8	172.1	185.1	189.2	196.5	196.2	198.6	201.0
% of Total	27.2%	30.4%	31.8%	32.7%	34.6%	35.4%	36.7%	34.0%	37.1%	34.4%	37.8%	38.1%	37.1%	36.4%	34.1%	33.6%	29.8%
% Change Year Ago	—	10.3%	2.2%	-15.3%	3.5%	6.6%	2.8%	5.0%	3.7%	3.4%	9.1%	7.5%	2.2%	3.8%	-0.1%	1.2%	1.2%
Jewelry and Silverware																	
United States	31.6	32.0	26.6	19.4	13.7	16.2	17.1	13.0	13.0	12.3	10.5	9.0	8.5	8.3	8.3	9.8	10.3
Japan	2.2	2.5	2.2	1.0	1.1	1.3	1.1	1.0	1.4	1.7	1.4	1.6	1.7	1.4	3.5	2.8	2.9
Western Europe	57.2	57.4	50.3	27.5	28.7	32.7	23.9	27.3	33.1	47.3	53.3	57.3	63.8	68.3	73.1	71.8	68.7
Other Countries	-	-	3.7	4.4	4.3	6.2	5.5	6.1	8.0	14.0	22.0	23.3	40.2	50.3	70.4	87.6	152.6
Subtotal	91.0	91.9	82.8	52.3	47.8	56.4	47.6	47.4	55.5	75.3	87.2	91.2	114.2	128.3	155.3	172.0	234.5
% of Total	19.1%	19.5%	18.0%	13.8%	12.9%	14.6%	12.5%	10.9%	13.5%	16.4%	19.1%	18.7%	22.4%	23.8%	27.0%	29.1%	34.8%
% Change Year Ago	—	1.0%	-10.0%	-36.9%	-8.6%	18.0%	-15.6%	-0.4%	17.1%	35.7%	15.7%	4.6%	25.2%	12.4%	21.1%	10.8%	36.3%
Electronics and Batteries																	
United States	37.1	36.8	38.1	33.8	30.2	31.9	28.9	28.3	30.0	31.1	25.2	25.5	26.3	25.8	21.4	21.4	23.1
Japan	6.9	7.0	8.9	7.6	6.4	6.6	7.7	7.8	7.5	6.8	7.0	8.4	9.5	9.7	9.7	8.4	8.7
Western Europe	34.7	35.5	33.4	29.8	25.6	23.2	23.8	26.2	27.2	28.5	28.9	31.5	34.8	34.7	34.8	32.4	32.1
Other Countries	-	-	-	-	-	0.9	0.5	0.8	3.1	3.0	8.3	9.2	9.7	14.1	17.8	19.1	19.7
Subtotal	78.7	79.3	80.4	71.2	62.2	62.6	60.9	63.1	67.8	69.4	69.4	74.6	80.3	84.3	83.7	81.3	83.6
% of Total	16.5%	16.9%	17.5%	18.8%	16.8%	16.2%	16.0%	14.6%	16.5%	15.1%	15.2%	15.3%	15.7%	15.6%	14.5%	13.7%	12.4%
% Change Year Ago	—	0.8%	1.4%	-11.4%	-12.6%	0.6%	-2.6%	3.6%	7.5%	2.4%	-0.1%	7.5%	7.7%	5.0%	-0.6%	-2.9%	2.9%
Other Uses																	
United States	31.2	27.1	26.6	21.8	21.8	19.1	18.5	18.3	17.7	20.1	19.4	15.0	20.0	23.2	23.0	23.3	23.7
Japan	22.9	24.0	25.5	20.3	18.2	18.7	22.4	28.7	28.3	23.1	31.8	33.8	38.2	36.9	37.9	37.4	41.6
Western Europe	33.4	32.9	30.4	24.5	21.8	20.3	16.5	17.8	17.3	18.0	17.7	18.5	20.9	20.7	21.3	21.2	17.1
Other Countries	-	-	3.7	4.4	4.3	4.5	4.5	4.5	4.7	5.0	9.7	10.4	15.1	21.2	27.5	30.6	37.7
Subtotal	87.5	84.0	86.2	71.0	66.1	62.6	61.9	69.3	68.0	66.2	78.5	77.8	94.2	102.0	109.7	112.5	120.1
% of Total	18.4%	17.9%	18.7%	18.7%	17.8%	16.3%	16.2%	16.0%	16.5%	14.4%	17.2%	16.0%	18.5%	18.9%	19.1%	19.0%	17.8%
% Change Year Ago	—	-4.0%	2.6%	-17.6%	-6.9%	-5.2%	-1.2%	12.0%	-1.9%	-2.7%	18.7%	-0.9%	21.1%	8.2%	7.6%	2.6%	6.7%
Other Countries	73.1	54.3	52.8	46.1	51.3	43.4	45.8	49.6	37.2	41.3	23.5	24.7	0.2	3.1	3.4	-0.4	5.0
% of Total	15.4%	11.5%	11.5%	12.2%	13.8%	11.3%	12.0%	11.4%	9.0%	9.0%	5.2%	5.1%	0.0%	0.6%	0.6%	-0.1%	0.7%
Net Imports into the																	
Transitional Economies	15.9	18.2	11.5	14.5	15.3	23.8	25.4	56.6	30.4	49.2	24.9	32.9	32.6	25.0	27.2	27.5	30.0
% Change Year Ago	—	14.2%	-36.7%	25.8%	5.7%	55.5%	6.9%	122.7%	-46.2%	61.8%	-49.5%	32.1%	-0.9%	-23.3%	8.9%	0.9%	9.1%
Total	475.8	470.6	459.7	378.8	370.7	385.2	381.8	433.3	411.6	459.2	455.5	486.2	510.6	539.1	575.6	591.5	674.3
% Change Year Ago	—	-1.1%	-2.3%	-17.6%	-2.1%	3.9%	-0.9%	13.5%	-5.0%	11.6%	-0.8%	6.7%	5.0%	5.6%	6.8%	2.8%	14.0%

Notes: Totals may not equal the sums of the categories due to rounding. The "Other Countries" categories for individual sectors include Mexico from 1982; India from 1987; Hong Kong from 1985; Thailand from 1986; Korea, Australia, Brazil, Colombia, Argentina, Chile, Pakistan, and Bangladesh from 1989; and Taiwan from 1990. In 2000, the transitional economies shifted from being net importers of silver to net exporters. See "silver statistical position" table for related statistics. Excludes coins.
Source: CPM Group
March 15, 2010

CPM Group — Silver Yearbook 2010 - Fabrication Demand

1994	1995	1996	1997	1998	1999	2000	2001	2002	2003	2004	2005	2006	2007	2008	2009	2010p	
																	Photography
71.0	72.9	78.3	84.6	91.0	96.0	104.0	102.0	104.0	103.0	99.0	88.0	75.0	69.0	58.0	52.0	49.0	United States
61.1	63.6	65.7	67.3	71.0	71.5	55.5	53.5	49.2	43.9	40.0	31.2	32.3	34.4	22.2	14.0	13.0	Japan
70.6	72.6	74.4	77.5	81.8	85.6	88.6	88.3	89.3	88.8	89.8	81.0	69.4	62.4	50.9	43.4	40.6	Western Europe
12.8	12.1	12.5	12.8	13.3	14.1	13.6	12.9	13.0	13.5	13.9	7.4	4.2	3.7	3.3	2.9	2.7	Other Countries
215.5	221.2	230.9	242.2	257.1	267.2	261.7	256.7	255.5	249.2	242.7	207.6	180.9	169.5	134.4	112.3	105.3	Subtotal
31.0%	30.5%	30.4%	30.1%	31.3%	32.8%	30.7%	31.7%	32.3%	31.6%	30.3%	25.7%	25.2%	23.4%	19.3%	18.2%	16.7%	% of Total
7.2%	2.6%	4.4%	4.9%	6.2%	3.9%	-2.1%	-1.9%	-0.5%	-2.5%	-2.6%	-14.5%	-12.9%	-6.3%	-20.7%	-16.5%	-6.2%	% Change Year Ago
																	Jewelry and Silverware
11.0	12.0	13.1	14.1	15.7	15.9	16.2	13.5	12.4	13.5	14.1	14.4	13.6	14.3	12.0	11.5	11.8	United States
2.7	2.4	2.7	2.7	2.3	2.0	3.0	2.8	2.6	2.9	3.0	3.1	3.0	3.2	3.0	3.2	3.2	Japan
74.3	80.9	74.0	78.0	92.4	90.4	86.5	82.4	69.0	71.2	72.7	67.7	64.9	66.3	66.6	60.4	61.8	Western Europe
146.5	149.9	172.4	188.3	183.1	183.4	179.8	188.9	186.9	177.4	153.0	203.6	160.5	177.8	179.5	167.1	169.5	Other Countries
234.5	245.2	262.2	283.1	293.5	291.7	285.5	287.6	270.9	264.9	242.8	288.8	241.9	261.6	261.0	242.1	246.3	Subtotal
33.8%	33.8%	34.6%	35.2%	35.7%	35.8%	33.5%	35.5%	34.3%	33.6%	30.3%	35.8%	33.7%	36.1%	37.6%	39.3%	39.0%	% of Total
0.0%	4.6%	6.9%	8.0%	3.7%	-0.6%	-2.1%	0.7%	-5.8%	-2.2%	-8.4%	19.0%	-16.2%	8.1%	-0.2%	-7.2%	1.7%	% Change Year Ago
																	Electronics and Batteries
23.1	25.0	26.8	31.3	33.3	34.2	37.9	34.8	32.7	33.8	34.9	36.5	38.0	39.9	41.2	40.3	42.0	United States
8.9	10.1	9.3	11.3	7.9	6.0	10.8	4.8	4.9	7.0	8.3	6.7	6.0	6.2	6.4	5.3	6.6	Japan
31.5	32.2	30.6	31.3	34.0	35.1	37.1	34.4	33.1	34.0	34.9	34.6	35.2	36.0	35.7	34.3	35.2	Western Europe
19.7	21.3	22.0	23.0	21.0	23.8	29.5	28.4	35.4	29.6	28.5	24.1	33.0	37.4	39.9	39.6	41.4	Other Countries
83.2	88.6	88.7	96.9	96.2	99.1	115.3	102.4	106.0	104.4	106.6	101.9	112.2	119.5	123.2	119.5	125.2	Subtotal
12.0%	12.2%	11.7%	12.1%	11.7%	12.2%	13.5%	12.6%	13.4%	13.2%	13.3%	12.6%	15.6%	16.5%	17.7%	19.4%	19.8%	% of Total
-0.5%	6.5%	0.1%	9.3%	-0.8%	3.1%	16.3%	-11.2%	3.6%	-1.6%	2.1%	-4.3%	10.0%	6.5%	3.1%	-3.0%	4.8%	% Change Year Ago
																	Other Uses
25.0	26.3	28.5	30.5	32.3	32.4	33.0	37.1	37.1	41.8	47.2	47.9	46.7	49.5	52.3	47.5	48.8	United States
42.8	46.4	45.8	45.4	38.4	36.7	56.1	30.9	31.2	42.2	60.3	62.2	48.7	42.2	39.5	22.9	30.6	Japan
20.8	20.0	19.7	20.2	22.1	23.1	23.8	22.2	23.7	31.9	47.1	46.8	35.1	31.5	29.0	23.7	24.4	Western Europe
40.6	44.4	48.5	49.2	44.5	47.7	70.5	67.4	59.3	46.8	46.7	38.1	40.8	38.9	45.4	40.8	42.2	Other Countries
129.2	137.0	142.5	145.2	137.3	139.8	183.4	157.6	151.4	162.7	201.3	195.0	171.3	162.1	166.3	134.9	146.0	Subtotal
18.6%	18.9%	18.8%	18.1%	16.7%	17.1%	21.5%	19.4%	19.1%	20.6%	25.1%	24.2%	23.9%	22.4%	23.9%	21.9%	23.1%	% of Total
7.6%	6.1%	4.0%	1.9%	-5.5%	1.8%	31.1%	-14.1%	-4.0%	7.5%	23.7%	-3.1%	-12.1%	-5.4%	2.6%	-18.9%	8.2%	% Change Year Ago
3.9	3.4	6.0	6.5	6.4	6.9	6.4	6.2	7.0	7.2	7.5	3.9	1.4	1.3	1.8	1.6	2.4	Other Countries
0.6%	0.5%	0.8%	0.8%	0.8%	0.8%	0.8%	0.8%	0.9%	0.9%	0.9%	0.5%	0.2%	0.2%	0.3%	0.3%	0.4%	% of Total
																	Net Imports into the
28.0	29.3	27.9	29.6	31.2	11.0	-	-	-	-	-	10.0	10.0	10.0	8.0	6.0	6.0	Transitional
-6.7%	4.7%	-4.8%	6.3%	5.3%	-64.7%	NA	NA	NA	NA	NA	NA	0.0%	0.0%	-20.0%	-25.0%	0.0%	% Change Year Ago
694.3	724.7	758.2	803.6	821.7	815.8	852.3	810.5	790.8	788.4	800.9	807.2	717.7	724.0	694.7	616.4	631.2	Total
3.0%	4.4%	4.6%	6.0%	2.3%	-0.7%	4.5%	-4.9%	-2.4%	-0.3%	1.6%	0.8%	-11.1%	0.9%	-4.0%	-11.3%	2.4%	% Change Year Ago

Silver Yearbook 2010 - Fabrication Demand CPM Group

U.S. Fabrication Demand

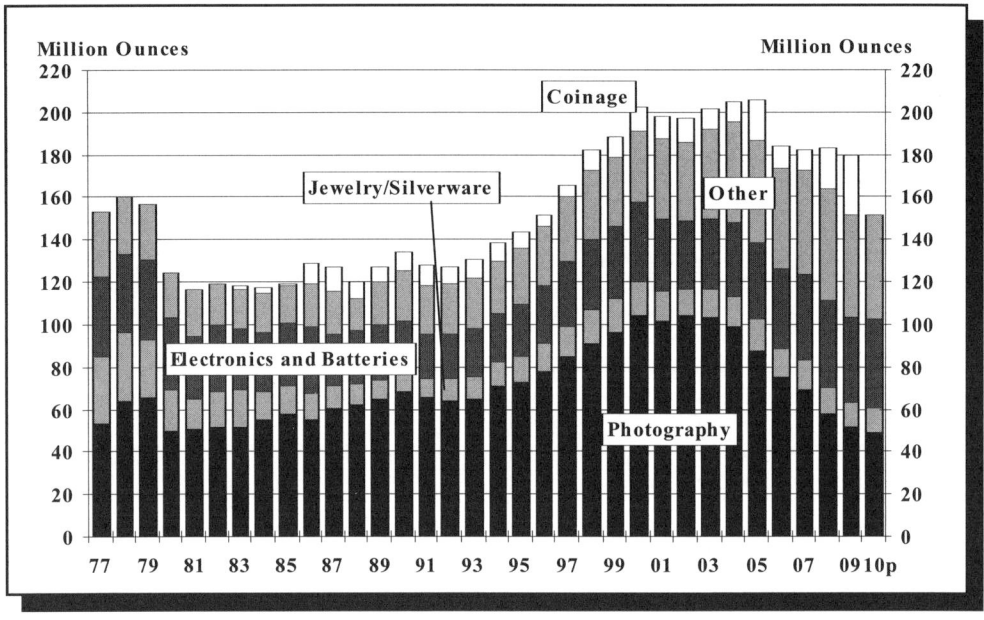

Indian Silver Fabrication Demand

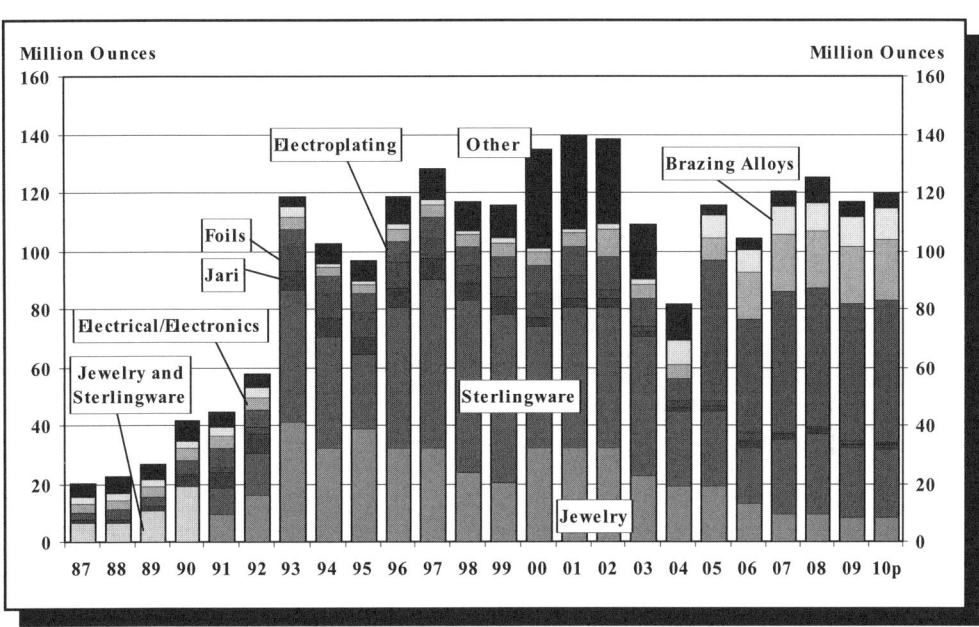

Silver Yearbook 2010 - Fabrication Demand — CPM Group

Italian Fabrication Demand

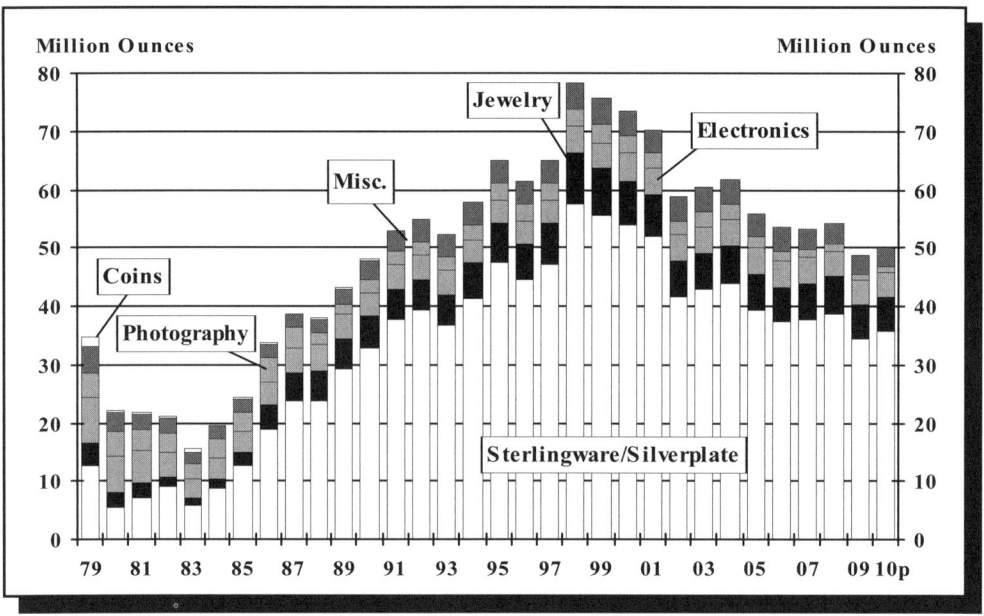

Japanese Fabrication Demand

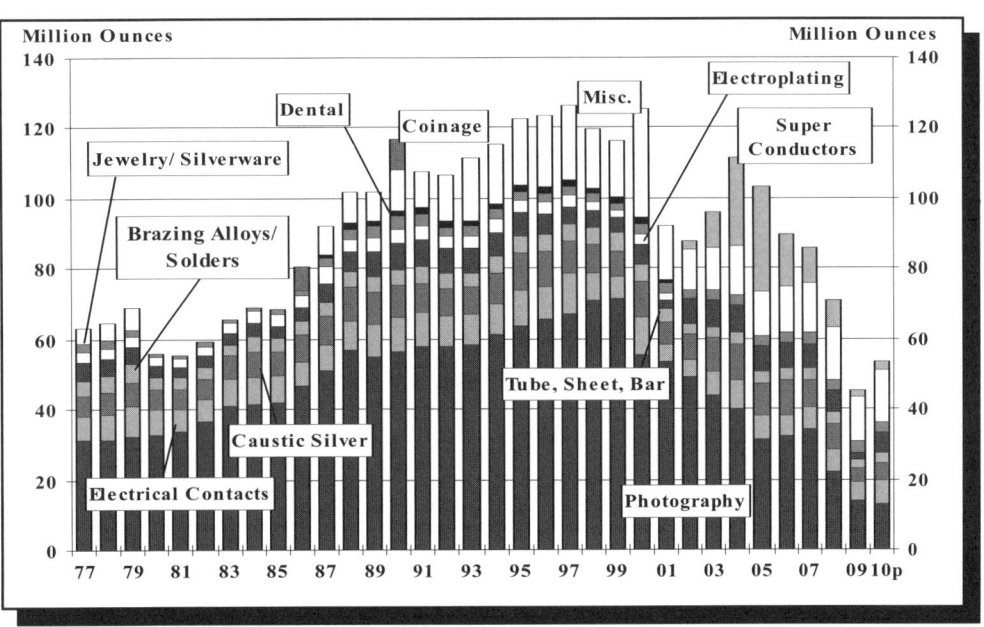

European Fabrication Demand

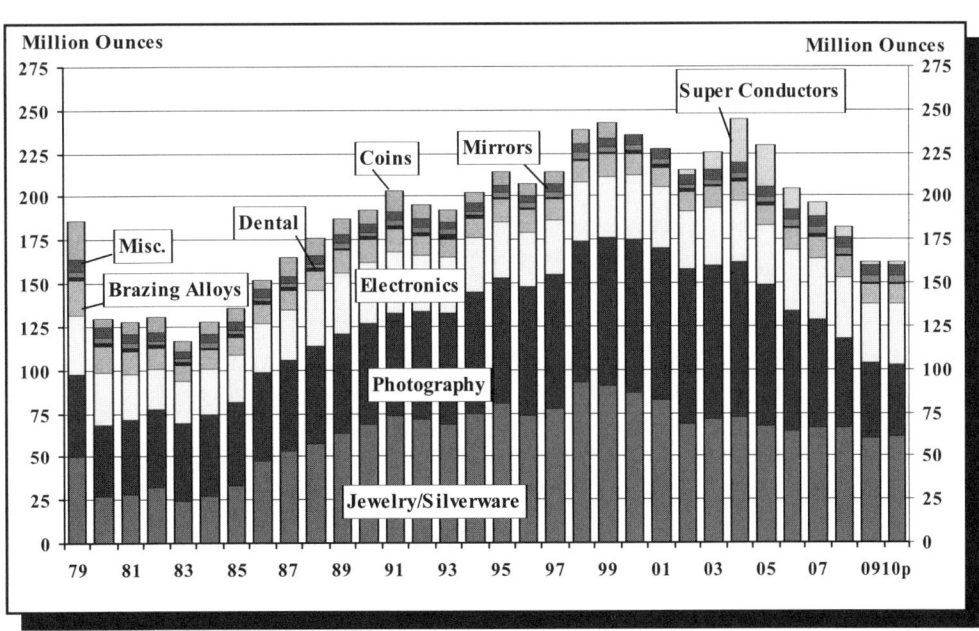

Silver Yearbook 2010 - Fabrication Demand CPM Group

Fabrication Demand by Country, 1960-2010p
Million Troy Ounces

Year	Germany	Italy	U.K.	France	Belgium	Other Europe	Subtotal
				Europe			
1960	40.2	-i-	16.5	13.0	-i-	-i-	69.7
1961	43.5	20.0	20.0	14.0	-i-	-i-	97.5
1962	41.8	22.0	20.0	13.5	-i-	-i-	97.3
1963	40.5	25.0	20.0	13.9	-i-	-i-	99.4
1964	46.3	25.0	23.0	14.8	-i-	-i-	109.1
1965	54.6	25.0	25.0	14.0	-i-	-i-	118.6
1966	48.2	30.0	25.0	14.7	-i-	-i-	117.9
1967	48.2	28.2	24.0	14.7	-i-	-i-	115.1
1968	50.0	22.5	23.0	18.0	-i-	-i-	113.5
1969	50.0	29.0	24.5	19.3	-i-	-i-	122.8
1970	48.2	32.0	25.0	15.5	-i-	-i-	120.7
1971	59.9	30.5	25.0	15.6	-i-	-i-	131.0
1972	60.0	32.0	27.0	16.5	-i-	-i-	135.5
1973	60.0	33.5	31.5	22.5	-i-	-i-	147.5
1974	55.0	30.0	33.0	21.0	-i-	-i-	139.0
1975	38.9	28.9	28.0	21.0	-i-	-i-	116.8
1976	52.9	38.5	27.6	31.8	-i-	-i-	150.8
1977	48.1	36.3	29.4	32.6	-i-	-i-	146.4
1978	42.0	31.0	29.0	24.6	-i-	-i-	126.6
1979	39.8	33.3	27.6	24.1	14.8	22.4	162.0
1980	31.9	21.8	19.5	19.8	14.6	15.6	123.2
1981	29.3	21.5	18.4	18.9	16.0	15.2	119.3
1982	32.7	20.8	18.1	17.1	17.0	15.4	121.1
1983	30.3	15.0	17.7	16.5	16.3	14.0	109.8
1984	32.2	19.4	19.2	17.1	16.8	14.2	118.9
1985	34.6	24.0	19.1	16.9	16.4	14.7	125.7
1986	36.3	33.5	19.1	17.0	17.6	21.4	144.9
1987	39.1	38.6	21.1	17.6	17.9	18.2	152.5
1988	44.1	43.0	22.7	21.3	19.2	14.0	164.3
1989	46.9	45.7	24.5	22.1	19.2	18.2	176.6
1990	48.4	47.9	24.4	22.4	19.4	20.2	182.7
1991	52.3	53.0	21.7	21.9	19.7	20.6	189.2
1992	49.1	54.9	21.7	21.7	20.4	19.8	187.6
1993	45.8	52.3	23.2	22.0	21.9	20.1	185.3
1994	45.8	58.0	24.4	23.3	24.5	21.2	197.2
1995	43.6	65.1	25.6	23.8	26.9	20.6	205.7
1996	41.1	61.5	27.5	22.4	28.5	17.6	198.7
1997	42.7	65.2	28.7	23.1	29.9	17.4	207.0
1998	47.5	78.4	31.2	23.7	31.8	17.7	230.3
1999	48.8	75.7	32.5	24.7	34.5	18.0	234.2
2000	47.0	73.5	34.8	27.2	37.0	16.5	236.0
2001	44.0	70.4	33.8	26.7	37.8	14.6	227.3
2002	44.6	58.7	33.4	25.4	39.5	13.5	215.1
2003	53.3	60.4	34.0	25.6	38.8	13.7	225.8
2004	69.0	61.8	34.3	26.1	39.2	14.1	244.5
2005	68.2	56.0	31.9	24.9	35.0	14.1	230.1
2006	54.2	53.5	29.0	22.2	32.0	13.7	204.6
2007	50.9	53.4	28.0	21.0	29.0	13.9	196.2
2008	46.1	54.2	25.2	18.8	24.0	14.0	182.2
2009	39.3	48.8	23.2	17.2	20.0	13.3	161.8
2010p	39.3	50.1	23.3	16.9	19.0	13.4	162.0

Notes: Excludes silver use in coinage. Totals may not equal the sums of countries due to rounding. "Other Europe" prior to 1979 is included in "Other." -i- included in Other.
In 2000, the transitional economies shifted from being net importers of silver to net exporters.

Silver Yearbook 2010 - Fabrication Demand

U.S.	Japan	India	Thailand	Canada	Mexico	Other	Tran. Econ.	Total	Year
102.0	21.6	1.5	-i-	4.3	6.8	31.9	-	237.8	1960
105.5	19.1	1.5	-i-	3.4	5.3	37.3	-	269.6	1961
110.4	19.6	1.5	-i-	3.3	5.2	38.2	-	275.5	1962
110.0	20.0	2.5	-i-	3.2	5.0	38.8	-	278.9	1963
123.0	20.0	12.0	-i-	4.1	6.4	43.6	-	318.2	1964
137.0	25.8	16.0	-i-	5.7	7.4	48.0	-	358.5	1965
183.7	31.5	16.0	-i-	5.8	6.1	56.1	-	417.1	1966
171.0	33.2	15.0	-i-	5.8	7.9	53.9	-	401.9	1967
145.3	35.0	16.0	-i-	6.2	7.9	50.1	-	373.9	1968
141.5	41.5	16.0	-i-	5.7	6.9	51.9	-	386.3	1969
128.4	46.0	16.0	-i-	6.0	8.5	50.4	-	376.0	1970
129.1	46.5	16.0	-i-	6.8	8.0	54.5	2.4	391.9	1971
151.7	54.3	13.0	-i-	8.3	11.0	63.8	6.2	437.6	1972
196.4	69.0	13.0	-i-	10.4	16.5	77.5	7.8	530.3	1973
176.0	57.7	14.0	-i-	10.3	10.2	71.9	9.1	479.1	1974
157.7	46.4	13.0	-i-	10.3	8.8	65.6	10.9	418.6	1975
170.6	60.8	18.0	-i-	9.3	10.2	86.1	21.1	505.8	1976
153.6	63.2	17.6	-i-	9.1	8.6	77.3	15.9	475.8	1977
160.2	64.9	21.0	-i-	9.6	9.1	79.2	18.2	470.6	1978
157.3	68.8	22.5	-i-	7.3	8.6	33.2	11.5	459.7	1979
124.7	61.5	22.5	-i-	8.7	4.9	33.3	14.5	378.8	1980
116.7	59.6	26.5	-i-	8.5	5.0	35.1	15.3	370.7	1981
118.8	63.2	23.0	-i-	9.0	5.7	44.4	23.8	385.2	1982
116.3	72.1	22.5	-i-	8.9	3.5	48.8	25.4	381.8	1983
114.8	78.8	20.9	-i-	9.0	5.5	85.4	56.6	433.3	1984
118.6	72.6	21.0	-i-	9.1	8.0	56.7	30.4	411.6	1985
118.9	78.6	19.3	5.9	9.6	7.7	74.4	49.2	459.2	1986
115.3	92.3	20.1	7.4	10.4	6.9	50.6	24.9	455.5	1987
112.0	102.0	22.4	8.2	11.0	7.1	59.1	32.9	486.2	1988
120.0	102.5	27.0	11.2	12.0	7.1	54.2	32.6	510.6	1989
125.1	106.9	41.8	11.0	12.5	7.2	26.9	25.0	539.1	1990
118.7	108.9	44.5	30.4	13.1	11.7	31.9	27.2	575.6	1991
118.9	106.5	57.8	34.5	13.6	14.7	30.4	27.5	591.5	1992
121.1	111.7	119.0	41.4	15.2	14.7	36.0	30.0	674.3	1993
130.1	115.5	102.9	49.7	15.1	15.0	41.0	28.0	694.3	1994
136.2	122.5	96.5	52.0	16.9	15.0	50.7	29.3	724.7	1995
146.7	123.5	119.0	55.1	17.7	15.3	54.3	27.9	758.2	1996
160.5	126.7	128.6	56.3	18.4	16.2	60.2	29.6	803.6	1997
172.3	119.6	116.8	59.0	19.1	18.8	54.7	31.2	821.7	1998
178.5	116.2	115.7	62.0	19.6	19.6	59.0	11.0	815.8	1999
191.1	125.4	134.8	64.0	18.5	20.8	61.7	-	852.3	2000
187.4	92.0	139.7	69.5	17.3	19.5	57.8	-	810.5	2001
186.2	87.9	138.3	66.5	16.9	20.0	59.9	-	790.8	2002
192.1	96.0	109.3	66.5	16.7	21.1	60.9	-	788.4	2003
195.2	111.6	81.7	66.5	16.8	22.0	62.6	-	800.9	2004
186.8	103.2	115.7	68.0	16.4	17.0	60.0	10.0	807.2	2005
173.3	90.0	104.8	47.5	15.4	15.1	57.0	10.0	717.7	2006
172.7	86.0	120.9	50.5	15.2	15.5	57.0	10.0	724.0	2007
163.5	71.1	125.3	48.5	15.1	16.0	65.0	8.0	694.7	2008
151.3	45.4	117.0	44.5	14.0	14.9	61.5	6.0	616.4	2009
151.6	53.4	119.8	45.2	14.5	14.9	63.8	6.0	631.2	2010p

See "silver statistical position" table for related statistics.
Sources: U.S. Bureau of Mines, Handy & Harman, trade sources, CPM Group.
March 15, 2010

Silver Yearbook 2010 - Fabrication Demand — CPM Group

European Silver Fabrication Demand
Million Troy Ounces

	1979	1980	1981	1982	1983	1984	1985	1986
Jewelry/Silverware	50.3	27.5	28.7	32.7	23.9	27.3	33.1	47.3
Photography	47.9	41.4	43.2	44.9	45.6	47.6	48.1	51.1
Electronics	33.4	29.8	25.6	23.2	23.8	26.2	27.2	28.5
Brazing Alloys/Solders	20.8	15.2	13.0	12.0	9.9	10.5	10.4	10.9
Dental	1.3	1.6	1.3	1.2	1.1	1.1	1.1	1.1
Mirrors	2.3	2.5	2.6	2.2	1.9	1.9	1.8	1.8
Miscellaneous	6.6	5.3	4.8	4.4	3.6	4.3	3.9	4.2
Total	162.0	123.2	119.3	121.1	109.8	118.9	125.7	144.9
% Change Year Ago	--	-24.0%	-3.2%	1.5%	-9.3%	8.3%	5.7%	15.3%
Coinage	22.6	5.8	7.0	8.5	5.8	7.8	8.1	5.3
Total Including Coinage	184.6	129.0	126.3	129.6	115.6	126.7	133.8	150.2
% Change Year Ago	--	-30.1%	-2.1%	2.6%	-10.8%	9.6%	5.6%	12.2%

	1987	1988	1989	1990	1991	1992	1993	1994
Jewelry/Silverware	53.3	57.3	63.8	68.3	73.1	71.8	68.7	74.3
Photography	52.6	57.0	57.1	59.0	60.0	62.2	63.9	70.6
Electronics	29.0	31.5	34.8	34.7	34.8	32.4	32.1	31.5
Brazing Alloys/Solders	11.0	11.4	13.0	13.3	13.5	13.4	12.9	12.6
Dental	1.1	1.2	1.1	1.0	1.2	1.2	1.1	1.1
Mirrors	1.4	1.5	2.0	2.0	2.0	2.0	2.3	2.5
Miscellaneous	4.0	4.6	4.8	4.4	4.6	4.6	4.2	4.6
Total	152.5	164.3	176.6	182.7	189.2	187.6	185.3	197.2
% Change Year Ago	5.3%	7.8%	7.5%	3.4%	3.6%	-0.8%	-1.2%	6.4%
Coinage	11.1	10.2	9.0	7.5	11.9	7.5	6.3	6.6
Total Including Coinage	163.5	174.6	185.6	190.2	201.1	195.1	191.6	203.8
% Change Year Ago	8.9%	6.7%	6.3%	2.5%	5.7%	-3.0%	-1.8%	6.4%

	1995	1996	1997	1998	1999	2000	2001	2002
Jewelry/Silverware	80.9	74.0	78.0	92.4	90.4	86.5	82.4	69.0
Photography	72.6	74.4	77.5	81.8	85.6	88.6	88.3	89.3
Electronics	32.2	30.6	31.3	34.0	35.1	37.1	34.4	33.1
Brazing Alloys/Solders	11.9	11.5	11.7	12.6	13.1	12.9	11.9	11.5
Dental	1.1	1.1	1.1	1.2	1.3	1.3	1.3	1.3
Mirrors	2.8	2.9	3.1	3.5	3.5	3.4	3.1	2.9
Miscellaneous	4.2	4.2	4.3	4.8	5.1	6.2	5.9	5.6
Super Conducters	-	-	-	-	-	-	-	2.5
Total	205.7	198.7	207.0	230.3	234.2	236.0	227.3	215.1
% Change Year Ago	4.3%	-3.4%	4.2%	11.2%	1.7%	0.8%	-3.7%	-5.4%
Coinage	8.2	7.2	7.63	8.6	8.1	-	-	-
Total Including Coinage	213.9	205.9	214.7	238.9	242.3	236.0	227.3	215.1
% Change Year Ago	5.0%	-3.7%	4.2%	11.3%	1.4%	-2.6%	-3.7%	-5.4%

	2003	2004	2005	2006	2007	2008	2009	2010p
Jewelry/Silverware	71.2	72.7	67.7	64.9	66.3	66.6	60.4	61.8
Photography	88.8	89.8	81.0	69.4	62.4	50.9	43.4	40.6
Electronics	34.0	34.9	34.6	35.2	36.0	35.7	34.3	35.2
Brazing Alloys/Solders	11.7	11.6	11.3	11.7	12.0	11.7	11.0	11.4
Dental	1.3	1.4	1.4	1.5	1.6	1.6	1.4	1.5
Mirrors	3.0	3.2	3.2	3.7	3.6	3.6	3.4	3.4
Miscellaneous	5.9	5.9	5.9	6.2	6.4	6.1	5.9	6.1
Super Conducters	10	25	25	12	8	6	2.0	2.0
Total	225.8	244.5	230.1	204.6	196.2	182.2	161.8	162.0
% Change Year Ago	5.0%	8.3%	-5.9%	-11.1%	-4.1%	-7.1%	-11.2%	0.1%
Coinage	-	-	-	-	-	-	-	-
Total Including Coinage	225.8	244.5	230.1	204.6	196.2	182.2	161.8	162.0
% Change Year Ago	5.0%	8.3%	-5.9%	-11.1%	-4.1%	-7.1%	-11.2%	0.1%

Notes: Totals may not equal the sums of categories due to rounding. Consumption of silver in semi-fabricated form is excluded.
Sources: European trade sources, CPM Group.
March 15, 2010

CPM Group   **Silver Yearbook 2010 - Fabrication Demand**

Italian Silver Fabrication Demand
Million Troy Ounces

	1986	1987	1988	1989	1990	1991	1992	1993
Sterlingware	18.5	23.2	23.2	28.9	32.2	37.0	38.6	36.3
Silverplate	0.4	0.4	0.4	0.4	0.6	0.6	0.6	0.6
Jewelry	4.1	5.0	5.4	5.0	5.5	5.5	5.5	5.2
Photography	4.2	3.5	1.9	1.6	2.3	2.3	2.5	2.5
Electronics	4.2	4.2	4.5	4.5	4.0	4.1	4.0	4.0
Brazing Alloys/Solders	1.1	1.1	1.2	1.3	1.6	1.8	1.9	1.9
Mirrors	0.3	0.3	0.3	0.3	0.8	0.8	0.8	0.8
Miscellaneous	0.9	0.9	1.0	1.1	1.0	1.0	1.0	1.0
Total	33.5	38.6	37.9	43.0	47.9	53.0	54.9	52.3
% Change Year Ago	39.9%	15.2%	-2.0%	13.7%	11.3%	10.6%	3.6%	-4.7%
Coinage	0.2	0.2	0.2	0.2	0.1	—	0.2	—
Total Including Coinage	33.7	38.8	38.0	43.3	48.0	53.0	55.1	52.3
% Change Year Ago	37.9%	15.1%	-2.0%	13.8%	10.9%	10.4%	4.0%	-5.1%

	1994	1995	1996	1997	1998	1999	2000	2001
Sterlingware	40.7	46.6	43.8	46.4	56.6	54.7	53.0	51.1
Silverplate	0.8	0.9	0.8	0.9	1.1	1.0	1.0	0.9
Jewelry	6.0	6.7	6.1	7.0	8.8	7.9	7.5	7.2
Photography	2.7	2.8	2.8	2.8	3.0	3.1	3.0	2.9
Electronics	4.0	4.0	4.0	4.0	4.4	4.5	4.8	4.4
Brazing Alloys/Solders	2.0	2.1	2.1	2.1	2.3	2.3	2.2	2.1
Mirrors	0.9	1.0	1.0	1.0	1.1	1.1	1.0	0.8
Miscellaneous	1.0	1.0	1.0	1.0	1.1	1.1	1.0	1.0
Total	58.0	65.1	61.5	65.2	78.4	75.7	73.5	70.4
% Change Year Ago	10.9%	12.2%	-5.8%	6.0%	20.2%	-3.4%	-2.9%	-4.2%

	2002	2003	2004	2005	2006	2007	2008	2009
Sterlingware	41.0	42.2	42.8	38.5	36.5	37.0	38.0	34.0
Silverplate	0.7	0.8	1.0	1.0	1.0	0.8	0.8	0.6
Jewelry	6.0	6.2	6.5	6.0	5.8	6.1	6.4	5.8
Photography	2.5	2.5	2.4	2.0	1.6	1.4	1.2	1.0
Electronics	4.5	4.6	4.8	4.5	4.6	4.4	4.2	4.0
Brazing Alloys/Solders	2.2	2.3	2.3	2.0	2.0	1.9	1.8	1.7
Mirrors	0.8	0.8	1.0	1.0	1.0	0.8	0.8	0.7
Miscellaneous	1.0	1.0	1.0	1.0	1.0	1.0	1.0	1.0
Total	58.7	60.4	61.8	56.0	53.5	53.4	54.2	48.8
% Change Year Ago	-16.6%	2.9%	2.3%	-9.4%	-4.5%	-0.2%	1.5%	-10.0%

	2010p
Sterlingware	35.0
Silverplate	0.7
Jewelry	6.0
Photography	0.9
Electronics	4.1
Brazing Alloys/Solders	1.7
Mirrors	0.7
Miscellaneous	1.0
Total	50.1
% Change Year Ago	2.7%

Notes: Totals may not equal the sums of categories due to rounding. Consumption of silver in semi-fabricated form is excluded.
Sources: European trade sources, CPM Group.
March 15, 2010

Silver Yearbook 2010 - Fabrication Demand — CPM Group

German Silver Fabrication Demand

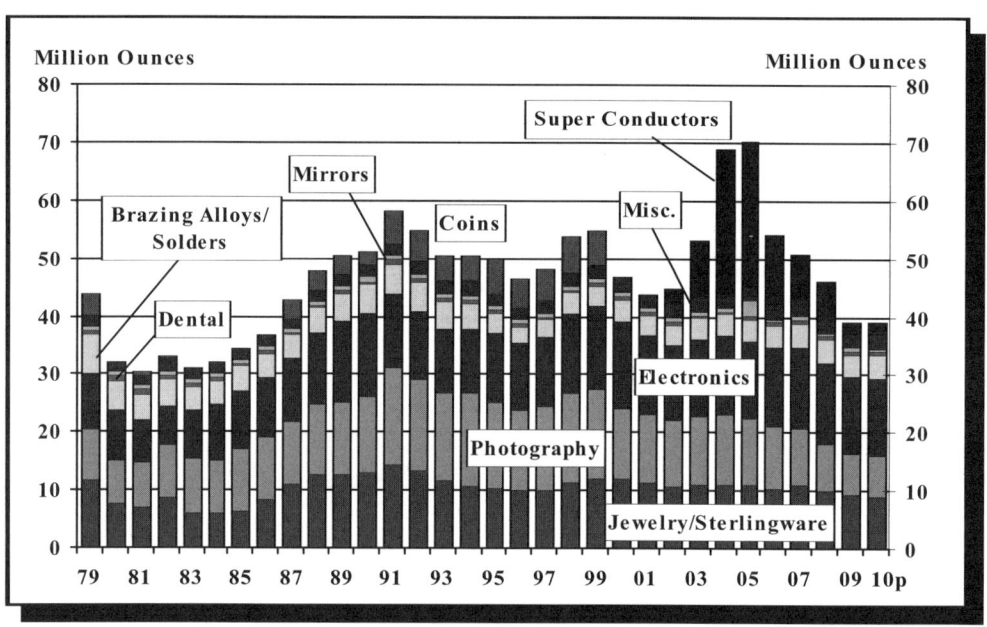

German Silver Fabrication Demand
Million Troy Ounces

	1979	1980	1981	1982	1983	1984	1985	1986
Jewelry/Silverware	11.8	7.6	6.9	8.7	6.1	5.9	6.4	8.5
Photography	8.7	7.3	7.8	8.9	9.2	9.2	10.6	10.4
Electronics	9.6	8.7	7.4	6.7	8.6	9.7	10.1	10.6
Brazing Alloys/Solders	6.7	5.3	4.5	4.7	3.9	4.0	4.2	4.0
Dental	0.5	0.7	0.5	0.5	0.4	0.3	0.3	0.4
Mirrors	0.5	0.5	0.5	0.5	0.5	0.5	0.5	0.5
Miscellaneous	2.0	1.8	1.8	2.4	1.9	2.1	2.0	1.9
Total	39.8	31.9	29.3	32.7	30.3	32.2	34.6	36.3
% Change Year Ago	—	-19.8%	-8.2%	11.6%	-7.3%	6.2%	7.5%	5.0%
Coinage	3.7	—	0.5	0.3	—	—	—	—
Total Including Coinage	43.5	31.9	29.8	33.0	30.3	32.2	34.6	36.3
% Change Year Ago	—	-26.7%	-6.6%	10.7%	-8.2%	6.2%	7.5%	5.0%

	1987	1988	1989	1990	1991	1992	1993	1994
Jewelry/Silverware	11.2	12.7	12.7	13.2	14.5	13.5	11.6	10.7
Photography	10.5	12.1	12.5	12.9	16.7	15.7	15.1	16.1
Electronics	10.9	12.3	13.8	14.3	12.7	11.6	11.3	11.2
Brazing Alloys/Solders	4.1	4.2	4.8	5.0	5.1	5.0	4.5	4.2
Dental	0.3	0.3	0.3	0.4	0.5	0.5	0.4	0.4
Mirrors	0.5	0.5	0.5	0.5	0.5	0.5	0.5	0.5
Miscellaneous	1.6	1.9	2.1	2.1	2.3	2.4	2.4	2.7
Total	39.1	44.1	46.9	48.4	52.3	49.1	45.8	45.8
% Change Year Ago	7.6%	12.8%	6.2%	3.3%	8.1%	-6.1%	-6.7%	0.1%
Coinage	3.2	3.2	3.2	2.4	5.5	5.3	4.5	4.2
Total Including Coinage	42.3	47.3	50.1	50.8	57.8	54.4	50.3	50.0
% Change Year Ago	16.5%	11.8%	5.8%	1.5%	13.9%	-6.0%	-7.5%	-0.6%

	1995	1996	1997	1998	1999	2000	2001	2002
Photography	14.8	13.8	14.5	15.4	15.5	12.0	11.7	11.6
Electronics	11.9	11.6	11.9	13.7	14.2	15.0	13.6	13.0
Brazing Alloys/Solders	3.5	2.9	3.1	3.5	3.6	4.0	3.6	3.4
Dental	0.4	0.4	0.4	0.4	0.5	0.5	0.5	0.5
Mirrors	0.5	0.5	0.6	0.7	0.7	0.7	0.6	0.5
Miscellaneous	2.2	2.0	2.1	2.3	2.3	2.8	2.6	2.5
Super Conducters	-	-	-	-	-	-	-	2.5
Total	43.6	41.1	42.7	47.5	48.8	47.0	44.0	44.6
% Change Year Ago	-4.8%	-5.6%	3.8%	11.2%	2.7%	-3.7%	-6.4%	1.4%
Coinage	5.8	5.1	5.5	6.5	6.0			
Total Including Coinage	49.4	46.2	48.2	54.0	54.8			
% Change Year Ago	-1.2%	-6.4%	4.2%	12.0%	1.5%			

	2003	2004	2005	2006	2007	2008	2009	2010p
Jewelry/Silverware	10.9	11.1	11.0	10.5	10.9	10.1	9.3	9.2
Photography	11.9	12.1	11.4	10.5	9.7	8.0	7.2	6.8
Electronics	13.3	13.6	13.5	13.7	14.2	14.0	13.4	13.6
Brazing Alloys/Solders	3.6	3.6	3.7	3.8	4.0	3.9	3.7	3.8
Dental	0.5	0.5	0.5	0.6	0.7	0.7	0.6	0.6
Mirrors	0.5	0.5	0.5	0.5	0.6	0.6	0.5	0.5
Miscellaneous	2.6	2.6	2.6	2.6	2.8	2.8	2.6	2.8
Super Conducters	10.0	25.0	25.0	12.0	8.0	6.0	2.0	2.0
Total	53.3	69.0	68.2	54.2	50.9	46.1	39.3	39.3
% Change Year Ago	19.5%	29.5%	-1.2%	-20.5%	-6.1%	-9.4%	-14.8%	0.0%

Notes: Totals may not equal the sums of categories due to rounding.
Sources: European trade sources, CPM Group.
March 15, 2010

Silver Yearbook 2010 - Fabrication Demand — CPM Group

U.K. Silver Fabrication Demand

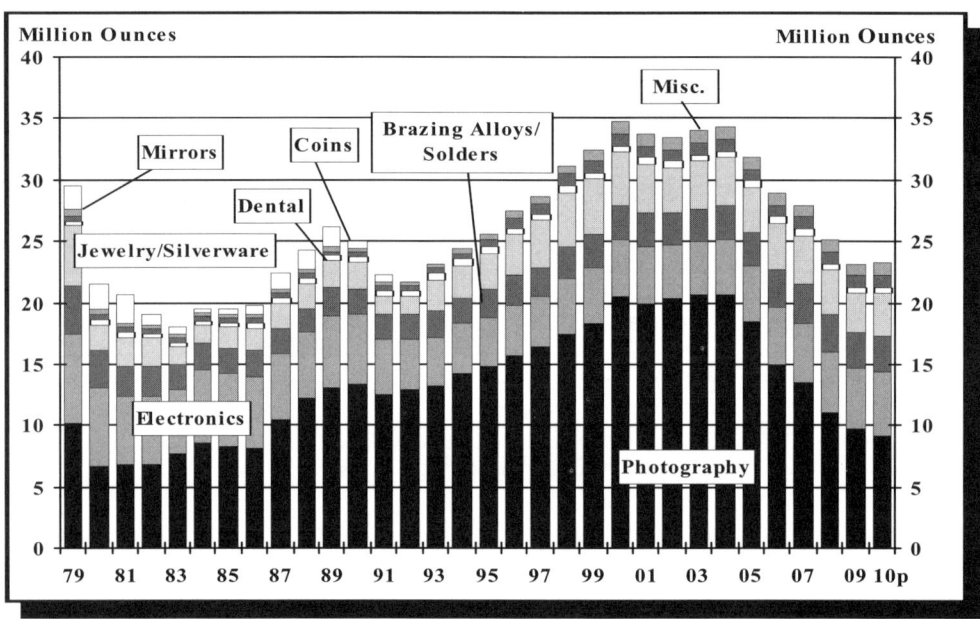

United Kingdom Silver Fabrication Demand
Million Troy Ounces

	1979	1980	1981	1982	1983	1984	1985	1986
Jewelry/Silverware	4.9	2.1	2.3	2.2	1.5	1.4	1.8	1.7
Photography	10.2	6.7	6.9	6.8	7.7	8.6	8.3	8.1
Electronics	7.3	6.4	5.4	5.5	5.3	5.9	5.9	5.8
Brazing Alloys/Solders	3.9	3.0	2.6	2.6	2.0	2.2	2.1	2.3
Dental	0.3	0.4	0.4	0.4	0.3	0.3	0.3	0.4
Mirrors	0.5	0.4	0.4	0.4	0.4	0.4	0.4	0.4
Miscellaneous	0.5	0.5	0.4	0.3	0.3	0.3	0.3	0.3
Total	27.6	19.5	18.4	18.1	17.7	19.2	19.1	19.1
% Change Year Ago	—	-29.3%	-5.6%	-1.6%	-2.2%	8.3%	-0.5%	0.2%
Coinage	2.0	2.1	2.2	0.9	0.6	0.3	0.4	0.8
Total Including Coinage	29.6	21.6	20.6	19.1	18.3	19.5	19.5	19.8
% Change Year Ago	—	-27.0%	-4.6%	-7.3%	-4.2%	6.4%	-0.1%	1.8%

	1987	1988	1989	1990	1991	1992	1993	1994
Jewelry/Silverware	2.0	2.0	2.2	2.1	1.5	1.5	2.6	2.7
Photography	10.4	12.3	13.0	13.4	12.5	13.0	13.2	14.3
Electronics	5.5	5.4	5.9	5.6	4.5	4.0	4.0	4.0
Brazing Alloys/Solders	2.0	1.9	2.3	2.1	2.0	2.0	2.1	2.1
Dental	0.5	0.5	0.5	0.5	0.5	0.5	0.5	0.5
Mirrors	0.4	0.4	0.4	0.4	0.4	0.4	0.5	0.5
Miscellaneous	0.3	0.3	0.3	0.3	0.3	0.3	0.3	0.4
Total	21.1	22.7	24.5	24.4	21.7	21.7	23.2	24.4
% Change Year Ago	10.5%	7.7%	7.9%	-0.5%	-11.1%	0.0%	6.7%	5.5%
Coinage	1.3	1.6	1.6	0.3	0.2	—	—	—
Total Including Coinage	22.4	24.3	26.1	24.7	21.9	21.7	23.2	24.4
% Change Year Ago	13.1%	8.7%	7.4%	-5.5%	-11.3%	-0.9%	6.9%	5.2%

	1995	1996	1997	1998	1999	2000	2001	2002
Jewelry/Silverware	3.0	3.4	3.8	4.4	4.5	4.3	4.0	3.7
Photography	14.8	15.7	16.4	17.5	18.3	20.5	20.0	20.4
Electronics	4.0	4.1	4.1	4.5	4.6	4.7	4.6	4.3
Brazing Alloys/Solders	2.2	2.4	2.4	2.6	2.7	2.8	2.7	2.6
Dental	0.5	0.5	0.5	0.5	0.5	0.5	0.5	0.5
Mirrors	0.6	0.8	0.9	1.0	1.0	1.0	1.0	0.9
Miscellaneous	0.5	0.6	0.6	0.7	0.9	1.0	1.0	1.0
Total	25.6	27.5	28.7	31.2	32.5	34.8	33.8	33.4
% Change Year Ago	4.9%	7.3%	4.4%	8.7%	4.2%	7.1%	-2.9%	-1.2%
Coinage	—	—	—	—	—	—	—	—
Total Including Coinage	25.6	27.5	28.7	31.2	32.5	34.8	33.8	33.4
% Change Year Ago	4.9%	7.3%	4.4%	8.7%	4.2%	7.1%	-2.9%	-1.2%

	2003	2004	2005	2006	2007	2008	2009	2010p
Jewelry/Silverware	3.8	3.9	3.7	3.8	4.0	3.6	3.3	3.5
Photography	20.6	20.7	18.5	15.0	13.5	11.1	9.7	9.1
Electronics	4.4	4.5	4.5	4.7	4.9	5.0	5.0	5.3
Brazing Alloys/Solders	2.7	2.7	2.7	3.0	3.1	3.0	2.8	2.9
Dental	0.5	0.5	0.5	0.5	0.5	0.5	0.4	0.5
Mirrors	1.0	1.0	1.0	1.0	1.0	1.0	1.0	1.0
Miscellaneous	1.0	1.0	1.0	1.0	1.0	1.0	1.0	1.0
Total	34	34.3	31.9	29	28	25.2	23.2	23.3
% Change Year Ago	1.8%	0.9%	-7.0%	-9.1%	-3.4%	-10.1%	-7.9%	0.5%
Coinage	—	—	—	—	—	—	—	—
Total Including Coinage	34	34.3	31.9	29	28	25.2	23.2	23.3
% Change Year Ago	1.8%	0.9%	-7.0%	-9.1%	-3.4%	-10.1%	-7.9%	0.5%

Notes: Totals may not equal the sums of categories due to rounding.
Sources: European trade sources, CPM Group.
March 15, 2010

Silver Yearbook 2010 - Fabrication Demand — CPM Group

Belgian Silver Fabrication Demand

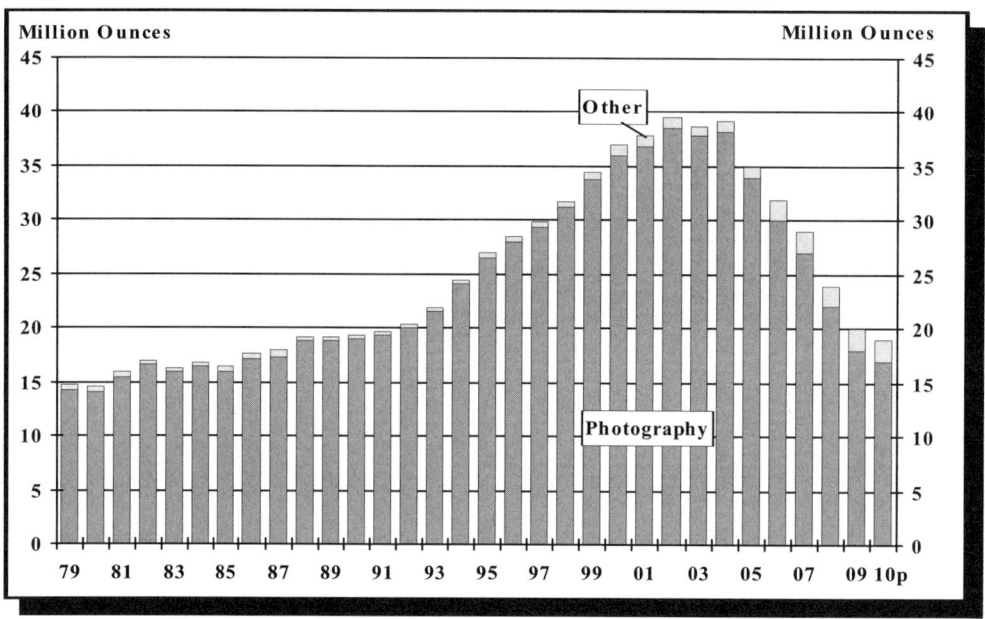

CPM Group   Silver Yearbook 2010 - Fabrication Demand

Belgian Silver Fabrication Demand

Million Troy Ounces

	1979	1980	1981	1982	1983	1984	1985	1986
Photography	14.2	14.1	15.5	16.6	15.9	16.4	16.0	17.2
Mirrors	0.1	0.1	0.1	0.3	0.3	0.3	0.3	0.3
Sterlingware/Jewelry	0.1	0.1	0.1					
Electronics	0.1	0.1	*	*	*	*	*	*
Dental	*	*	*	*				
Miscellaneous	0.2	0.2	0.2	0.1	0.1	0.1	0.1	0.1
Total	14.8	14.6	16.0	17.0	16.3	16.8	16.4	17.6
% Change Year Ago	-----	-1.4%	9.5%	6.4%	-4.1%	3.4%	-2.4%	7.3%

	1987	1988	1989	1990	1991	1992	1993	1994
Photography	17.4	18.8	18.8	19.0	19.3	20.0	21.5	24.1
Mirrors	0.3	0.3	0.3	0.3	0.3	0.3	0.3	0.3
Sterlingware/Jewelry								
Electronics	*	*	*	*	*	*	*	*
Dental								
Miscellaneous	0.2	0.1	0.1	0.1	0.1	0.1	0.1	0.1
Total	17.9	19.2	19.2	19.4	19.7	20.4	21.9	24.5
% Change Year Ago	1.7%	7.3%	-0.2%	1.0%	1.5%	3.6%	7.4%	11.7%

	1995	1996	1997	1998	1999	2000	2001	2002
Photography	26.5	28.0	29.4	31.2	33.8	36.0	36.8	38.6
Mirrors	0.4	0.4	0.4	0.5	0.5	0.5	0.5	0.5
Sterlingware/Jewelry								
Electronics	*	*	*	*	*	*	*	*
Dental								
Miscellaneous	0.1	0.1	0.1	0.2	0.2	0.5	0.5	0.4
Total	26.9	28.5	29.9	31.8	34.5	37.0	37.8	39.5
% Change Year Ago	10.0%	6.1%	4.7%	6.4%	8.3%	7.4%	2.2%	4.5%

	2003	2004	2005	2006	2007	2008	2009	2010p
Photography	37.8	38.2	34.0	30.0	27.0	22.0	18.0	17.0
Mirrors	0.5	0.5	0.5	1	1	1	1	1
Sterlingware/Jewelry								
Electronics	*	*	*	*	*	*	*	*
Dental								
Miscellaneous	0.5	0.5	0.5	1	1	1	1	1
Total	38.8	39.2	35.0	32.0	29.0	24.0	20.0	19.0
% Change Year Ago	-1.8%	1.0%	-10.7%	-8.6%	-9.4%	-17.2%	-16.7%	-5.0%

Notes: Totals may not equal the sums of categories due to rounding. Asterisks indicate that consumption in individual industries totaled less than 100,000 ounces.
Sources: European trade sources, CPM Group.
March 15, 2010

Silver Yearbook 2010 - Fabrication Demand — CPM Group

French Silver Fabrication Demand

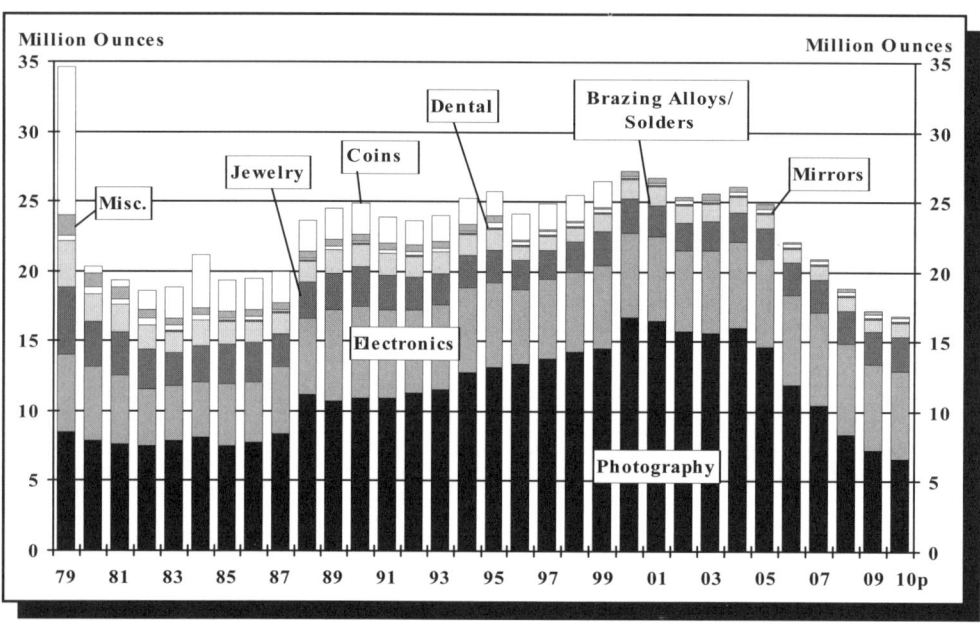

French Silver Fabrication Demand
Million Troy Ounces

	1979	1980	1981	1982	1983	1984	1985	1986
Jewelry/Silverware	4.7	3.2	3.0	2.8	2.4	2.6	2.8	2.8
Photography	8.5	7.9	7.7	7.5	7.9	8.1	7.6	7.7
Electronics	5.6	5.3	4.9	4.1	3.9	3.9	4.4	4.4
Brazing Alloys/Solders	3.4	2.0	2.0	1.8	1.5	1.8	1.6	1.6
Dental	—	—	—	—	0.1	0.1	0.1	0.1
Mirrors	0.4	0.4	0.4	0.4	0.3	0.3	0.2	0.2
Miscellaneous	1.4	1.0	0.8	0.5	0.4	0.3	0.3	0.3
Total	24.1	19.8	18.9	17.1	16.5	17.1	16.9	17.0
% Change Year Ago	—	-17.8%	-4.5%	-9.5%	-3.5%	3.7%	-0.9%	0.4%
Coinage	10.6	0.1	0.1	1.4	2.2	3.9	2.2	2.2
Total Including Coinage	34.7	19.9	19.0	18.5	18.7	21.0	19.1	19.2
% Change Year Ago	—	-42.7%	-4.5%	-2.6%	1.1%	12.3%	-8.9%	0.3%

	1987	1988	1989	1990	1991	1992	1993	1994
Jewelry/Silverware	2.3	2.5	2.7	2.8	2.5	2.3	2.3	2.3
Photography	8.4	11.2	10.8	11.0	10.9	11.3	11.6	12.9
Electronics	4.8	5.5	6.4	6.5	6.3	6.0	6.0	6.0
Brazing Alloys/Solders	1.5	1.5	1.6	1.6	1.6	1.5	1.5	1.5
Dental	0.1	0.1	0.1	0.1	0.1	0.1	0.1	0.1
Mirrors	0.2	0.2	0.2	0.2	0.2	0.2	0.2	0.2
Miscellaneous	0.3	0.3	0.3	0.3	0.3	0.3	0.3	0.3
Total	17.6	21.3	22.1	22.5	21.9	21.7	22.0	23.3
% Change Year Ago	3.4%	20.9%	3.9%	1.9%	-2.8%	-0.9%	1.4%	5.8%
Coinage	2.2	2.2	2.2	2.2	1.8	1.8	1.8	1.8
Total Including Coinage	19.8	23.4	24.3	24.7	23.7	23.5	23.8	25.1
% Change Year Ago	3.0%	18.5%	3.6%	1.8%	-4.2%	-0.7%	1.3%	5.4%

	1995	1996	1997	1998	1999	2000	2001	2002
Jewelry/Silverware	2.4	2.1	2.1	2.2	2.4	2.5	2.3	2.0
Photography	13.2	13.5	13.8	14.3	14.5	16.7	16.5	15.8
Electronics	6.0	5.3	5.7	5.7	6.0	6.1	6.0	5.8
Brazing Alloys/Solders	1.5	1.0	1.0	1.0	1.3	1.3	1.3	1.2
Dental	0.1	0.1	0.1	0.1	0.1	0.1	0.1	0.1
Mirrors	0.3	0.2	0.2	0.2	0.2	0.2	0.2	0.2
Miscellaneous	0.3	0.2	0.2	0.2	0.2	0.3	0.3	0.3
Total	23.8	22.4	23.1	23.7	24.7	27.2	26.7	25.4
% Change Year Ago	2.2%	-6.0%	3.3%	2.6%	4.2%	10.1%	-1.8%	-4.9%
Coinage	1.8	1.8	1.8	1.8	1.8			
Total Including Coinage	25.6	24.2	24.9	25.5	26.5			
% Change Year Ago	2.1%	-5.6%	3.1%	2.4%	3.9%			

	2003	2004	2005	2006	2007	2008	2009	2010p
Jewelry/Silverware	2.1	2.1	2.2	2.3	2.4	2.4	2.3	2.4
Photography	15.6	16.0	14.7	12.0	10.5	8.4	7.3	6.6
Electronics	6.0	6.2	6.3	6.4	6.6	6.5	6.2	6.4
Brazing Alloys/Solders	1.2	1.1	1.0	1.0	1.0	1.0	0.9	1.0
Dental	0.1	0.1	0.1	0.1	0.1	0.1	0.1	0.1
Mirrors	0.2	0.2	0.2	0.2	0.2	0.2	0.2	0.2
Miscellaneous	0.4	0.4	0.4	0.2	0.2	0.2	0.2	0.2
Total	25.6	26.1	24.9	22.2	21	18.8	17.2	16.9
% Change Year Ago	0.8%	2.0%	-4.6%	-10.8%	-5.4%	-10.5%	-8.5%	-1.7%

Notes: Totals may not equal the sums of categories due to rounding. Asterisks indicate that consumption in individual industries totaled less than 100,000 ounces.
Sources: European trade sources, CPM Group.
March 15, 2010

Austrian Silver Fabrication Demand

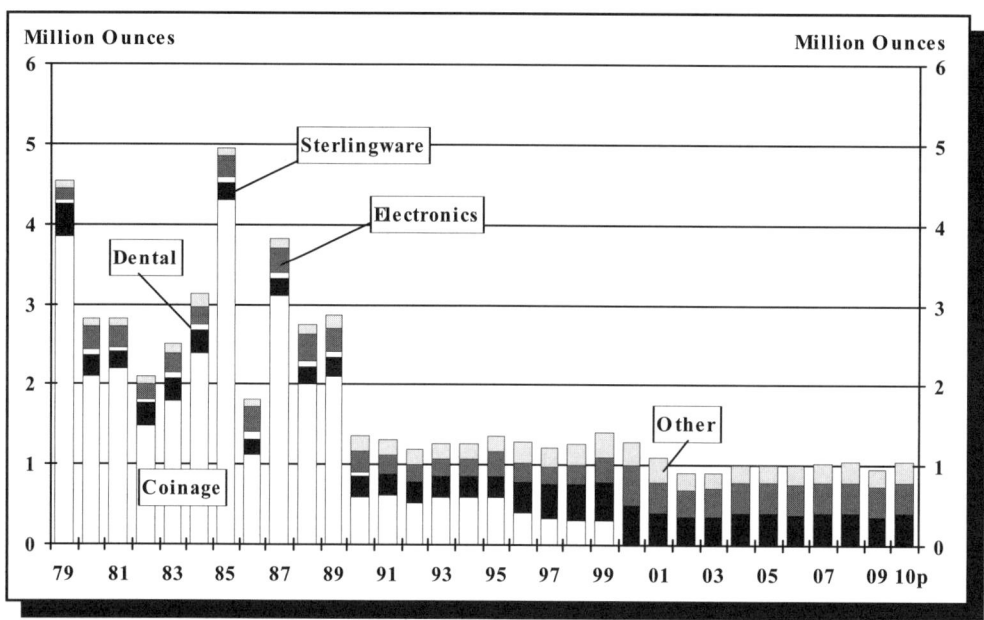

CPM Group — Silver Yearbook 2010 - Fabrication Demand

Austrian Silver Fabrication Demand
Million Troy Ounces

	1979	1980	1981	1982	1983	1984	1985	1986
Sterlingware/Jewelry	0.40	0.26	0.21	0.29	0.30	0.28	0.21	0.21
Dental	0.06	0.07	0.06	0.05	0.07	0.07	0.07	0.09
Electronics	0.13	0.30	0.26	0.18	0.24	0.21	0.26	0.32
Brazing Alloys/Solders	*	0.06	0.06	0.06	0.06	0.10	0.11	0.10
Medals/Medallions	*	*	*	*	*	*	*	*
Miscellaneous	*	*	*	*	*	0.1	*	*
Total	0.59	0.69	0.59	0.58	0.67	0.73	0.66	0.71
% Change Year Ago	—	17.5%	-14.0%	-2.2%	15.5%	8.1%	-9.3%	7.8%
Coinage	3.85	2.10	2.20	1.48	1.78	2.40	4.30	1.11
Total Including Coinage	4.44	2.79	2.79	2.06	2.46	3.13	4.96	1.82
% Change Year Ago	—	-37.2%	0.1%	-26.1%	19.0%	27.3%	58.6%	-63.2%

	1987	1988	1989	1990	1991	1992	1993	1994
Sterlingware/Jewelry	0.21	0.23	0.24	0.26	0.27	0.26	0.26	0.26
Dental	0.08	0.07	0.06	0.06	*	*	*	*
Electronics	0.32	0.33	0.30	0.26	0.23	0.23	0.22	0.22
Brazing Alloys/Solders	0.11	0.12	0.15	0.18	0.19	0.18	0.18	0.18
Medals/Medallions	*	*	*	*	*	*	*	*
Miscellaneous	*	*	*	*	*	*	*	*
Total	0.73	0.76	0.76	0.75	0.68	0.67	0.66	0.66
% Change Year Ago	2.3%	4.0%	0.4%	-0.8%	-9.4%	1.5%	-1.5%	0.0%
Coinage	3.10	2.00	2.10	0.60	0.62	0.52	0.60	0.60
Total Including Coinage	3.83	2.76	2.86	1.35	1.30	1.19	1.26	1.26
% Change Year Ago	109.8%	-28.0%	3.7%	-52.7%	-3.5%	-8.7%	6.1%	0.0%

	1995	1996	1997	1998	1999	2000	2001	2002
Sterlingware/Jewelry	0.26	0.40	0.42	0.46	0.50	0.50	0.40	0.35
Dental	*	*	*	*	*	*	*	*
Electronics	0.30	0.23	0.23	0.25	0.30	0.50	0.40	0.35
Brazing Alloys/Solders	0.20	0.09	0.09	0.10	0.10	0.10	0.10	0.10
Medals/Medallions	*	*	*	*	*	*	*	*
Miscellaneous	*	0.17	0.15	0.16	0.20	0.20	0.20	0.10
Total	0.76	0.89	0.89	0.97	1.10	1.30	1.10	0.90
% Change Year Ago	15.2%	17.1%	0.4%	8.5%	13.4%	18.2%	-15.4%	-18.2%
Coinage	0.60	0.40	0.33	0.30	0.30			
Total Including Coinage	1.36	1.29	1.22	1.27	1.40			
% Change Year Ago	7.6%	-5.1%	-5.1%	3.8%	10.2%			

	2003	2004	2005	2006	2007	2008	2009	2010p
Sterlingware/Jewelry	0.35	0.40	0.40	0.38	0.40	0.40	0.37	0.40
Dental	*	*	*	*	*	*	*	*
Electronics	0.36	0.40	0.40	0.38	0.38	0.40	0.37	0.40
Brazing Alloys/Solders	0.10	0.10	0.10	0.12	0.12	0.12	0.11	0.12
Medals/Medallions	*	*	*	*	*	*	*	*
Miscellaneous	0.10	0.10	0.10	0.12	0.12	0.12	0.11	0.12
Total	0.91	1.00	1.00	1.00	1.02	1.04	0.96	1.04
% Change Year Ago	1.1%	9.9%	-	-	2.0%	2.0%	-7.7%	8.3%

Notes: Totals may not equal the sums of categories due to rounding. Asterisks indicate that consumption in individual industries totaled less than 50,000 ounces.
Sources: European trade sources, CPM Group.
March 15, 2010

Silver Yearbook 2010 - Fabrication Demand — CPM Group

Netherlands Silver Fabrication Demand

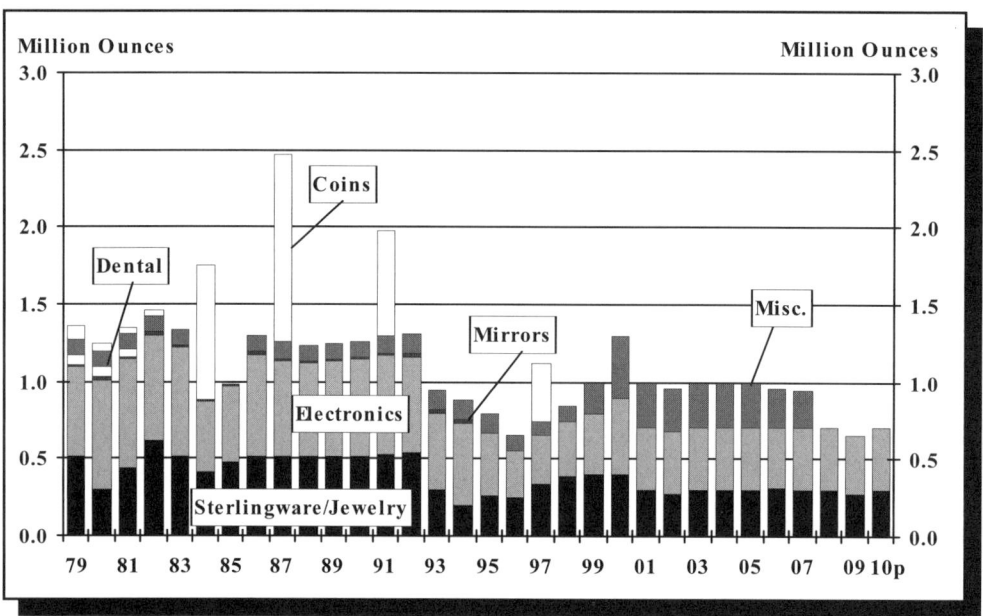

CPM Group Silver Yearbook 2010 - Fabrication Demand

Netherlands Silver Fabrication Demand
Million Troy Ounces

	1979	1980	1981	1982	1983	1984	1985	1986
Sterlingware/Jewelry	0.52	0.31	0.44	0.62	0.52	0.41	0.48	0.52
Electronics	0.58	0.71	0.71	0.68	0.71	0.45	0.48	0.66
Mirrors	*	*	*	*	*	*	*	*
Dental	0.06	0.06	0.05	—	—	—	—	—
Miscellaneous	0.10	0.10	0.10	0.10	0.10	—	—	0.10
Total	1.26	1.18	1.30	1.40	1.32	0.86	0.98	1.28
% Change Year Ago	—	-6.5%	10.0%	8.3%	-5.7%	-34.4%	11.5%	32.1%
Coinage	0.08	0.05	0.02	0.03	—	0.87	—	—
Total Including Coinage	1.34	1.23	1.32	1.44	1.32	1.74	0.98	1.28
% Change Year Ago	—	-8.5%	7.5%	8.9%	-7.8%	30.8%	-43.5%	30.4%

	1987	1988	1989	1990	1991	1992	1993	1994
Sterlingware/Jewelry	0.52	0.51	0.52	0.52	0.53	0.54	0.30	0.28
Electronics	0.62	0.61	0.61	0.62	0.64	0.62	0.50	0.53
Mirrors	*	*	*	*	*	*	*	*
Dental	—	—	—	—	—	—	—	—
Miscellaneous	0.10	0.10	0.10	0.10	0.11	0.13	0.13	0.13
Total	1.29	1.23	1.29	1.29	1.29	1.29	0.98	0.99
% Change Year Ago	-3.0%	-1.4%	1.2%	0.6%	3.3%	0.3%	-24.0%	1.0%
Coinage	1.21	—	—	—	0.67	—	—	—
Total Including Coinage	2.50	1.23	1.29	1.29	1.96	1.29	0.98	0.99
% Change Year Ago	95.9%	-51.0%	4.9%	0.5%	51.9%	-34.2%	-24.0%	1.0%

	1995	1996	1997	1998	1999	2000	2001	2002
Sterlingware/Jewelry	0.27	0.25	0.34	0.39	0.40	0.40	0.30	0.28
Electronics	0.40	0.30	0.31	0.35	0.40	0.50	0.40	0.40
Mirrors	*	*	*	*	*	*	*	*
Dental	—	—	—	—	—	—	—	—
Miscellaneous	0.13	0.10	0.10	0.11	0.20	0.40	0.30	0.28
Total	0.80	0.65	0.75	0.85	1.00	1.30	1.00	0.96
% Change Year Ago	-19.3%	-18.7%	15.4%	13.3%	17.6%	30.0%	-23.1%	-4.0%
Coinage	—	—	0.38					
Total Including Coinage	0.80	0.65	1.13					
% Change Year Ago	-19.2%	-18.8%	73.6%					

	2003	2004	2005	2006	2007	2008	2009	2010p
Sterlingware/Jewelry	0.30	0.30	0.30	0.31	0.30	0.30	0.28	0.30
Electronics	0.40	0.40	0.40	0.40	0.40	0.40	0.38	0.40
Mirrors	*	*	*	*	*	*	*	*
Dental	—	—	—	—	—	—	—	—
Miscellaneous	0.30	0.30	0.30	0.25	0.25	—	—	—
Total	1.00	1.00	1.00	0.96	0.95	0.70	0.66	0.70
% Change Year Ago	4.2%	0.0%	0.0%	-4.0%	-1.0%	-26.3%	-5.7%	6.1%

Notes: Totals may not equal the sums of categories due to rounding. *Mirrors absorb around 2,000 ounces annually.
Sources: European trade sources, CPM Group.
March 15, 2010

Silver Yearbook 2010 - Fabrication Demand CPM Group

Annual U.S. Silver Fabrication Demand, 1986 - 1997
Million Troy Ounces

	1986	1987	1988	1989	1990	1991
Photography	55.4	60.2	62.5	65.2	68.0	66.0
Electrical Contacts and Conductors	27.4	22.7	23.0	23.5	22.8	18.3
Batteries	3.7	2.4	2.5	2.8	3.0	3.1
Sterling Ware	3.9	3.8	3.5	3.4	3.5	3.5
Jewelry	4.6	4.2	2.9	2.4	2.0	2.0
Silverplate	3.7	2.5	2.6	2.7	2.8	2.8
Brazing Alloys and Solders	6.4	5.6	5.5	6.0	6.2	6.4
Catalysts	2.3	2.4	2.6	2.8	3.0	3.3
Medallions and Commemorative Objects	4.0	4.2	—	—	—	—
Dental and Medical Supplies	1.5	1.3	1.4	1.7	1.8	—
Mirrors	1.0	1.0	1.1	1.1	1.2	1.1
Bearings	0.4	0.3	—	—	—	—
Miscellaneous	4.6	4.5	4.4	8.4	11.0	12.2
Total Industrial	118.9	115.3	112.0	120.0	125.3	118.7
% Change Year Ago	0.3%	-3.1%	-2.8%	7.1%	4.4%	-5.3%
Coinage	10.3	12.2	7.9	6.8	9.1	9.1
Total Fabrication	129.2	127.5	119.9	126.8	134.4	127.8
% Change Year Ago	8.7%	-1.4%	-5.9%	5.8%	6.0%	-4.9%

	1992	1993	1994	1995	1996	1997
Photography	64.4	65.0	71.0	72.9	78.3	84.6
Electrical Contacts and Conductors	18.3	18.8	19.5	20.9	22.3	26.5
Batteries	3.1	3.3	3.6	4.1	4.5	4.8
Sterling Ware	3.9	4.0	4.2	4.4	4.8	5.1
Jewelry	3.0	3.3	3.7	4.1	4.4	4.9
Silverplate	2.9	3.0	3.1	3.5	3.9	4.1
Brazing Alloys and Solders	7.1	7.2	7.5	7.7	8.2	8.9
Catalysts	3.8	4.0	4.2	4.9	5.5	5.7
Medallions and Commemorative Objects	—	—	—	—	—	—
Dental and Medical Supplies	—	—	—	—	—	—
Mirrors	1.2	1.3	1.5	1.7	2.1	2.4
Biocides	—	—	—	—	—	—
Miscellaneous	11.2	11.2	11.8	12.0	12.7	13.5
Total Industrial	118.9	121.1	130.1	136.2	146.7	160.5
% Change Year Ago	0.2%	1.9%	7.4%	4.7%	7.7%	9.4%
Coinage	8.1	8.9	8.1	7.5	5.0	5.3
Total Fabrication	127.0	130.0	138.2	143.7	151.7	165.8
% Change Year Ago	-0.6%	2.4%	6.3%	4.0%	5.6%	9.3%

Silver YEARBOOK 2010 - Fabrication Demand

Annual U.S. Silver Fabrication Demand, 1998 - 2010p
Million Troy Ounces

	1998	1999	2000	2001	2002	2003	2004
Photography	91.0	96.0	104.0	102.0	104.0	103.0	99.0
Electrical Contacts and Conductors	28.4	29.2	32.7	29.5	27.3	28.3	29.4
Batteries	4.9	5.0	5.2	5.3	5.4	5.5	5.5
Sterling Ware	5.7	5.8	5.6	4.6	4.4	4.5	4.7
Jewelry	5.5	5.7	6.1	4.9	4.2	5.0	5.3
Silverplate	4.5	4.4	4.5	4.0	3.8	4.0	4.1
Brazing Alloys and Solders	9.3	9.1	8.6	8.5	8.2	8.0	8.2
Catalysts	5.9	5.9	6.3	6.1	6.0	6.3	6.5
Medallions and Commemorative Objects	—	—	—	—	—	—	—
Dental and Medical Supplies	—	—	—	—	—	—	—
Mirrors	2.6	2.6	2.6	2.5	2.4	2.5	2.5
Bearings	—	—	—	—	1.0	3.0	5.0
Miscellaneous	14.5	14.8	15.5	20.0	19.5	22.0	25.0
Total Industrial	172.3	178.5	191.1	187.4	186.2	192.1	195.2
% Change Year Ago	7.4%	3.6%	7.1%	-1.9%	-0.6%	3.2%	1.6%
Coinage	10.3	10.2	11.5	10.5	11.1	9.9	9.9
Total Fabrication	182.6	188.7	202.6	197.9	197.3	202.0	205.1
% Change Year Ago	10.1%	3.3%	7.4%	-2.3%	-0.3%	2.4%	1.5%

	2005	2006	2007	2008	2009	2010p
Photography	88.0	75.0	69.0	58.0	52.0	49.0
Electrical Contacts and Conductors	30.7	32.0	33.5	34.5	33.5	35.0
Batteries	5.8	6.0	6.4	6.7	6.8	7.0
Sterling Ware	4.7	4.4	4.5	3.2	3.0	3.0
Jewelry	5.5	5.2	5.9	5.0	4.8	5.0
Silverplate	4.2	4.0	3.9	3.8	3.7	3.8
Brazing Alloys and Solders	8.5	8.8	9.2	9.3	8.8	9.0
Catalysts	6.7	6.9	7.0	7.0	7.1	7.2
Medallions and Commemorative Objects	—	—	—	—	—	—
Dental and Medical Supplies	—	—	—	—	—	—
Mirrors	2.5	2.4	2.5	2.5	2.4	2.4
Biocides	5.2	5.6	5.8	6.0	5.2	5.2
Miscellaneous	25.0	23.0	25.0	27.5	24.0	25.0
Total Industrial	186.8	173.3	172.7	163.5	151.3	151.6
% Change Year Ago	-4.3%	-7.2%	-0.3%	-5.3%	-7.5%	0.2%
Coinage	19.5	11.0	9.9	19.5	28.8	
Total Fabrication	206.3	184.3	182.6	183.0	180.1	151.6
% Change Year Ago	0.6%	-10.7%	-0.9%	0.2%	-1.6%	-15.8%

Notes: Totals may not equal the sums of components due to rounding.
Categories marked with dashes are included in miscellaneous.
Sources: U.S. Bureau of Mines, trade sources, CPM Group.
March 15, 2010

Silver Yearbook 2010 - Fabrication Demand   CPM Group

Japanese Silver Fabrication Demand, 1973-1990
Million Troy Ounces

	1973	1974	1975	1976	1977	1978	1979	1980	1981
Photography	25.0	22.6	23.0	27.3	31.2	31.4	32.2	32.6	33.9
Electrical Contacts	11.1	9.2	5.6	6.8	6.9	7.0	8.9	7.6	6.4
Caustic Silver	4.4	2.9	2.6	4.7	5.8	6.5	6.6	5.6	5.6
Brazing Alloys and Solders	7.3	5.9	2.9	4.7	4.3	4.7	5.3	3.5	3.1
Tube, Sheet, and Bar	6.5	4.8	3.5	5.9	5.6	5.1	4.9	3.2	3.0
Electroplating	4.3	2.8	2.3	3.4	2.8	2.9	2.8	2.5	2.4
Jewelry and Silverware	3.9	1.8	1.4	2.0	2.2	2.5	2.2	1.0	1.1
Miscellaneous	6.5	7.7	5.1	6.0	4.4	4.8	5.9	5.5	4.1
Total	69.0	57.7	46.4	60.8	63.2	64.9	68.8	61.5	59.6
% Change Year Ago		-16.4%	-19.6%	31.0%	3.9%	2.7%	6.0%	-10.6%	-3.1%
Coinage	—	—	—	—	—	—	—	—	—
Total Including Coinage	69.0	57.7	46.4	60.8	63.2	64.9	68.8	61.5	59.6
% Change Year Ago	—	-16.4%	-19.6%	31.0%	3.9%	2.7%	6.0%	-10.6%	-3.1%

	1982	1983	1984	1985	1986	1987	1988	1989	1990
Photography	36.6	40.9	41.3	42.2	47.0	51.3	56.8	54.8	56.5
Electrical Contacts	6.6	7.7	7.8	7.5	6.8	7.0	8.4	9.5	9.7
Caustic Silver	5.5	6.7	7.6	6.8	7.6	8.3	9.6	9.0	9.0
Brazing Alloys and Solders	3.3	3.2	3.9	3.7	3.7	3.8	4.4	4.6	4.5
Tube, Sheet, and Bar	3.6	3.2	3.9	3.6	4.1	5.3	5.6	6.9	7.6
Electroplating	2.3	2.8	3.7	3.2	3.2	4.9	3.6	3.8	4.1
Jewelry and Silverware	1.3	1.1	1.0	1.4	1.7	2.2	3.0	3.5	3.8
Dental	—	—	—	—	—	1.4	1.6	1.7	1.4
Miscellaneous	4.0	6.5	9.6	4.2	4.4	8.1	9.0	8.7	10.3
Total	63.2	72.1	78.8	72.6	78.5	92.3	102.0	102.5	106.9
% Change Year Ago	6.0%	14.1%	9.3%	-7.9%	8.1%	17.6%	10.5%	0.5%	4.3%
Coinage	—	—	—	—	6.4	—	—	—	8.9
Total Including Coinage	63.2	72.1	78.8	72.6	84.9	92.3	102.0	102.5	115.8
% Change Year Ago	6.0%	14.1%	9.3%	-7.9%	16.9%	8.7%	10.5%	0.5%	13.0%

Notes: Totals may not equal the sums of components due to rounding. There was
no silver use in coinage in Japan prior to 1986. * - unidentified uses included.
Sources: Japanese trade sources, CPM Group.
March 15, 2010

Japanese Silver Fabrication Demand, 1991-2010p
Million Troy Ounces

	1991	1992	1993	1994	1995	1996	1997	1998	1999	2000
Photography	57.8	58.0	58.5	61.1	63.6	65.7	67.3	71.0	71.5	55.5
Electrical Contacts	9.7	8.4	8.7	8.9	10.1	9.3	11.3	7.9	6.0	10.8
Caustic Silver	8.4	7.9	7.5	8.9	10.9	10.0	9.1	8.0	7.4	10.0
Brazing Alloys and Solders	4.8	4.2	3.8	4.5	4.9	4.7	5.2	5.0	5.5	4.9
Tube, Sheet, and Bar	7.5	7.2	7.2	7.1	6.8	6.0	4.8	4.5	4.3	5.5
Electroplating	4.1	3.4	3.5	3.6	3.3	3.2	3.0	2.5	2.0	3.0
Jewelry and Silverware	3.5	2.8	2.9	2.7	2.4	2.7	2.7	2.3	2.0	3.0
Dental	1.7	1.6	1.4	1.6	1.7	1.8	1.8	1.6	1.5	2.0
Miscellaneous	11.4	13.0	18.2	17.1	18.8	20.1	21.5	16.8	16.0	30.7
Total	108.9	106.5	111.7	115.5	122.5	123.5	126.7	119.6	116.2	125.4
% Change Year Ago	1.9%	-2.2%	4.9%	3.4%	6.1%	0.8%	2.6%	-5.6%	-2.8%	7.9%
Coinage	—	—	—	—	—	—	—	—	—	—
Total Including Coinage	108.9	106.5	111.7	115.5	122.5	123.5	126.7	119.6	116.2	125.4
% Change Year Ago	-6.0%	-2.2%	4.9%	3.4%	6.1%	0.8%	2.6%	-5.6%	-2.8%	7.9%

	2001	2002	2003	2004	2005	2006	2007	2008	2009	2010p
Photography	53.5	49.2	43.9	40.0	31.2	32.3	34.4	22.2	14.0	13.0
Electrical Contacts	4.8	4.9	7.0	8.3	6.7	6.0	6.2	6.4	5.3	6.6
Caustic Silver	6.5	7.1	9.5	9.9	9.6	9.9	7.7	7.2	4.0	5.0
Brazing Alloys and Solders	3.6	3.2	3.1	3.4	3.3	3.4	3.4	3.1	2.4	3.0
Tube, Sheet, and Bar	2.8	6.9	7.3	8.0	6.9	7.1	6.8	6.3	2.0	5.6
Electroplating	1.6	—	—	—	—	—	—	—	—	—
Jewelry and Silverware	2.8	2.6	2.9	3.0	3.1	3.0	3.2	3.0	3.2	3.2
Dental	1.0	—	—	—	—	—	—	—	—	—
Miscellaneous	15.4	11.5	12.3	14.0	12.4	13.3	14.3	14.9	12.5	15.0
Super Conductors	—	2.5	10.0	25.0	30.0	15.0	10.0	8.0	2.0	2.0
Total	92.0	87.9	96.0	111.6	103.2	90.0	86.0	71.1	45.4	53.4
% Change Year Ago	-26.6%	-4.5%	9.2%	16.2%	-7.5%	-12.8%	-4.4%	-17.3%	-36.1%	17.6%
Coinage	—	—	—	—	—	—	—	—	—	—
Total Including Coinage	92.0	87.9	96.0	111.6	103.2	90.0	86.0	71.1	45.4	53.4
% Change Year Ago	-26.6%	-4.5%	9.2%	16.2%	-7.5%	-12.8%	-4.4%	-17.3%	-36.1%	17.6%

Silver Yearbook 2010 - Fabrication Demand — CPM Group

Thai Silver Fabrication Demand

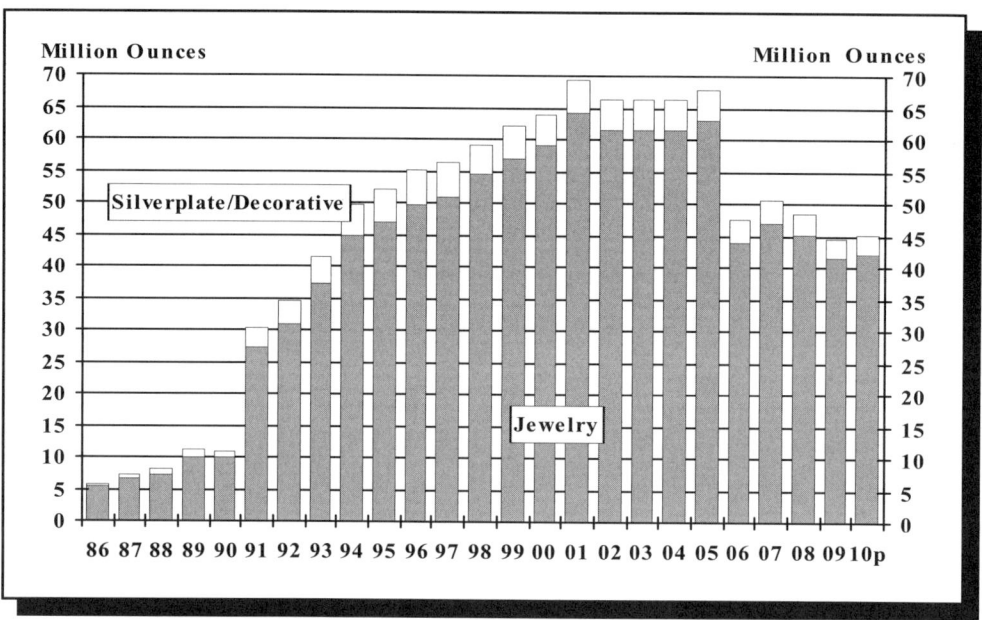

Thai Silver Fabrication Demand
Million Troy Ounces

	1986	1987	1988	1989	1990	1991
Jewelry	5.3	6.6	7.4	10.1	9.9	27.3
Silverplate/Decorative	0.6	0.7	0.8	1.1	1.1	3.0
Total Demand	5.9	7.4	8.2	11.2	11.0	30.4
% Change Year Ago	—	25.0%	11.1%	36.7%	-1.9%	176.2%
	1992	1993	1994	1995	1996	1997
Jewelry	31.0	37.3	44.7	46.9	49.8	50.8
Silverplate/Decorative	3.4	4.1	5.0	5.1	5.4	5.5
Total Demand	34.5	41.4	49.7	52.0	55.1	56.3
% Change Year Ago	13.5%	20.0%	20.0%	4.7%	6.0%	2.1%
	1998	1999	2000	2001	2002	2003
Jewelry	54.5	57.0	59.0	64.2	61.5	61.5
Silverplate/Decorative	4.5	5.0	5.0	5.3	5.0	5.0
Total Demand	59.0	62.0	64.0	69.5	66.5	66.5
% Change Year Ago	4.8%	5.1%	3.2%	8.6%	-4.3%	0.0%
	2004	2005	2006	2007	2008	2009
Jewelry	61.5	63.0	44.0	47.0	45.1	41.5
Silverplate/Decorative	5.0	5.0	3.5	3.5	3.4	3.0
Total Demand	66.5	68.0	47.5	50.5	48.5	44.5
% Change Year Ago	0.0%	2.3%	-30.1%	6.3%	-4.0%	-8.2%
	2010p					
Jewelry	42.0					
Silverplate/Decorative	3.2					
Total Demand	45.2					
% Change Year Ago	1.6%					

Notes: Totals may not equal the sums of categories due to rounding.
Sources: Thai trade sources, CPM Group.
March 15, 2010

Silver Yearbook 2010 - Fabrication Demand — CPM Group

South Korean Silver Fabrication Demand

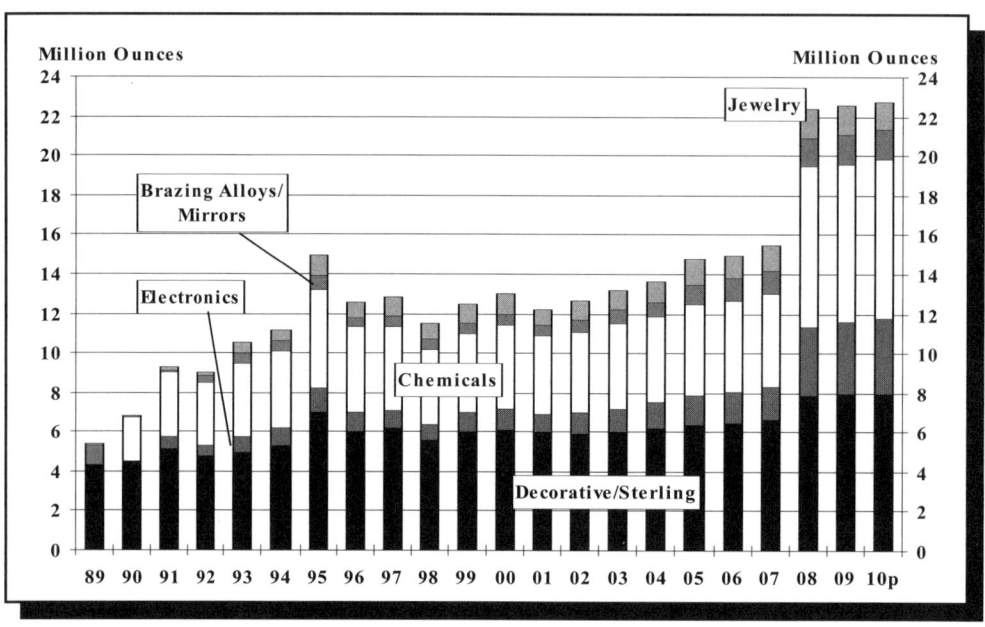

South Korean Silver Fabrication Demand
Million Troy Ounces

	1989	1990	1991	1992	1993	1994	1995
Decorative/Sterling	4.3	4.5	5.1	4.8	5.0	5.3	7.0
Electronics	0.0	0.0	0.6	0.5	0.8	0.9	1.2
Chemicals	0.0	2.2	3.2	3.2	3.7	3.9	5.0
Brazing Alloys	1.0	0.1	0.2	0.3	0.5	0.5	0.7
Jewelry	0.0	0.0	0.2	0.2	0.5	0.6	1.1
Total	5.4	6.8	9.3	9.0	10.5	11.2	15.0
% Change Year Ago	—	27.4%	36.2%	-3.1%	16.2%	6.7%	33.9%

	1996	1997	1998	1999	2000	2001	2002
Decorative/Sterling	6.0	6.2	5.6	6.0	6.1	6.0	5.9
Electronics	1.0	0.9	0.8	1.0	1.1	0.9	1.1
Chemicals	4.3	4.2	3.8	4.0	4.2	4.0	4.1
Brazing Alloys	0.5	0.6	0.5	0.5	0.6	0.5	0.6
Jewelry	0.8	0.9	0.8	1.0	1.0	0.8	1.0
Total	12.6	12.8	11.5	12.5	13.0	12.2	12.7
% Change Year Ago	-16.0%	1.6%	-10.2%	8.7%	4.0%	-6.2%	4.1%

	2003	2004	2005	2006	2007	2008	2009
Decorative/Sterling	6.0	6.2	6.4	6.5	6.6	7.9	8.0
Electronics	1.2	1.3	1.5	1.6	1.7	3.4	3.6
Chemicals	4.3	4.4	4.6	4.6	4.7	8.2	8.0
Mirrors	-	-	-	-	-	-	-
Brazing Alloys	0.7	0.7	1.0	1.1	1.2	1.4	1.5
Jewelry	1.0	1.0	1.3	1.2	1.3	1.5	1.5
Total	13.2	13.6	14.8	15.0	15.5	22.4	22.6
% Change Year Ago	3.9%	3.0%	8.8%	1.4%	3.3%	44.5%	0.9%

	2010p
Decorative/Sterling	8.0
Electronics	3.8
Chemicals	8.0
Mirrors	0.0
Brazing Alloys	1.5
Jewelry	1.5
Total	22.8
% Change Year Ago	0.9%

Notes: Totals may not equal sums of categories due to rounding. Consumption in individual industries prior to 1989 totaled less than 100,000 ounces.
Dashes indicate that consumption was less than 100,000 ounces.
Sources: Trade sources, CPM Group
March 15, 2010

Silver Yearbook 2010 - Fabrication Demand — CPM Group

Taiwan Silver Fabrication Demand

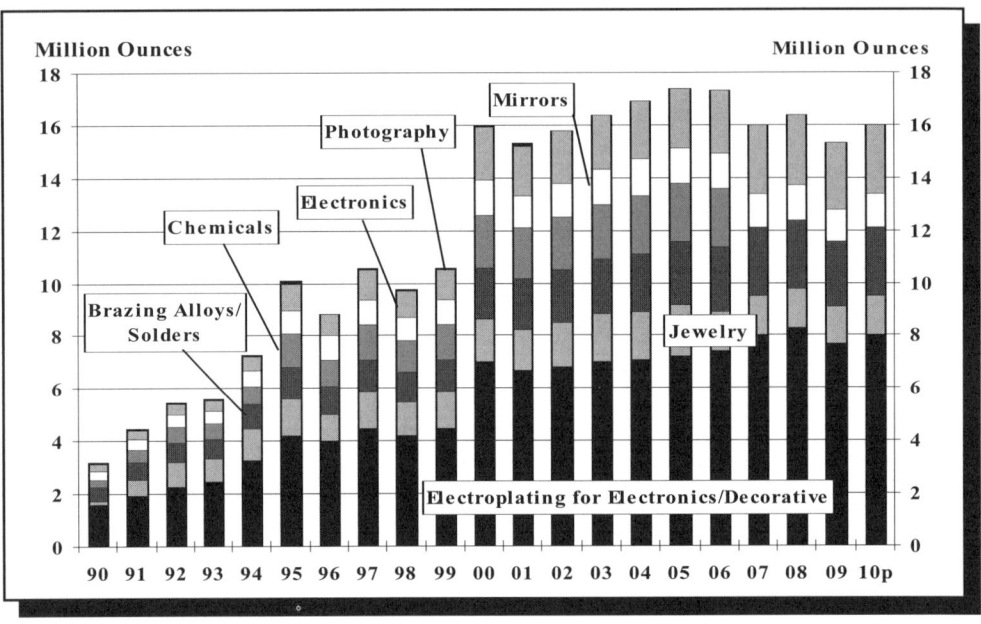

Taiwan Silver Fabrication Demand
Million Troy Ounces

	1990	1991	1992	1993	1994	1995	1996	1997
Photography	0.1	0.1	0.1	0.1	0.1	0.1	0.0	0.1
Electronics	0.3	0.3	0.4	0.4	0.5	1.0	0.8	1.1
Electroplating for Electronics and Decorative	1.6	1.9	2.3	2.5	3.3	4.2	4.0	4.5
Chemicals	0.3	0.5	0.6	0.6	0.7	1.3	1.0	1.3
Mirrors	0.3	0.4	0.5	0.5	0.6	0.9	0.9	1.0
Brazing Alloys and Solders	0.5	0.6	0.7	0.7	0.9	1.2	1.1	1.2
Jewelry	0.1	0.6	1.0	0.9	1.2	1.4	1.0	1.4
Total	3.2	4.5	5.5	5.6	7.3	10.1	8.8	10.6
% Change Year Ago	—	40.5%	23.0%	2.2%	29.5%	38.4%	-12.9%	20.5%

	1998	1999	2000	2001	2002	2003	2004	2005
Photography	0.1	0.1	0.1	0.1	0.0	0.0	0.0	0.0
Electronics	1.0	1.1	2.0	1.9	2.0	2.1	2.2	2.3
Electroplating for Electronics and Decorative	4.2	4.5	7.0	6.7	6.8	7.0	7.1	7.2
Chemicals	1.2	1.3	2.0	1.9	2.0	2.1	2.2	2.2
Mirrors	0.9	1.0	1.3	1.2	1.3	1.3	1.4	1.3
Brazing Alloys and Solders	1.1	1.2	2.0	2.0	2.0	2.1	2.2	2.4
Jewelry	1.3	1.4	1.6	1.5	1.7	1.8	1.8	2.0
Total	9.8	10.6	16.0	15.3	15.8	16.4	16.9	17.4
% Change Year Ago	-7.5%	8.2%	50.9%	-4.4%	3.3%	3.8%	3.0%	3.0%

	2006	2007	2008	2009	2010p
Photography	0.0	0.0	0.0	0.0	0.0
Electronics	2.4	2.6	2.7	2.5	2.6
Electroplating for Electronics and Decorative	7.4	8.0	8.3	7.7	8.0
Chemicals	2.2	0.0	0.0	0.0	0.0
Mirrors	1.3	1.3	1.3	1.2	1.3
Brazing Alloys and Solders	2.5	2.6	2.6	2.5	2.6
Jewelry	1.5	1.5	1.5	1.4	1.5
Total	17.3	16.0	16.4	15.3	16.0
% Change Year Ago	-0.6%	-7.5%	2.5%	-6.7%	4.6%

Notes: Totals may not equal sums of categories due to rounding. Consumption in individual industries prior to 1990 totaled less than 100,000 ounces.
Sources: Trade sources, CPM Group.
March 15, 2010

Silver Yearbook 2010 - Fabrication Demand — CPM Group

Hong Kong Silver Fabrication Demand

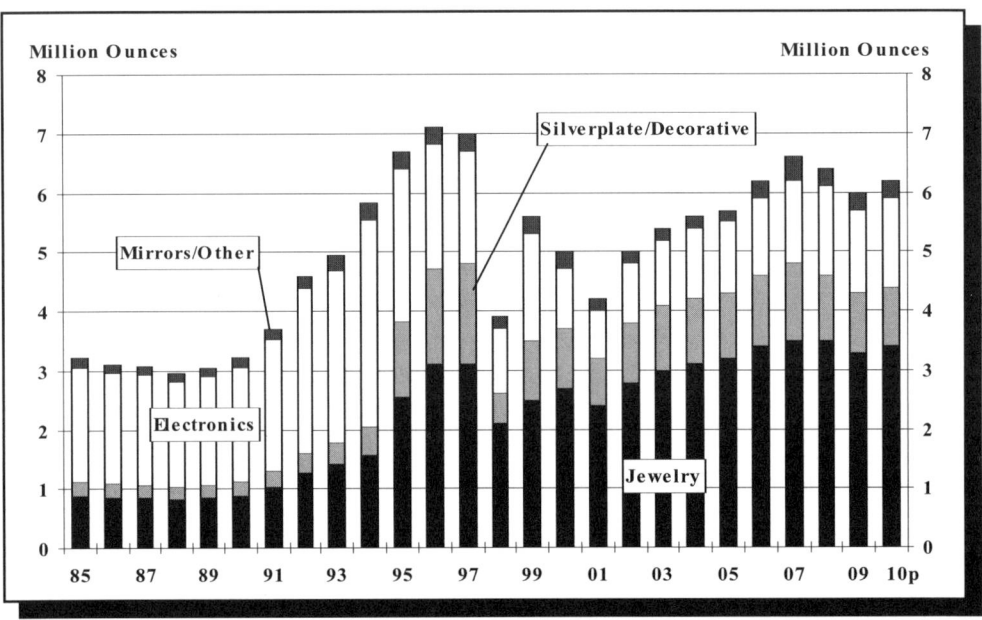

CPM Group　　　　　　　　　　　　Silver Yearbook 2010 - Fabrication Demand

Hong Kong Silver Fabrication Demand
Million Troy Ounces

	1986	1987	1988	1989	1990	1991
Jewelry	0.9	0.9	0.8	0.9	0.9	1.0
Silverplate/decorative	0.2	0.2	0.2	0.2	0.2	0.3
Electronics	1.9	1.9	1.8	1.8	1.9	2.2
Mirrors/other	0.2	0.2	0.1	0.2	0.2	0.2
Total Demand	3.1	3.1	3.0	3.1	3.2	3.7
% Change Year Ago	-3.0%	-1.0%	-4.2%	3.3%	5.3%	15.0%

	1992	1993	1994	1995	1996	1997
Jewelry	1.3	1.4	1.6	2.5	3.1	3.1
Silverplate/decorative	0.3	0.4	0.5	1.3	1.6	1.7
Electronics	2.8	2.9	3.5	2.6	2.1	1.9
Mirrors/other	0.2	0.3	0.3	0.3	0.3	0.3
Total Demand	4.6	4.9	5.8	6.7	7.1	7.0
% Change Year Ago	24.4%	7.5%	17.9%	14.9%	6.0%	-1.4%

	1998	1999	2000	2001	2002	2003
Jewelry	2.1	2.5	2.7	2.4	2.8	3.0
Silverplate/decorative	0.5	1.0	1.0	0.8	1.0	1.1
Electronics	1.1	1.8	1.0	0.8	1.0	1.1
Mirrors/other	0.2	0.3	0.3	0.2	0.2	0.2
Total Demand	3.9	5.6	5.0	4.2	5.0	5.4
% Change Year Ago	-44.3%	43.6%	-10.7%	-16.0%	19.0%	8.0%

	2004	2005	2006	2007	2008	2009
Jewelry	3.1	3.2	3.4	3.5	3.5	3.3
Silverplate/decorative	1.1	1.1	1.2	1.3	1.1	1.0
Electronics	1.2	1.2	1.3	1.4	1.5	1.4
Mirrors/other	0.2	0.2	0.3	0.4	0.3	0.3
Total Demand	5.6	5.7	6.2	6.6	6.4	6.0
% Change Year Ago	3.7%	1.8%	8.8%	6.5%	-3.0%	-6.3%

	2010p
Jewelry	3.4
Silverplate/decorative	1.0
Electronics	1.5
Mirrors/other	0.3
Total Demand	6.2
% Change Year Ago	3.3%

Notes: Totals may not equal the sums of categories due to rounding. Consumption in individual industries prior to 1985 totaled less than 100,000 ounces.
Sources: Hong Kong trade sources, CPM Group.
March 15, 2010

Silver Yearbook 2010 - Fabrication Demand — CPM Group

Indian Silver Fabrication Demand

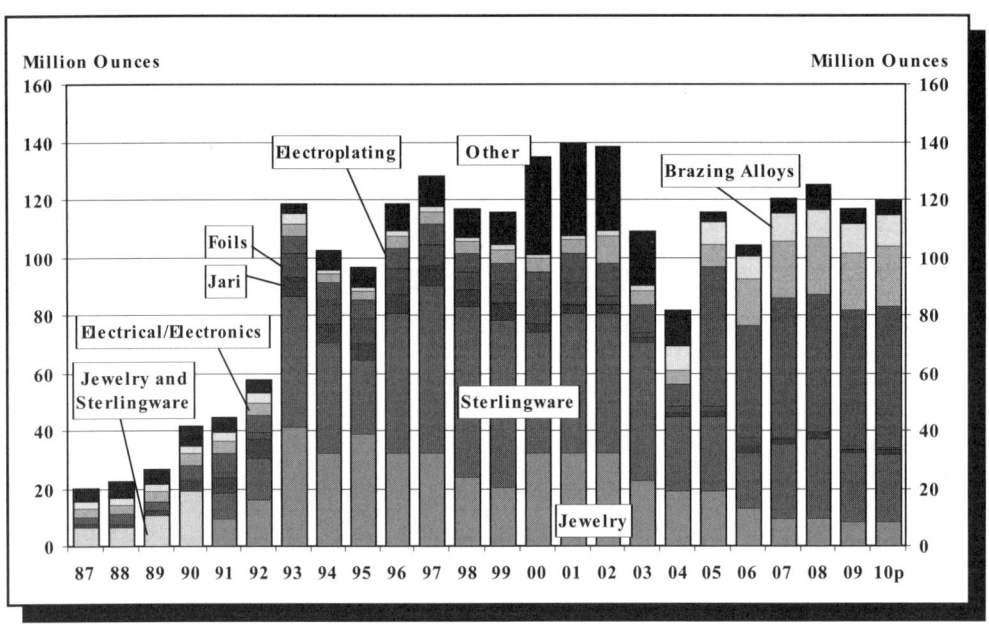

CPM Group — Silver Yearbook 2010 - Fabrication Demand

Indian Silver Fabrication Demand
Million Troy Ounces

	1987	1988	1989	1990	1991	1992	1993	1994	1995	1996	1997	1998
Industrial Uses												
Photography	4.1	4.8	4.8	5.6	2.6	2.6	2.3	1.6	0.6	0.6	0.6	0.6
Electoplating	2.7	3.2	3.2	4.8	6.4	6.4	6.4	6.4	6.4	7.2	7.2	6.6
Electrical/Electronics	2.7	3.2	3.2	4.0	4.2	4.2	4.2	2.6	3.2	4.0	4.2	4.0
Brazing Alloys	2.2	2.4	2.4	2.4	3.2	3.2	3.2	1.6	1.0	1.6	1.6	1.3
Jari	1.4	1.6	1.6	3.2	5.1	6.4	6.4	6.4	6.4	7.1	7.1	6.0
Foils	—	—	—	1.0	1.6	2.3	8.0	8.0	8.0	8.8	7.6	5.7
Chemicals	—	—	—	—	—	—	—	2.3	3.2	3.2	4.0	3.8
Mirrors and Bangels										1.6	1.9	1.6
Miscellaneous	0.7	0.8	0.8	1.4	2.6	2.3	1.6	3.2	3.2	4.3	4.3	4.0
Subtotal	13.8	16.0	16.1	22.5	25.7	27.3	32.2	32.1	32.2	38.6	38.6	33.6
% Change Year Ago	-	15.9%	0.5%	39.8%	-12.5%	6.2%	18.0%	-0.3%	0.3%	20.0%	0.0%	-12.9%
Jewelry and Silverware												
Jewelry	—	—	—	—	9.6	16.1	41.3	32.2	38.6	32.2	32.2	24.0
Silverware	—	—	—	—	9.2	14.4	45.5	38.6	25.7	48.2	57.9	59.2
Subtotal	6.3	6.4	10.9	19.3	18.8	30.5	86.8	70.7	64.3	80.4	90.0	83.1
% Change Year Ago	—	1.6%	70.3%	77.1%	-2.6%	62.2%	184.6%	-18.5%	-9.1%	25.0%	12.0%	-7.7%
Total	20.1	22.4	27.0	41.8	44.5	57.8	119.0	102.9	96.5	119.0	128.6	116.8
% Change Year Ago	—	11.4%	20.4%	54.8%	6.5%	29.9%	105.9%	-13.5%	-6.2%	23.3%	8.1%	-9.2%

	1999	2000	2001	2002	2003	2004	2005	2006	2007	2008	2009	2010p
Industrial Uses												
Photography	1.0	—	—	—	—	—	—	—	—	—	—	—
Electoplating	7.4	9.6	9.6	11.3	9.6	8.0	48.2	38.6	48.2	47.9	47.0	48.6
Electrical/Electronics	4.5	4.8	4.8	9.7	4.8	4.8	8.0	16.1	19.3	19.3	20.0	20.8
Brazing Alloys	1.7	1.6	1.6	1.6	1.6	8.0	8.0	8.0	9.6	9.6	10.3	10.7
Jari	6.0	3.2	3.2	3.2	1.6	0.8	1.6	2.4	1.6	1.6	1.5	1.6
Foils	6.5	8.0	8.0	3.2	1.6	2.3	1.6	3.2	1.0	1.0	1.0	1.0
Chemicals	4.5	20.9	19.3	16.1	9.6	7.7	0.6	2.4	1.9	4.8	2.0	2.5
Mirrors & Bangles	2.3	3.2	3.2	3.2	2.4	2.3	—	—	—	—	—	—
Miscellaneous	3.7	9.6	9.6	9.7	7.2	2.7	2.6	1.9	3.9	4.1	3.2	3.3
Total	37.6	60.9	59.3	57.9	38.6	36.7	70.7	72.6	85.6	88.4	85.0	88.5
% Change Year Ago	11.8%	62.0%	-2.6%	-2.4%	-33.4%	-5.0%	93.0%	2.7%	17.8%	3.3%	-3.8%	4.1%
Jewelry and Silverware												
Jewelry	20.2	32.1	32.1	32.2	22.5	19.3	19.3	12.9	9.6	9.6	8.4	8.3
Silverware	57.9	41.8	48.3	48.2	48.2	25.7	25.7	19.3	25.7	27.3	23.6	23.4
% Change Year Ago	78.1	73.9	80.4	80.4	70.7	45.0	45.0	32.2	35.3	36.9	32.0	31.7
	-6.0%	-5.4%	8.8%	0.0%	-12.0%	-36.4%	0.0%	-28.6%	9.8%	4.5%	-13.3%	-0.9%
Total	115.7	134.8	139.7	138.3	109.3	81.7	115.7	104.8	120.9	125.3	117.0	120.2
% Change Year Ago	-0.9%	16.5%	3.6%	-1.0%	-20.9%	-25.3%	41.7%	-9.5%	15.4%	3.7%	-6.6%	2.7%

Note: Totals may not equal the sums of categories due to rounding. Photography included in chemical from 2000.
Silver Nitrate in miscellaneous, mirrors and bangles in plating, 2005-2010.
Silverware includes some kilo bars, tola bars, coins, and medallions for investment purposes
Sources: Indian trade sources, CPM Group.
March 12, 2010

Silver Yearbook 2010 - Fabrication Demand — CPM Group

Pakistan Silver Fabrication Demand

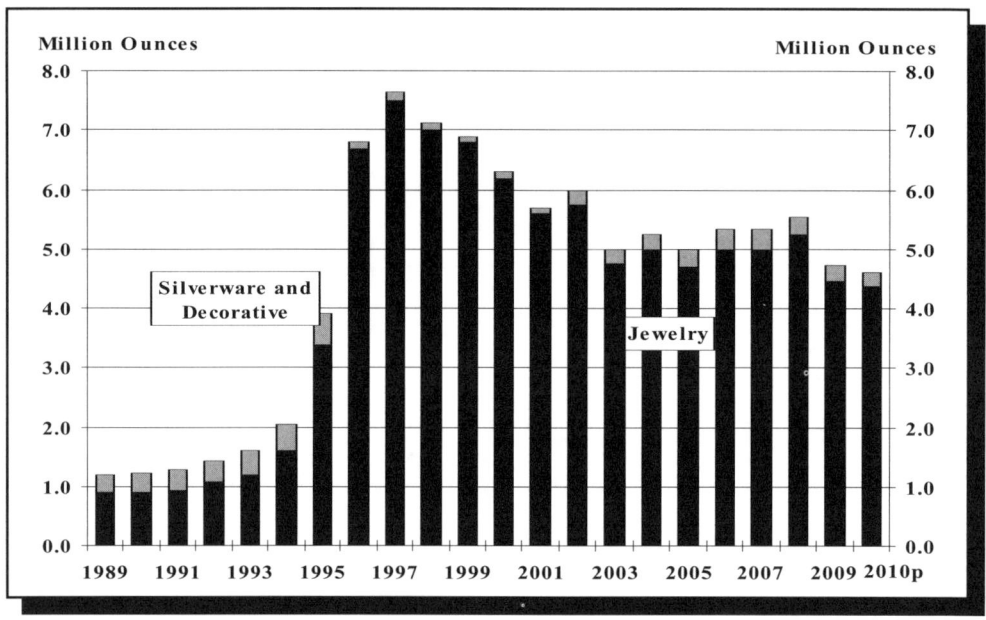

Pakistan Silver Fabrication Demand
Million Troy Ounces

	1989	1990	1991	1992	1993	1994	1995
Jewelry	0.90	0.91	0.94	1.08	1.21	1.60	3.40
Silverware and Decorative	0.30	0.32	0.35	0.35	0.40	0.43	0.50
Total	1.20	1.23	1.29	1.43	1.61	2.03	3.90
% Change Year Ago	—	2.5%	4.9%	10.9%	12.5%	26.2%	92.1%
	1996	1997	1998	1999	2000	2001	2002
Jewelry	6.70	7.50	7.00	6.80	6.20	5.60	5.75
Silverware and Decorative	0.10	0.15	0.13	0.10	0.10	0.10	0.25
Total	6.80	7.65	7.13	6.90	6.30	5.70	6.00
% Change Year Ago	74.4%	12.5%	-6.8%	-3.2%	-8.7%	-9.5%	5.3%
	2003	2004	2005	2006	2007	2008	2009
Jewelry	4.75	5.00	4.70	5.00	5.00	5.25	4.46
Silverware and Decorative	0.25	0.25	0.30	0.35	0.35	0.30	0.26
Total	5.00	5.25	5.00	5.35	5.35	5.55	4.72
% Change Year Ago	-16.7%	5.0%	-4.8%	7.0%	0.0%	3.7%	-15.0%

	2010p
Jewelry	4.37
Silverware and Decorative	0.25
Total	4.62
% Change Year Ago	-2.1%

Note: Totals may not equal the sums of categories due to rounding.
Sources: Trade sources, CPM Group.
March 15, 2010

Silver Yearbook 2010 - Fabrication Demand   CPM Group

Bangladesh Silver Fabrication Demand

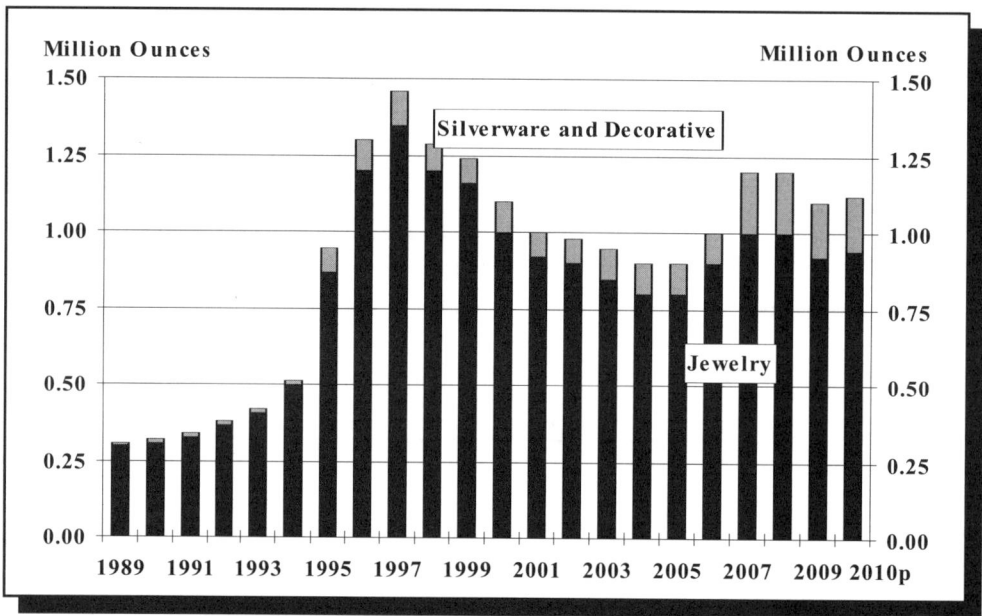

Bangladesh Silver Fabrication Demand
Million Troy Ounces

	1989	1990	1991	1992	1993
Jewelry	0.30	0.31	0.33	0.37	0.41
Silverware and Decorative	0.01	0.01	0.01	0.01	0.01
Total	0.31	0.32	0.34	0.38	0.42
% Change Year Ago	—	3.2%	6.3%	11.8%	10.5%
	1995	1996	1997	1998	1999
Jewelry	0.87	1.20	1.35	1.20	1.16
Silverware and Decorative	0.08	0.10	0.11	0.09	0.08
Total	0.95	1.30	1.46	1.29	1.24
% Change Year Ago	82.7%	36.8%	12.3%	-11.6%	-3.9%
	2001	2002	2003	2004	2005
Jewelry	0.92	0.90	0.85	0.80	0.80
Silverware and Decorative	0.08	0.08	0.10	0.10	0.10
Total	1.00	0.98	0.95	0.90	0.90
% Change Year Ago	-9.1%	-2.0%	-3.1%	-5.3%	0.0%
	2007	2008	2009	2010p	
Jewelry	1.00	1.00	0.92	0.94	
Silverware and Decorative	0.20	0.20	0.18	0.18	
Total	1.20	1.20	1.10	1.12	
% Change Year Ago	20.0%	0.0%	-8.3%	1.8%	

Note: Totals may not equal the sums of categories due to rounding.
Sources: Trade sources, CPM Group.
March 15, 2010

Silver Yearbook 2010 - Fabrication Demand — CPM Group

Mexican Silver Fabrication Demand

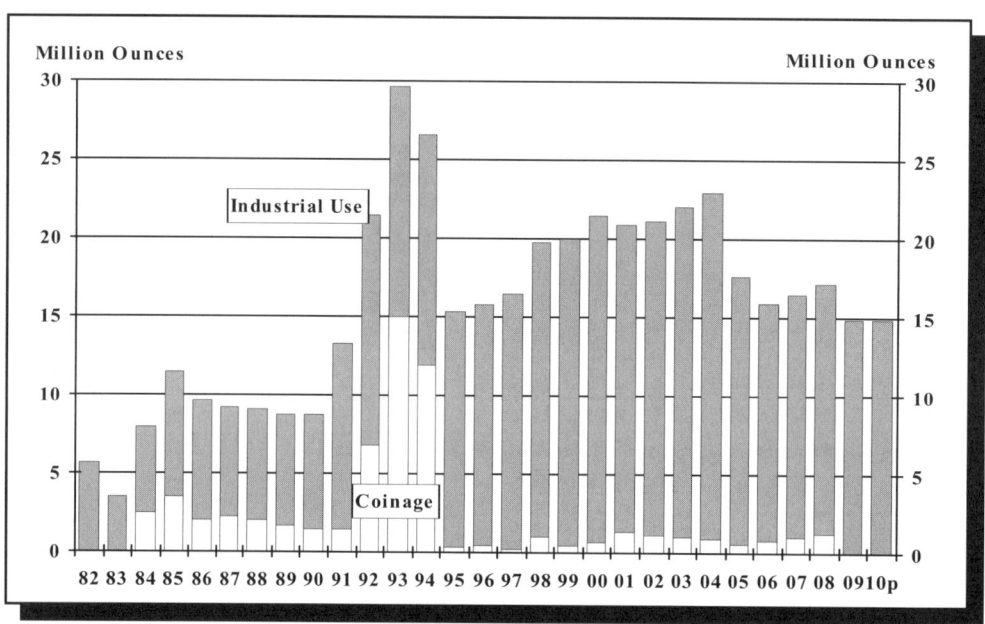

Mexican Silver Fabrication Demand
Million Troy Ounces

	1982	1983	1984	1985	1986	1987	1988	1989
Industrial								
Photography	3.2	2.0	3.1	4.5	4.3	3.9	4.0	4.0
Jewelry and Decorative	1.7	1.0	1.6	2.3	2.2	2.0	2.1	2.1
Electronics and Electrical Contacts	0.9	0.5	0.8	1.2	1.2	1.0	1.0	1.1
Subtotal	5.7	3.5	5.5	8.0	7.7	6.9	7.1	7.1
% Change Year Ago	-	-38.6%	57.1%	45.5%	-3.8%	-10.4%	2.9%	0.0%
Coinage			2.5	3.5	2.0	2.3	2.0	1.7
% Change Year Ago	-	NM	NM	40.0%	-42.9%	15.0%	-13.0%	-15.0%
Total Fabrication Demand	5.7	3.5	8.0	11.5	9.7	9.2	9.1	8.8
% Change Year Ago	-	-38.6%	128.6%	43.8%	-15.7%	-5.2%	-1.1%	-3.3%

	1990	1991	1992	1993	1994	1995	1996	1997
Industrial								
Photography	4.0	6.6	8.1	8.1	8.1	8.3	8.3	8.4
Jewelry and Decorative	2.1	3.4	4.4	4.4	4.4	4.5	4.6	5.1
Electronics and Electrical Contacts	1.1	1.8	2.2	2.2	2.2	2.3	2.4	2.7
Subtotal	7.2	11.8	14.7	14.7	14.7	15.0	15.3	16.2
% Change Year Ago	1.4%	63.2%	25.1%	0.0%		2.0%	2.0%	5.9%
Coinage	1.5	1.5	6.8	15.0	11.9	0.3	0.5	0.3
% Change Year Ago	-11.8%	0.0%	353.3%	120.6%	-20.7%	-97.5%	66.7%	-49.2%
Total Fabrication Demand	8.7	13.3	21.5	29.7	26.6	15.3	15.8	16.5
% Change Year Ago	-1.1%	52.3%	62.3%	38.1%	-10.4%	-42.5%	3.3%	4.1%

	1998	1999	2000	2001	2002	2003	2004	2005
Industrial								
Photography	8.8	9.2	10.0	9.3	9.5	10.0	10.4	5.0
Jewelry and Decorative	7.2	7.5	7.6	7.2	7.5	8.0	8.4	8.8
Electronics and Electrical Contacts	2.8	2.9	3.2	3.0	3.0	3.1	3.2	3.2
Subtotal	18.8	19.6	20.8	19.5	20.0	21.1	22.0	17.0
% Change Year Ago	16.0%	4.3%	6.1%	-6.3%	2.6%	5.5%	4.3%	-22.7%
Coinage	1.0	0.4	0.7	1.4	1.1	1.0	0.9	0.6
% Change Year Ago	293.6%	-60.0%	75.0%	100.0%	-21.4%	-9.1%	-10.0%	-33.3%
Total Fabrication Demand	19.8	20.0	21.5	20.9	21.1	22.1	22.9	17.6
% Change Year Ago	20.3%	1.0%	7.5%	-2.8%	1.0%	4.7%	3.6%	-23.1%

	2006	2007	2008	2009	2010p
Industrial					
Photography	2.5	2.2	2.0	1.8	1.7
Jewelry and Decorative	9.2	9.7	10.2	9.5	9.4
Electronics and Electrical Contacts	3.4	3.6	3.8	3.6	3.8
Subtotal	15.1	15.5	16.0	14.9	14.9
% Change Year Ago	-11.2%	2.6%	3.2%	-6.9%	0.0%
Coinage	0.8	1.0	1.2		
% Change Year Ago	33.3%	25.0%	20.0%		
Total Fabrication Demand	15.9	16.5	17.2	14.9	14.9
% Change Year Ago	-9.7%	3.8%	4.2%	-13.4%	0.0%

Notes: Totals may not equal the sums of categories because of rounding. NM - Not Meaningful.
Sources: Industry sources, CPM Group.
March 15, 2010

Silver Yearbook 2010 - Fabrication Demand — CPM Group

Brazilian Silver Fabrication Demand

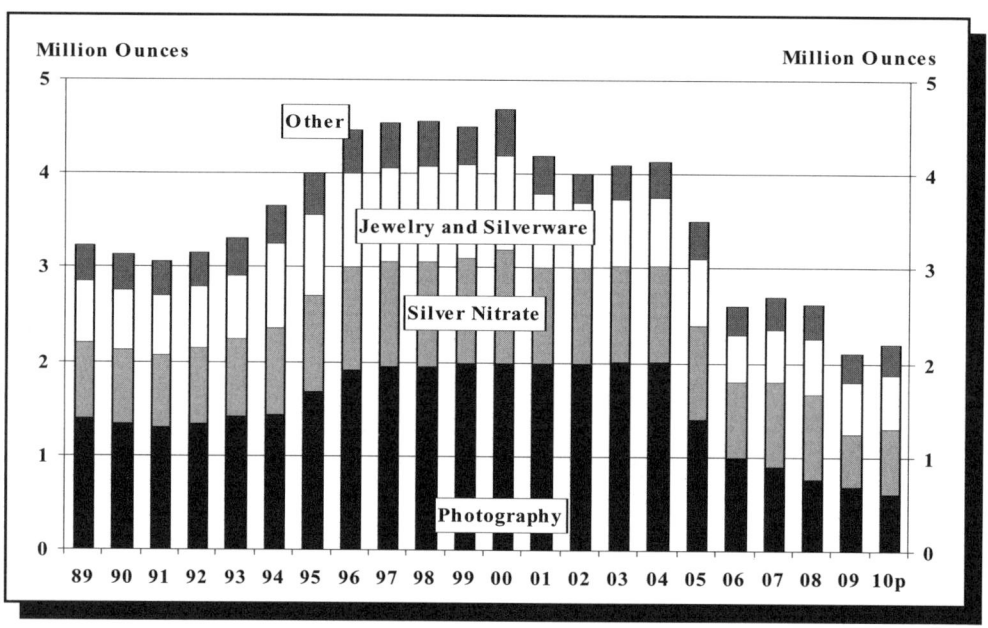

Brazilian Silver Fabrication Demand
Million Troy Ounces

	1989	1990	1991	1992	1993	1994	1995
Photography	1.40	1.34	1.30	1.34	1.41	1.43	1.68
Silver Nitrate	0.80	0.78	0.76	0.80	0.84	0.93	1.02
Jewelry and Silverware	0.65	0.64	0.64	0.65	0.67	0.89	0.87
Other	0.39	0.38	0.37	0.38	0.39	0.41	0.43
Total	3.24	3.14	3.07	3.17	3.31	3.66	4.00
% Change Year Ago	—	-3.1%	-2.2%	3.3%	4.4%	10.6%	9.2%

	1996	1997	1998	1999	2000	2001	2002
Photography	1.92	1.95	1.96	2.00	2.00	2.00	2.00
Silver Nitrate	1.09	1.11	1.10	1.10	1.20	1.00	1.00
Jewelry and Silverware	1.00	1.01	1.02	1.00	1.00	0.80	0.70
Other	0.46	0.47	0.48	0.40	0.50	0.40	0.30
Total	4.47	4.54	4.56	4.50	4.70	4.20	4.00
% Change Year Ago	11.9%	1.6%	0.4%	-1.3%	4.4%	-10.6%	-4.8%

	2003	2004	2005	2006	2007	2008	2009
Photography	2.02	2.02	1.40	1.00	0.90	0.77	0.69
Silver Nitrate	1.01	1.01	1.00	0.80	0.90	0.90	0.55
Jewelry and Silverware	0.71	0.73	0.70	0.50	0.55	0.60	0.56
Other	0.36	0.38	0.40	0.30	0.35	0.35	0.30
Total	4.10	4.14	3.50	2.60	2.70	2.62	2.10
% Change Year Ago	2.5%	1.0%	-15.5%	-25.7%	3.8%	-3.0%	-19.8%

	2010p
Photography	0.62
Silver Nitrate	0.68
Jewelry and Silverware	0.58
Other	0.32
Total	2.20
% Change Year Ago	4.8%

Note: Totals may not equal the sums of categories due to rounding.
Sources: Centromin, Doe Run Peru, industry sources, CPM Group.
March 15, 2010

Silver Yearbook 2010 - Fabrication Demand — CPM Group

Peruvian Silver Fabrication Demand

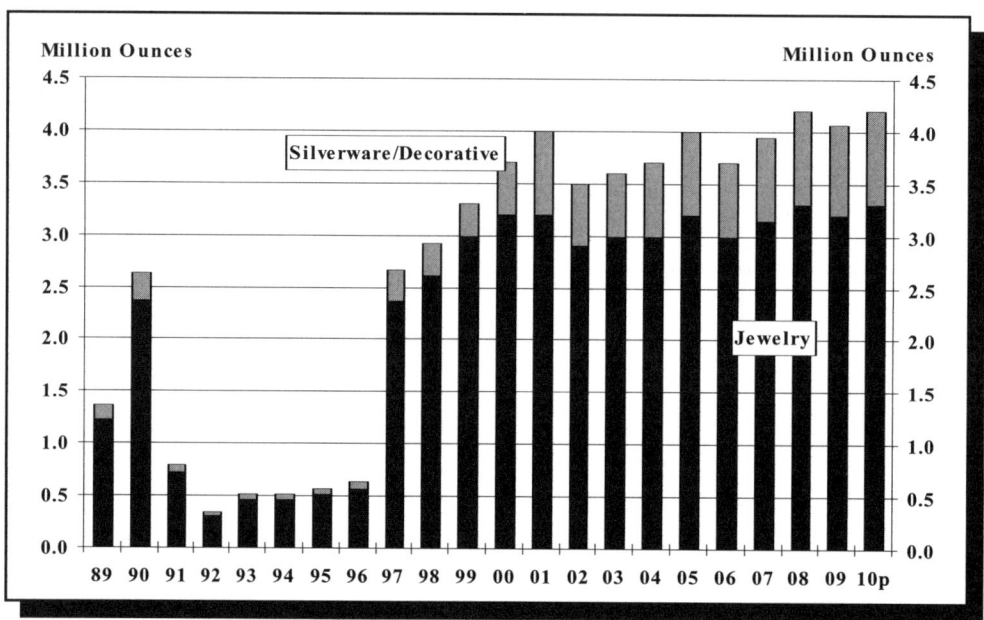

Peruvian Silver Fabrication Demand
Million Troy Ounces

	1989	1990	1991	1992	1993	1994	1995
Jewelry	1.24	2.37	0.72	0.32	0.46	0.47	0.51
Silverplate/ Decorative	0.14	0.26	0.08	0.04	0.05	0.05	0.06
Total	1.37	2.64	0.80	0.35	0.51	0.52	0.57
% Change Year Ago	—	92.0%	-69.5%	-56.0%	45.5%	1.1%	10.5%

	1996	1997	1998	1999	2000	2001	2002
Jewelry	0.57	2.37	2.61	3.00	3.20	3.20	2.90
Silverplate/ Decorative	0.07	0.29	0.31	0.30	0.50	0.80	0.60
Total	0.64	2.66	2.92	3.30	3.70	4.00	3.50
% Change Year Ago	11.6%	314.7%	9.8%	13.0%	12.1%	8.1%	-12.5%

	2003	2004	2005	2006	2007	2008	2009
Jewelry	3.00	3.00	3.20	3.00	3.15	3.30	3.20
Silverplate/ Decorative	0.60	0.70	0.80	0.70	0.80	0.90	0.87
Total	3.60	3.70	4.00	3.70	3.95	4.20	4.07
% Change Year Ago	2.9%	2.8%	8.1%	-7.5%	6.8%	6.3%	-3.1%

	2010p
Jewelry	3.30
Silverplate/ Decorative	0.90
Total	4.20
% Change Year Ago	3.2%

Note: Totals may not equal the sums of categories due to rounding.
Sources: Centromin, Doe Run Peru, industry sources, CPM Group.
March 15, 2010

Silver Yearbook 2010 - Fabrication Demand — CPM Group

Canadian Silver Fabrication Demand

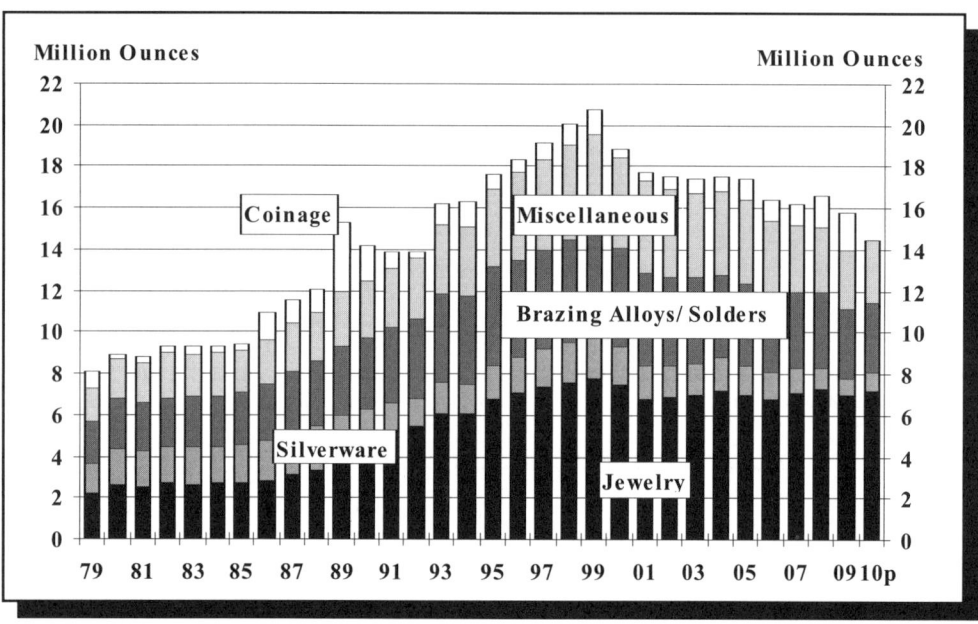

CPM Group — Silver Yearbook 2010 - Fabrication Demand

Canadian Silver Fabrication Demand
Million Troy Ounces

	1979	1980	1981	1982	1983	1984	1985	1986	1987
Jewelry	2.2	2.6	2.6	2.7	2.7	2.7	2.7	2.9	3.1
Silverware	1.5	1.7	1.7	1.8	1.8	1.8	1.8	1.9	2.1
Brazing Alloys/Solders	2.0	2.4	2.4	2.3	2.4	2.4	2.5	2.7	2.9
Miscellaneous	1.6	1.9	1.9	2.2	2.0	2.1	2.0	2.1	2.3
Total	7.3	8.7	8.5	9.0	8.9	9.0	9.1	9.6	10.4
% Change Year Ago	—	19.2%	-2.3%	5.9%	-1.1%	1.1%	1.1%	5.5%	8.3%
Coinage	0.8	0.2	0.3	0.3	0.4	0.3	0.3	1.3	1.2
Total Including Coinage	8.1	8.9	8.8	9.3	9.3	9.3	9.4	10.9	11.6
% Change Year Ago	—	9.9%	-1.1%	5.7%	0.0%	0.0%	1.1%	16.0%	6.4%

	1988	1989	1990	1991	1992	1993	1994	1995	1996
Jewelry	3.3	3.6	3.8	5.2	5.4	6.1	6.0	6.8	7.1
Silverware	2.2	2.4	2.5	1.3	1.4	1.5	1.5	1.7	1.8
Brazing Alloys/Solders	3.1	3.4	3.5	3.7	3.8	4.3	4.2	4.7	4.6
Miscellaneous	2.4	2.6	2.8	2.9	3.0	3.3	3.3	3.7	4.2
Total	11.0	12.0	12.5	13.1	13.6	15.2	15.1	16.9	17.7
% Change Year Ago	5.8%	9.1%	4.2%	4.8%	3.8%	11.8%	-0.7%	11.9%	4.7%
Coinage	1.1	3.3	1.7	0.8	0.3	1.0	1.2	0.7	0.7
Total Including Coinage	12.1	15.3	14.2	13.9	13.9	16.2	16.3	17.6	18.4
% Change Year Ago	4.3%	26.4%	-7.2%	-2.1%	0.0%	16.5%	0.6%	8.0%	4.5%

	1997	1998	1999	2000	2001	2002	2003	2004	2005
Jewelry	7.4	7.6	7.8	7.5	6.8	6.9	7.0	7.2	7.0
Silverware	1.8	1.9	1.9	1.8	1.6	1.5	1.5	1.6	1.4
Brazing Alloys/Solders	4.8	5.0	5.1	4.8	4.5	4.3	4.2	4.0	4.0
Miscellaneous	4.4	4.6	4.8	4.4	4.4	4.2	4.0	4.0	4.0
Total	18.4	19.1	19.6	18.5	17.3	16.9	16.7	16.8	16.4
% Change Year Ago	4.0%	3.8%	2.6%	-5.6%	-6.5%	-2.3%	-1.2%	0.6%	-2.4%
Coinage	0.8	1.0	1.2	0.4	0.4	0.6	0.7	0.7	1.0
Total Including Coinage	19.2	20.1	20.8	18.9	17.7	17.5	17.4	17.5	17.4
% Change Year Ago	4.2%	4.9%	3.5%	-9.1%	-6.3%	-1.1%	-0.6%	0.6%	-0.6%

	2006	2007	2008	2009	2010p
Jewelry	6.8	7.1	7.3	7.0	7.2
Silverware	1.3	1.2	1.0	0.8	0.9
Brazing Alloys/Solders	3.9	3.7	3.7	3.4	3.4
Miscellaneous	3.4	3.2	3.1	2.8	3.0
Total	15.4	15.2	15.1	14.0	14.5
% Change Year Ago	-6.1%	-1.3%	-0.7%	-7.3%	3.6%
Coinage	1.0	1.0	1.5	1.8	
Total Including Coinage	16.4	16.2	16.6	15.8	
% Change Year Ago	-5.7%	-1.2%	2.5%	-4.8%	

Notes: Totals may not equal the sums of categories due to rounding.
Sources: Statistics Canada, trade sources, CPM Group.
March 15, 2010

Silver Yearbook 2010 - Fabrication Demand — CPM Group

Australian Silver Fabrication Demand

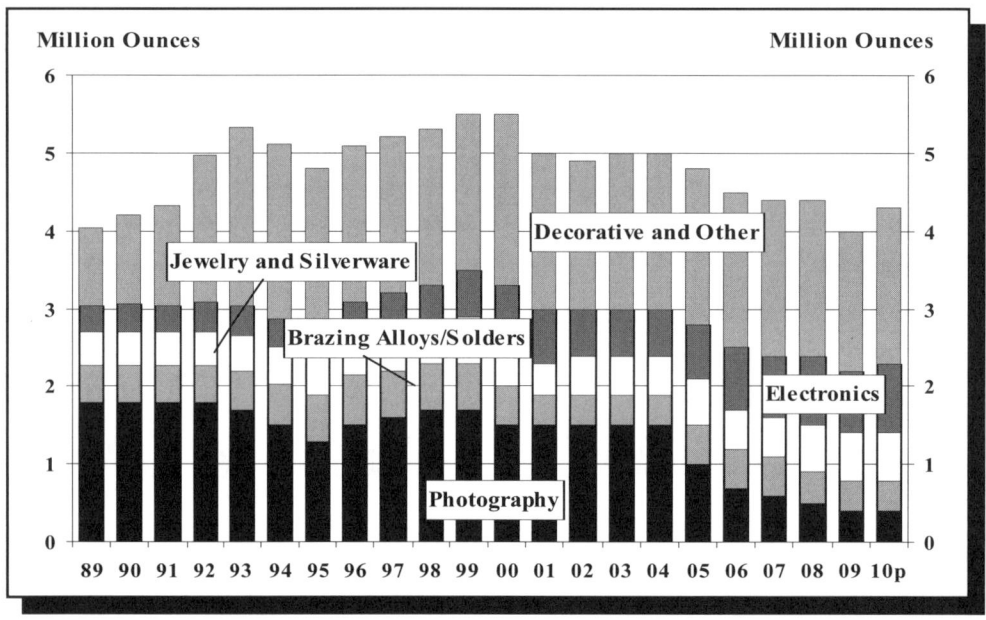

CPM Group　　　　　　　　　　　　　　Silver Yearbook 2010 - Fabrication Demand

Australian Silver Fabrication Demand
Million Troy Ounces

	1989	1990	1991	1992	1993	1994	1995
Photography	1.8	1.8	1.8	1.8	1.7	1.5	1.3
Brazing Alloys and Solders	0.5	0.5	0.5	0.5	0.5	0.5	0.6
Jewelry and Silverware	0.4	0.4	0.4	0.4	0.5	0.5	0.5
Electrical/Electronics	0.3	0.4	0.4	0.4	0.4	0.4	0.4
Other	1.0	1.1	1.3	1.9	2.3	2.2	2.0
Total	4.0	4.2	4.3	5.0	5.3	5.1	4.8
% Change Year Ago	—	5.0%	2.4%	16.3%	6.0%	-3.9%	-6.3%

	1996	1997	1998	1999	2000	2001	2002
Photography	1.5	1.6	1.7	1.7	1.5	1.5	1.5
Brazing Alloys and Solders	0.6	0.6	0.6	0.6	0.5	0.4	0.4
Jewelry and Silverware	0.5	0.5	0.5	0.6	0.5	0.4	0.5
Electrical/Electronics	0.5	0.5	0.5	0.6	0.8	0.7	0.6
Other	2.0	2.0	2.0	2.0	2.2	2.0	1.9
Total	5.1	5.2	5.3	5.5	5.5	5.0	4.9
% Change Year Ago	6.0%	2.2%	1.9%	3.8%	0.0%	-9.1%	-2.0%

	2003	2004	2005	2006	2007	2008	2009
Photography	1.5	1.5	1.0	0.7	0.6	0.5	0.4
Brazing Alloys and Solders	0.4	0.4	0.5	0.5	0.5	0.4	0.4
Jewelry and Silverware	0.5	0.5	0.6	0.5	0.5	0.6	0.6
Electrical/Electronics	0.6	0.6	0.7	0.8	0.8	0.9	0.8
Other	2.0	2.0	2.0	2.0	2.0	2.0	1.8
Total	5.0	5.0	4.8	4.5	4.4	4.4	4.0
% Change Year Ago	2.0%	0.0%	-4.0%	-6.3%	-2.2%	0.0%	-9.1%

	2010p
Photography	0.4
Brazing Alloys and Solders	0.4
Jewelry and Silverware	0.6
Electrical/Electronics	0.9
Other	2.0
Total	4.3
% Change Year Ago	7.5%

Note: Other includes small amount of decorative silver use. Totals may not equal the sums of categories due to rounding.
Sources: Australian trade sources, CPM Group.
March 15, 2010

Investment Demand

Investment Demand

Silver investment demand played a central role in determining the price of the metal during 2009. Investors purchased large amounts of the metal as a hedge against global economic, financial, and political problems; as a portfolio diversifier; and in expectation of potential further price appreciation. This trend continued during the first two months of 2010, and is expected to remain in place at least in the near future.

Recently there have been signs of improvement in the global economy. This has resulted in some investors liquidating their silver investment positions. It should be noted, however, that there still is a fair amount of uncertainty regarding the pace and strength of this recovery. Most investors purchasing silver for its safe haven attributes are expected to continue buying the metal or are expected to remain invested in the metal, at least as long as this uncertainty prevails.

Another set of investors, those with a longer investment horizon, have been buying silver to profit from the metal's price appreciation associated with increased fabrication demand. Fabrication demand is expected to rise at a rapid pace when the global economy is on a firmer footing. These investors are expected to be buyers on price dips.

In addition to these two factors that have played and are expected to continue playing an important role in determining investment demand for silver during

Annual Net Investment Demand and Prices

Prices Through 2009.

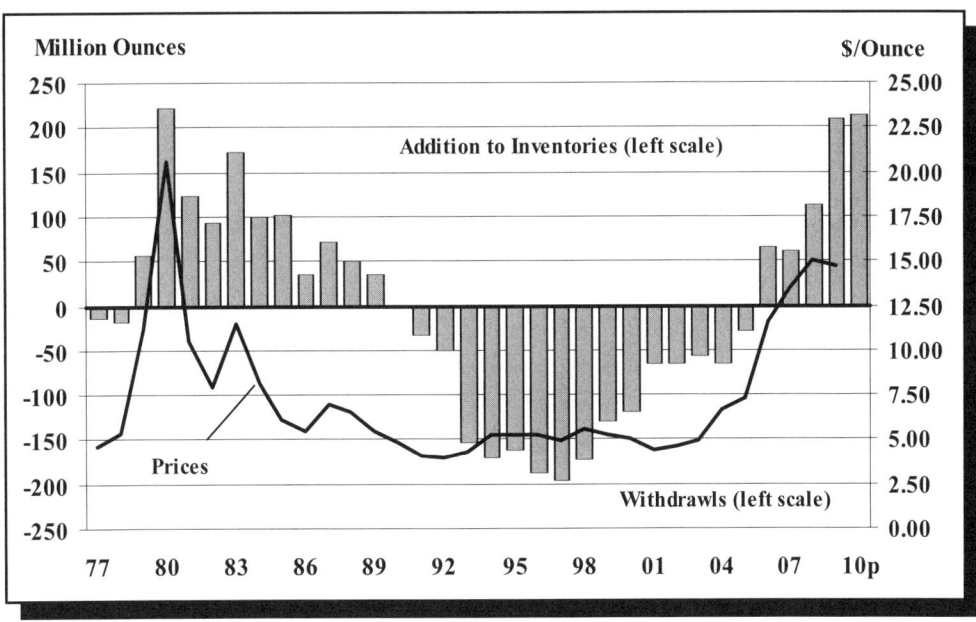

2010, the metal also works very well as a portfolio diversifier. An asset with a low correlation with other assets in a portfolio is typically considered a good portfolio diversifier. This is because such an asset helps reduce the overall risk of the portfolio.

Silver has a very weak correlation with other asset classes such as stocks and bonds. Studying the correlation between annual silver prices and broad indices that track the stock market such as the Dow Jones Industrial Average (DJIA) and the Standard and Poor's Index (S&P Index) between 1979 and 2009 reveals a very weak positive correlation. Over this period the correlation of silver with the DJIA stood at 4.3%, meanwhile, it stood at 2.1% with the S&P Index. Even though these are positive correlations they are so low that it can be said that there is virtually no relation between silver prices and these stock market indices.

The metal's relation with the bond markets is only slightly greater than its relation with the stock market, but it is still very weak. Silver's correlation with T-bills stood at 7.3% and with T-bonds 14.5% between 1979 and 2009.

The correlation between silver and the Commodity Research Bureau Index, which tracks a basket of commodities, stood at 2.6% between 1979 and 2009.

Silver's low correlation with other assets coupled with an overall increase in investor interest in commodities has helped boost investment demand for silver. The relatively recent introduction of silver exchange traded funds (ETF) has also helped divert an increased amount of investor dollars toward silver, by making it easier for investors to participate in the physical silver market.

As a result of this, investors have been accumulating silver over the past four years on a net basis. The net surplus in the silver market is a direct measure of the apparent amount of net investment demand in the silver market. The net additions of silver to investment inventories is projected at 213.9 million ounces during 2010. This would be an increase over last year's net surplus, or net accumulation of bullion inventories, of 209.7 million ounces. The forecast net surplus during 2010 is positive for silver prices, however, since it reflects net investor demand driving prices higher. Net investor buying pushes the market into a surplus of newly refined metal entering the market relative to fabrication demand, as investors bid the price higher, encouraging increased supplies and discouraging or squeezing out fabrication demand for silver.

Exchange Traded Funds

Exchange traded funds were one of the most important components of investment demand for silver during 2009. Their importance has grown in recent years as a result of increased investor interest in commodities as an asset class and the transparent, easy to understand nature of these investment vehicles. As a percentage of apparent investment demand for physical silver, ETFs have become much more important than they are in gold.

Investors made net additions of 150.9 million ounces to silver ETF holdings during 2009. As a result of these additions, combined silver ETF holdings stood at 464.8 million ounces at the end of 2009. The net additions to silver ETF holdings during 2009 were around 81% higher than the additions made in 2008. Investor interest in ETFs is forecast to remain healthy during 2010. The rate of growth in silver ETF holdings seen during 2009 may not be replicated during 2010. That said any growth will be from an already high base and therefore is expected to be a substantial increase. Combined silver ETF holdings rose around 2% during the first two months of 2010. This 2% increase is equivalent to a net addition of around 9.2 million ounces.

The proportion of net additions made to silver ETF holdings in relation to the total supply of silver has been rising over the past several years, standing at 9.8% in 2007, 10.3% in 2008, and 18.2% in 2009.

Exchange Traded Funds' Physical Silver Holdings

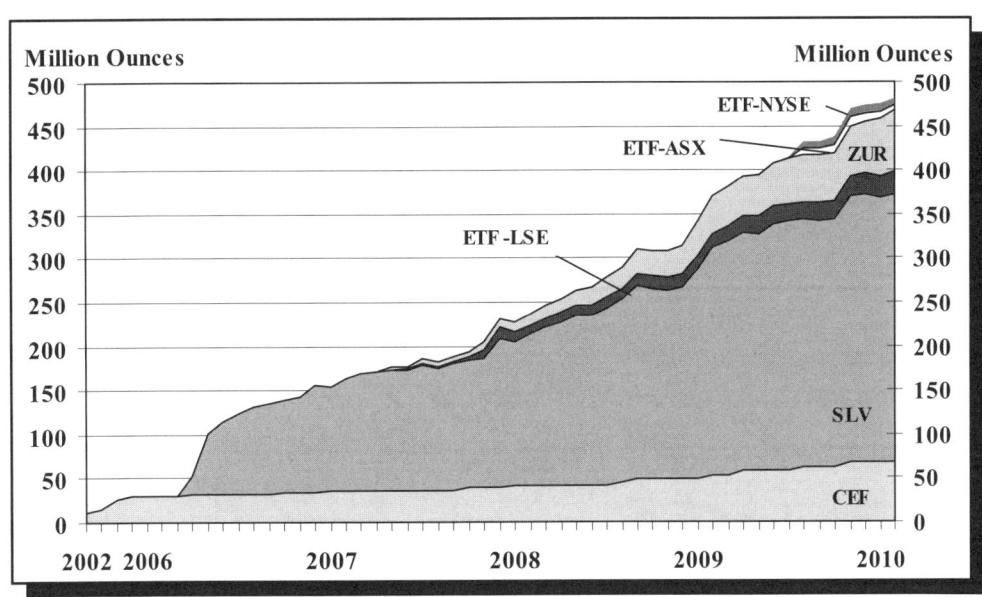

Note: CEF-Central Fund of Canada traded on the Toronto Stock Exchange. SLV-iShares Silver Trust traded on the American Stock Exchange. ZKB-Zurich Cantonal traded on the Swiss Exchange. ETF-LSE ETF Securities' silver ETF traded on the London Stock Exchange. ETF-ASX ETF Securities' silver ETF traded on the Australian Stock Exchange. ETF-NYSE ETF Securities' silver ETF traded on the NewYork Stock Exchange. Data as of 5 March 2010.

Silver Yearbook 2010 - Investment Demand   CPM Group

Exchange Traded Fund Activity

The largest additions to combined silver ETF holdings during 2009 were made by iShares Silver Trust, traded on the American Stock Exchange (AMEX). This ETF added a massive 86.8 million ounces of silver to its holdings during 2009. The additions made by this fund accounted for around 57% of total net additions made to silver ETF holdings during 2009. This ETF held 305.2 million ounces of silver on 31 December 2009, which was around 66% of the total silver held by ETFs on that day. Investors liquidated some of their positions in this fund during the first two months of 2010. Holdings declined to a low of 300.3 million ounces on 14 January. Holdings in this fund had risen back to 304.7 million ounces by the end of February 2010, however.

The Toronto Stock Exchange traded Central Fund of Canada added around 18.8 million ounces of silver to its holdings during 2009. This was a 127% increase over net additions made to this fund in 2008. This fund was the second largest at the end of 2009, based on net silver holdings. There were no changes to holdings in this fund during the first two months of 2010. This had resulted in the fund losing its position as the second largest fund to Zurich Cantonal Bank's silver ETF, at the end of February 2010.

Zurich Cantonal Bank's (ZKB) silver ETF was backed by around 59.4 million ounces of silver on 31 December 2009,

Silver Price and Total ETF Holdings
Daily, Through 5 March 2010.

making it the third largest ETF on that day. The fund added 26.6 million ounces of silver to its holdings in 2009, or around 45% of the fund's total holdings at the end of 2009. This ETF added around 9.6 million ounces of silver to its holdings during the first two months of 2010.

ETF Securities' London Stock Exchange traded silver ETF grew by 9.1 million ounces during 2009. This was an increase of 389% over the fund's 2008 net additions to holdings. As a result, the fund was the fastest growing in percentage terms, if not volume, of the four funds that traded during 2008. The fund added around 2.8 million ounces of silver to its holdings during the first two months of 2010.

The launch of two ETFs by ETF Securities - one on the New York Stock Exchange (NYSE) and the other on the Australian Stock Exchange (ASX) - during 2009 were partly responsible for the sharp increase in total net additions to silver ETF holdings during 2009.

The ASX listed ETF was launched in the middle of January 2009. The fund's holdings rose at a rapid pace during the first six months of the year. Little activity was seen between 2 July and 31 December. After rising to 345,724 ounces on 1 July from 325,516 ounces on 30 June, holdings declined slightly to 344,790 ounces on 11 September. Holdings remained steady at this level until 28 October when they rose to 409,472 ounces. Holdings remained at this level until 28

Monthly Change in Silver ETF Holdings & Percent Change in Price
Monthly, Through February 2010.

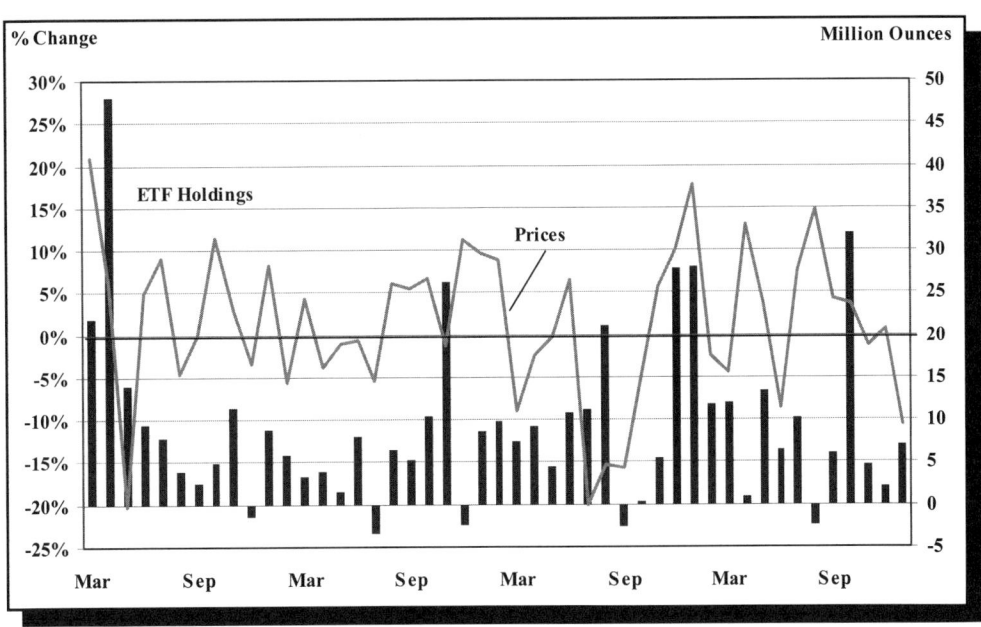

Silver Yearbook 2010 - Investment Demand — CPM Group

Exchange Traded Funds Physical Silver Holdings
Troy Ounces, Month-end

		CEF TSX	SLV AMEX	ETF Securities -LSE	Zurich Cantonal	ETF Securities - ASX	ETF Securites-NYSE	Total
2002	December	11,946,381	-	-	-	-	-	11,946,381
2003	December	14,846,381	-	-	-	-	-	14,846,381
2004	December	26,173,714	-	-	-	-	-	26,173,714
2005	December	30,973,714	-	-	-	-	-	30,973,714
2006	January	30,973,714	-	-	-	-	-	30,973,714
	February	30,973,714	-	-	-	-	-	30,973,714
	March	30,973,714	-	-	-	-	-	30,973,714
	April	31,847,514	20,999,769	-	-	-	-	52,847,283
	May	31,847,514	68,993,652	-	-	-	-	100,841,166
	June	31,847,514	82,953,516	-	-	-	-	114,801,030
	July	31,847,514	92,416,063	-	-	-	-	124,263,577
	August	31,847,514	100,368,644	-	-	-	-	132,216,158
	September	31,847,514	104,323,655	-	-	-	-	136,171,169
	October	33,995,514	104,776,594	-	-	-	-	138,772,108
	November	33,995,514	109,721,369	-	-	-	-	143,716,883
	December	33,995,514	121,144,585	-	-	-	-	155,140,099
2007	January	36,630,054	117,108,946	-	-	-	-	153,739,000
	February	36,630,054	126,026,951	-	-	-	-	162,657,005
	March	36,630,054	131,952,261	-	-	-	-	168,582,315
	April	36,630,054	134,883,938	455,210	-	-	-	171,969,202
	May	36,630,054	135,821,755	875,325	2,519,319	-	-	175,846,453
	June	36,630,054	136,263,707	1,545,090	2,985,405	-	-	177,424,256
	July	36,630,054	141,671,812	2,454,288	4,755,567	-	-	185,511,721
	August	36,630,054	138,135,340	2,308,437	4,940,104	-	-	182,013,935
	September	36,630,054	143,536,762	2,557,523	5,775,334	-	-	188,499,674
	October	40,252,756	143,977,750	3,302,735	6,253,930	-	-	193,787,171
	November	40,252,756	145,408,391	9,850,360	8,657,648	-	-	204,169,155
	December	40,252,756	168,652,106	12,353,908	9,138,141	-	-	230,396,911
2008	January	41,523,556	162,640,046	12,779,113	11,047,284	-	-	227,989,999
	February	41,523,556	172,488,301	9,633,153	12,959,546	-	-	236,604,557
	March	41,523,556	179,367,462	10,623,604	14,872,644	-	-	246,387,266
	April	41,523,556	185,719,016	10,859,679	15,823,277	-	-	253,925,529
	May	41,523,556	192,569,101	11,281,913	17,729,784	-	-	263,104,354
	June	41,523,556	192,981,804	11,021,803	22,030,653	-	-	267,557,816
	July	41,523,556	201,805,748	11,789,947	23,169,561	-	-	278,288,812
	August	44,893,456	208,145,125	12,219,034	24,302,148	-	-	289,559,763
	September	48,527,624	220,304,639	13,589,476	28,205,795	-	-	310,627,534
	October	48,527,624	217,056,464	14,229,780	28,183,648	-	-	307,997,516
	November	48,527,624	214,983,945	14,283,674	31,024,364	-	-	308,819,607
	December	48,527,626	218,399,706	14,225,172	32,724,158	-	-	313,876,662
2009	January	48,527,624	239,624,280	14,879,759	38,700,275	74,911	-	341,806,849
	February	52,460,793	259,063,967	15,300,523	42,826,610	114,146	-	369,766,039
	March	52,460,793	266,752,572	17,063,707	45,071,442	185,670	-	381,534,184
	April	58,648,793	270,484,575	17,808,178	46,296,679	275,789	-	393,514,013
	May	58,648,793	268,400,196	19,989,984	47,069,223	299,959	-	394,408,155
	June	58,648,793	280,510,677	19,567,271	48,799,986	325,516	-	407,852,243
	July	58,648,793	283,831,312	18,787,735	52,343,842	345,724	299,993	414,257,398
	August	62,115,879	281,064,152	19,629,158	54,396,034	345,724	6,900,000	424,450,947
	September	62,115,879	280,553,742	20,185,507	54,396,034	345,724	7,096,781	424,693,666
	October	62,115,879	281,126,170	21,004,574	54,762,924	409,472	8,693,067	428,112,088
	November	67,322,479	302,370,919	22,951,072	57,366,621	409,472	9,688,852	460,109,415
	December	67,322,479	305,205,951	23,370,555	59,370,030	409,472	9,185,591	464,864,079
2010	January	67,322,479	301,734,131	23,698,224	65,808,720	408,513	7,987,168	466,959,235
	February	67,322,479	304,689,792	26,126,095	68,978,972	444,095	6,489,437	474,050,870

Note: CEF-Central Fund of Canada traded on the Toronto Stock Exchange. SLV-iShares Silver Trust traded on the American Stock Exchange. ZKB-Zurich Cantonal traded on the Swiss Exchange. ETF-LSE ETF Securities' silver ETF traded on the London Stock Exchange. ETF-ASX ETF Securities' silver ETF traded on the Australian Stock Exchange. ETF-NYSE ETF Securities' silver ETF traded on the NewYork Stock Exchange.
CPM Group
March 12, 2010

January 2010. Holdings then spiked up at the end of February to 444,095 ounces.

ETF Securities' other newer offering, the NYSE listed fund, began trading during the last week of July 2009. Holdings in this fund rose at a rapid pace, standing at 10.1 million ounces on 4 December. Holdings remained at this level for most of the month of December, briefly declining to around 8.7 million ounces on 22 December. Holdings rose back to approximately 9.2 million ounces on 24 December and remained at around that level until the middle of January 2010. By the end of February 2010, holdings were down to 6.5 million ounces.

Collectively the two U.S. silver ETFs, iShare's Silver Trust and ETF Securities' NYSE listing, accounted for around 65% of total silver ETF holdings at the end of February 2010. This underscores the strong investor interest in these ETFs from both U.S. investors as well as investors from other parts of the world who prefer to invest through U.S. markets. There has been a tendency for investors from many parts of the world to prefer to invest in U.S. listed securities, most likely due to a perception of more stringent investment regulations in the United States, which provide a sense of security to international investors. It should be noted, however, that the portion of silver ETF holdings held in the United States has declined from 68% at the end of 2009 to 65% at the end of February 2010. That said, these two ETFs still account for the majority of global ETF investments.

Coins

Concerns regarding the health of the global economy drove demand for the U.S. Mint's Silver Eagle coins sharply higher during 2009. Investors typically increase their purchases of precious metals, as safe haven investments, during times of troubled economic conditions and financial markets. Sales of these coins totaled 28.8 million ounces during 2009 a 47.4% increase over 2008 coin sales.

Silver is significantly less expensive per ounce than gold and shares similar safe haven attributes to gold. This makes it a popular choice among retail investors, who are the largest buyers of silver in this form.

Investors have continued to aggressively purchase these coins during 2010. In the first month of the year sales totaled 3.6 million ounces. This was a record high for monthly sales. Combined sales during the first two months of the year stood at 5.6 million ounces, which was a 40.2% increase over the corresponding period of 2009.

Coin sales are likely to continue growing at a robust pace during the remainder of 2010. Investor demand appears likely to remain high. Investors might remain interested in buying silver coins on the one hand, if they remain concerned about the potential of renewed economic and financial problems derailing the nascent global economic recovery. However, if investors back away from

Recent Trends in U.S. Eagle Sales
Monthly, Through February 2010.

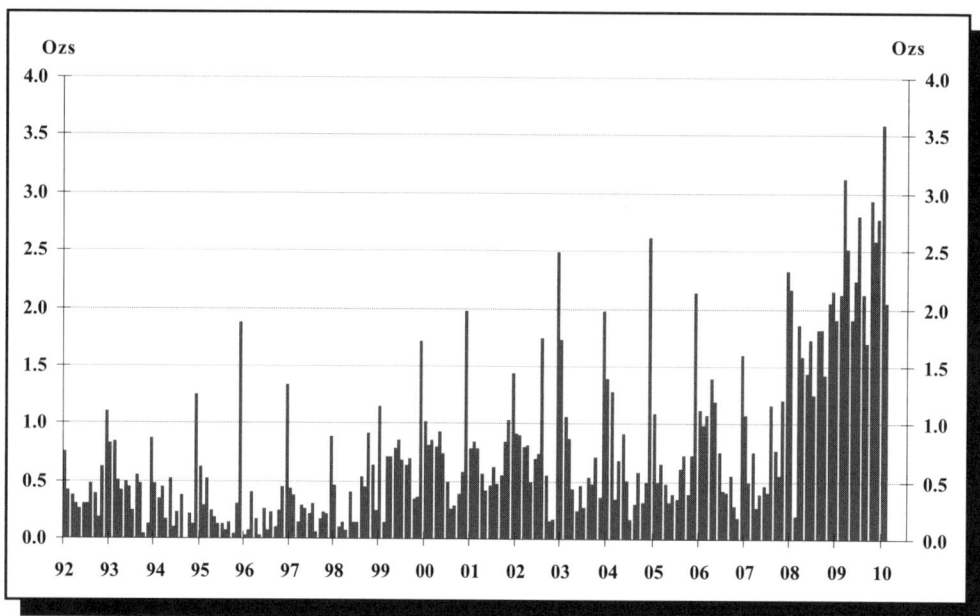

One Month Implied Lease Rate
Daily, Through 5 March 2010.

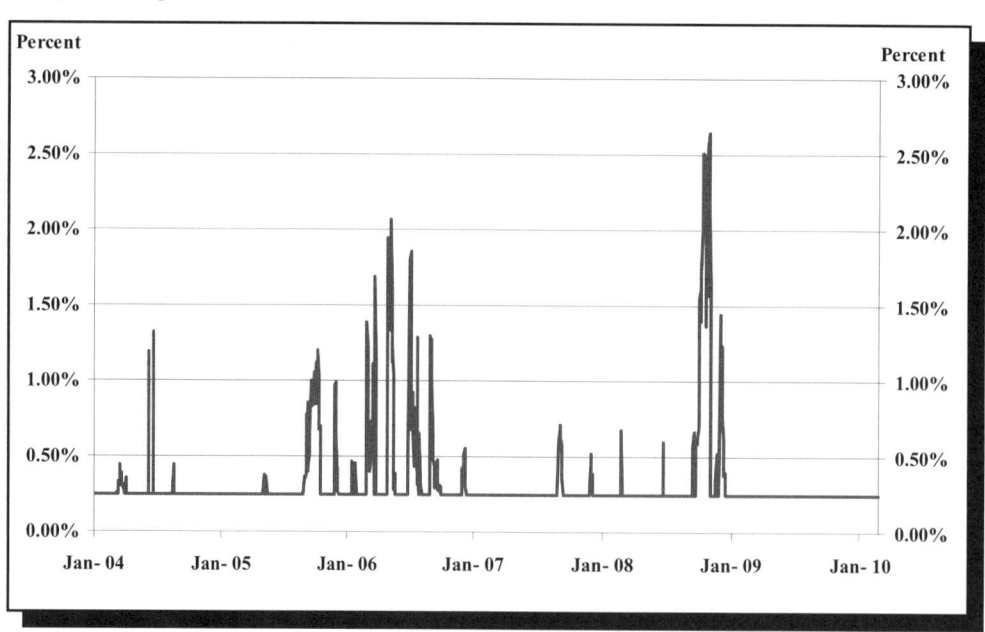

concerns over hostile economic conditions, they may remain interested in buying silver as an investment likely to benefit from strong and rising fabrication demand.

Silver Lease Rates

The one month implied silver lease rate stood unchanged at 0.25% during 2009 and the first two months of 2010. As no official figures for silver lease rates are available, an indicative lease rate is calculated using one-month Libor rate and the silver forward spread. Actual market lease rates tend to vary greatly from such implied lease rates.

Futures and Options

Large non-commercial market participants largely remained bullish on silver during 2009. Net long positions held by these participants rose swiftly between 21 July and 20 October 2009. Net long positions rose to 266 million ounces on 20 October, up from 115 million ounces on 21 July. An increase in gross long positions and a simultaneous decline in gross short positions were responsible for the increase in net long positions during this period. Net long positions slipped lower over the remainder of 2009, but were still significantly higher than levels seen in the second half of 2008 and the first half of 2009.

Comex Disaggragated Non-Commercial Positions
Weekly, Through 2 March 2010.

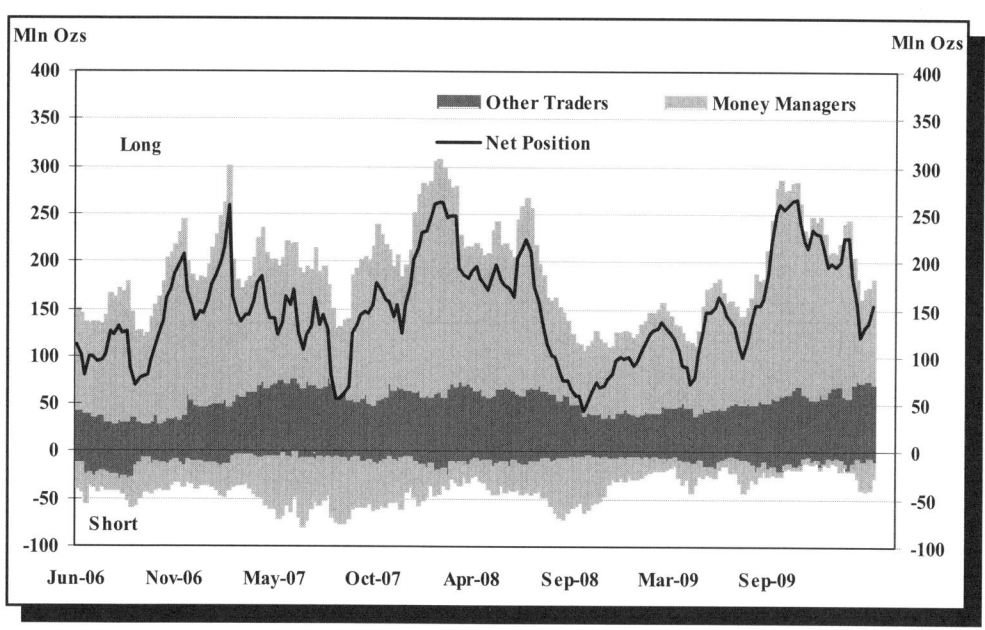

Net long positions held by these market participants declined rapidly between 19 January and 9 February 2010. Net long positions stood at 120.6 million ounces on 9 February, down from 224.3 million ounces on 19 January. This decline can be explained, to some extent, by the increase in silver prices during the first half of January. This is likely to have stimulated profit-taking resulting in long liquidation. The resultant decline in price also pushed higher the build-up of gross short positions, further accelerating the decline in price and net long positions. Gross short positions during this period doubled to 40 million ounces on 9 February, from 20 million ounces on 19 January.

Disaggregated Commitment of Traders Reports

The Commodity Futures Trade Commission began to release Disaggregated Commitment of Traders Reports on 1 September 2009. These reports include categories that are both non-commercial and commercial. The intent was to provide greater detail as to the types of companies holding positions on commodities futures exchanges. The categorizations are somewhat vague, however, and not well defined, so that the new reports provide only marginally better insights than the previous Commitment of Traders reports.

One category- producers/merchant/processor/user - includes entities which

Large Non-Commercial Comex Silver Positions
Weekly, Through 2 March 2010.

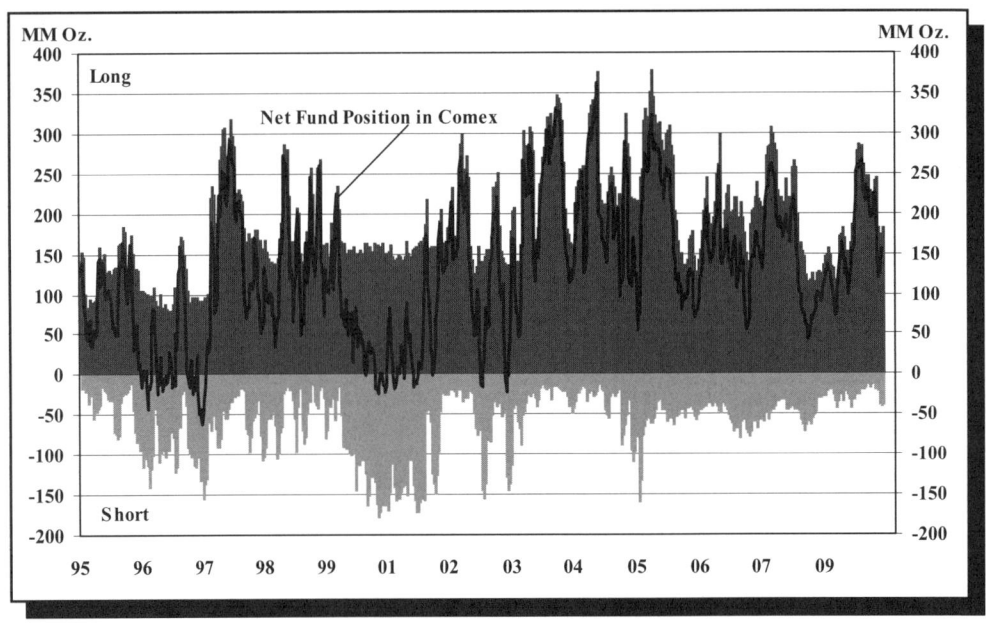

deal with the physical commodity and use futures and options to manage or hedge risks. Most of the trades most likely are executed by merchants. Few producers, processors, or users trade directly on the Comex. Another new category is termed Swap dealers. In the past producers/merchants/processors/users' and swap dealers' positions were included in the commercial category in the previous Commitment of Traders Reports. The following two categories meanwhile were included in non-commercial data in the Commitment of Traders Reports. Money managers, non-commercial entities, are funds investing in or trading futures on behalf of clients. "Other traders," the final category, do not fit in the other three categories of the disaggregated reports.

Money managers have held the majority of the gross long and the gross short positions over the past several years. Other traders meanwhile have been mostly long. On 6 January 2009 non-commercial net long positions were 99.7 million ounces. By 20 October non-commercial net long positions had reached a high of 266.0 million ounces. Non-commercial net long positions have come off since then and were 154.5 million ounces as of 2 March 2010.

Silver Yearbook 2010 - Investment Demand — CPM Group

Silver Coinage
Million Troy Ounces

Year	United States	Canada	Austria	France	Germany	Mexico	Other	Transitional Economies	Total
1960	46.0	7.5	-i-	12.2	-i-	-i-	38.2	-	103.9
1961	56.0	5.1	-i-	23.8	-i-	-i-	51.1	-	136.0
1962	78.0	10.9	-i-	13.7	-i-	-i-	25.0	-	127.6
1963	112.0	13.0	-i-	12.2	-i-	-i-	29.2	-	166.4
1964	203.0	13.7	-i-	10.7	-i-	-i-	39.7	-	267.1
1965	320.3	24.4	2.7	7.2	2.7	-i-	27.8	-	385.1
1966	53.6	15.5	3.3	8.7	2.9	-i-	45.5	-	129.5
1967	43.8	8.8	3.2	9.6	3.1	-i-	36.8	-	105.3
1968	36.8	7.4	2.2	2.9	4.2	-i-	35.8	-	89.3
1969	19.6	0.0	1.9	0.7	2.9	-i-	7.6	-	32.7
1970	0.7	0.0	4.0	3.5	7.4	-i-	7.8	-	23.4
1971	2.5	0.2	3.2	0.4	19.2	-i-	2.3	-	27.8
1972	2.3	0.1	5.8	0.3	22.6	-i-	7.0	-	38.1
1973	0.9	6.6	6.3	0.1	7.0	-i-	7.6	-	28.5
1974	1.0	9.0	5.7	3.6	7.6	-i-	4.7	-	31.6
1975	2.7	10.4	9.1	1.8	5.4	-i-	4.0	-	33.4
1976	1.3	8.4	6.9	6.2	1.8	-i-	5.4	-	30.0
1977	0.1	0.5	8.9	7.1	4.6	4.2	9.1	-	34.5
1978	0.0	1.0	9.6	9.0	3.6	6.6	9.7	-	39.5
1979	0.2	0.8	4.0	10.6	3.7	5.0	6.7	-	31.0

Notes: Excludes transitional economies prior to 1990.
i -- included in Other. na -- not available.
Sources: U.S. Mint; Energy, Mines, and Resources Canada;
Silver Institute; Handy & Harman; Bank of Mexico; trade sources;

CPM Group.
March 11, 2010

CPM Group　　　　　　　　　　　　　Silver Yearbook 2010 - Investment Demand

Silver Coinage
Million Troy Ounces

Year	United States	Canada	Austria	France	Germany	Mexico	Other	Transitional Economies	Total
1980	0.1	0.2	2.3	0.1	0.0	6.1	6.2	-	15.0
1981	0.2	0.3	3.1	0.1	0.5	0.0	5.3	-	9.5
1982	1.8	0.3	4.5	1.4	0.3	0.0	3.7	-	12.0
1983	2.1	0.4	1.8	2.2	0.0	0.0	3.7	-	10.2
1984	2.0	0.3	2.4	3.9	0.0	2.5	2.6	-	13.7
1985	0.4	0.3	4.6	2.2	0.0	3.5	2.4	-	13.4
1986	10.3	1.3	1.1	2.2	0.0	2.0	9.9	-	26.8
1987	12.2	1.2	3.1	2.2	3.2	2.3	6.2	-	30.4
1988	7.9	1.1	2.0	2.2	3.2	2.0	6.9	-	25.3
1989	6.8	3.3	2.1	2.2	3.2	1.7	7.0	-	26.3
1990	9.1	1.7	0.6	2.2	2.4	1.5	10.9	1.4	29.8
1991	9.1	0.8	0.6	1.8	5.5	1.5	7.5	0.9	27.7
1992	8.1	0.3	0.5	1.8	5.3	6.8	6.0	0.6	29.4
1993	8.9	1.0	0.6	1.8	4.5	15.0	5.6	0.6	38.0
1994	8.1	1.2	0.6	1.8	4.2	11.9	5.2	0.5	33.5
1995	7.5	0.7	0.6	1.8	5.8	0.3	5.0	0.3	22.0
1996	5.0	0.7	0.4	1.8	5.1	0.5	4.4	0.2	18.1
1997	5.3	0.8	0.3	1.8	5.5	0.3	4.7	0.2	18.9
1998	5.6	1.0	0.3	1.8	6.3	1.0	8.8	0.2	25.0
1999	9.9	1.2	0.3	1.8	6.0	0.4	9.7	0.2	29.5
2000	10.3	0.4	na	na	na	0.7	13.8	na	25.2
2001	10.2	0.4	na	na	na	1.4	5.6	na	17.6
2002	11.5	0.6	na	na	na	1.1	7.3	na	20.5
2003	10.5	0.7	na	na	na	1.0	5.5	na	17.7
2004	11.1	0.7	na	na	na	0.9	5.5	na	18.2
2005	9.9	1.0	na	na	na	0.6	5.0	na	16.5
2006	11.0	1.0	0.5	na	na	0.8	4.5	na	17.8
2007	9.9	1.0	0.5	na	na	1.0	5.0	na	17.4
2008	19.5	1.5	0.5	na	na	1.2	5.5	na	28.2
2009	28.8	1.8	0.5	na	na	1.5	5.7	na	38.3

Silver Yearbook 2010 - Investment Demand — CPM Group

U.S. Mint Silver Coin Sales
Troy Ounces

	1986	1987	1988	1989	1990	1991	1992
Uncirculated Eagles							
January	-	715,000	790,000	416,000	1,616,000	1,800,000	756,000
February	-	775,000	700,000	700,000	450,000	1,235,000	415,000
March	-	1,355,000	130,000	1,755,000	700,000	880,000	385,000
April	-	1,060,000	780,000	325,000	250,000	508,000	310,000
May	-	1,280,000	650,000	500,000	340,000	210,000	260,000
June	-	1,125,000	50,000	460,000	360,000	170,000	300,000
July	-	0	100,000	150,000	160,000	210,000	310,000
August	-	100,000	226,000	365,000	420,000	160,000	480,000
September	-	300,000	353,000	450,000	250,000	150,000	400,000
October	-	800,000	305,000	350,000	955,000	260,000	195,000
November	1,400,000	1,250,000	400,000	150,000	330,000	250,000	625,000
December	3,696,000	660,000	215,000	150,000	1,416,000	1,119,000	1,108,000
Subtotal	5,096,000	9,420,000	4,699,000	5,771,000	7,247,000	6,952,000	5,544,000
% Change	-	84.9%	-50.1%	22.8%	25.6%	-4.1%	-20.3%
Proof Eagles	1,446,778	904,732	557,370	617,694	695,510	511,924	498,543
Commemoratives	-	-	-	-	1,172,463	1,645,499	1,305,112
% Change	-	-	-	-	-	40.3%	-20.7%
Proof Coin Sets	-	-	-	-	-	-	792,040
Total	6,542,778	10,324,732	5,256,370	6,388,694	9,114,973	9,109,423	8,139,695
% Change	-	57.8%	-49.1%	21.5%	42.7%	-0.1%	-10.6%

	1993	1994	1995	1996	1997	1998	1999
Uncirculated Eagles							
January	825,000	480,000	625,000	30,000	435,000	460,000	1,145,000
February	850,000	345,000	285,000	75,000	385,000	100,000	149,000
March	510,000	450,000	525,000	413,000	150,000	145,000	718,000
April	425,000	175,000	250,000	175,000	286,000	75,000	716,000
May	500,000	525,000	185,000	25,000	265,000	410,000	792,000
June	455,000	100,000	135,000	260,000	220,000	150,000	863,000
July	250,000	230,000	125,000	75,000	305,000	140,000	678,500
August	550,000	375,000	75,000	230,000	65,000	535,000	644,500
September	480,000	0	150,000	105,000	180,000	450,000	694,000
October	50,000	225,000	50,000	250,000	240,000	920,000	349,000
November	125,000	125,000	310,000	450,000	225,000	635,000	366,000
December	870,000	1,250,500	1,875,000	1,343,000	890,000	250,000	1,718,000
Subtotal	5,890,000	4,280,500	4,590,000	3,431,000	3,646,000	4,270,000	8,833,000
% Change	6.2%	-27.3%	7.2%	-25.3%	6.3%	17.1%	106.9%
Proof Eagles	405,913	372,168	437,924	498,293	440,315	450,728	549,330
Commemoratives	2,081,825	2,606,920	2,000,000	553,872	727,933	400,000	300,000
% Change	59.5%	25.2%	-23.3%	-72.3%	31.4%	-45.0%	-25.0%
Proof Coin Sets	449,677	700,000	458,989	522,713	498,260	492,828	200,000
Total	8,827,415	7,959,588	7,486,913	5,005,878	5,312,508	5,613,556	9,882,330
% Change	8.4%	-9.8%	-5.9%	-33.1%	6.1%	5.7%	76.0%

CPM Group   **Silver Yearbook 2010 - Investment Demand**

U.S. Mint Silver Coin Sales
Troy Ounces

	2000	2001	2002	2003	2004	2005	2006
Uncirculated Eagles							
January	1,011,500	779,500	913,500	1,725,000	1,392,500	1,095,000	1,115,000
February	808,500	846,500	905,000	1,055,000	1,281,000	500,000	993,000
March	851,500	786,000	797,000	876,000	348,000	650,000	1,072,000
April	804,500	562,000	815,000	434,000	680,000	480,000	1,395,000
May	925,000	426,000	495,000	245,000	914,500	315,000	1,186,000
June	738,500	467,000	695,000	468,000	505,000	400,000	760,000
July	499,500	624,500	740,000	280,000	170,000	355,000	417,000
August	255,500	474,500	1,745,000	535,000	311,000	615,000	413,000
September	296,500	550,000	550,000	475,000	580,000	725,000	550,000
October	386,500	843,500	155,000	705,500	320,000	400,000	285,000
November	580,500	1,031,500	175,000	370,000	492,500	725,000	195,000
December	1,975,000	1,436,500	2,490,000	1,985,000	2,622,500	2,145,000	1,600,000
Subtotal	9,133,000	8,827,500	10,475,500	9,153,500	9,617,000	8,405,000	9,981,000
% Change	3.4%	-3.3%	18.7%	-12.6%	5.1%	-12.6%	18.8%
Proof Eagles	600,743	746,398	647,342	747,831	801,602	711,606	
Commemoratives	474,073	611,256	347,665	571,740	717,488	776,097	
% Change	58.0%	28.9%	-43.1%	64.5%	25.5%	8.2%	
Proof Coin Sets	100,000						
Total	10,307,816	10,185,154	11,470,507	10,473,071	11,136,090	9,892,703	9,981,000
% Change	4.3%	-1.2%	12.6%	-8.7%	6.3%	-11.2%	0.9%

	2007	2008	2009	2010
Uncirculated Eagles				
January	1,070,000	2,170,000	1,900,000	3,592,500
February	500,000	200,000	2,125,000	2,050,000
March	762,000	1,855,000	3,132,000	
April	280,000	1,584,000	2,518,000	
May	395,000	1,443,500	1,904,500	
June	470,000	1,735,500	2,245,000	
July	405,000	1,251,500	2,810,000	
August	1,165,000	1,813,000	2,130,000	
September	765,000	1,825,000	1,703,000	
October	550,000	1,425,000	2,939,000	
November	1,200,500	2,050,000	2,586,500	
December	2,324,500	2,158,500	2,773,500	
Subtotal	9,887,000	19,511,000	28,766,500	5,642,500
% Change	-0.9%	97.3%	47.4%	40.2%
Proof Eagles				
Commemoratives				
% Change				
Proof Coin Sets				
Total	9,887,000	19,511,000	28,766,500	5,642,500
% Change	-0.9%	97.3%	47.4%	

Notes: The U.S. Eagle program was introduced in November 1986.
Proof coin sets and commemoratives end-year. NA - not available.
Proof Eagles as of 30 September 2005, year-end through 2004.
Source: U.S. Mint, CPM Group.
March 11, 2010

Silver and U.S. Inflation

Quarterly, Through Fourth Quarter 2009.

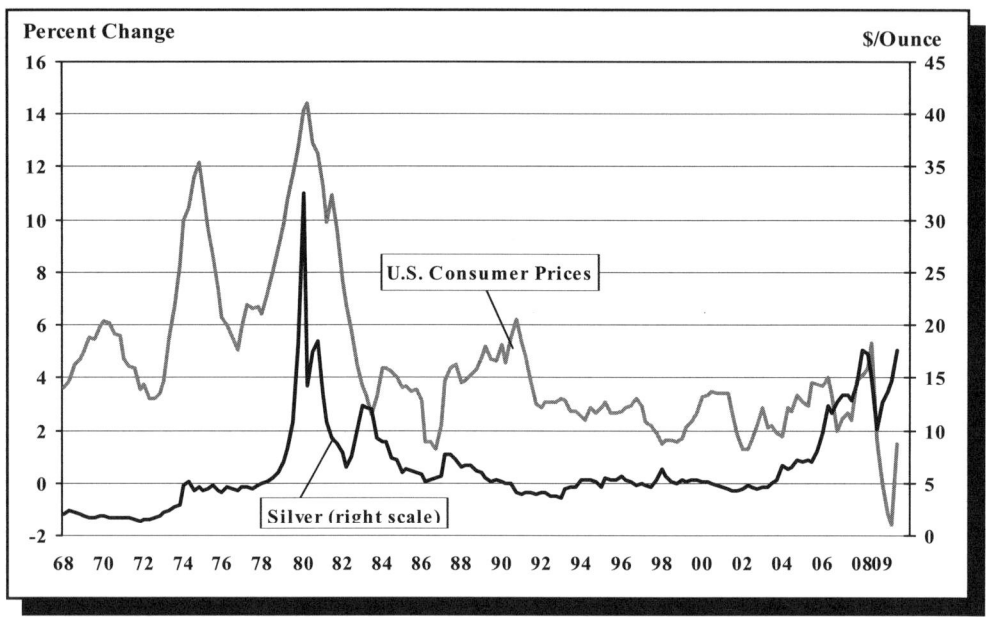

Interest Rates and Silver Prices

Quarterly, Through Fourth Quarter 2009.

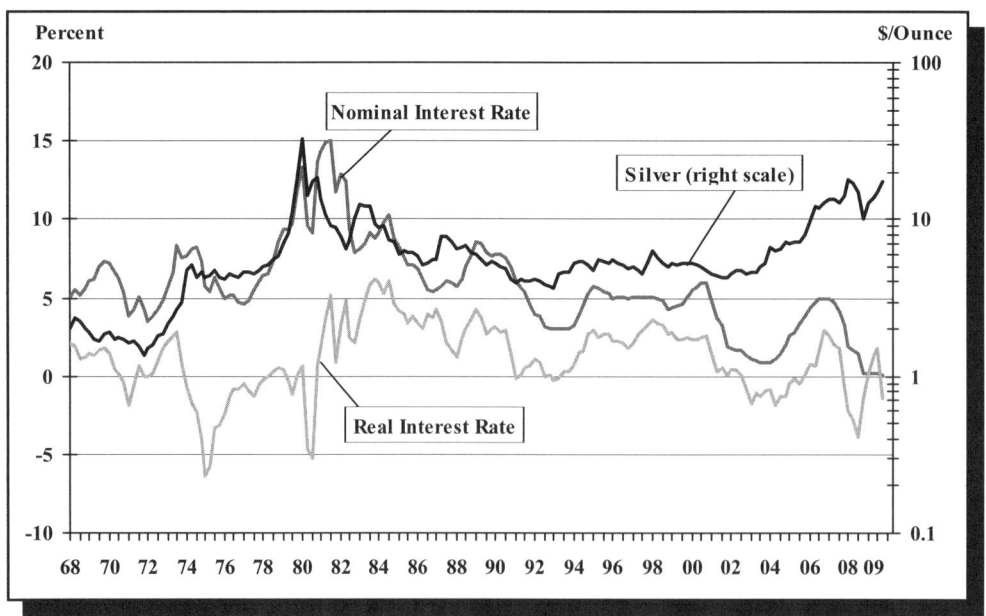

Silver and the U.S. Dollar

Quarterly, Through Fourth Quarter 2009. Dollar is the J.P. Morgan Index.

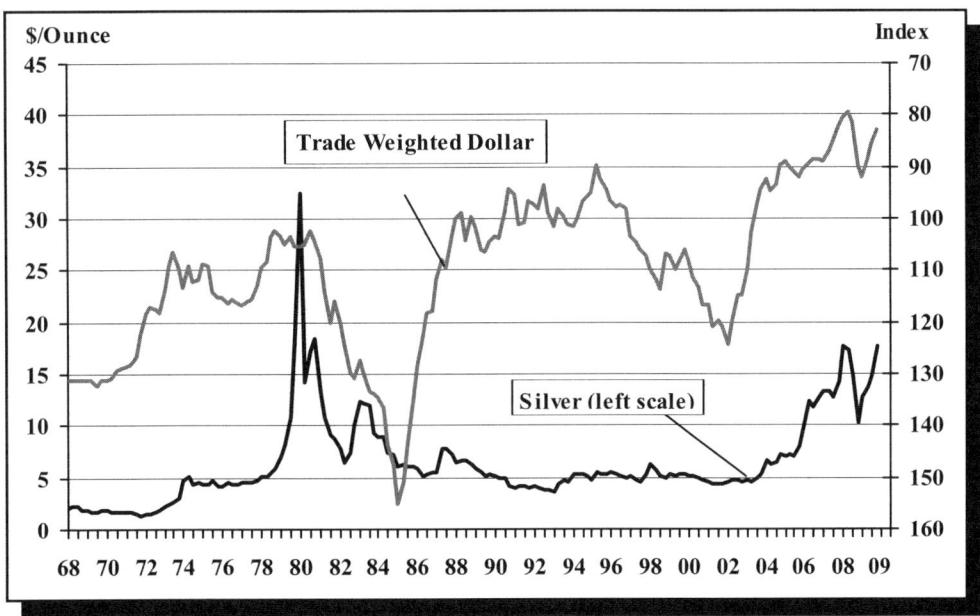

Silver and the 30-Year U.S. Treasury Bond

Monthly, Through February 2010.

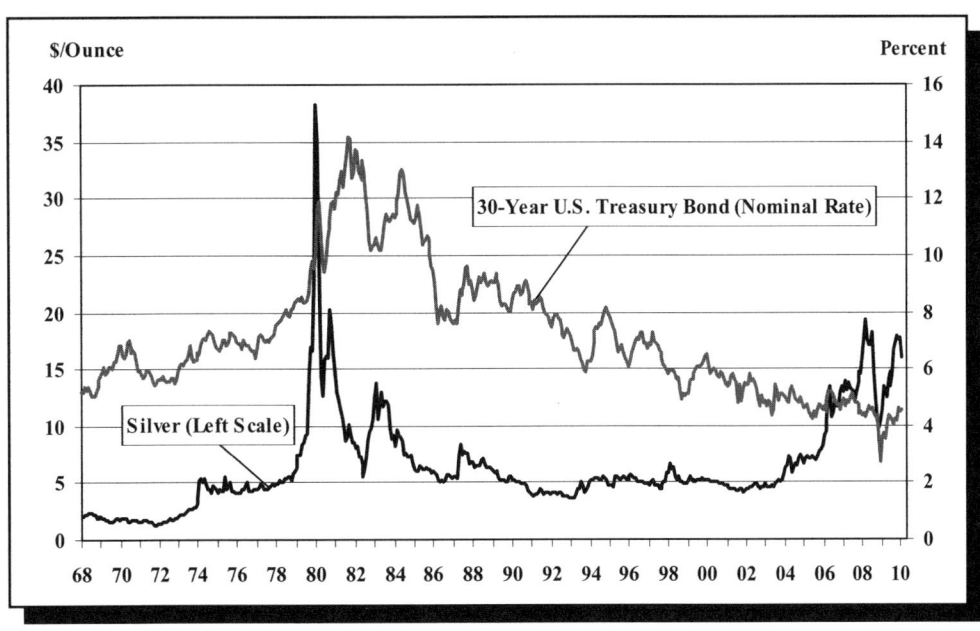

Comparative Investments

	1968-2009		1984-2009		1991-2009	
	Average Return	Average Risk	Average Return	Average Risk	Average Return	Average Risk
Gold	11.33%	11.03%	5.01%	6.92%	6.57%	6.74%
Silver	10.82%	18.65%	4.71%	12.16%	9.54%	12.63%
Platinum	7.65%	13.25%	7.36%	11.29%	8.66%	10.83%
T-Bonds	7.29%	0.39%	6.88%	0.36%	5.90%	0.31%
S&P 500	7.16%	8.85%	8.91%	8.29%	6.89%	7.72%
DJIA	7.08%	8.69%	9.73%	8.05%	7.66%	7.37%
T-Bills	5.78%	0.47%	4.61%	0.39%	3.65%	0.37%
CRB	3.44%	7.30%	0.79%	7.10%	2.10%	8.26%
TWDollar	-0.74%	3.48%	-1.58%	3.66%	-0.42%	3.47%

Note: Calculated on a 12-month moving basis. Risk is defined as the first-order standard deviation of the return over any given 12-month period. Returns based on capital appreciation only.
Source: CPM Group
March 12, 2010

Inventories

Inventories

Silver inventories are an important component of the silver market. They consist of reported and unreported inventories. Inventories that lie untouched are sterile in their impact on the market. However, at times inventories become mobilized, as investors add to their stocks or sell inventories into the market. It is the flow of metal into and out of inventories that affects silver prices.

Unreported inventories appear to be large, held by large and small investors around the world. The volumes of silver held by investors away from public and regulatory scrutiny only can be estimated or inferred based on data from other segments of the silver market over many years, and by the 'shadows' these unreported inventories cast in the market.

There are times when it is obvious that silver held in unreported inventories is being sold, appearing in the market and depressing prices. At other times it is clear that investors are buying metal in bullion and coin form, and taking silver out of circulation, pushing prices higher.

Total inventories also include reported silver stocks held at various depositories that serve as registered vaults for various exchanges, with governments, and at vaults holding silver for exchange traded funds. While estimates of unreported silver bullion inventories held outside of these sources are subject to a great margin of error, the reported stock levels are accurate. Thousands of years of mining and hoarding the metal has made it difficult to account for the unreported silver.

Market and Reported Inventories and Prices

Quarterly, Through Fourth Quarter 2009.

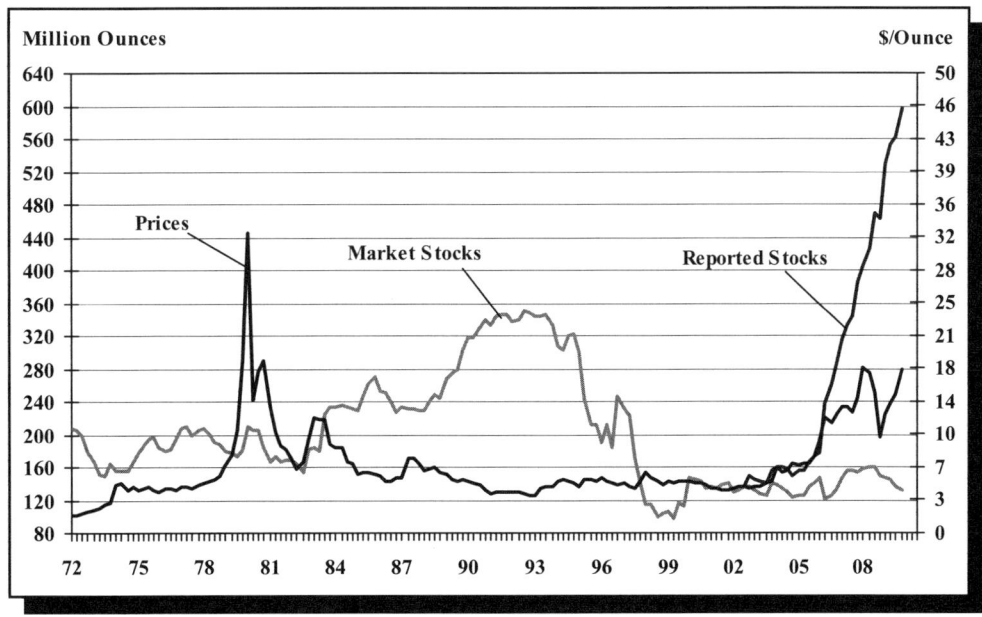

Most of this silver is presumed to have been used, lost, or is tied up in jewelry, or in decorative and religious objects. Some of that gets converted into bullion from time to time. At present silver bullion inventories are estimated to be somewhere between 600 and 900 million ounces.

Market silver inventories declined for the second consecutive year during 2009. These inventories are made up of stocks held at the New York Comex, NYSE Liffe (formerly the Chicago Board of Trade or CBOT), and Tokyo Commodity Exchange. They also include metal held by fabricating and refining companies in the United States and Japan. These inventories stood at 132.7 million ounces at the end of 2009. This was down from 148.8 million ounces at the end of 2008. The largest decline was in Comex registered inventories, which stood at 111.8 million ounces at the end of 2009, down from 127.7 million ounces at the end of 2008. Metal held by Comex registered depositories accounted for around 84% of the total market inventories. NYSE Liffe inventories stood at 2.3 million ounces, Tocom inventories stood at 290,000 ounces, and metal held by refiners, producers, and trading companies in the United States and Japan stood at 18.4 million ounces. These levels were marginally lower compared with 2008 levels.

Reported inventories, which include inventories held by silver exchange traded funds (ETFs) in addition to market silver inventories mentioned above, rose during 2009. In fact, silver held by ETFs now far exceeds the volumes of silver held in exchange registered and reported inventories. Reported market inventories stood at 597.6 million ounces at the end of 2009. This was an increase of 29.2% over levels at the end of 2008. These inventories have been in a rising trend since 2004, when they stood at 149.4 million ounces. Much of this increase can be attributed to silver exchange traded funds, which have gained popularity in recent years. Total silver ETF holdings stood at 464.9 million ounces at the end of 2009. This was an increase of 48.1% from the end of 2008. Silver ETF holdings have grown sharply from the 11.9 million ounces they held in 2002 to their present status.

Comex Inventories

Comex reported stocks are broken down in to two categories: eligible stocks and registered stocks. Registered stocks comprise silver that meets the standards for delivery as stated in the Comex rules and for which a warehouse receipt has been delivered to the Comex clearing house, registering the metal with the exchange. Eligible stocks are those which meet the exchange standard for delivery but are not registered with the exchange as the owner has not delivered the depository receipt to the clearing house. Both eligible and registered inventories can be delivered against open Comex contracts. The eligible

Reported and Estimated Silver Inventories

Million Troy Ounces, Year-End Data

Mid-Point Estimates	1998	2001	2002	2003	2004	2005	2006	2007	2008	2009	December 2009 Percent Change From Dec. 1998
Market *											
Comex *	75.8	104.5	107.4	124.3	103.6	120.0	111.1	132.6	127.7	111.8	47.4%
Tocom	1.6	1.4	1.7	0.7	1.2	0.6	0.4	0.2	0.3	0.3	-82.1%
NYSE Liffe	4.4	3.7	3.9	-	-	2.2	2.3	2.3	2.3	2.3	-47.4%
U.S. and Japanese Industry	21.0	30.6	23.2	16.2	18.4	18.8	19.6	18.5	18.5	18.4	-12.4%
Exchange Traded Funds		-	11.9	14.8	26.2	31.0	155.1	230.4	313.9	464.9	48.1%
Total Market	102.8	140.3	148.2	156.0	149.4	172.5	288.5	384.0	462.7	597.6	481.4%
Inferred, Unreported											
Other U.S. depositories and private holdings	140.0	30-90	60.0	38.0	30.0	30.0	40.0	43.0	49.7	87.5	-37.5%
European depositories * and private holdings	200.0	140-180	160.0	150.0	125.3	125.0	85.0	57.3	70.0	79.0	-60.5%
Asia, Latin America	42.9	90.0	55.0	35.0	25.0	25.0	20.0	10.0	14.0	42.0	-2.1%
Subtotal, Inferred	382.9	360.0	275.0	223.0	180.3	180.0	145.0	110.3	133.7	208.5	-45.5%
Subtotal, Bullion	485.7	620.0-720.0	423.2	379.0	329.7	352.5	433.5	494.3	596.4	806.1	66.0%
Unreported Coins*											
Bullion	394.0	465.5	485.5	495.5	506.0	522.5	540.3	557.7	585.9	624.2	58.4%
Bags of U.S. monetized coins	18.0	2.0	2.0	2.0	2.0	2.0	2.0	1.0	1.0	1.0	-94.4%
Subtotal, Coins	412.0	467.5	487.5	497.5	508.0	524.5	542.3	558.7	586.9	625.2	51.7%
Total, Bullion and Coins	897.7	1,087.5-1,187.5	910.7	876.5	837.7	877.0	975.8	1,053	1,183	1,431	59.4%
Government Stocks	161.5	127.2	123.2	123.2	122.7	87.7	63.7	55.7	55.7	55.7	-65.5%
Total, with Government	1,059	1,214.7-1,314.7	1,034	999.7	960.4	964.7	1,040	1,109	1,239	1,487	40.4%

Notes: The total reported and unreported inventory figures cited in this table represent CPM Group's mid-point estimate of silver stocks, based on discussions with industry sources. CPM Group also derives low-end and high-end estimates from this information. It must be emphasized that these figures represent CPM Group's best estimates. There are no official data regarding unreported silver inventories, and there is a wide range between our high, low, and mid-point estimates. * Market stocks data reported by respective exchanges and industry groups. Comex includes registered and eligible stocks. European estimates include London and Zurich bullion banks. NYSE Liffe formerly Chicago Board of Trade. Coin bags exclude private holdings of old coins, which are included in private holdings.
Source: CPM Group
March 12, 2010

stocks merely require that the owner deliver the depository receipt to the clearing house. Registered stocks also can be used as a margin against long or short positions. Comex reports both of these categories of inventories to increase transparency in the market about the total amount of the metal in the depositories that could be delivered against the futures contracts in a short span of time.

Registered inventories declined to 54.4 million ounces at the end 2009 from around 66.9 million ounces at the end of 2008. The decline gained momentum during the second half of the year. The decrease in registered inventories during 2009 suggests strong physical demand for silver that year. Eligible inventories also declined, to 57.4 million ounces at the end of 2009 from 60.7 million ounces at the end of 2008.

There are four silver depositories approved by Comex. These depositories are operated by Scotia Mocatta, HSBC Bank, Brinks, and the Delaware Depository Service Co. Registered and eligible stocks rose at all of the depositories expect HSBC during 2009. The decline in stocks at HSBC was not offset by the increases in the other three depositories, however. Total stocks (eligible plus registered) at HSBC declined to 53.3 million ounces at the end of 2009, down 24.8 million ounces from the end of 2008. The combined increase in total stocks at the other three depositories was 8.9 million ounces during 2009. As a result, combined silver inventories fell to 111.8 million ounces at the end of 2009 from 127.7 million ounces at the end of 2008.

Government Inventories

Governments across the globe also are holders of silver inventories. These holdings have slipped over time, however. Silver formerly was used in circulating coinage, so that governments held silver as part of their monetary systems. The U.S. government removed silver from its circulating currency in the 1960s, while many other governments, from Europe to Asia, followed suit over the 1970s. As governments moved away from using silver in coinage, they tended to sell off their remaining inventories.

Governments held around 359 million ounces of silver in 1970. These holdings had declined to 55.7 million ounces in 2007. Governments have not sold any silver since then, resulting in inventories remaining at 55.7 million ounces at the end of 2009. The United States and India were the largest holders of silver inventory as of 2009. The United States held 19.9 million ounces and India held 19.1 million ounces that year. Mexico's government is the third largest holder of silver, with around seven million ounces of the metal in inventories during 2009.

CPM Group   Silver Yearbook 2010 - Inventories

Government Silver Inventories

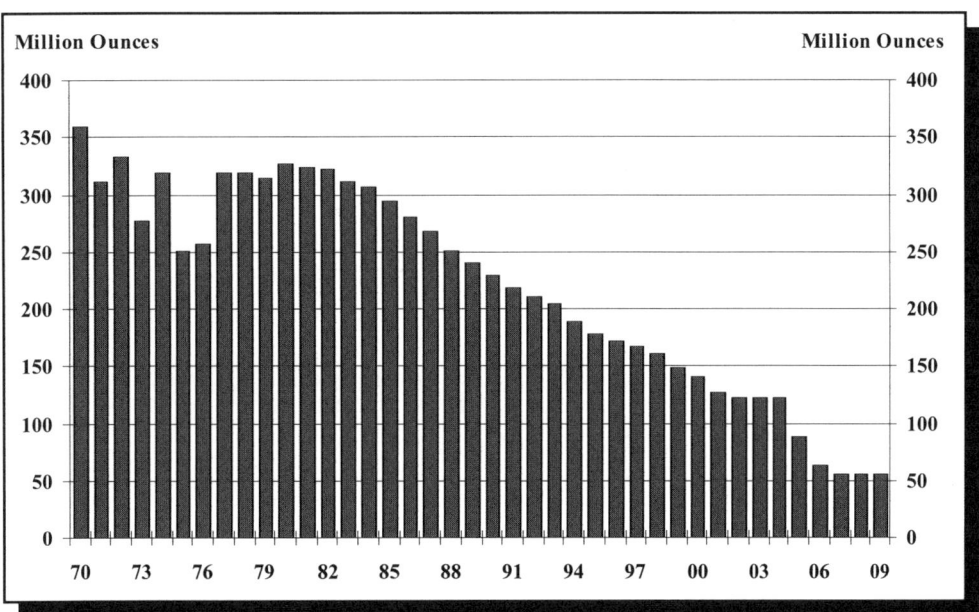

Comex Stocks
Month-End, Through December 2009.

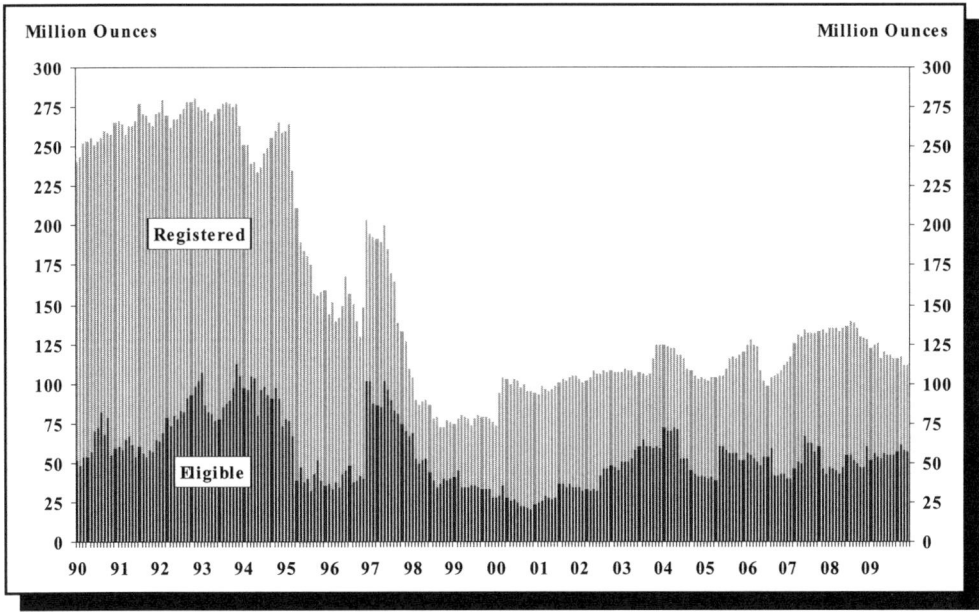

Note: Comex began reporting Wilmington Trust stocks eligible for Comex delivery in the fourth quarter of 1996. Wilmington became a licensed Comex silver depository as of 1 January 1997.

Silver Yearbook 2010 - Inventories — CPM Group

Government Silver Inventories
Million Troy Ounces

	1970	1980	1993	1994	1995	1996	1997	1998	1999	2000	2001	2002	2003	2004	2005	2006	2007	2008	2009
Afghanistan	8.3	8.3	i	i	i	i	i	i	i	i	i	i	i	i	i	i	i	i	i
Austria	1.1	0.6	i	i	i	i	i	i	i	i	i	i	i	i	i	i	i	i	i
Belgium	6.3	2.7	i	i	i	i	i	i	i	i	i	i	i	i	i	i	i	i	i
Australia	1.2	0.0	i	i	i	i	i	i	i	i	i	i	i	i	i	i	i	i	i
Canada	0.9	0.9	i	i	i	i	i	i	i	i	i	i	i	i	i	i	i	i	i
Colombia	0.0	0.3	i	i	i	i	i	i	i	i	i	i	i	i	i	i	i	i	i
Ethiopia	0.2	0.2	i	i	i	i	i	i	i	i	i	i	i	i	i	i	i	i	i
Finland	1.6	2.5	i	i	i	i	i	i	i	i	i	i	i	i	i	i	i	i	i
France	3.4	3.4	i	i	i	i	i	i	i	i	i	i	i	i	i	i	i	i	i
Germany	28.0	6.6	i	i	i	i	i	i	i	i	i	i	i	i	i	i	i	i	i
Greece	3.6	3.6	i	i	i	i	i	i	i	i	i	i	i	i	i	i	i	i	i
Guatemala	1.1	1.3	i	i	i	i	i	i	i	i	i	i	i	i	i	i	i	i	i
India, Reserve Bank	2.6	69.0	67.5	67.5	67.5	67.5	67.5	67.5	67.5	67.5	67.5	67.5	67.5	67.0	32.0	8.0	0.0	0.0	0.0
India, non-RBI	-	-	19.1	19.1	19.1	19.1	19.1	19.1	19.1	19.1	19.1	19.1	19.1	19.1	19.1	19.1	19.1	19.1	19.1
Italy	9.9	9.9	i	i	i	i	i	i	i	i	i	i	i	i	i	i	i	i	i
Japan	3.2	3.5	i	i	i	i	i	i	i	i	i	i	i	i	i	i	i	i	i
Mexico	50.7	11.9	10.0	10.0	6.0	6.0	6.0	6.0	7.0	7.0	7.0	7.0	7.0	7.0	7.0	7.0	7.0	7.0	7.0
Nepal	4.4	4.5	i	i	i	i	i	i	i	i	i	i	i	i	i	i	i	i	i
Netherlands	0.6	0.1	i	i	i	i	i	i	i	i	i	i	i	i	i	i	i	i	i
Norway	0.2	0.2	i	i	i	i	i	i	i	i	i	i	i	i	i	i	i	i	i
Philippines	0.2	2.5	i	i	i	i	i	i	i	i	i	i	i	i	i	i	i	i	i
Pakistan	49.9	0.0	i	i	i	i	i	i	i	i	i	i	i	i	i	i	i	i	i
Portugal	4.0	1.8	i	i	i	i	i	i	i	i	i	i	i	i	i	i	i	i	i
Saudia Arabia	4.3	4.7	i	i	i	i	i	i	i	i	i	i	i	i	i	i	i	i	i
South Africa	1.4	1.2	i	i	i	i	i	i	i	i	i	i	i	i	i	i	i	i	i
Sweden	0.2	0.2	i	i	i	i	i	i	i	i	i	i	i	i	i	i	i	i	i
Switzerland	4.6	5.9	i	i	i	i	i	i	i	i	i	i	i	i	i	i	i	i	i
Taiwan	2.1	2.0	i	i	i	i	i	i	i	i	i	i	i	i	i	i	i	i	i
Thailand	0.7	0.3	i	i	i	i	i	i	i	i	i	i	i	i	i	i	i	i	i
United States	163.9	179.6	92.3	83.2	75.5	70.5	65.2	59.2	46.1	37.1	23.9	19.9	19.9	19.9	19.9	19.9	19.9	19.9	19.9
Others	0.1	0.1	15.7	9.9	9.7	9.7	9.7	9.7	9.7	9.7	9.7	9.7	9.7	9.7	9.7	9.7	9.7	9.7	9.7
Total	359.0	327.8	204.6	189.7	177.8	172.8	167.5	161.5	149.4	140.4	127.2	123.2	123.2	122.7	87.7	63.7	55.7	55.7	55.7

Notes: i - included in "Others".
Source: CPM Group.
March 12, 2010

Silver in Comex Approved Depositories
Troy Ounces

	12/29/2006	12/31/2007	12/31/2008	12/31/2009
Scotia Mocatta				
Registered	10,839,746	29,487,270	22,250,730	18,157,470
Eligible	9,475,446	9,768,610	5,353,280	13,139,260
Total	20,315,192	39,255,880	27,604,010	31,296,730
HSBC Bank (NY)				
Registered	41,706,029	45,805,100	34,389,100	28,327,950
Eligible	22,959,013	23,998,170	43,711,770	24,980,230
Total	64,665,042	69,803,270	78,100,870	53,308,180
Brink's Inc.				
Registered	11,767,819	10,342,000	7,352,000	6,050,170
Eligible	4,497,721	1,951,530	2,261,000	6,327,130
Total	16,265,540	12,293,530	9,613,000	12,377,300
Delaware Depository				
Registered	3,778,475	3,793,010	3,007,060	1,841,170
Eligible	6,046,523	7,480,420	9,367,230	12,947,030
Total	9,824,998	11,273,430	12,374,290	14,788,200
Combined Totals				
Registered	68,092,069	89,427,380	66,998,890	54,376,760
Eligible	42,978,703	43,198,730	60,693,280	57,393,650
Total	111,070,772	132,626,110	127,692,170	111,770,410

Source: Comex, CPM Group.
March 12, 2010

Silver Yearbook 2010 - Inventories — CPM Group

Ratio Between Silver Demand and Reported Stocks
Weeks of Demand Covered by Inventories

Year		Including Eligible Comex Stocks	Excluding Eligible Comex Stocks	Year		Including Eligible Comex Stocks	Excluding Eligible Comex Stocks
1972	1st Qtr.	23.02	-	1982	1st Qtr.	22.90	-
	2nd Qtr.	22.78	-		2nd Qtr.	22.05	-
	3rd Qtr.	22.02	-		3rd Qtr.	20.67	-
	4th Qtr.	19.80	-		4th Qtr.	24.44	-
1973	1st Qtr.	15.63	-	1983	1st Qtr.	25.11	-
	2nd Qtr.	14.25	-		2nd Qtr.	24.50	-
	3rd Qtr.	14.10	-		3rd Qtr.	30.55	-
	4th Qtr.	15.52	-		4th Qtr.	31.94	-
1974	1st Qtr.	16.17	-	1984	1st Qtr.	27.92	-
	2nd Qtr.	16.18	-		2nd Qtr.	28.25	-
	3rd Qtr.	16.24	-		3rd Qtr.	27.99	-
	4th Qtr.	17.19	-		4th Qtr.	27.78	-
1975	1st Qtr.	20.82	-	1985	1st Qtr.	28.84	-
	2nd Qtr.	21.88	-		2nd Qtr.	31.10	-
	3rd Qtr.	22.82	-		3rd Qtr.	32.95	-
	4th Qtr.	23.18	-		4th Qtr.	34.25	-
1976	1st Qtr.	18.49	-	1986	1st Qtr.	28.68	-
	2nd Qtr.	18.11	-		2nd Qtr.	28.32	-
	3rd Qtr.	18.37	-		3rd Qtr.	27.17	-
	4th Qtr.	19.61	-		4th Qtr.	25.59	-
1977	1st Qtr.	22.80	-	1987	1st Qtr.	28.68	-
	2nd Qtr.	23.03	-		2nd Qtr.	28.28	-
	3rd Qtr.	21.73	-		3rd Qtr.	28.28	-
	4th Qtr.	22.50	-		4th Qtr.	25.36	-
1978	1st Qtr.	22.89	-	1987	1st Qtr.	26.78	-
	2nd Qtr.	22.33	-		2nd Qtr.	26.33	-
	3rd Qtr.	21.12	-		3rd Qtr.	26.46	-
	4th Qtr.	20.82	-		4th Qtr.	26.14	-
1979	1st Qtr.	20.25	-	1988	1st Qtr.	24.62	-
	2nd Qtr.	19.99	-		2nd Qtr.	25.70	23.67
	3rd Qtr.	19.63	-		3rd Qtr.	26.49	24.31
	4th Qtr.	20.54	-		4th Qtr.	26.07	24.16
1980	1st Qtr.	28.68	-	1989	1st Qtr.	27.26	24.30
	2nd Qtr.	28.28	-		2nd Qtr.	27.92	24.74
	3rd Qtr.	28.28	-		3rd Qtr.	28.43	24.51
	4th Qtr.	25.36	-		4th Qtr.	30.81	26.04
1981	1st Qtr.	23.46	-	1990	1st Qtr.	30.66	25.41
	2nd Qtr.	24.30	-		2nd Qtr.	30.73	23.90
	3rd Qtr.	23.46	-		3rd Qtr.	31.98	25.40
	4th Qtr.	23.53	-		4th Qtr.	32.77	27.00

Note: Based on end-quarter data.
Sources: CPM Group, New York Commodity Exchange, Tokyo Commodity Exchange,
NYSE Liffe (formerly Chicago Board of Trade), London Metal Exchange,
Japanese Ministry of Trade and Industry, trade sources.
March 12, 2010

Ratio Between Silver Demand and Reported Stocks
Weeks of Demand Covered by Inventories

Year		Including Eligible Comex Stocks	Excluding Eligible Comex Stocks	Year		Including Eligible Comex Stocks	Excluding Eligible Comex Stocks
1991	1st Qtr.	30.06	24.20	2001	1st Qtr.	8.74	6.85
	2nd Qtr.	31.09	26.17		2nd Qtr.	8.66	6.85
	3rd Qtr.	31.31	26.39		3rd Qtr.	8.87	6.63
	4th Qtr.	31.24	25.38		4th Qtr.	9.00	6.77
1992	1st Qtr.	29.61	22.69	2002	1st Qtr.	8.54	6.35
	2nd Qtr.	29.91	23.09		2nd Qtr.	8.63	6.52
	3rd Qtr.	30.82	22.80		3rd Qtr.	8.96	5.92
	4th Qtr.	30.60	21.64		4th Qtr.	8.96	5.95
1993	1st Qtr.	30.25	22.98	2003	1st Qtr.	8.83	5.49
	2nd Qtr.	26.46	20.47		2nd Qtr.	8.50	4.46
	3rd Qtr.	26.73	19.81		3rd Qtr.	8.34	4.36
	4th Qtr.	25.61	17.51		4th Qtr.	9.31	5.35
1994	1st Qtr.	23.05	15.15	2004	1st Qtr.	9.04	4.48
	2nd Qtr.	22.60	15.40		2nd Qtr.	8.72	5.29
	3rd Qtr.	23.95	17.12		3rd Qtr.	8.49	5.54
	4th Qtr.	24.08	18.54		4th Qtr.	8.00	5.25
1995	1st Qtr.	21.56	16.78	2005	1st Qtr.	8.04	5.35
	2nd Qtr.	17.53	14.81		2nd Qtr.	8.05	4.16
	3rd Qtr.	15.20	12.08		3rd Qtr.	8.79	5.16
	4th Qtr.	15.27	12.69		4th Qtr.	9.12	5.77
1996	1st Qtr.	13.10	10.49	2006	1st Qtr.	10.59	6.76
	2nd Qtr.	14.49	11.38		2nd Qtr.	8.84	4.94
	3rd Qtr.	12.53	9.60		3rd Qtr.	9.13	6.10
	4th Qtr.	16.86	9.89		4th Qtr.	9.66	6.55
1997	1st Qtr.	14.93	9.36	2007	1st Qtr.	10.55	7.24
	2nd Qtr.	14.38	8.17		2nd Qtr.	11.17	6.34
	3rd Qtr.	11.10	5.83		3rd Qtr.	11.15	6.99
	4th Qtr.	9.05	4.67		4th Qtr.	11.04	7.93
1998	1st Qtr.	7.30	4.15	2008	1st Qtr.	11.78	8.43
	2nd Qtr.	7.21	4.39		2nd Qtr.	11.80	7.71
	3rd Qtr.	6.31	3.96		3rd Qtr.	11.81	8.09
	4th Qtr.	6.50	3.99		4th Qtr.	11.03	6.53
1999	1st Qtr.	6.72	4.49	2009	1st Qtr.	11.96	7.59
	2nd Qtr.	6.21	3.94		2nd Qtr.	11.82	7.33
	3rd Qtr.	7.46	5.31		3rd Qtr.	11.07	6.38
	4th Qtr.	7.23	5.45		4th Qtr.	10.77	6.11
2000	1st Qtr.	9.01	6.80				
	2nd Qtr.	8.78	7.12				
	3rd Qtr.	8.69	7.29				
	4th Qtr.	8.17	6.73				

Silver Yearbook 2010 - Inventories   CPM Group

Market Silver Inventories
Million Troy Ounces

		Comex	NYSE Liffe	LME	Tocom	Industry	Total
1972	1st Qtr.	109.1	15.0	6.7	--	77.0	207.8
	2nd Qtr.	98.6	17.3	6.4	--	83.4	205.7
	3rd Qtr.	92.8	19.9	7.7	--	78.4	198.8
	4th Qtr.	77.6	22.8	7.5	--	70.9	178.8
1973	1st Qtr.	69.1	26.5	9.1	--	60.9	165.6
	2nd Qtr.	56.1	23.1	12.3	--	59.5	151.0
	3rd Qtr.	47.5	29.4	15.4	--	57.1	149.4
	4th Qtr.	64.3	27.4	16.3	--	56.4	164.4
1974	1st Qtr.	64.4	25.9	14.8	--	50.9	156.0
	2nd Qtr.	74.3	20.3	13.5	--	48.0	156.1
	3rd Qtr.	68.2	20.0	11.5	--	57.0	156.7
	4th Qtr.	68.0	19.5	12.0	--	66.3	165.8
1975	1st Qtr.	70.3	25.0	12.2	--	69.1	176.6
	2nd Qtr.	78.3	40.3	14.6	--	52.4	185.6
	3rd Qtr.	82.6	42.8	16.4	--	51.8	193.6
	4th Qtr.	85.7	38.5	17.8	--	54.6	196.6
1976	1st Qtr.	79.8	39.4	15.3	--	48.5	183.0
	2nd Qtr.	65.2	47.9	17.5	--	48.7	179.3
	3rd Qtr.	50.0	53.6	29.8	--	48.4	181.8
	4th Qtr.	54.8	61.0	28.5	--	49.8	194.1
1977	1st Qtr.	63.2	64.4	27.5	--	53.5	208.6
	2nd Qtr.	69.4	63.9	25.1	--	52.3	210.7
	3rd Qtr.	64.8	61.3	18.8	--	53.9	198.8
	4th Qtr.	68.4	62.2	19.2	--	56.1	205.9
1978	1st Qtr.	74.1	62.5	19.2	--	51.3	207.1
	2nd Qtr.	72.8	64.0	18.0	--	47.3	202.1
	3rd Qtr.	67.8	62.2	18.2	--	42.9	191.1
	4th Qtr.	58.2	59.9	23.0	--	47.3	188.4
1979	1st Qtr.	49.6	55.3	21.3	--	52.8	179.0
	2nd Qtr.	54.1	56.8	18.8	--	47.0	176.7
	3rd Qtr.	51.5	65.3	15.9	--	40.8	173.5
	4th Qtr.	74.8	58.3	13.1	--	35.4	181.6
1980	1st Qtr.	83.6	57.8	17.8	-	49.7	208.9
	2nd Qtr.	82.0	45.8	28.0	-	50.2	206.0
	3rd Qtr.	82.1	46.1	26.6	-	51.2	206.0
	4th Qtr.	86.6	34.2	27.3	-	36.6	184.7
1981	1st Qtr.	85.4	18.9	24.5	-	38.4	167.2
	2nd Qtr.	86.7	20.4	25.8	-	40.3	173.2
	3rd Qtr.	77.4	21.2	29.7	-	38.9	167.2
	4th Qtr.	77.6	18.9	32.2	-	39.0	167.7
1982	1st Qtr.	77.1	18.6	33.2	-	40.7	169.6
	2nd Qtr.	70.8	15.2	35.7	-	41.6	163.3
	3rd Qtr.	61.5	13.5	36.9	-	41.2	153.1
	4th Qtr.	90.7	15.5	35.2	-	39.6	181.0

CPM Group Silver Yearbook 2010 - Inventories

Market Silver Inventories
Million Troy Ounces

		Comex	NYSE Liffe	LME	Tocom	Industry	Total
1983	1st Qtr.	97.2	15.5	34.1	-	37.6	184.4
	2nd Qtr.	90.9	19.0	35.4	-	34.6	179.9
	3rd Qtr.	129.3	21.1	37.7	-	36.2	224.3
	4th Qtr.	127.4	23.8	45.4	-	37.9	234.5
1984	1st Qtr.	116.8	23.4	50.0	-	42.4	232.6
	2nd Qtr.	120.9	21.3	51.7	-	41.5	235.4
	3rd Qtr.	115.0	21.2	52.6	-	44.4	233.2
	4th Qtr.	118.5	19.1	51.6	-	42.3	231.5
1985	1st Qtr.	106.6	17.4	54.1	-	50.2	228.3
	2nd Qtr.	132.4	14.9	50.5	2.1	46.3	246.2
	3rd Qtr.	144.0	16.6	55.0	2.4	42.8	260.8
	4th Qtr.	155.3	17.8	51.2	2.7	44.1	271.1
1986	1st Qtr.	148.2	17.6	40.8	2.9	43.8	253.3
	2nd Qtr.	151.9	17.5	35.8	3.3	41.6	250.1
	3rd Qtr.	157.2	16.5	25.2	3.6	37.4	239.9
	4th Qtr.	145.4	16.7	23.1	4.0	36.8	226.0
1987	1st Qtr.	157.9	15.0	21.8	4.2	35.7	234.6
	2nd Qtr.	152.5	14.0	23.1	4.2	36.8	230.6
	3rd Qtr.	155.7	12.6	21.1	4.4	38.0	231.8
	4th Qtr.	155.3	13.5	20.1	4.5	35.5	228.9
1988	1st Qtr.	155.8	13.5	18.7	4.4	37.8	230.2
	2nd Qtr.	168.2	13.8	14.8	5.3	38.2	240.3
	3rd Qtr.	178.8	13.8	15.1	5.8	34.2	247.7
	4th Qtr.	174.4	12.0	15.0	8.0	34.3	243.7
1989	1st Qtr.	194.8	11.4	11.8	9.8	39.8	267.6
	2nd Qtr.	206.1	13.2	-	10.8	44.0	274.1
	3rd Qtr.	212.3	12.7	-	9.8	44.3	279.1
	4th Qtr.	238.8	11.8	-	10.5	41.4	302.5
1990	1st Qtr.	252.1	11.9	-	10.3	43.6	317.8
	2nd Qtr.	251.6	12.1	-	11.2	43.7	318.6
	3rd Qtr.	260.2	12.9	-	11.4	47.1	331.6
	4th Qtr.	265.4	12.3	-	14.2	47.8	339.7
1991	1st Qtr.	257.9	12.0	-	14.0	48.8	332.7
	2nd Qtr.	266.1	12.1	-	13.9	52.1	344.2
	3rd Qtr.	269.7	12.1	-	13.4	51.5	346.6
	4th Qtr.	270.7	12.1	-	12.1	50.9	345.8
1992	1st Qtr.	262.2	12.1	-	12.1	50.5	336.9
	2nd Qtr.	267.8	11.7	-	10.8	49.9	340.2
	3rd Qtr.	278.6	11.7	-	9.3	51.0	350.6
	4th Qtr.	276.6	11.7	-	8.8	51.0	348.1
1993	1st Qtr.	271.8	11.7	-	7.8	52.8	344.1
	2nd Qtr.	273.9	11.5	-	7.6	50.0	343.1
	3rd Qtr.	276.8	10.7	-	7.6	51.6	346.6
	4th Qtr.	263.1	10.7	-	7.5	50.8	332.1

Silver Yearbook 2010 - Inventories

Market Silver Inventories
Million Troy Ounces

		Comex	NYSE Liffe	LME	Tocom	Industry	Total
1994	1st Qtr.	239.4	10.7	-	7.5	50.2	307.8
	2nd Qtr.	237.2	10.7	-	7.2	46.6	301.8
	3rd Qtr.	255.2	10.7	-	6.7	47.2	319.8
	4th Qtr.	258.6	10.7	-	6.2	46.0	321.6
1995	1st Qtr.	235.1	10.7	-	6.4	48.3	300.5
	2nd Qtr.	184.6	10.6	-	6.2	43.0	244.4
	3rd Qtr.	156.5	10.2	-	5.1	40.0	211.9
	4th Qtr.	159.1	10.2	-	4.5	39.0	212.8
1996	1st Qtr.	139.7	10.2	-	4.1	37.0	191.0
	2nd Qtr.	167.6	6.4	-	4.0	33.3	211.3
	3rd Qtr.	139.3	6.3	-	3.8	33.3	182.7
	4th Qtr.*	203.5	6.1	-	3.6	32.7	245.8
1997	1st Qtr.	191.7	5.5	-	2.5	31.0	230.7
	2nd Qtr.	185.5	5.5	-	2.4	28.8	222.2
	3rd Qtr.	138.1	5.4	-	2.4	25.5	171.5
	4th Qtr.	109.8	4.8	-	2.2	23.0	139.8
1998	1st Qtr.	86.9	4.4	-	2.0	22.0	115.3
	2nd Qtr.	86.2	4.4	-	1.8	21.5	113.9
	3rd Qtr.	72.8	4.1	-	1.5	21.3	99.7
	4th Qtr.	75.8	4.4	-	1.6	21.0	102.8
1999	1st Qtr.	79.6	4.3	-	1.5	20.0	105.4
	2nd Qtr.	73.5	4.3	-	1.5	18.0	97.4
	3rd Qtr.	79.4	4.2	-	1.5	32.0	117.1
	4th Qtr.	76.0	4.0	-	1.4	32.0	113.4
2000	1st Qtr.	104.3	4.0	-	1.5	38.0	147.7
	2nd Qtr.	102.7	4.0	-	1.7	35.6	144.0
	3rd Qtr.	99.6	4.0	-	1.7	37.2	142.4
	4th Qtr.	94.0	4.0	-	1.7	34.1	133.8
2001	1st Qtr.	96.7	3.9	-	1.6	34.0	136.3
	2nd Qtr.	98.7	3.7	-	1.6	30.8	134.9
	3rd Qtr.	101.5	3.7	-	1.6	30.9	137.8
	4th Qtr.	104.5	3.7	-	1.6	30.6	140.5
2002	1st Qtr.	102.2	3.9	-	1.6	22.0	129.8
	2nd Qtr.	106.6	3.9	-	1.6	19.0	131.1
	3rd Qtr.	107.5	3.9	-	1.7	23.0	136.2
	4th Qtr.	107.4	3.9	-	1.7	23.2	136.3
2003	1st Qtr.	108.7	-	-	0.0	23.4	132.1
	2nd Qtr.	107.2	-	-	0.0	19.9	127.1
	3rd Qtr.	105.9	-	-	0.5	20.1	126.5
	4th Qtr.	124.3	-	-	0.7	16.2	141.1

CPM Group   Silver Yearbook 2010 - Inventories

Market Silver Inventories
Million Troy Ounces

Year	Quarter	Comex	NYSE Liffe	LME	Tocom	Industry	Total
2004	1st Qtr.	122.1	-	-	0.5	16.7	139.2
	2nd Qtr.	118.4	-	-	0.6	15.3	134.3
	3rd Qtr.	107.8	-	-	0.4	22.5	130.7
	4th Qtr.	103.6	-	-	1.2	18.4	123.2
2005	1st Qtr.	103.6	-	-	1.0	20.2	124.8
	2nd Qtr.	104.7	-	-	0.9	19.3	124.9
	3rd Qtr.	116.7	-	-	0.9	18.8	136.4
	4th Qtr.	120.0	2.2	-	0.6	18.8	141.5
2006	1st Qtr.	125.0	2.3	-	0.6	18.3	146.2
	2nd Qtr.	102.3	2.3	-	0.6	16.9	122.0
	3rd Qtr.	105.2	2.3	-	0.4	18.2	126.1
	4th Qtr.	111.1	2.3	-	0.4	19.6	133.4
2007	1st Qtr.	125.8	2.3	-	0.3	18.5	146.8
	2nd Qtr.	134.1	2.3	-	0.4	18.8	155.6
	3rd Qtr.	132.6	2.3	-	0.4	19.9	155.2
	4th Qtr.	132.6	2.3	-	0.2	18.5	153.6
2008	1st Qtr.	135.9	2.3	-	0.3	20.4	158.9
	2nd Qtr.	136.0	2.3	-	0.3	20.5	159.1
	3rd Qtr.	135.5	2.3	-	0.7	20.8	159.3
	4th Qtr.	127.7	2.3	-	0.3	18.5	148.8
2009	1st Qtr.	125.4	2.3	-	0.3	19.5	147.5
	2nd Qtr.	117.6	2.3	-	0.3	25.6	145.7
	3rd Qtr.	115.4	2.3	-	0.2	18.5	136.4
	4th Qtr.	111.8	2.3	-	0.3	18.4	132.7

Notes: Industry stocks include dealer, importer, and refiner stocks, in the United States and Japan. The London Metal Exchange ceased its silver contract in June 1989. Stocks formerly registered against the contracts now are held in private hands. The London Metal Exchange re-launched its silver contract in May 1999, but does not publicly report warehouse stocks. *Comex began reporting Wilmington Trust stocks eligible for Comex delivery in the fourth quarter of 1996. Wilmington Trust became a licensed Comex silver depository on January 1, 1997. NA -- not available.
Sources: Comex, NYSE Liffe (formerly Chicago Board of Trade), Tokyo Commodity Exchange, London Metal Exchange, U.S. Bureau of Mines, Japanese Ministry of Trade and Industry, CPM Group.
March 12, 2010

Silver Yearbook 2010 - Inventories — CPM Group

Reported Market Inventories
Quarterly, Through Fourth Quarter 2009.

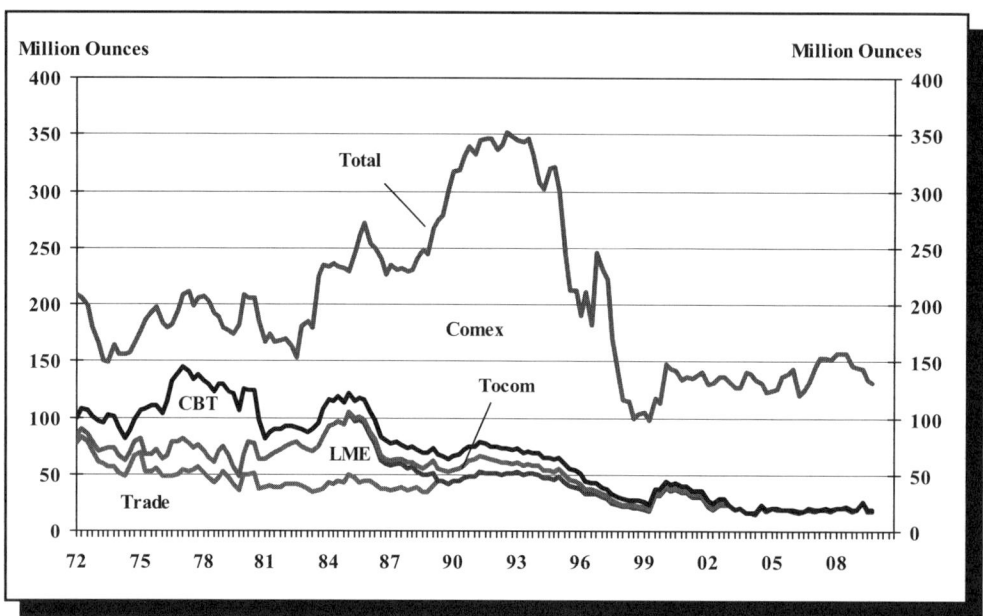

Market Stocks
Quarterly, Through Fourth Quarter 2009.

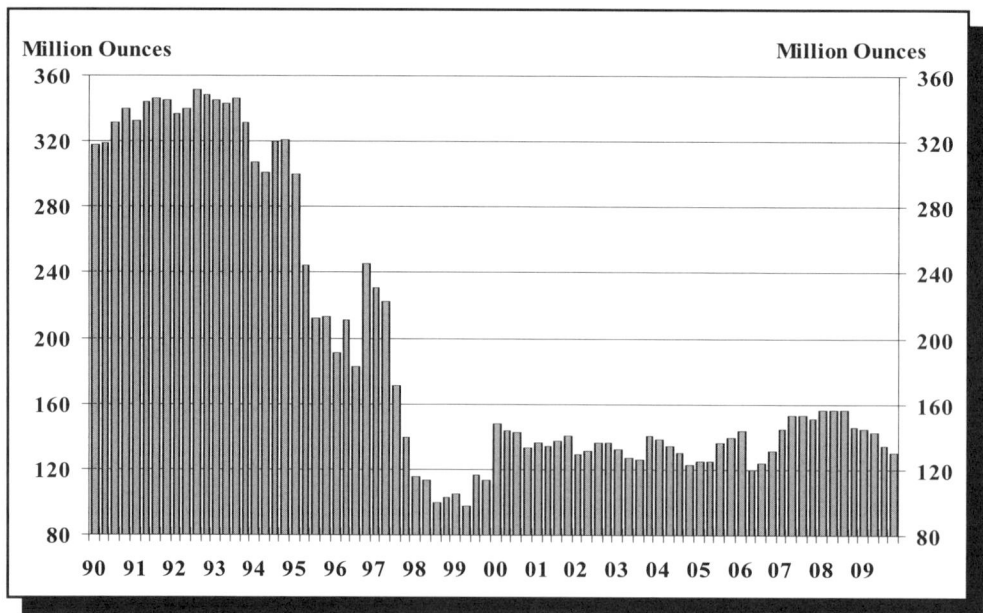

CPM Group Silver YEARBOOK 2010 - Inventories

Reported and Unreported Silver Holdings
Million Troy Ounces

| | | Reported Stock Levels | | | | Year-to-Year Changes | | |
	Government	Exchange	ETFs	Dealer	Total	Reported Stocks	Unreported Stocks	Total
1970	359.0	135.0	-	82.2	217.2	NA	NA	NA
1971	311.9	135.7	-	57.1	192.8	-24.4	-11.6	-36.0
1972	333.6	107.9	-	70.9	178.8	-14.0	-82.6	-96.6
1973	277.2	108.0	-	56.4	164.4	-14.4	-114.6	-129.0
1974	319.2	99.5	-	66.3	165.8	1.4	-53.4	-52.0
1975	250.8	142.0	-	54.6	196.6	30.8	-40.9	-10.1
1976	257.0	144.3	-	49.8	194.1	-2.5	-23.2	-25.7
1977	319.0	149.8	-	56.1	205.9	11.8	-60.9	-49.1
1978	318.8	141.1	-	47.3	188.4	-17.5	-39.6	-57.1
1979	314.6	146.2	-	35.4	181.6	-6.8	32.7	25.9
1980	327.8	148.1	-	50.2	198.3	16.7	190.5	207.2
1981	323.8	128.7	-	40.3	169.0	-29.3	143.6	114.3
1982	322.8	141.4	-	41.6	183.0	14.0	66.5	80.5
1983	311.7	196.6	-	34.6	231.2	48.2	114.3	162.5
1984	307.0	189.2	-	41.5	230.7	-0.5	86.2	85.7
1985	294.0	227.0	-	46.3	273.3	42.6	45.6	88.2
1986	280.0	189.2	-	41.6	230.8	-42.5	50.9	8.4
1987	267.8	193.4	-	36.8	230.2	-0.6	41.3	40.7
1988	251.6	209.4	-	38.2	247.6	17.4	6.9	24.3
1989	240.9	261.1	-	44.0	305.1	57.5	-49.2	8.3
1990	229.9	291.9	-	43.7	335.6	30.5	-59.4	-28.9
1991	218.4	294.9	-	52.1	347.0	11.4	-71.6	-60.2
1992	210.3	367.8 *	-	49.9	417.7	70.7	-150.5 *	-79.7
1993	204.6	373.3	-	50.0	423.3	5.6	-194.6	-189.0
1994	189.7	347.4	-	46.0	393.4	-29.9	-174.7	-204.6
1995	177.8	233.2	-	39.0	272.2	-121.2	-63.5	-184.7
1996	172.8	213.1	-	32.7	245.8	-26.3	-179.1	-205.4
1997	167.5	116.8	-	23.0	139.8	-106.0	-108.3	-214.3
1998	161.5	81.8	-	21.0	102.8	-37.0	-160.7	-197.8
1999	149.4	81.4	-	32.0	113.4	10.6	-169.5	-158.9
2000	140.4	99.7	-	34.1	133.8	20.5	-164.5	-144.1
2001	127.2	109.9	-	30.6	140.5	6.7	-89.9	-83.3
2002	123.2	113.1	11.9	23.2	148.2	7.7	-93.7	-86.0
2003	123.2	124.9	14.8	16.2	156.0	7.8	-83.1	-75.3
2004	122.7	104.8	26.2	18.4	149.4	-6.6	-76.6	-83.2
2005	87.7	120.5	31.0	18.8	170.3	21.0	-66.1	-45.1
2006	63.7	113.8	155.1	19.6	288.5	118.2	-70.4	47.9
2007	55.7	135.1	230.4	18.5	384.0	95.5	-51.4	44.1
2008	55.7	130.3	313.9	18.5	462.7	78.6	5.4	84.0
2009	55.7	114.3	464.9	18.4	597.6	135.0	36.5	171.5

Notes: Changes in total stocks represents the change in the supply/demand balance of new metal. Market stocks include reported U.S. dealer inventories and exchange registered stocks. New York Commodity Exchange stocks also include eligible stocks. Changes in market stocks are end-year; 2004 change is through end-December. Changes in unreported stocks is the change in the supply/demand balance of new metal, adjusted for changes in reported inventories. End of year data. *Adjusted to include Wilmington Trust stocks that would have been eligible for Comex delivery. Wilmington Trust became a licensed Comex silver depository on January 1, 1997. Includes ETF and CEF stocks as of 2008.
Sources: U.S. Bureau of the Mint; U.S. Bureau of Mines; New York Commodity Exchange; London Metal Exchange; Chicago Board of Trade; Tokyo Commodity Exchange; CPM Group.
March 12, 2010

Silver Yearbook 2010 - Inventories CPM Group

Comex Inventories
Troy Ounces

		Eligible	Registered	Total
1988	January			
	February			
	March			
	April	20,931,178	137,735,862	158,667,040
	May	23,267,595	141,080,749	164,348,344
	June	19,048,467	149,149,501	168,197,968
	July	22,419,309	147,324,079	169,743,388
	August	20,844,158	154,751,024	175,595,182
	September	20,430,956	158,341,924	178,772,880
	October	20,595,315	154,686,825	175,282,140
	November	18,220,714	160,236,251	178,456,965
	December	17,859,494	158,060,356	175,919,850
1989	January	19,160,193	163,496,673	182,656,866
	February	23,131,632	167,111,383	190,243,015
	March	28,976,762	165,825,629	194,802,391
	April	38,647,464	162,347,967	200,995,431
	May	35,066,425	168,140,357	203,206,782
	June	31,200,288	174,848,870	206,049,158
	July	31,155,105	176,130,744	207,285,849
	August	32,577,746	177,807,340	210,385,086
	September	38,453,219	173,830,263	212,283,482
	October	45,019,114	181,551,266	226,570,380
	November	43,900,831	194,045,589	237,946,420
	December	46,787,483	191,985,060	238,772,543
1990	January	52,157,110	188,639,227	240,796,337
	February	48,801,419	194,619,375	243,420,794
	March	54,362,447	197,741,690	252,104,137
	April	54,149,135	199,623,503	253,772,638
	May	57,134,847	198,286,005	255,420,852
	June	70,866,114	180,759,827	251,625,941
	July	72,595,954	180,730,153	253,326,107
	August	82,219,388	173,594,421	255,813,809
	September	68,279,740	191,904,669	260,184,409
	October	79,486,485	179,127,685	258,614,170
	November	55,330,949	202,354,370	257,685,319
	December	59,768,672	205,570,595	265,339,267
1991	January	61,113,795	205,092,178	266,205,973
	February	58,398,935	205,433,464	263,832,399
	March	64,871,675	192,979,471	257,851,146
	April	66,858,781	196,704,194	263,562,975
	May	62,069,034	201,617,049	263,686,083
	June	54,444,776	211,641,952	266,086,728
	July	60,249,532	216,711,025	276,960,557
	August	56,648,508	214,155,505	270,804,013
	September	54,478,488	215,182,765	269,661,253
	October	58,918,511	206,955,342	265,873,853
	November	57,058,278	205,776,673	262,834,951
	December	64,848,241	205,886,040	270,734,281
1992	January	63,890,330	207,801,743	271,692,073
	February	69,174,680	209,815,116	278,989,796
	March	78,754,912	190,820,207	269,575,119
	April	73,747,831	188,491,645	262,239,476
	May	79,940,269	187,062,531	267,002,800
	June	77,623,785	190,194,292	267,818,077
	July	83,215,228	188,044,215	271,259,443
	August	82,821,967	190,920,787	273,742,754
	September	91,230,401	187,344,698	278,575,099
	October	92,762,047	185,764,386	278,526,433
	November	98,153,181	182,558,939	280,712,120
	December	101,939,323	173,216,882	275,156,205

Comex Inventories
Troy Ounces

		Eligible	Registered	Total
1993	January	106,998,830	165,825,641	272,824,471
	February	86,961,954	186,667,499	273,629,453
	March	82,662,229	189,193,714	271,855,943
	April	80,895,709	185,391,189	266,286,898
	May	77,063,808	193,735,970	270,799,778
	June	77,578,847	196,367,983	273,946,830
	July	85,711,618	191,516,305	277,227,923
	August	87,728,399	191,016,115	278,744,514
	September	89,815,975	187,003,403	276,819,378
	October	97,885,085	177,485,327	275,370,412
	November	112,165,854	165,500,524	277,666,378
	December	105,016,928	158,120,600	263,137,528
1994	January	97,437,653	154,247,251	251,684,904
	February	95,900,884	154,829,493	250,730,377
	March	105,568,497	133,805,368	239,373,865
	April	104,233,160	136,059,600	240,292,760
	May	79,737,856	154,212,232	233,950,088
	June	96,149,822	141,224,293	237,374,115
	July	98,196,337	148,094,476	246,290,813
	August	93,530,348	155,886,182	249,416,530
	September	91,233,359	163,964,469	255,197,828
	October	97,483,828	162,150,002	259,633,830
	November	91,432,535	174,277,752	265,710,287
	December	73,964,895	184,653,457	258,618,352
1995	January	77,729,176	181,925,185	259,654,361
	February	77,301,784	186,743,449	264,045,233
	March	66,693,322	168,421,093	235,114,415
	April	38,952,612	172,075,316	211,027,928
	May	47,374,096	142,293,524	189,667,620
	June	37,984,494	146,585,835	184,570,329
	July	40,169,295	141,099,427	181,268,722
	August	32,983,203	142,780,620	175,763,823
	September	43,442,226	113,101,277	156,543,503
	October	52,007,958	103,983,191	155,991,149
	November	38,836,229	119,188,166	158,024,395
	December	35,831,045	123,280,548	159,111,593
1996	January	36,940,389	107,025,922	143,966,311
	February	33,366,191	117,967,447	151,333,638
	March	38,068,627	101,672,254	139,740,881
	April	34,243,584	107,567,990	141,811,574
	May	43,247,715	106,072,060	149,319,775
	June	45,337,013	122,259,056	167,596,069
	July	49,138,317	107,484,770	156,623,087
	August	38,299,394	112,452,911	150,752,305
	September	38,911,341	100,411,090	139,322,431
	October	42,753,103	87,275,643	130,028,746
	November	39,979,743	108,471,715	148,451,458
	December*	101,619,515	101,831,268	203,450,783
1997	January	101,738,914	93,110,545	194,849,459
	February	87,402,640	105,816,663	193,219,303
	March	86,111,053	105,600,425	191,711,478
	April	85,722,960	104,078,774	189,801,734
	May	101,394,054	98,802,811	200,196,865
	June	95,997,795	89,531,201	185,528,996
	July	90,018,293	79,591,120	169,609,413
	August	83,284,069	81,012,292	164,296,361
	September	81,331,218	56,818,062	138,149,280
	October	74,874,064	58,051,601	132,925,665
	November	70,579,064	56,460,142	127,039,206
	December	67,618,752	42,229,326	109,848,078

Silver Yearbook 2010 - Inventories — CPM Group

Comex Inventories
Troy Ounces

		Eligible	Registered	Total
1998	January	68,780,324	35,324,866	104,105,190
	February	53,563,944	36,531,320	90,095,264
	March	49,746,209	37,179,714	86,925,923
	April	52,506,354	36,050,079	88,556,433
	May	52,985,545	37,347,768	90,333,313
	June	44,538,232	41,707,022	86,245,254
	July	38,926,117	39,581,321	78,507,438
	August	35,148,850	43,532,564	78,681,414
	September	37,194,347	35,602,263	72,796,610
	October	40,196,352	32,862,795	73,059,147
	November	39,129,372	37,688,599	76,817,971
	December	39,731,390	36,076,073	75,807,463
1999	January	41,143,162	34,025,293	75,168,455
	February	45,015,339	33,119,380	78,134,719
	March	34,966,954	44,638,085	79,605,039
	April	34,623,366	44,195,505	78,818,871
	May	34,889,797	42,621,838	77,511,635
	June	35,536,370	37,977,406	73,513,776
	July	35,374,638	42,217,393	77,592,031
	August	34,472,469	45,133,568	79,606,037
	September	33,824,345	45,566,758	79,391,103
	October	33,608,471	45,546,418	79,154,889
	November	33,551,213	44,864,649	78,415,862
	December	27,938,474	48,056,048	75,994,522
2000	January	28,218,317	45,730,145	73,948,462
	February	28,778,744	65,003,696	93,782,440
	March	36,268,761	67,990,735	104,259,496
	April	28,224,388	74,364,580	102,588,968
	May	26,381,397	72,903,682	99,285,079
	June	27,253,384	75,459,430	102,712,814
	July	25,114,032	77,176,922	102,290,954
	August	23,216,925	74,661,578	97,878,503
	September	22,905,824	76,645,930	99,551,754
	October	21,975,302	73,773,921	95,749,223
	November	20,492,787	75,224,472	95,717,259
	December	23,581,876	70,401,291	93,983,167
2001	January	24,818,365	68,376,467	93,194,832
	February	25,978,135	72,680,650	98,658,785
	March	29,548,156	67,145,444	96,693,600
	April	28,577,377	67,167,204	95,744,581
	May	27,393,422	68,696,703	96,090,125
	June	28,204,631	70,495,433	98,700,064
	July	36,392,330	64,102,014	100,494,344
	August	36,440,680	66,328,997	102,769,677
	September	34,839,925	66,698,130	101,538,055
	October	36,640,993	67,340,623	103,981,616
	November	34,934,455	70,300,573	105,235,028
	December	34,715,333	69,832,178	104,547,511
2002	January	34,494,716	67,900,097	102,394,813
	February	32,428,939	68,554,133	100,983,072
	March	33,243,387	68,932,187	102,175,574
	April	32,389,844	71,533,549	103,923,393
	May	33,757,824	74,068,776	107,826,600
	June	32,133,892	74,432,507	106,566,399
	July	42,706,117	63,434,826	106,140,943
	August	46,886,596	61,202,926	108,089,522
	September	46,218,923	61,322,723	107,541,646
	October	48,334,900	59,547,885	107,882,785
	November	47,645,570	59,458,840	107,104,410
	December	45,734,368	61,660,853	107,395,221

Comex Inventories
Troy Ounces

		Eligible	Registered	Total
2003	January	50,562,260	56,514,494	107,076,754
	February	50,484,559	58,647,084	109,131,643
	March	50,500,867	58,189,084	108,689,951
	April	53,168,722	54,999,604	108,168,326
	May	59,025,032	46,067,341	105,092,373
	June	61,179,745	46,042,085	107,221,830
	July	65,315,896	41,186,781	106,502,677
	August	60,982,910	43,861,897	104,844,807
	September	60,407,335	45,451,486	105,858,821
	October	60,061,555	55,401,789	115,463,344
	November	60,430,739	64,104,546	124,535,285
	December	59,970,714	64,300,016	124,270,730
2004	January	72,056,800	52,123,986	124,180,786
	February	70,368,603	52,825,960	123,194,563
	March	70,198,328	51,889,166	122,087,494
	April	72,266,724	50,420,414	122,687,138
	May	71,605,034	46,867,062	118,472,096
	June	52,764,168	65,605,072	118,369,240
	July	52,976,426	63,276,608	116,253,034
	August	52,632,893	56,678,487	109,311,380
	September	45,350,018	62,439,079	107,789,097
	October	42,970,021	61,654,128	104,624,149
	November	41,511,949	61,319,474	102,831,423
	December	42,302,549	61,287,203	103,589,752
2005	January	40,765,019	61,594,562	102,359,581
	February	40,435,337	61,058,686	101,494,023
	March	41,688,765	61,938,594	103,627,359
	April	38,851,493	65,143,967	103,995,460
	May	60,118,068	44,910,706	105,028,774
	June	60,314,695	44,404,436	104,719,131
	July	58,880,816	50,585,264	109,466,080
	August	56,040,938	59,547,308	115,588,246
	September	56,338,376	60,348,359	116,686,735
	October	56,707,193	59,549,790	116,256,983
	November	52,036,979	65,570,801	117,607,780
	December	51,925,748	68,048,244	119,973,992
2006	January	56,693,377	68,099,235	124,792,612
	February	55,602,621	72,295,794	127,898,415
	March	52,883,807	72,134,632	125,018,439
	April	50,366,357	73,306,429	123,672,786
	May	49,035,059	59,806,533	108,841,592
	June	53,888,844	48,379,108	102,267,952
	July	54,581,537	44,427,711	99,009,248
	August	59,789,785	43,844,166	103,633,951
	September	41,860,766	63,359,473	105,220,239
	October	41,936,630	63,967,485	105,904,115
	November	43,854,607	63,915,798	107,770,405
	December	42,978,703	68,092,069	111,070,772
2007	January	40,230,953	73,738,727	113,969,680
	February	40,175,700	77,017,356	117,193,056
	March	46,099,254	79,676,282	125,775,536
	April	50,705,366	80,682,365	131,387,731
	May	50,263,196	80,233,963	130,497,159
	June	67,326,637	66,743,167	134,069,804
	July	62,688,362	69,417,607	132,105,969
	August	63,230,331	68,668,082	131,898,413
	September	57,805,695	74,818,218	132,623,913
	October	60,122,505	73,582,186	133,704,691
	November	46,197,101	88,171,409	134,368,510
	December	43,199,020	89,427,093	132,626,113

Silver Yearbook 2010 - Inventories — CPM Group

Comex Inventories
Troy Ounces

		Eligible	Registered	Total
2008	January	47,252,737	88,233,925	135,486,662
	February	46,691,952	88,344,972	135,036,924
	March	45,296,025	90,584,666	135,880,691
	April	42,910,257	90,602,091	133,512,348
	May	47,534,597	87,539,541	135,074,138
	June	55,099,430	80,859,308	135,958,738
	July	55,310,523	83,903,309	139,213,832
	August	51,690,290	86,891,886	138,582,176
	September	50,157,896	85,345,613	135,503,509
	October	47,535,910	82,653,850	130,189,760
	November	47,851,650	80,738,570	128,590,220
	December	60,693,580	66,998,730	127,692,310
2009	January	52,483,320	69,741,600	122,224,920
	February	56,197,070	67,925,340	124,122,410
	March	53,835,410	71,557,460	125,392,870
	April	52,816,330	63,402,220	116,218,550
	May	56,325,360	63,763,270	120,088,630
	June	55,366,350	62,208,560	117,574,910
	July	55,119,710	62,590,550	117,710,260
	August	54,714,670	61,659,060	116,373,730
	September	57,721,030	57,692,160	115,413,190
	October	61,961,990	55,346,290	117,308,280
	November	58,875,300	52,718,400	111,593,700
	December	57,393,650	54,376,760	111,770,410

Notes: Stocks are month-end. *Comex began reporting Wilmington Trust stocks eligible for The Comex deliver in the fourth quarter of 1996. Wilmington became a licensed Comex silver depository as of January 1, 1997.
Source: Comex.
March 12, 2010

Markets

Markets

Trading in the major international silver markets was 85.7 billion ounces in 2009, down from 102.0 billion ounces in 2008. The dollar value of silver market transactions was $1.26 trillion last year, down from a record $1.53 trillion in 2008. However, last year's dollar value of the silver market was the second highest since clearing volume data for the London bullion market began to be published and included in these statistics in 1997. Despite the decline last year, silver market volumes remained healthy overall.

The physical flow of newly refined silver from mines and scrap recycling accounted for slightly less than 1.0% of silver market trading in 2009. This is not an unusual figure since most of the trading that occurs in the silver market is more related to investment and trading activity, and is settled for cash. Trading volume through futures and options exchanges accounted for 70.5% of these trades, while the remaining 28.5% of the silver volumes was cleared through the over the counter market centered in London.

Investors remained active market participants in the silver market in 2009. Even though trading volumes were off from 2008 levels, they were still high by historical standards. Activity remained at high levels from both short-term and longer term investors. As discussed elsewhere in this report investors have been buying a great deal of physical silver over the past two years.

The Silver Market
Annual Total, Through 2009.

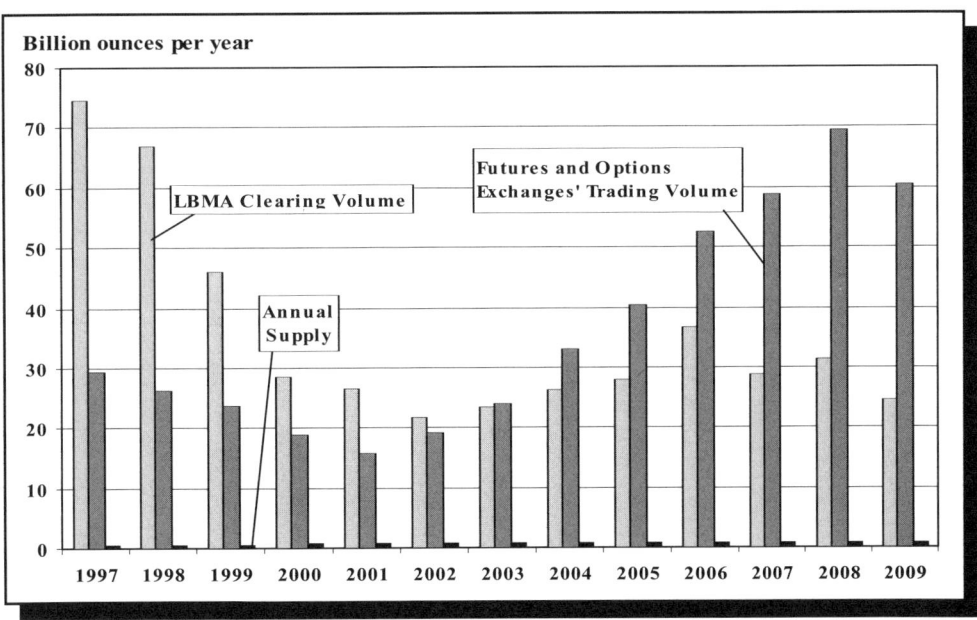

Silver Yearbook 2010 - Markets — CPM Group

The Silver Market 1997 - 2009
Million Ounces

	1997	1998	1999	2000	2001	2002	2003	2004	2005	2006	2007	2008	2009
Annual Supply	608.1	649.0	686.3	733.5	744.8	725.3	730.8	736.0	778.6	783.4	785.5	806.9	826.1
Futures and Options Exchanges Trading Volume	29,478.1	26,218.9	23,885.3	19,032.3	15,911.0	19,259.9	23,974.6	33,205.8	40,496.4	52,458.4	58,725.8	69,641.2	60,428.4
London Bullion Market Association Clearing Volume	74,573.9	67,059.3	46,111.9	28,475.4	26,552.5	21,888.9	23,460.0	26,402.5	27,886.4	36,784.7	28,951.3	31,517.8	24,454.4
Total	104,660.1	93,927.2	70,683.5	48,241.1	43,208.3	41,874.1	48,165.4	60,344.3	69,161.4	90,026.4	88,462.6	101,965.9	85,708.9
Ratio: Trading: Annual Supply	171:1	144:1	102:1	65:1	57:1	57:1	65:1	81:1	88:1	114:1	112:1	125:1	103:1
Average Price	$4.91	$5.53	$5.23	$5.00	$4.38	$4.60	$4.90	$6.70	$7.35	$11.61	$13.45	$14.97	$14.67
Dollar Value ($Bil)	$514	$519	$370	$241	$189	$193	$236	$404	$508	$1,045	$1,190	$1,526	$1,258

Source: CPM Group
March 10, 2010

Trading activity in the silver futures and options markets declined in 2009, after reaching record levels in 2008. Despite the decline in trading activity last year, combined volumes were still the second highest on record. In 2008 there was a record combined trading volume of silver futures and options, measuring 69.6 billion ounces. This activity fell to 60.4 million ounces last year, down sharply from the prior year, but higher than 58.7 billion ounces traded in 2007.

Combined futures and options data here includes the New York Commodities Exchange (Comex), the Tokyo Commodities Exchange (Tocom), the NYSE Liffe (formerly the Chicago Board of Trade or CBOT), and the Multi Commodity Exchange of India (MCX). The Comex and the CBOT became part of the CME Group in 2008. The NYSE Euronext group acquired the CBOT's gold and silver trading operations in September 2008. Silver is traded on other markets around the world, but these four exchanges represent the bulk of silver futures and options trading.

There have been reports from officials at the Shanghai Futures Exchange (SHFE) that silver futures trading may eventually begin at the SHFE. Other futures products also are being discussed. Gold futures trading was launched at the SHFE in 2008. Volumes are low compared to Comex, the largest gold futures exchange, but activity is on par with the other exchanges that trade gold futures.

London Bullion Market Association

Clearing volume handled by members of the London Bullion Market Association also declined last year. Volume fell to 24.5 billion ounces, the lowest level since 2003, when clearing volume was 23.5 billion ounces. Over the past several years trading activity has been moving toward the futures and options markets.

London clearing volumes hit a low of 21.9 billion ounces in 2003. After that clearing volumes rose, peaking in 2006 at 36.8 billion ounces. The LBMA first began to make clearing statistics publicly available in October 1996. The first full year of statistics was for 1997.

The decline in clearing activity since 2006 reflects several factors. The most significant factor behind it probably was the move away from proprietary trading in silver by major bullion banks and trading companies in the years 2007 - 2009. The proprietary trading of these banks is estimated to have represented the bulk of the enormous clearing volumes of 1997 - 1998. Volumes fell sharply from that point forward, until 2003, as banks liquidated or severely cut back their proprietary trading desks. The often-temporary marked to market losses that banks suffered when gold prices spiked sharply higher in September and October 1999 served as an impetus for many bullion trading banks and brokerage companies to pull back from their proprietary trading, as the price spike emphasized the risks the banks were taking on in these trades. Many banks already had been considering cutting back or closing their precious metals and commodities trading operations at that time, and the events of late 1999 only served to help convince the banks' managements that they should reduce their exposure to commodities. Banks stayed out of the markets until 2003 and 2004, by which time commodities were becoming a hot and marketable product to investors. The banks began to rebuild their commodities operations, including some increases in proprietary trading, somewhat in the period 2003 - 2006, but the financial crunch that began to emerge in 2007 put an end to many of these programs once again.

Additionally, part of the decline since 2006 may have reflected a move from over the counter forwards and options to organized futures and options exchanges. Last year's clearing activity through LBMA members was less than half of the 60.4 billion ounces traded through organized exchanges. The last time LBMA activity was higher than combined trading activity of organized exchanges was in 2002.

The LBMA provides three basic monthly data sets which include the average daily clearing volume, the average daily value of all trades cleared, and the average number of transfers per day. This data enables the calculation of other data series, including the average trade size in ounces. The average trade size in

London Bullion Market Association - Average Transaction Size

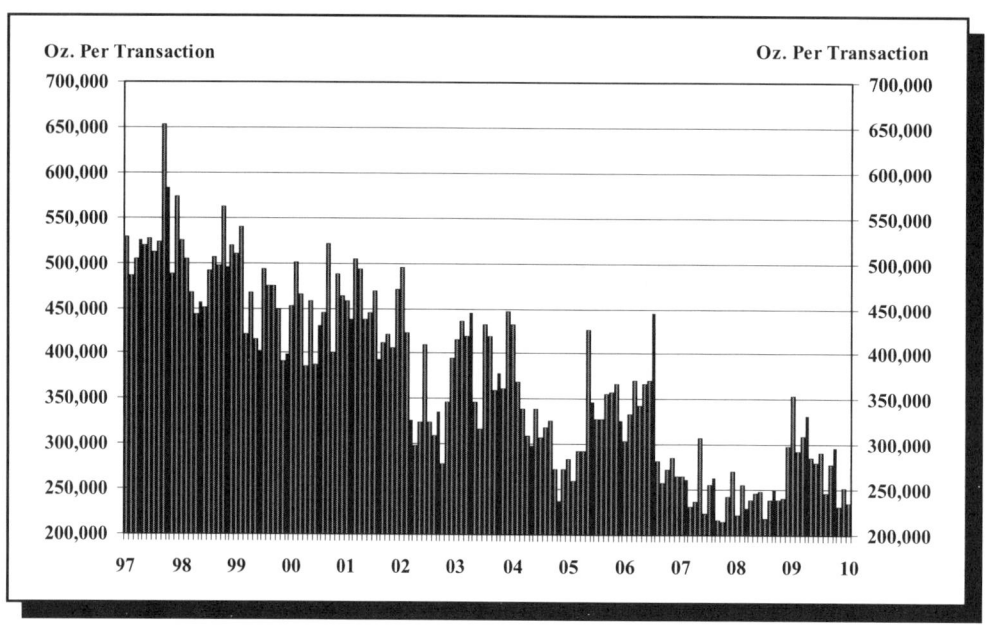

2009 was 287,483 ounces, up from 244,061 ounces in the prior year. The sharp increase in the average trade size was off sharply from the average trade size of 398,978 ounces between October 1996 and 2007, however.

The average value per trade also increased in 2009, to $4.17 million from $3.63 million in 2008. Last year's average value per trade was a record, topping 2006's average value per trade of $3.75 million.

Trading activity through the LBMA remains healthy despite the decline seen in various areas of clearing data. The 24.5 billion ounces cleared through the LBMA in 2009 was still 30 times greater than the physical flow of newly refined silver last year.

Futures and Options

Combined futures trading volume of the Comex, MCX, NYSE Liffe, and Tocom was 55.1 billion ounces in 2009, down 9.9% from a record 61.1 billion ounces in 2008. The decline in combined trading volume last year was the first since 2001, when trading volume was 13.5 billion ounces. Despite the decline in futures trading activity last year, the volume was four times greater than trading activity in 2001. Last year's combined futures trading volume also was the second highest on record, surpassing 52.4 billion ounces traded in 2007.

Trading Volumes on Major Silver Exchanges

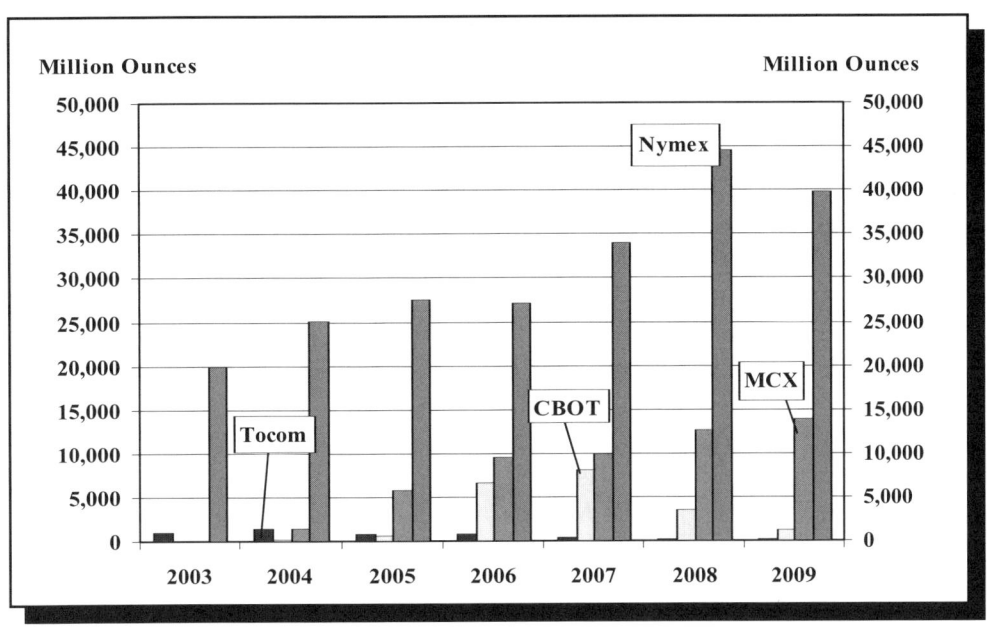

Trading activity during the first two months of this year was 11.9 billion ounces. At this pace, futures trading volume could reach 71 billion ounces, a record level. Although trading volumes may not keep up this pace, trading activity should be expected to be at very high levels again this year.

The Comex remained the largest futures trading venue in 2009, accounting for 72.5% of all silver futures traded at these major exchanges around the world. (There are other exchanges that trade smaller volumes of silver, not included in these figures.) Futures trading volume at the Comex was 39.9 billion ounces last year, down from a record 44.6 billion ounces in 2008. Last year's volume was the second highest on record, topping 34.0 billion ounces in 2007. Trading activity remained healthy during the first couple of months of 2010, reaching 9.1 billion ounces. As with the total futures volumes, the Comex volumes in the first two months of 2010 are running at a record pace.

The MCX, the second largest futures exchange by volume since 2005, continued to see annual trading volumes rise last year. This marked the fifth consecutive year of rising volumes, since 2004. The MCX began trading silver futures contracts on 10 November 2003. Trading activity at the MCX was 13.8 billion ounces in 2009, up from 12.7 billion ounces in 2008. This increase in futures trading volume at the MCX pushes the exchange's market share of silver futures activity to 25.2% from 20.7% in 2008.

Silver futures trading volume at NYSE Liffe was 1.19 billion ounces in 2009. This was off sharply from 3.6 billion ounces in 2008. Trading volume during the first two months of 2010 suggests a possible increase to 1.4 billion ounces this year.

Tocom silver futures trading volume was 107.7 million ounces in 2009, down from 290.5 million ounces in 2008. Last year's trading activity at Tocom was a record low since the exchange began trading silver futures in 1985. Tocom has been aggressively trying to recoup market share over the past few years. Trading volumes were 28.9 million ounces during the first two months of 2010. On an annualized basis could rise to 170 million ounces.

Combined open interest of silver futures was 657.3 million ounces at the end of 2009, up from 461.9 million ounces in 2008. Combined open interest ended last year relatively high, compared to the average year-end open interest from 1985 to 2009 of 522.5 million ounces.

Comex accounted for the majority of year-end open interest last year, 94.4% of the total at 620.3 million ounces. Open interest rose from 429.6 million ounces at the end of 2008. By the end of February 2010 open interest had declined to 538.2 million ounces from end 2009.

Open interest of silver futures on the MCX was 22.5 million ounces at the end of 2009, up from 12.8 million ounces at year-end 2008. Although the MCX accounted for around a quarter of combined futures trading volume in 2009, it only accounted for 3.4% of combined open interest at the end of last year.

The NYSE Liffe had silver futures open interest at 11.3 million ounces at the end of 2009, down from 14.2 million ounces at the end of 2008. Open interest had declined to 10.8 million ounces by the end of February 2010.

At the end of 2009 open interest of silver futures on the Tocom was 3.2 million ounces, down from 5.3 million ounces at the end of 2008. Similar to the trend in silver futures trading volume at the Tocom, open interest at the end of last year was a record low since Tocom began its silver futures operation in 1985. At the end of February of this year open interested was 3.7 million ounces.

Trading volume of combined Comex put and call options in 2009 fell to 5.4 billion ounces, down from a record 8.5 billion ounces in 2008. Despite the sharp decline in options trading volume it was still a healthy figure. Trading volume of call options was 3.0 billion ounces last year, down from 5.3 billion ounces in the prior year. Trading volume of put options meanwhile fell to 2.4 billion ounces from 3.2 billion ounces in 2008. Part of the decline in options trading activity may reflect the decline in price volatility levels from 2008 to 2009.

Additionally, with silver prices at elevated levels there has been a marked reduction in silver hedging using options by industrial users, which have shown reluctance to hedge at higher prices. There also has been a decline in hedging byproduct silver production by mining companies, further reducing options volumes.

Open interest of combined Comex put and call options was 539.3 million ounces at the end of 2009, up from 456.2 million ounces at the end of 2008. Last year's year-end open interest was the third highest since 1985, when the Comex first began trading silver options. At the end of 2009 open interest of call options was 346.4 million ounces, up from 333.5 million ounces at the end of 2008. Year-end 2009 open interest of put options was 192.9 million ounces, up from 122.7 million ounces at the end of 2008.

The put to call ratio was 0.36:1 at the beginning of 2009. Many market participants on the Comex began to purchase an increased amount of call options during the second half of 2008 into 2009. This may have been based on rising demand for silver as a safe haven and an expectation that prices could rise. Investors may have wanted to have the option of buying silver. This occurred during the depths of the recession, but by the end of 2009 the put to call ratio had increased to 0.55:1.

Silver Yearbook 2010 - Markets — CPM Group

London Bullion Market Clearing Turnover
Daily Averages

Ounces Transferred (Million Ounces)

	1996	1997	1998	1999	2000	2001	2002	2003	2004	2005	2006	2007	2008	2009	2010
January	-	294.4	330.4	214.2	149.2	105.1	175.7	89.7	143.4	76.9	124.5	98.8	117.6	111.7	70.4
February	-	275.0	347.8	277.3	172.7	102.0	108.7	107.5	121.5	77.5	152.9	108.1	132.4	105.8	
March	-	284.1	272.1	188.8	134.0	131.3	77.9	90.0	128.7	93.8	187.9	112.0	154.7	98.8	
April	-	253.0	230.7	198.2	106.9	121.6	68.8	79.2	133.8	87.6	238.1	105.7	119.2	101.1	
May	-	236.6	266.5	189.0	121.0	110.2	99.9	78.9	94.7	152.1	205.7	137.5	121.2	97.5	
June	-	270.5	217.9	161.3	97.0	99.8	107.2	61.3	95.1	123.4	164.3	112.4	119.5	100.0	
July	-	270.6	233.5	191.3	93.3	99.5	72.9	108.3	93.6	95.1	169.5	114.9	105.5	90.5	
August	-	263.3	223.4	196.1	100.5	89.4	66.2	97.8	82.5	104.4	94.7	120.8	149.8	79.3	
September	-	314.3	232.2	176.3	117.0	96.7	61.7	96.2	82.3	126.8	110.4	108.1	143.7	113	
October	279.4	345.5	249.4	182.4	82.2	101.9	67.5	101.3	92.0	124.7	98.6	106.4	136.2	101.1	
November	244.3	327.9	169.1	125.9	97.6	91.4	58.2	89.6	75.5	132	108.8	129	107.6	81	
December	248.8	395.8	202.2	119.9	116.4	147.3	79.1	110.1	102.2	131.3	107.7	119.1	102.1	88	

Value in Billions of Dollars

	1996	1997	1998	1999	2000	2001	2002	2003	2004	2005	2006	2007	2008	2009	2010
January	-	1.4	1.9	1.1	0.77	0.49	0.77	0.43	0.91	0.51	1.14	1.27	1.88	1.26	1.23
February	-	1.4	2.4	1.5	0.91	0.46	0.48	0.50	0.78	0.54	1.46	1.50	2.33	1.42	
March	-	1.5	1.7	1.0	0.68	0.58	0.35	0.41	0.93	0.68	1.95	1.48	3.02	1.30	
April	-	1.2	1.5	1.0	0.54	0.53	0.31	0.36	0.94	0.62	3.00	1.45	2.09	1.27	
May	-	1.1	1.5	1.0	0.60	0.49	0.47	0.37	0.55	1.07	2.80	1.81	2.07	1.37	
June	-	1.3	1.1	0.8	0.48	0.44	0.52	0.28	0.56	0.90	1.77	1.48	2.03	1.46	
July	-	1.2	1.3	1.0	0.46	0.42	0.36	0.52	0.59	0.67	1.90	1.48	1.90	1.21	
August	-	1.2	1.2	1.0	0.49	0.38	0.30	0.49	0.55	0.74	1.15	1.49	2.20	1.14	
September	-	1.5	1.2	0.9	0.57	0.42	0.28	0.50	0.53	0.91	1.29	1.39	1.78	1.85	
October	1.4	1.7	1.2	1.0	0.40	0.45	0.30	0.51	0.65	0.96	1.14	1.45	1.42	1.74	
November	1.2	1.7	0.8	0.6	0.46	0.38	0.26	0.46	0.57	1.04	1.41	1.90	1.06	1.39	
December	1.2	2.3	1.0	0.6	0.54	0.64	0.37	0.62	0.73	1.13	1.44	1.72	1.05	1.55	

Number of Transfers

	1996	1997	1998	1999	2000	2001	2002	2003	2004	2005	2006	2007	2008	2009	2010
January	-	557	630	420	329	229	355	216	332	272	410	374	529	315	298
February	-	565	690	514	344	233	257	247	329	299	457	415	517	362	
March	-	562	581	448	288	260	239	215	380	321	506	484	676	319	
April	-	482	520	423	277	246	230	178	431	299	693	446	500	305	
May	-	455	583	454	264	252	307	228	317	357	561	446	490	342	
June	-	513	484	400	250	224	262	193	280	355	442	503	480	358	
July	-	528	474	387	217	212	224	251	305	289	380	449	481	310	
August	-	503	441	413	226	227	214	233	259	318	337	458	625	322	
September	-	481	466	371	224	235	184	267	252	356	427	497	576	406	
October	481	592	443	407	205	242	243	268	337	349	361	496	569	341	
November	484	671	341	322	200	225	168	248	319	359	381	533	446	350	
December	493	691	389	300	251	312	200	246	375	403	406	439	343	348	

Note: * partly estimated.
Value is calculated using the monthly average London fixing for silver. Allocations between Clearing Members where the sole purpose is for overnight credit and physical movements arranged by Clearing Members in locations other than London are excluded.
Source: London Bullion Market Association, CPM Group.
March 10, 2010

London Bullion Market Association - Ounces of Silver Transferred

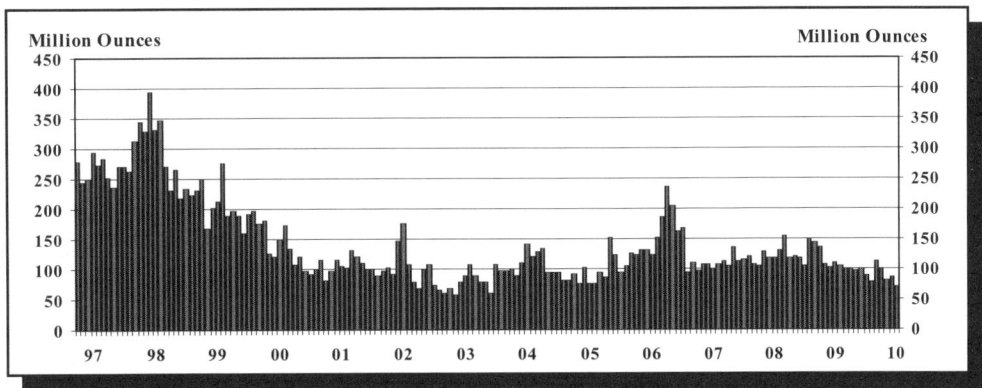

Value of Silver Transferred

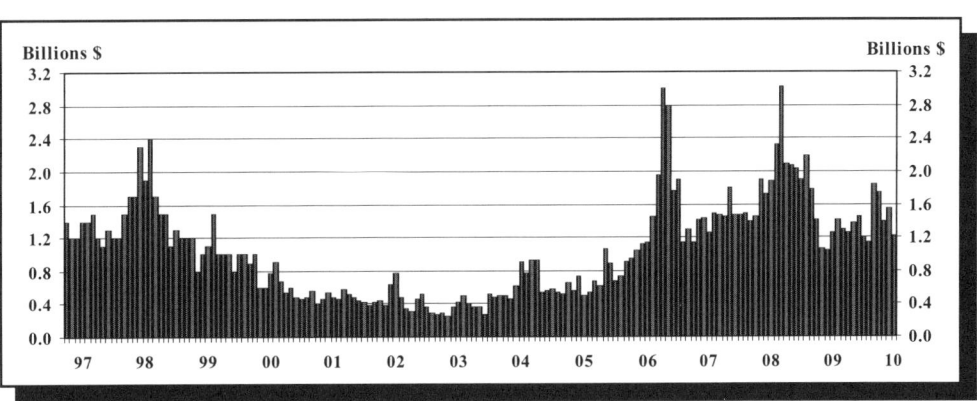

Number of Transfers

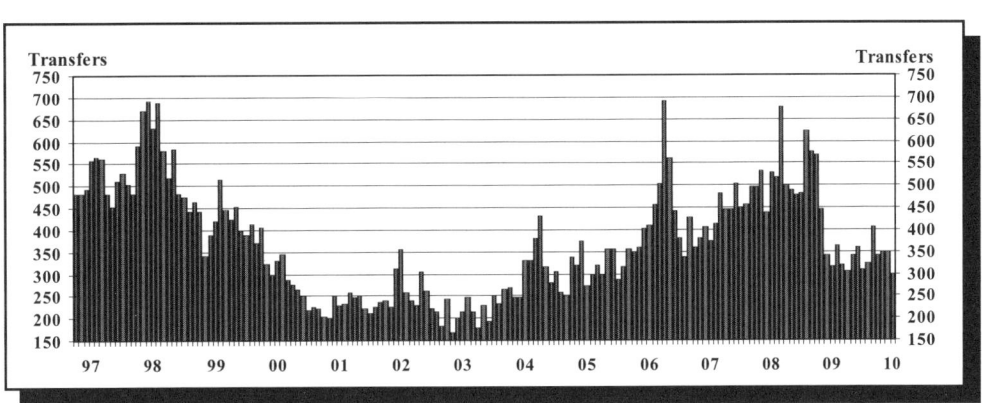

Trading Volume in the Futures Markets
Annual Total, Through 2009.

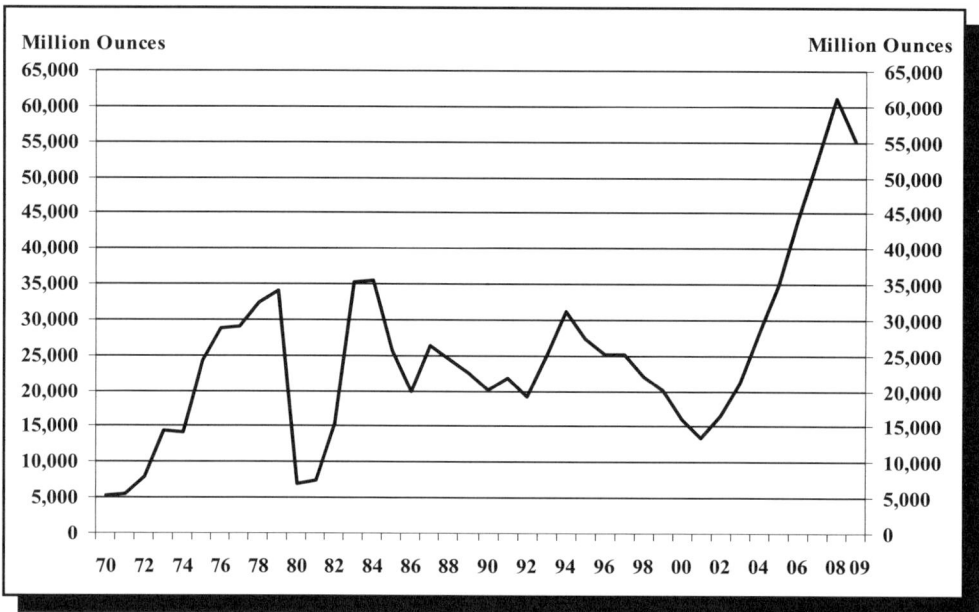

Open Interest in the Futures Markets
Year-end, Through 2009. 2010 Through end-February.

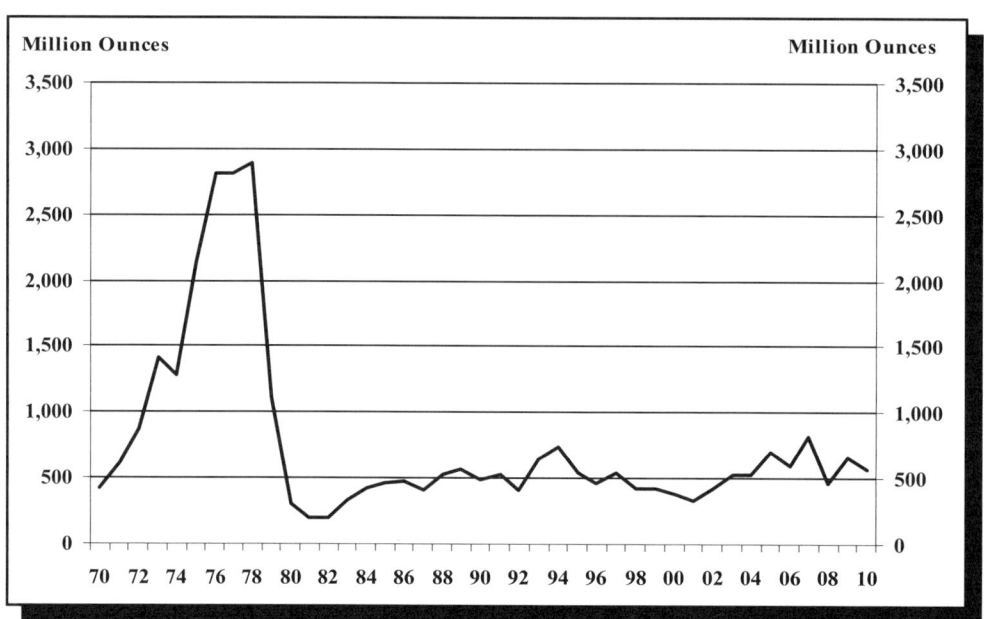

Trading Volume in the Options Market - Puts and Calls
Annual Total, Through 2009.

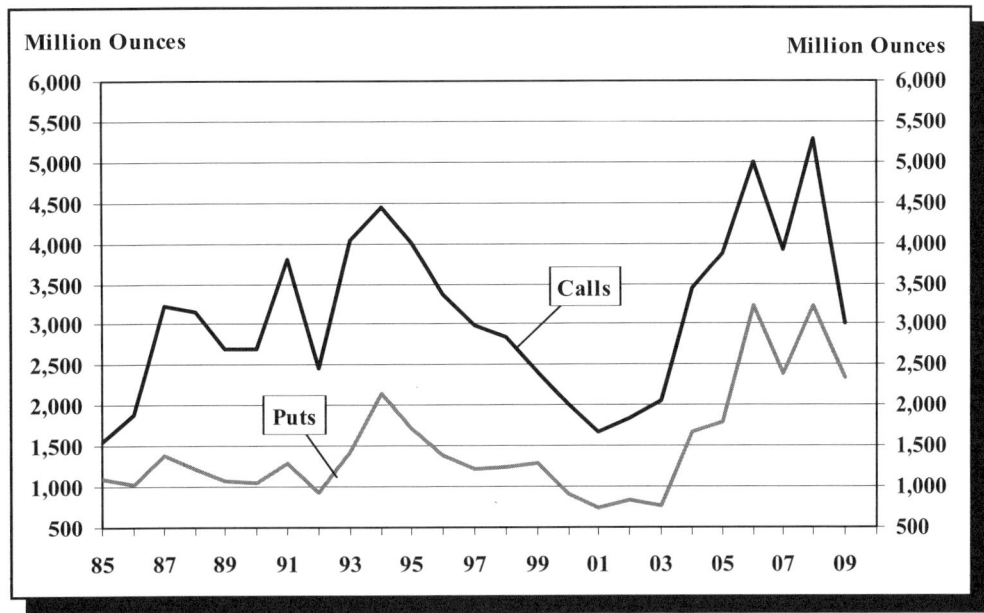

Open Interest in the Options Market - Puts and Calls
Year-end, Through 2009.

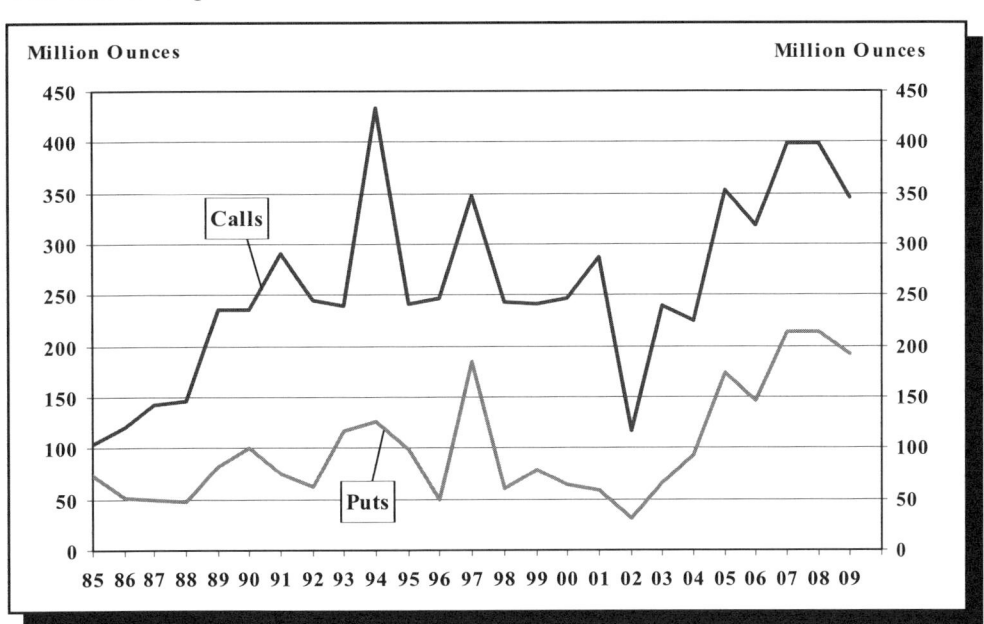

Silver YearBook 2010 - Markets — CPM Group

Silver Futures Exchange Activity
Million Troy Ounces

	\multicolumn{5}{c}{Trading Volume}				
	Comex	NYSE Liffe	Tocom	MCX	Total
1970	3,468.5	1,813.1	—	—	5,281.6
1971	3,081.2	2,520.5	—	—	5,601.7
1972	4,074.5	3,770.2	—	—	7,844.7
1973	6,189.3	8,153.0	—	—	14,342.3
1974	6,829.6	7,314.0	—	—	14,143.6
1975	14,511.6	9,763.5	—	—	24,275.1
1976	18,709.5	10,055.2	—	—	28,764.7
1977	17,700.2	11,285.3	—	—	28,985.5
1978	19,110.4	13,289.2	—	—	32,399.6
1979	20,403.1	13,602.9	—	—	34,006.0
1980	5,293.7	1,705.2	—	—	6,998.9
1981	6,203.6	1,257.3	—	—	7,460.9
1982	14,188.1	1,163.6	—	—	15,351.7
1983	32,619.9	2,750.5	—	—	35,370.4
1984	33,712.5	1,887.3	—	—	35,599.8
1985	24,106.0	1,034.8	591.1	—	25,731.9
1986	19,248.4	511.2	227.1	—	19,986.7
1987	25,278.3	597.0	473.2	—	26,348.5
1988	23,323.3	502.4	740.2	—	24,565.8
1989	21,833.1	266.7	420.8	—	22,520.6
1990	19,568.5	192.0	486.4	—	20,246.9
1991	20,773.5	117.5	1,020.1	—	21,911.1
1992	18,941.6	55.1	223.6	—	19,220.3
1993	24,279.6	94.3	639.9	—	25,013.8
1994	29,971.7	139.8	1,005.2	—	31,116.7
1995	25,773.7	139.9	1,389.2	—	27,302.7
1996	24,354.0	42.1	726.3	—	25,122.5
1997	24,467.6	31.2	764.7	—	25,263.5
1998	20,473.1	35.5	1,620.1	—	22,128.7
1999	19,234.5	21.2	932.5	—	20,188.2
2000	15,585.2	12.6	538.9	—	16,136.7
2001	12,846.0	10.5	637.4	—	13,493.9
2002	15,677.8	8.1	897.9	—	16,583.8
2003	20,020.2	34.8	1,119.4	0.1	21,174.5
2004	25,030.6	266.2	1,421.1	1,376.1	28,094.1
2005	27,681.8	594.5	788.6	5,772.6	34,837.5
2006	27,165.3	6,589.5	827.7	9,641.0	44,223.6
2007	34,036.1	8,018.3	517.5	9,866.4	52,438.3
2008	44,585.9	3,601.0	290.5	12,659.4	61,136.8
2009	39,909.4	1,187.0	107.7	13,871.1	55,075.3
2010YTD	9,105.2	240.6	28.9	2,568.9	11,943.5

Notes: Trading volume is the total for the year. 2010 through February. Open interest is month-end, 2010 through February. Sources: New York Commodity Exchange, Silver futures trading on CBOT was acquired by NYSE Liffe as of September 2008. Tokyo Commodity Exchange , Multi Commodity Exchange.
March 9, 2010

Silver Futures Exchange Activity
Million Troy Ounces

	Open Interest				
Comex	NYSE Liffe	Tocom	MCX	Total	
230.9	191.2	—	—	422.1	1970
245.5	366.7	—	—	612.2	1971
327.8	544.7	—	—	872.5	1972
428.0	981.6	—	—	1,409.6	1973
658.4	623.5	—	—	1,281.9	1974
1,276.4	864.5	—	—	2,140.9	1975
2,138.7	680.3	—	—	2,819.0	1976
1,404.9	1,409.8	—	—	2,814.7	1977
1,549.0	1,343.9	—	—	2,892.9	1978
636.8	468.7	—	—	1,105.5	1979
166.2	143.1	—	—	309.3	1980
140.0	56.3	—	—	196.3	1981
169.0	34.8	—	—	203.8	1982
301.7	32.4	—	—	334.1	1983
401.5	26.8	—	—	428.3	1984
430.7	18.5	17.6	—	466.8	1985
449.1	12.7	12.3	—	474.1	1986
371.2	11.2	24.8	—	407.2	1987
470.0	13.5	47.2	—	530.7	1988
474.2	9.7	80.2	—	564.1	1989
421.7	10.9	49.8	—	482.3	1990
488.8	6.1	38.0	—	532.9	1991
381.3	6.1	15.7	—	403.2	1992
578.9	7.0	62.1	—	648.0	1993
652.3	36.0	47.8	—	736.0	1994
492.8	2.5	51.9	—	547.2	1995
423.5	1.8	30.4	—	455.7	1996
494.5	1.2	42.5	—	538.2	1997
376.8	1.1	41.3	—	419.2	1998
381.9	1.2	35.6	—	418.8	1999
360.6	1.3	18.9	—	380.7	2000
315.5	0.3	15.4	—	331.2	2001
404.6	0.3	19.1	—	424.0	2002
511.3	1.4	21.0	0.0	533.7	2003
502.9	5.3	16.6	9.8	534.6	2004
656.1	10.8	16.3	19.6	702.9	2005
507.1	54.8	14.5	17.2	593.5	2006
770.6	28.3	9.2	11.3	819.4	2007
429.6	14.2	5.3	12.8	461.9	2008
620.3	11.3	3.2	22.5	657.3	2009
538.2	10.8	3.7	15.6	568.2	2010YTD

Comex - Trading Volume
Monthly, Through February 2010.

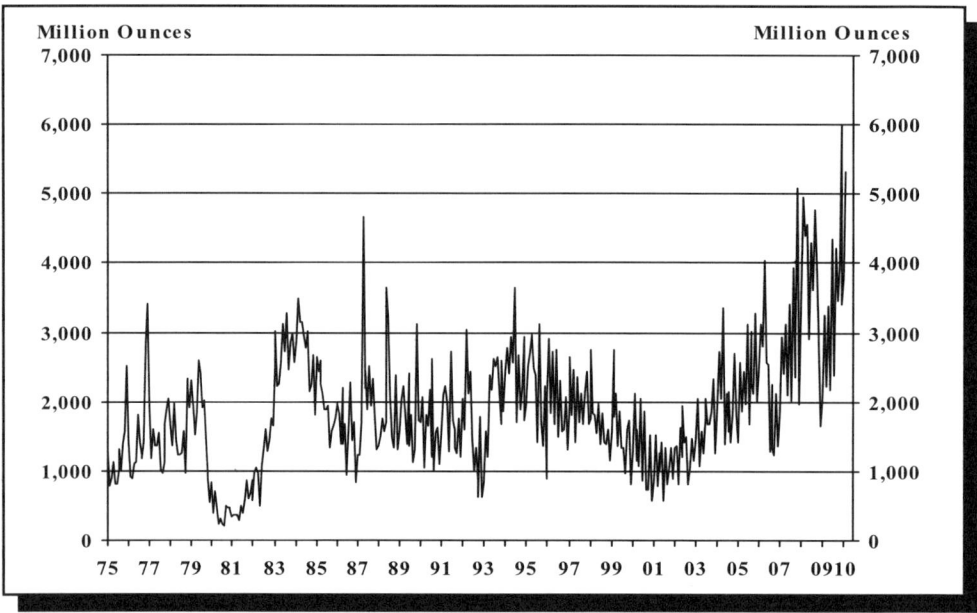

Comex - Open Interest
Month-end, Through February 2010.

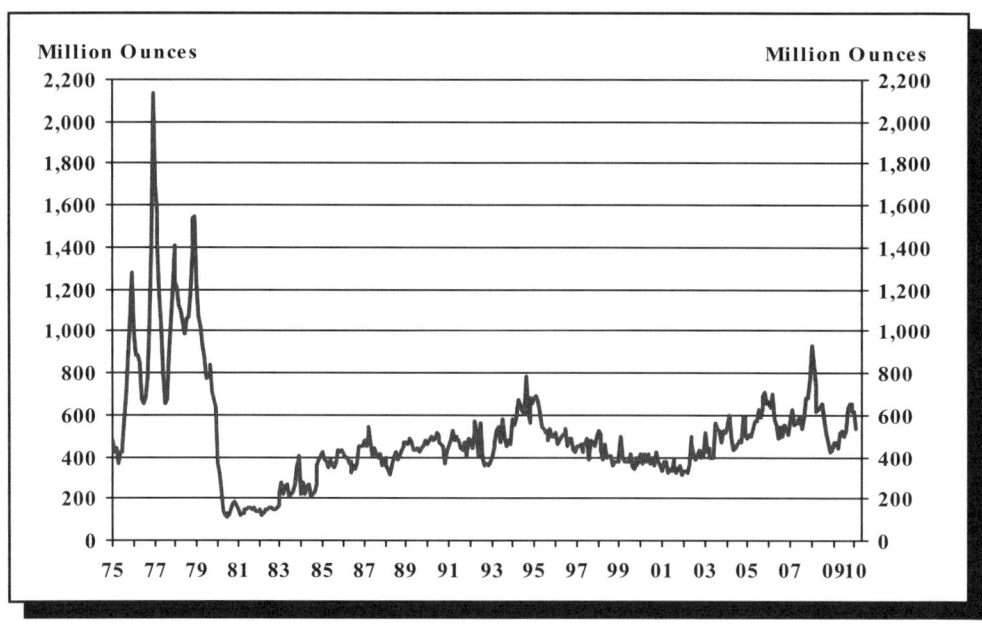

Tocom - Trading Volume

Monthly, Through February 2010.

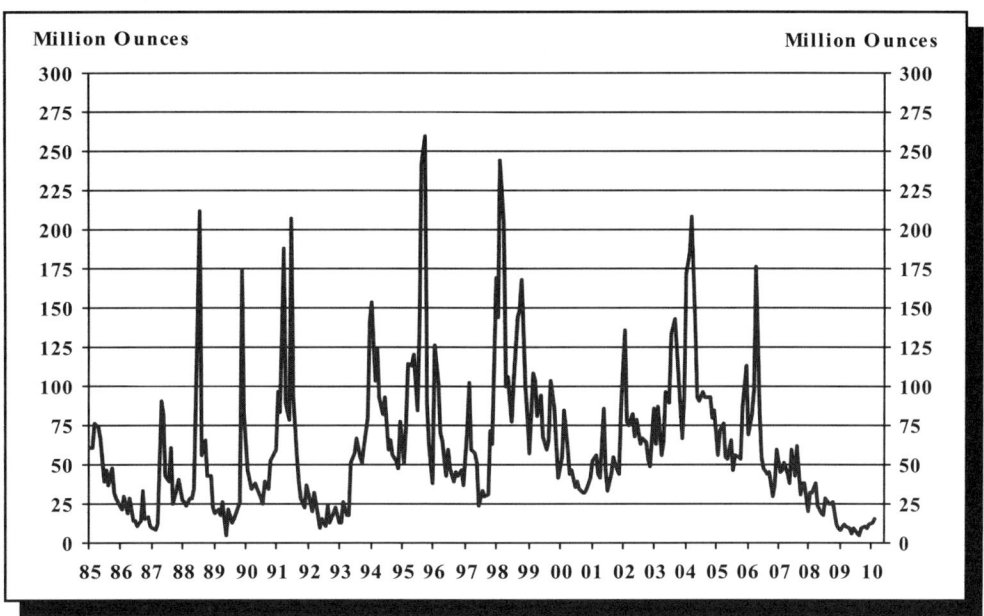

Tocom - Open Interest

Month-end, Through February 2010.

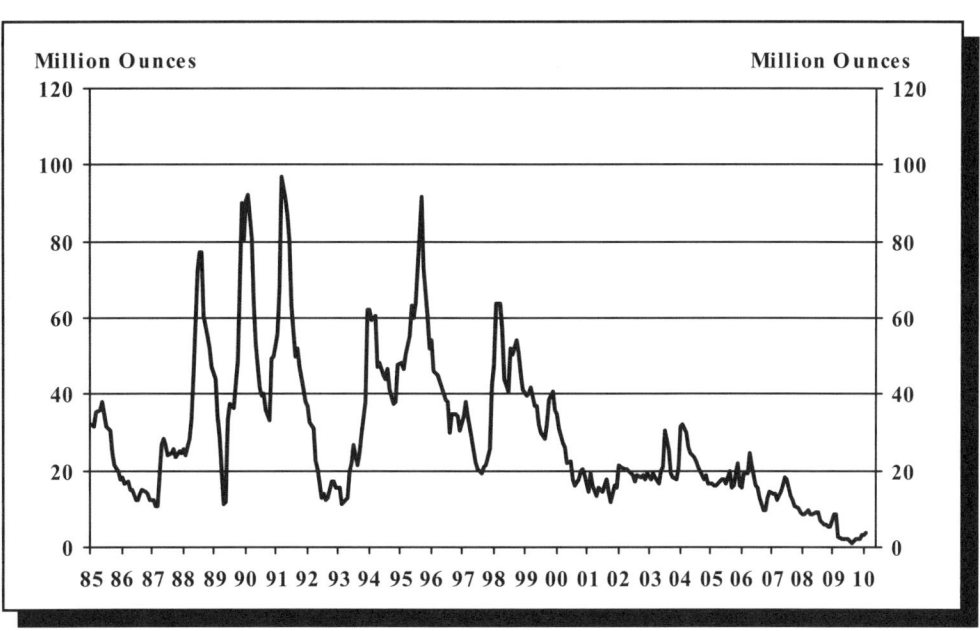

Silver Yearbook 2010 - Markets   CPM Group

Comex Trading Volume
Thousand Ounces

	1975	1976	1977	1978	1979	1980
January	1,277,415	1,414,390	1,927,810	1,650,015	2,299,675	838,665
February	777,410	912,215	1,191,535	1,353,430	1,941,390	380,785
March	897,705	904,350	1,593,455	1,954,990	1,522,985	717,365
April	1,118,530	1,092,145	1,371,570	1,437,350	1,836,625	469,865
May	809,070	1,129,005	1,367,295	1,224,720	2,587,495	233,090
June	825,540	1,814,445	1,545,700	1,236,180	2,402,495	316,300
July	1,024,830	1,426,260	1,010,710	1,270,555	1,919,265	228,240
August	1,322,000	1,229,505	970,615	1,580,935	2,020,290	208,930
September	987,705	1,175,930	1,114,725	960,045	1,465,965	504,555
October	1,393,015	1,403,615	1,671,705	2,345,235	958,500	464,595
November	1,573,875	2,792,515	1,899,965	2,189,865	892,995	478,115
December	2,504,480	3,415,165	2,035,150	1,907,105	555,415	453,165
Total	14,511,575	18,709,540	17,700,235	19,110,425	20,403,095	5,293,670

	1981	1982	1983	1984	1985	1986
January	353,450	563,915	2,554,445	2,853,930	2,659,165	1,970,040
February	355,225	969,410	3,007,130	3,493,840	2,439,950	1,844,575
March	374,555	1,057,695	2,233,185	3,478,740	2,592,200	1,387,955
April	363,075	964,700	2,264,275	3,149,325	2,248,800	2,194,000
May	290,245	498,490	2,580,325	3,133,730	2,123,830	1,400,655
June	486,960	1,086,795	3,118,505	2,936,830	1,889,500	1,680,350
July	386,770	1,315,360	2,726,465	2,773,345	1,888,405	939,480
August	580,055	1,586,215	3,282,270	3,007,745	1,942,655	1,588,995
September	859,335	1,290,145	2,460,115	2,156,285	1,338,265	2,273,190
October	607,240	1,444,480	2,844,905	2,246,105	1,569,820	1,433,400
November	682,895	1,753,185	2,984,705	2,671,160	1,663,850	1,694,670
December	863,795	1,657,705	2,563,585	1,811,505	1,749,590	841,125
Total	6,203,600	14,188,095	32,619,910	33,712,540	24,106,030	19,248,435

	1987	1988	1989	1990	1991	1992
January	1,236,730	1,370,490	1,585,760	1,715,875	1,549,205	2,040,895
February	1,239,790	1,505,595	2,042,425	2,066,435	2,100,460	1,601,130
March	1,715,890	1,744,525	2,236,615	1,050,965	2,232,455	3,036,685
April	4,663,655	1,569,635	1,771,175	1,820,275	1,979,785	2,127,235
May	2,193,070	1,705,725	1,392,480	1,644,520	1,277,740	2,426,950
June	2,432,050	3,634,300	2,423,555	2,169,240	2,737,475	1,476,790
July	1,893,700	3,194,670	1,361,270	1,211,440	1,723,415	989,730
August	2,513,645	2,058,325	1,801,905	2,624,075	1,603,195	1,331,735
September	1,951,330	1,499,290	1,124,630	1,006,365	1,343,300	865,825
October	2,340,320	1,341,915	1,305,510	1,542,245	1,264,915	627,685
November	1,779,465	2,376,870	3,110,615	1,618,320	1,748,490	1,778,640
December	1,318,615	1,321,935	1,727,115	1,098,790	1,213,085	638,270
Total	25,278,260	23,323,275	21,883,055	19,568,545	20,773,520	18,941,570

Notes: Monthly total.
Source: New York Commodity Exchange.
March 3, 2010

CPM Group　　　　　　　　　　　　　　　　　　　Silver Yearbook 2010 - Markets

Comex Trading Volume
Thousand Ounces

	1993	1994	1995	1996	1997	1998
January	836,005	2,445,275	1,952,265	2,079,005	2,009,975	1,763,440
February	1,579,580	2,775,680	2,507,270	2,918,835	2,652,570	2,754,000
March	1,214,870	2,420,670	2,709,035	1,840,875	1,804,355	1,840,635
April	2,382,770	2,925,290	2,963,100	2,738,145	2,469,995	1,800,650
May	2,167,300	2,581,980	2,502,610	1,674,865	1,402,680	1,550,650
June	2,619,805	3,647,070	2,382,405	2,748,155	2,361,530	1,969,855
July	2,519,675	1,696,490	1,403,255	1,484,525	1,701,225	1,393,870
August	2,658,860	2,678,610	3,131,785	2,303,430	2,127,355	1,836,285
September	2,141,830	1,887,700	1,720,910	1,581,830	1,677,000	1,417,375
October	1,690,945	2,225,245	1,361,810	1,608,905	2,151,985	1,400,330
November	2,602,955	2,946,100	2,235,475	2,077,205	2,440,120	1,596,080
December	1,865,025	1,741,615	903,775	1,298,265	1,668,810	1,149,910
Total	24,279,620	29,971,725	25,773,695	24,354,040	24,467,600	20,473,080

	1999	2000	2001	2002	2003	2004
January	1,575,825	1,290,265	875,130	1,328,865	1,455,600	1,925,425
February	2,751,355	2,129,550	1,510,175	1,356,465	2,048,685	2,724,695
March	1,777,795	1,156,680	778,290	819,490	1,083,300	2,042,235
April	2,124,110	1,593,760	1,262,430	1,629,445	1,576,200	3,355,885
May	1,370,010	1,084,690	1,022,760	1,217,375	1,255,480	1,393,515
June	1,868,310	2,037,275	1,409,230	1,948,990	1,762,820	2,127,505
July	1,342,400	876,175	564,780	1,406,070	2,039,655	1,581,320
August	1,336,625	1,853,695	1,338,555	1,482,895	1,677,540	2,139,865
September	968,140	730,035	801,645	822,685	1,677,540	1,408,685
October	1,591,280	746,260	1,051,330	1,046,245	1,867,965	1,820,790
November	1,721,445	1,518,365	1,330,385	1,464,305	2,321,220	2,706,830
December	807,170	568,435	901,280	1,154,990	1,254,175	1,803,875
Total	19,234,465	15,585,185	12,845,990	15,677,820	20,020,180	25,030,625

	2005	2006	2007	2008	2009	2010
January	1,427,245	2,478,245	1,822,825	3,596,540	2,077,905	3,779,315
February	2,568,085	3,122,455	2,946,660	4,948,005	3,260,305	5,325,840
March	1,851,690	2,811,650	2,399,480	4,408,880	2,168,785	
April	2,429,160	4,036,345	3,125,115	4,564,760	2,878,570	
May	1,960,780	2,569,110	2,086,715	2,904,795	2,091,695	
June	3,108,235	2,543,730	3,403,060	4,299,880	4,345,565	
July	1,674,515	1,278,885	2,020,540	3,613,315	2,382,960	
August	3,004,805	2,262,755	3,920,445	4,765,615	4,214,520	
September	2,275,165	1,341,965	2,347,295	3,960,360	3,282,790	
October	2,124,860	1,220,760	2,905,310	2,971,535	4,008,420	
November	3,264,585	2,123,855	5,092,475	2,890,045	5,796,520	
December	1,992,630	1,375,560	1,966,215	1,662,185	3,401,390	
Total	27,681,755	27,165,315	34,036,135	44,585,915	39,909,425	9,105,155

Silver Yearbook 2010 - Markets — CPM Group

Comex Open Interest
Thousand Ounces

	1975	1976	1977	1978	1979	1980
January	475,905	995,275	1,705,165	1,236,140	1,226,220	365,205
February	426,820	886,325	1,560,845	1,208,870	1,067,780	318,680
March	443,215	883,435	1,413,210	1,127,325	1,018,345	243,685
April	372,680	844,265	1,175,485	1,091,580	928,155	136,080
May	425,065	849,795	1,035,510	1,043,645	871,710	119,275
June	427,075	676,175	792,900	985,085	771,940	114,845
July	447,710	652,680	650,945	1,059,995	785,475	125,395
August	578,225	684,615	675,750	1,067,020	789,760	121,190
September	698,145	771,720	895,200	1,184,620	838,615	149,920
October	880,275	1,035,445	1,053,655	1,394,035	712,765	174,300
November	1,055,395	1,399,210	1,204,240	1,536,055	670,490	180,660
December	1,276,405	2,138,745	1,404,875	1,548,985	636,765	166,160

	1981	1982	1983	1984	1985	1986
January	142,830	136,765	221,475	308,785	421,865	409,745
February	119,310	127,025	276,220	326,170	383,330	395,040
March	129,055	146,315	221,295	364,160	376,670	392,030
April	129,650	142,810	255,600	321,500	352,650	369,340
May	143,370	136,755	269,870	332,050	382,365	376,080
June	149,690	141,355	214,205	286,280	359,550	322,390
July	156,200	141,575	223,320	326,660	364,700	356,190
August	154,930	135,575	234,185	299,945	352,415	338,690
September	145,315	126,370	263,985	323,620	369,640	369,475
October	158,600	145,060	257,130	359,480	428,955	449,990
November	140,845	156,335	281,440	385,260	426,830	454,760
December	140,005	169,040	301,670	401,500	430,700	449,110

	1987	1988	1989	1990	1991	1992
January	478,360	397,350	470,890	464,460	448,630	481,715
February	447,190	355,010	459,550	476,570	483,065	438,035
March	503,755	343,540	486,585	493,760	526,675	518,290
April	544,410	311,780	469,245	482,715	475,815	568,620
May	469,015	355,415	435,830	487,845	494,445	513,940
June	403,725	397,155	428,945	511,780	485,810	401,915
July	441,385	419,795	441,760	500,960	482,645	561,920
August	411,800	384,350	420,060	467,520	439,900	397,630
September	392,865	409,515	440,555	459,035	434,090	359,445
October	414,900	430,450	443,810	447,070	468,735	365,230
November	355,845	455,520	452,395	368,535	405,200	362,335
December	371,165	469,950	474,215	421,715	488,835	381,320

Notes: Month-end data.
Source: New York Commodity Exchange.
March 3, 2010

Comex Open Interest
Thousand Ounces

	1993	1994	1995	1996	1997	1998
January	404,500	560,010	679,610	518,975	449,660	525,760
February	447,180	548,910	690,380	462,005	453,520	509,935
March	473,365	592,320	662,620	480,960	456,620	429,930
April	522,800	676,560	606,420	493,065	425,875	384,410
May	547,515	641,145	542,205	504,065	459,665	457,855
June	473,075	617,190	531,150	517,960	456,385	399,490
July	577,030	609,295	514,280	532,645	485,215	405,720
August	497,920	782,415	523,800	451,485	388,125	404,915
September	453,315	609,710	479,905	490,550	477,945	358,895
October	481,785	564,990	530,310	483,890	473,355	373,610
November	464,030	682,760	494,645	430,240	450,630	373,790
December	578,860	652,255	492,775	423,465	494,530	376,765

	1999	2000	2001	2002	2003	2004
January	404,975	411,470	333,090	327,300	517,550	546,340
February	494,770	370,350	374,600	327,400	421,010	552,890
March	391,300	411,940	376,770	319,525	443,555	601,640
April	376,640	372,965	325,305	368,090	391,685	489,325
May	378,675	413,250	339,770	496,100	394,355	428,480
June	381,370	366,485	335,610	463,950	395,780	445,665
July	412,285	394,065	388,080	412,065	560,055	459,250
August	347,410	389,285	361,180	389,720	531,255	476,150
September	339,055	359,970	322,815	405,850	527,710	466,045
October	397,525	424,205	338,720	436,010	471,745	586,640
November	357,870	374,150	359,835	394,870	520,610	584,790
December	381,935	360,605	315,505	404,600	511,250	502,930

	2005	2006	2007	2008	2009	2010
January	483,325	666,295	571,680	927,700	464,950	616,965
February	508,190	639,195	623,485	833,390	470,510	538,175
March	496,255	698,075	552,745	733,160	472,530	
April	536,320	581,270	557,235	619,205	446,315	
May	566,790	551,190	562,815	623,275	513,155	
June	575,105	489,370	583,525	630,605	522,970	
July	621,890	495,710	592,750	657,995	497,055	
August	586,780	544,270	537,120	577,950	525,285	
September	633,980	495,035	588,215	519,060	638,360	
October	690,690	551,185	681,965	468,895	652,135	
November	704,540	533,335	679,570	421,010	657,580	
December	656,145	507,060	770,620	429,615	620,285	

Tocom Trading Volume
Thousand Troy Ounces

	1985	1986	1987	1988	1989	1990	1991	1992	1993
January	60,287	21,080	8,997	26,654	18,755	46,351	96,887	25,596	13,031
February	60,308	29,469	8,553	24,096	21,235	39,883	83,567	20,471	26,421
March	76,384	18,465	11,568	29,009	17,754	34,587	187,591	32,075	17,538
April	73,794	28,215	90,571	28,551	26,398	38,128	89,526	17,447	17,434
May	66,243	14,395	82,387	34,931	5,208	34,139	79,162	8,981	51,215
June	38,716	13,697	43,302	154,434	20,843	28,381	206,990	15,890	56,594
July	46,170	10,392	38,845	212,471	13,688	25,326	93,472	10,531	66,842
August	36,881	14,802	60,997	56,233	15,669	39,002	55,688	24,277	55,091
September	47,415	33,814	24,700	65,511	18,566	35,046	39,417	13,272	51,530
October	32,279	15,460	35,049	42,711	26,164	52,113	28,101	19,571	62,037
November	28,872	16,901	40,719	43,175	174,388	54,194	22,404	22,865	80,212
December	23,739	10,440	27,509	22,473	83,680	59,288	37,271	12,662	142,004
Annual Total	591,087	227,130	473,199	740,247	442,347	486,439	1,020,075	223,638	639,949

	1994	1995	1996	1997	1998	1999	2000	2001	2002
January	153,885	51,637	126,413	73,756	144,202	57,563	55,006	52,224	135,362
February	102,995	73,714	102,148	102,339	244,629	108,836	84,051	55,453	77,411
March	124,089	113,865	70,336	59,463	203,117	104,147	58,938	43,761	74,575
April	92,452	113,422	66,005	56,609	100,016	80,435	43,725	41,433	81,626
May	81,909	120,048	43,418	50,990	106,201	94,430	46,490	86,240	67,522
June	92,995	84,000	60,082	24,073	77,664	67,622	35,983	46,066	78,295
July	59,589	141,165	47,497	32,765	103,742	60,101	38,714	33,287	62,822
August	65,357	241,263	38,772	30,247	144,509	65,534	34,491	43,711	67,067
September	55,610	259,723	45,365	30,597	149,036	104,080	32,413	55,282	64,419
October	52,196	89,288	43,452	71,609	167,862	85,676	32,373	49,464	53,678
November	47,042	63,417	45,900	63,421	98,538	62,396	34,787	43,949	48,995
December	77,088	37,653	36,893	168,846	80,539	41,716	41,974	86,546	86,086
Annual Total	1,005,209	1,389,196	726,279	764,715	1,620,055	932,536	538,945	637,417	897,859

	2003	2004	2005	2006	2007	2008	2009	2010
January	63,255	171,313	55,719	69,479	45,553	32,111	8,868	13,584
February	86,947	185,212	70,914	82,211	46,430	31,736	12,121	15,299
March	55,581	208,210	76,459	97,864	51,419	38,615	10,397	
April	63,980	132,987	55,254	176,621	44,633	23,911	9,058	
May	95,955	93,337	53,457	83,476	37,720	19,454	5,488	
June	88,802	90,302	64,927	54,767	59,338	18,124	9,789	
July	133,415	96,282	46,041	47,183	43,175	28,126	5,544	
August	143,118	93,117	56,455	44,491	62,364	25,141	4,787	
September	124,166	93,154	54,704	44,714	30,934	25,506	9,544	
October	104,828	92,821	54,078	30,208	37,822	26,343	10,855	
November	67,067	80,157	87,010	37,281	38,331	11,950	9,357	
December	92,276	84,203	113,598	59,410	19,758	9,511	11,863	
Annual Total	1,119,389	1,421,096	788,616	827,707	517,478	290,529	107,669	28,884

Notes: Monthly total.
Source: Tokyo Commodity Exchange.
March 3, 2010

Tocom Open Interest
Thousand Troy Ounces

	1985	1986	1987	1988	1989	1990	1991	1992	1993
January	32,081	18,424	12,141	25,931	43,845	90,795	55,759	36,758	15,729
February	31,384	16,535	10,851	23,938	34,474	92,016	67,521	32,821	11,407
March	35,193	17,039	10,489	28,131	28,894	80,726	97,007	31,148	11,920
April	35,981	14,962	26,807	33,494	11,208	63,777	91,167	22,321	12,840
May	38,086	14,879	28,590	45,741	12,048	53,238	86,944	20,200	19,850
June	34,687	12,147	26,846	72,179	33,433	42,022	80,315	12,931	22,225
July	31,613	12,156	23,987	77,375	37,394	39,830	63,273	13,960	26,752
August	30,309	14,148	24,707	76,950	36,279	40,426	50,039	12,553	21,648
September	24,405	14,980	25,512	60,474	42,976	35,808	51,783	12,839	24,739
October	21,588	14,268	23,596	54,930	48,627	33,393	46,960	17,226	29,524
November	19,989	14,148	25,181	52,071	90,100	49,366	41,240	17,050	38,215
December	17,612	12,154	24,757	47,181	80,200	49,750	38,012	15,718	62,113

	1994	1995	1996	1997	1998	1999	2000	2001	2002
January	62,094	48,006	54,321	34,438	47,484	39,450	34,846	14,717	21,284
February	59,259	46,867	45,997	38,046	63,737	40,312	31,209	19,070	20,969
March	60,269	50,513	44,758	34,061	63,623	41,701	27,387	16,165	20,315
April	47,360	55,028	43,178	28,225	56,866	36,965	26,057	13,169	20,286
May	48,373	63,228	41,934	25,216	44,005	36,977	21,759	15,645	19,723
June	45,259	59,931	38,491	21,787	40,818	32,320	22,584	14,891	18,668
July	44,163	63,852	38,190	20,283	52,027	30,118	17,732	14,602	17,259
August	46,568	81,741	30,010	19,261	50,166	28,467	16,123	17,454	18,840
September	41,173	91,636	34,937	20,886	54,207	32,367	17,417	14,546	18,069
October	37,475	72,928	34,628	21,463	51,103	38,768	20,040	11,773	18,532
November	38,259	60,329	34,289	25,863	45,299	40,513	20,437	16,228	17,910
December	47,813	51,925	30,419	42,479	41,326	35,628	18,864	15,398	19,071

	2003	2004	2005	2006	2007	2008	2009	2010
January	17,619	31,866	16,347	15,546	13,915	8,355	4,916	3,276
February	19,050	32,393	16,166	19,245	14,152	8,820	3,145	3,683
March	18,180	30,192	16,317	19,203	12,351	9,752	2,452	
April	16,723	26,468	17,000	24,399	14,545	8,812	2,274	
May	20,053	24,897	17,743	21,300	15,807	8,662	2,329	
June	21,053	23,359	17,656	15,805	18,020	9,207	2,313	
July	30,437	22,533	16,676	15,642	17,736	8,863	2,060	
August	25,878	20,943	19,611	12,882	13,453	6,784	1,212	
September	19,320	18,924	15,285	9,625	12,545	6,066	1,706	
October	18,237	17,468	15,863	9,385	10,724	5,722	2,080	
November	17,802	18,913	21,727	12,783	9,963	5,608	2,283	
December	20,981	16,594	16,298	14,475	9,203	5,270	3,188	

Notes: Month-end data.
Source: Tokyo Commodity Exchange.
March 3, 2010

Multi Commodity Exchange Silver Trading Volume
Thousand Ounces

	2003	2004	2005	2006	2007	2008	2009	2010
January	-	523	271,814	837,462	937,610	1,101,315	1,179,112	1,029,145
February	-	2,001	385,303	458,768	871,683	1,040,379	1,159,141	1,539,790
March	-	5,294	431,363	817,263	976,270	1,183,279	1,126,540	
April	-	14,212	417,323	1,195,571	725,486	909,127	848,131	
May	-	13,169	408,402	938,309	677,561	759,235	947,636	
June	-	30,709	451,328	820,512	724,762	880,879	1,311,398	
July	-	63,895	324,738	659,254	644,731	1,077,776	841,178	
August	-	124,859	408,049	809,700	833,252	1,116,783	1,037,505	
September	-	178,684	536,125	855,400	764,512	1,466,777	1,340,760	
October	-	297,014	674,890	768,593	921,579	1,226,704	1,253,394	
November	40	302,863	636,050	729,435	1,105,288	948,701	1,462,441	
December	78	342,869	827,266	750,762	683,672	948,438	1,363,907	
Total	118	1,376,092	5,772,649	9,641,029	9,866,406	12,659,393	13,871,143	2,568,935

Notes: Monthly total volume.
Source: Multi Commodity Exchange of India.
March 9, 2010

Multi Commodity Exchange Silver Open Interest
Thousand Ounces

	2003	2004	2005	2006	2007	2008	2009	2010
January	-	46	10,309	25,156	11,103	16,501	17,413	20,660
February	-	145	6,576	17,020	8,302	15,749	9,164	15,591
March	-	401	8,023	14,515	12,783	7,680	9,266	
April	-	344	12,401	8,659	13,553	6,520	8,326	
May	-	533	17,026	8,589	17,106	6,302	20,158	
June	-	649	10,151	5,231	17,817	5,398	20,231	
July	-	2,143	10,000	6,399	15,236	7,762	12,646	
August	-	2,033	19,575	8,219	14,509	12,881	17,365	
September	-	4,572	21,320	15,222	12,940	19,544	18,401	
October	-	5,199	21,941	9,876	13,202	24,052	18,401	
November	8	5,296	25,706	10,161	12,942	16,814	17,003	
December	14	9,821	19,602	17,233	11,297	12,837	22,549	

Notes: Month-end data.
Source: Multi Commodity Exchange of India.
March 9, 2010

Trading Volume on Comex and Tocom
Annual Totals Through 2009.

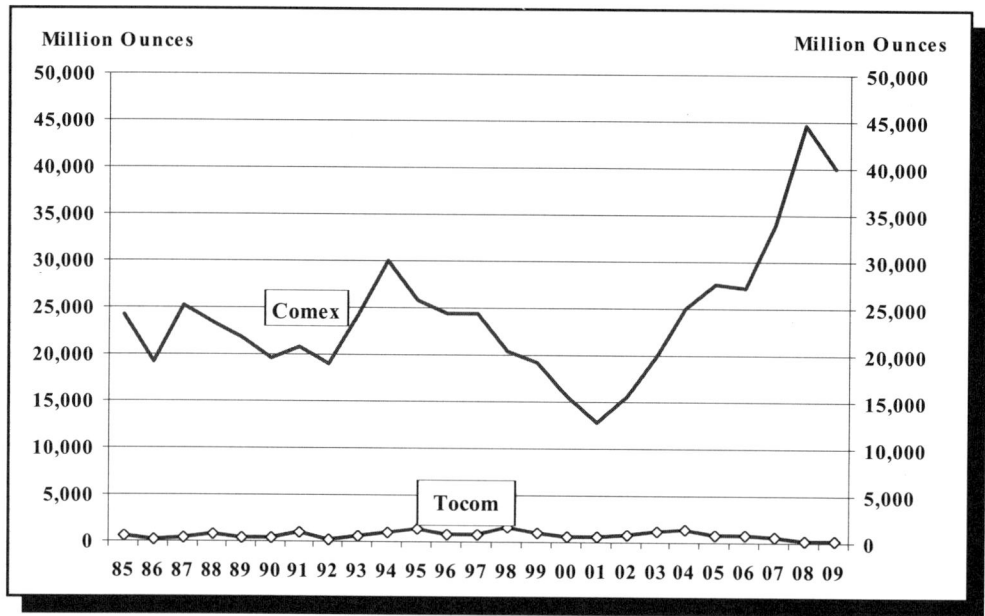

Open Interest on Comex and Tocom
Year-End, Through 2009.

CPM Group Silver Yearbook 2010 - Markets

Trading Volume in Comex Silver Options
Monthly Total, Through December 2009.

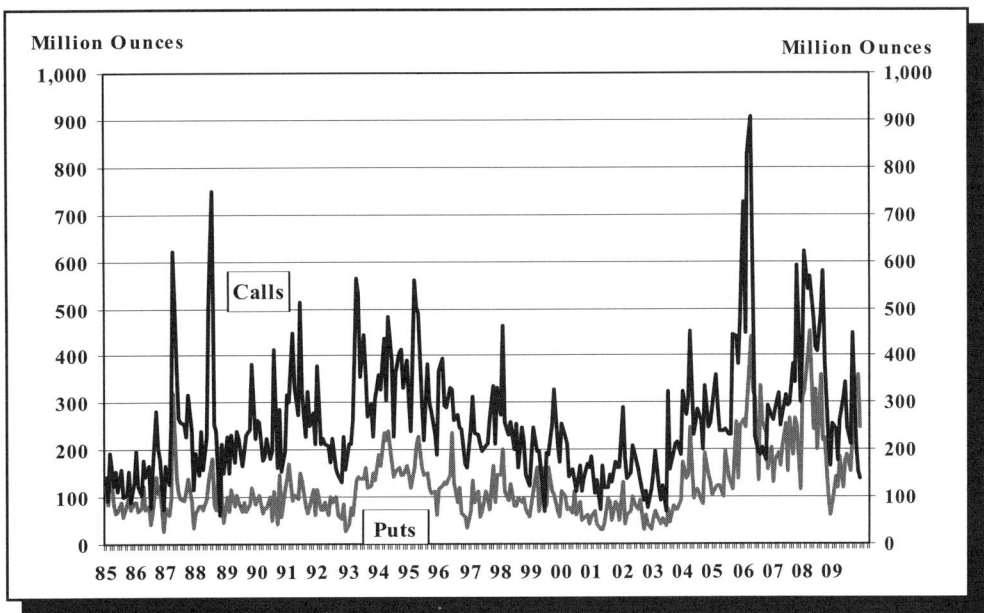

Open Interest in Comex Silver Options
Month-end, Through December 2009.

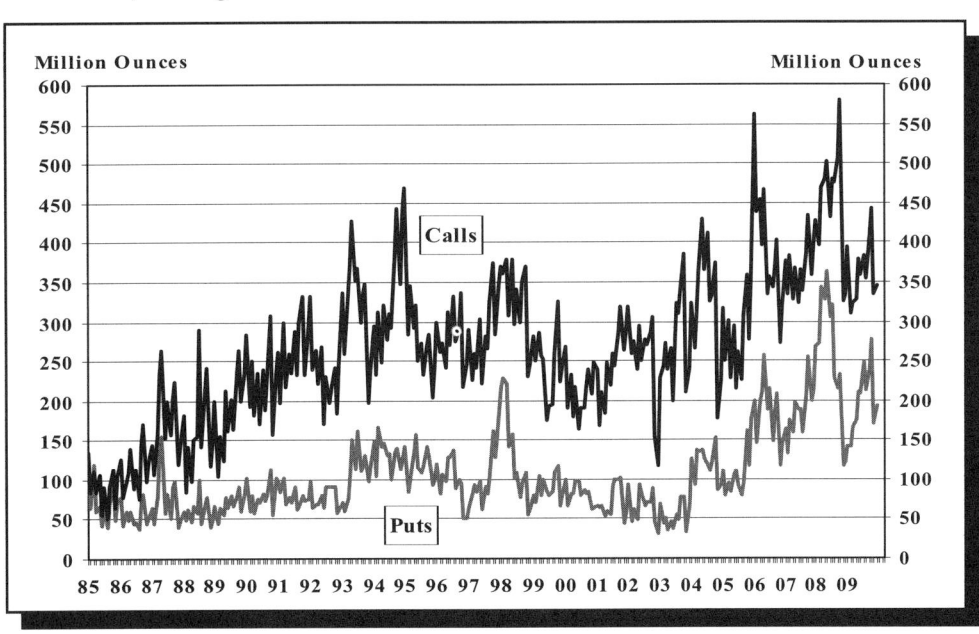

Annual Silver Options Activity
Troy Ounces

	Trading Volume		
	Puts	Calls	Total
1985	1,095,955,000	1,563,237,744	2,659,192,744
1986	1,018,975,000	1,878,150,000	2,897,125,000
1987	1,373,015,000	3,217,305,000	4,590,320,000
1988	1,211,685,000	3,148,845,000	4,360,530,000
1989	1,070,900,000	2,692,325,000	3,763,225,000
1990	1,040,990,000	2,696,505,000	3,737,495,000
1991	1,292,890,000	3,802,575,000	5,095,465,000
1992	930,160,000	2,452,555,000	3,382,715,000
1993	1,424,615,000	4,048,895,000	5,473,510,000
1994	2,145,140,000	4,438,110,000	6,583,250,000
1995	1,722,725,000	4,009,840,000	5,732,565,000
1996	1,385,065,000	3,361,130,000	4,746,195,000
1997	1,216,195,000	2,998,420,000	4,214,615,000
1998	1,252,370,000	2,837,895,000	4,090,265,000
1999	1,280,270,000	2,407,960,000	3,688,230,000
2000	900,820,000	1,994,605,000	2,895,425,000
2001	735,975,000	1,680,955,000	2,416,930,000
2002	825,100,000	1,851,020,000	2,676,120,000
2003	753,045,000	2,047,045,000	2,800,090,000
2004	1,678,040,000	3,433,700,000	5,111,740,000
2005	1,797,130,000	3,861,815,000	5,658,945,000
2006	3,231,580,000	5,003,215,000	8,234,795,000
2007	2,378,655,000	3,908,870,000	6,287,525,000
2008	3,214,560,000	5,289,850,000	8,504,410,000
2009	2,352,685,000	3,000,485,000	5,353,170,000

Notes: Trading volume is through December 2009. Open interest is month-end through December 2009.
Sources: New York Commodity Exchange.
March 3, 2010

Annual Silver Options Activity
Troy Ounces

	Open Interest		
	Puts	Calls	Total
1985	72,470,000	103,565,000	176,035,000
1986	50,745,000	121,025,000	171,770,000
1987	48,825,000	143,570,000	192,395,000
1988	47,830,000	145,455,000	193,285,000
1989	81,520,000	235,390,000	316,910,000
1990	100,935,000	235,110,000	336,045,000
1991	74,975,000	290,255,000	365,230,000
1992	62,745,000	244,670,000	307,415,000
1993	116,695,000	239,840,000	356,535,000
1994	126,165,000	433,525,000	559,690,000
1995	99,035,000	240,585,000	339,620,000
1996	50,115,000	246,480,000	296,595,000
1997	184,180,000	347,110,000	531,290,000
1998	61,145,000	243,145,000	304,290,000
1999	78,820,000	242,225,000	321,045,000
2000	64,570,000	247,515,000	312,085,000
2001	57,815,000	287,930,000	345,745,000
2002	31,180,000	116,650,000	147,830,000
2003	65,580,000	238,745,000	304,325,000
2004	93,095,000	225,090,000	318,185,000
2005	174,560,000	353,105,000	527,665,000
2006	146,765,000	319,030,000	465,795,000
2007	213,515,000	398,410,000	611,925,000
2008	122,720,000	333,465,000	456,185,000
2009	192,915,000	346,380,000	539,295,000

Silver Yearbook 2010 - Markets   CPM Group

Comex Options Trading Volume
Thousand Troy Ounces

	1985	1986	1987	1988	1989	1990	1991	1992	1993
January	266,155	283,135	243,530	260,255	326,100	351,820	455,335	496,310	252,505
February	179,250	195,970	190,630	225,560	221,965	360,135	467,925	283,225	286,850
March	362,940	183,260	347,870	321,835	345,745	243,400	538,570	297,650	327,035
April	206,795	299,430	945,225	232,870	252,785	260,485	440,300	299,875	696,420
May	216,150	215,220	506,820	324,425	344,900	302,005	370,280	271,110	677,550
June	182,095	247,170	372,460	645,510	312,370	279,455	664,690	271,725	492,825
July	244,780	120,225	354,450	933,410	236,075	247,270	456,225	311,570	583,330
August	161,630	213,200	348,845	338,190	283,860	527,835	309,320	260,655	528,445
September	187,605	423,115	339,310	313,690	303,620	206,060	390,850	207,155	390,540
October	261,770	314,195	455,155	263,655	327,215	434,325	332,210	186,370	420,030
November	163,820	302,435	333,900	305,765	502,655	213,035	395,445	310,170	378,770
December	223,585	99,770	152,125	195,365	305,935	311,670	274,315	186,900	439,210
Annual Total	2,656,575	2,897,125	4,590,320	4,360,530	3,763,225	3,737,495	5,095,465	3,382,715	5,473,510

	1994	1995	1996	1997	1998	1999	2000	2001	2002
January	548,670	452,490	483,725	317,940	420,735	270,725	366,635	242,055	421,655
February	492,030	358,520	517,680	447,155	661,555	358,085	330,765	176,300	221,855
March	674,380	725,320	426,195	323,710	371,550	360,525	283,655	175,735	199,715
April	526,010	710,335	417,865	341,010	323,130	269,575	221,300	103,170	219,640
May	721,560	715,680	479,015	269,430	383,405	261,070	224,230	198,700	309,380
June	563,825	458,570	566,080	268,035	284,010	231,560	249,495	161,660	280,275
July	369,530	366,635	393,025	320,655	339,270	272,945	174,000	217,925	233,240
August	520,840	533,140	364,485	309,160	260,295	353,350	254,810	236,630	228,620
September	565,350	421,810	365,725	337,060	333,590	366,300	161,705	182,685	122,495
October	561,175	390,415	309,060	501,140	310,510	430,410	191,215	265,120	171,205
November	481,075	349,335	226,845	301,360	218,150	281,820	231,040	243,560	120,210
December	558,805	250,315	196,495	477,960	184,065	231,865	206,575	213,390	147,830
Annual Total	6,583,250	5,732,565	4,746,195	4,214,615	4,090,265	3,688,230	2,895,425	2,416,930	2,676,120

	2003	2004	2005	2006	2007	2008	2009
January	203,425	498,645	393,505	986,950	390,680	721,630	339,560
February	268,410	414,935	479,425	693,410	462,540	944,405	388,145
March	170,395	455,450	415,890	1,140,020	513,010	941,980	297,765
April	132,650	698,660	361,955	1,349,000	418,440	1,019,520	444,910
May	178,030	326,550	339,990	866,375	485,230	721,420	427,365
June	109,695	366,240	440,205	540,845	569,640	745,150	520,465
July	399,880	401,150	370,275	329,370	446,460	608,260	435,620
August	205,265	356,115	356,755	523,235	560,810	851,285	365,355
September	271,490	287,275	558,540	465,955	571,765	801,980	681,210
October	286,150	526,985	696,855	412,740	608,090	610,050	550,060
November	292,015	392,650	519,975	451,690	841,860	311,720	513,230
December	282,685	387,085	725,575	475,205	419,000	227,010	389,485
Annual Total	2,800,090	5,111,740	5,658,945	8,234,795	6,287,525	8,504,410	5,353,170

Notes: Trading volume is monthly total.
Source: Commodity Exchange.
March 3, 2010

Comex Options Open Interest
Thousand Troy Ounces

	1985	1986	1987	1988	1989	1990	1991	1992	1993
January	219,055	204,515	207,985	242,625	266,925	385,315	358,125	431,075	406,805
February	148,085	120,100	151,910	131,335	149,570	252,850	283,280	304,560	320,210
March	231,150	156,565	238,970	204,905	219,330	328,815	400,995	332,460	407,475
April	142,695	156,265	377,555	144,165	181,185	239,710	285,830	290,010	475,835
May	174,595	200,845	418,485	216,535	289,250	310,815	337,185	346,090	578,575
June	99,180	132,485	210,490	211,685	226,145	242,260	305,360	235,335	463,325
July	157,860	159,270	283,145	388,425	280,305	320,725	379,515	320,485	528,930
August	91,515	112,365	207,630	186,240	229,415	261,730	294,955	287,775	409,290
September	161,095	215,180	292,925	273,145	311,650	303,570	365,130	306,585	453,095
October	206,415	252,110	320,620	319,745	353,130	419,310	411,695	331,025	479,230
November	113,150	143,105	160,320	155,965	259,805	212,025	304,455	241,035	294,735
December	176,035	171,770	192,395	193,285	316,910	336,045	365,230	307,415	356,535

	1994	1995	1996	1997	1998	1999	2000	2001	2002
January	443,185	610,590	419,115	353,730	584,920	361,045	367,085	304,155	410,015
February	335,945	365,810	342,685	307,710	587,555	322,380	256,900	231,015	305,145
March	479,455	446,475	378,225	352,385	599,130	389,170	315,225	277,320	336,555
April	390,795	426,695	339,025	325,560	449,470	337,735	262,440	237,395	289,480
May	466,270	477,200	440,945	400,040	534,975	351,355	314,200	306,720	387,385
June	406,460	366,575	397,165	282,000	398,915	260,380	262,060	274,070	331,735
July	442,100	381,215	469,815	373,810	449,195	272,945	271,260	349,560	344,750
August	392,015	349,310	362,860	348,095	378,335	279,640	277,910	343,485	341,560
September	517,915	410,215	389,480	425,600	445,540	365,650	297,870	384,070	355,545
October	582,300	412,080	432,590	535,050	478,860	442,525	322,880	420,300	394,565
November	459,940	296,680	268,005	410,865	286,200	289,510	269,730	307,070	202,600
December	559,690	339,620	296,595	531,290	304,290	321,045	312,085	345,745	147,830

	2003	2004	2005	2006	2007	2008	2009
January	297,640	449,970	427,405	763,120	541,740	694,305	535,690
February	287,330	356,735	329,865	583,560	466,465	668,830	451,380
March	323,630	451,915	396,300	652,210	556,805	811,665	487,955
April	274,100	499,605	312,320	606,220	485,560	808,105	504,275
May	311,185	567,325	402,720	723,110	562,655	865,570	589,075
June	237,585	492,255	326,880	523,790	511,195	735,635	565,110
July	376,705	528,925	355,515	569,530	553,330	801,385	632,795
August	357,770	437,040	306,470	492,410	500,225	704,060	565,355
September	415,155	454,810	403,430	553,950	591,840	722,975	645,950
October	462,220	525,675	521,465	611,550	689,355	813,530	720,600
November	242,925	263,175	395,530	389,385	558,365	442,020	503,525
December	304,325	318,185	527,665	465,795	611,925	456,185	539,295

Notes: Open interest is month-end.
Source: Commodity Exchange.
March 3, 2010

Comex Options Put/Call Ratio

Monthly, Through December 2009.

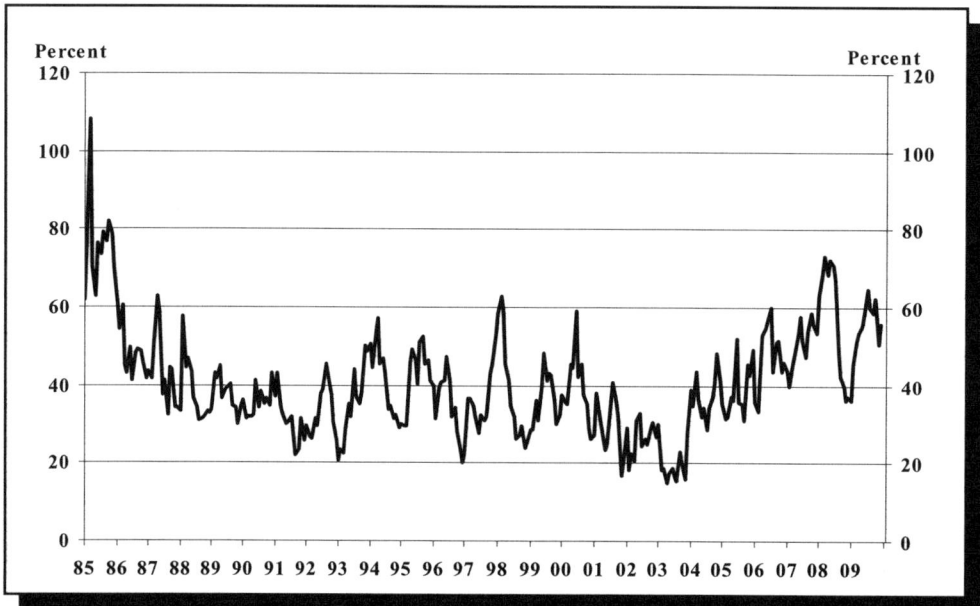

Note: Open interest of puts as a percentage of open interest of calls.

Prices

Prices

On an annual average price basis the silver price declined 2.0% in 2009, to $14.67 from an annual average price of $14.97 in 2008. Last year's annual average price was the third highest annual silver price on record, topped only by 2008 and 1980, when the average annual price was $20.65 and prices had spiked to $50. This relatively flat change in annual average price masks a tremendous amount of volatility in silver prices over the past two years.

Silver price volatility remained at a high level in 2009, although lower than in 2008. Silver traded in an $8.89 range last year on a settlement basis, down from a $12 range in 2008. On an intraday basis silver's range in 2009 was $9.18, from $10.32 on 15 January to $19.50 on 3 December. Despite silver trading in a narrower range last year, between $10.44 and $19.33 from $8.79 and $20.79 in 2008, silver's price range was the second highest since 1980, when silver traded in a $37.90 band.

Silver prices, basis the nearby active Comex futures settlement price, rallied 49.1% last year to end 2009 at $16.85, up from a settlement of $11.30 at the end of 2008. Last year's sharp price increase followed a 24.3% decline at the end of 2008 from the end of the prior year. Silver prices had been strong during the first half of 2008, but fell sharply as the financial crisis led to heavy liquidation of leveraged silver trades, push-

Weekly Average Silver Prices
Comex Nearby Active Settlement, Through 5 March 2010.

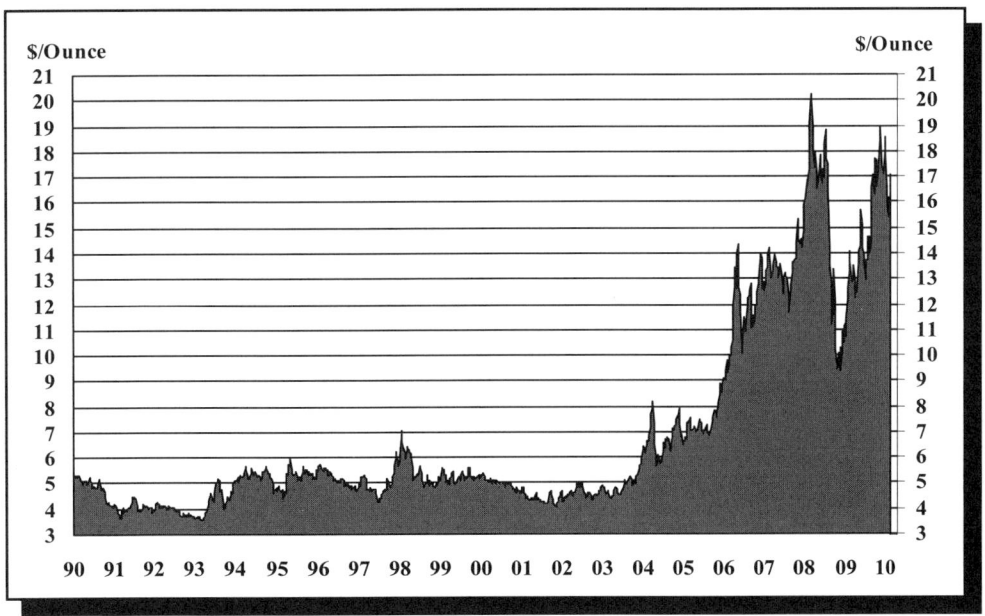

Silver Yearbook 2010 - Prices   **CPM Group**

High, Low, and Average Silver Prices
Annual, Comex nearby active settlement, Through 11 March 2010

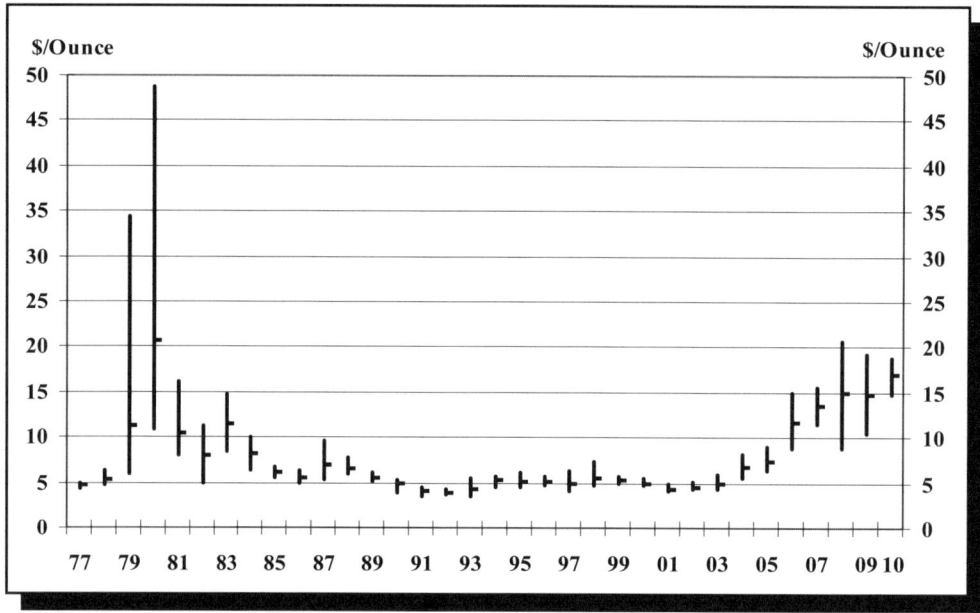

High, Low, and Settlement Prices in 2005-2010
Daily, Through 11 March 2010, Basis nearby active Comex contract.

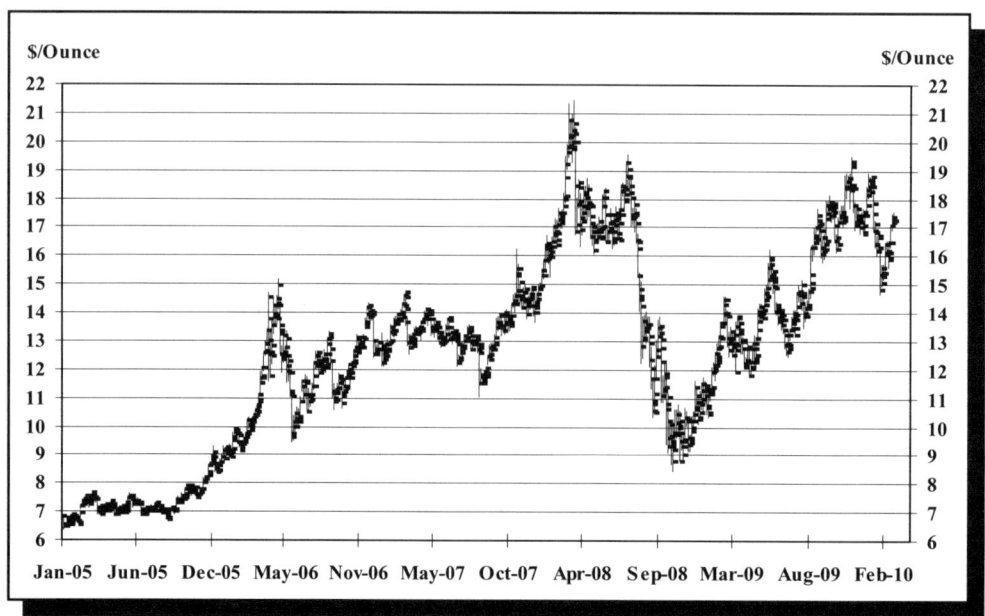

ing prices lower, in the final months of 2008. Prices remained weak in early 2009, but rose sharply as the year progressed.

Trading activity from both short-term and longer term investors was at pronounced levels again last year, contributing to the high level of price volatility. Investors remained concerned about financial markets and economic conditions, and political developments around the world. Investors continued to add physical silver on a net basis to their investment holdings. Silver prices trended higher overall over the course of 2009, reflecting strong and sustained levels of demand for silver.

As economic conditions deteriorated sharply and financial market losses surged during the second half of 2008 and into 2009 silver price volatility rose. Investors increased their silver purchases based on the metal's reputation as a financial safe haven and as a hedge against many financial market problems that were occurring at the time. Fabrication demand meanwhile was declining as demand for silver-bearing products was contracting. There also were some investors who were monetizing their silver holdings to meet other obligations.

During the early part of 2009 fabrication demand began to stabilize, while investors continued to increase their

Monthly Silver Price Volatility

Through February 2010.

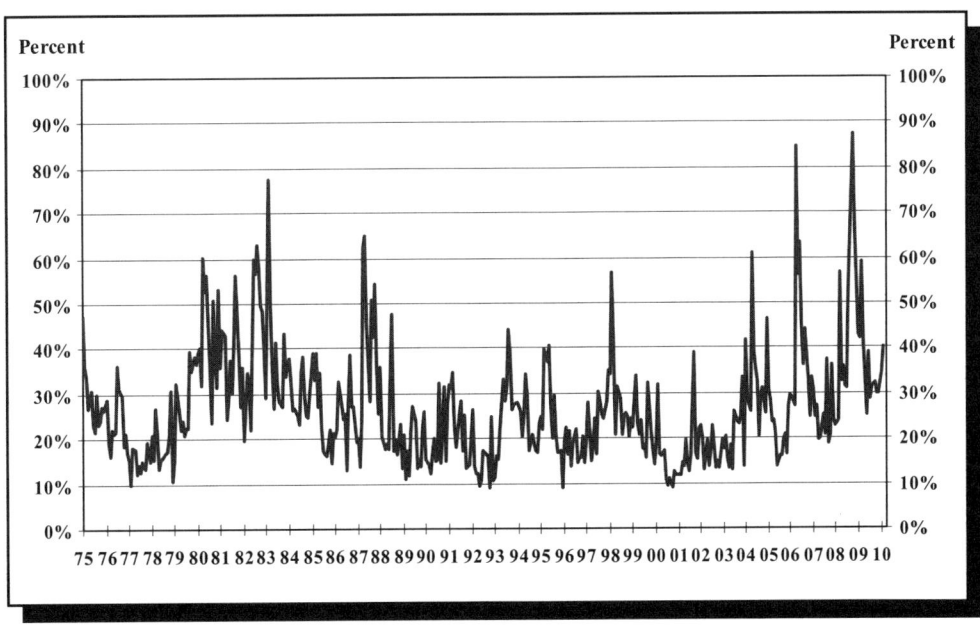

Silver Yearbook 2010 - Prices — CPM Group

physical silver holdings. Demand for silver from manufacturing users rose as the year progressed and investors continued to buy silver. This was reflected in the silver price trend during 2009.

Monthly price volatility began 2009 at 42.8%, down from 54.6% in December 2008. Despite this decline, price volatility was still high in January by historical standards. Price volatility remained above 41.5% over the next few months, until falling to 25.0% in May. That month would be the lowest level of price volatility in 2009, as volatility quickly picked up in June to 38.8%. For the remainder of the year volatility would range from 28.7% to 32.4%.

Monthly price volatility picked up once more in 2010, reaching 40.1% in February. Volatility is calculated as the standard deviation of the daily logarithmic settlement price changes.

The silver market was tight in 2009. This was evident in a narrow contango, which ranged from 0.5% to 1.7% last year. This was much narrower than the 0.2% to 6.8% range in 2008. The silver price contango is the spread between the nearby and forward silver price; it is annualized and expressed in percentage terms. The narrow contango last year showed that there was strong demand for silver and that readily available supplies were limited.

Silver Contango and Backwardation

Difference between Comex nearby active and forward active prices, annualized and expressed in percentage terms. Daily, Through 3 March 2010.

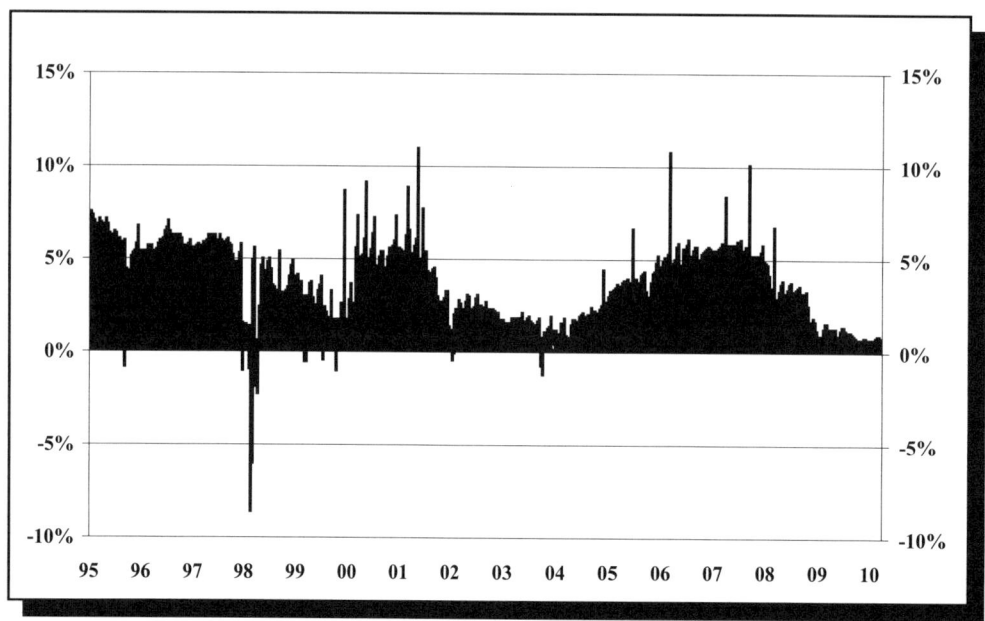

The typical price pattern for silver over the past several years has been that they rise during the last quarter of the year into the first three to four months of the following year, before declining during the middle of the year. This is the seasonal pattern for the silver price. Prices do not always follow this pattern, but it is more typical than unusual for silver prices to be strong at the start and end of a year, and to weaken in the second and third quarters. This silver price seasonality is due to fabrication and investment demand patterns. Both investors and fabricators tend to increase buying activity during the last part of a year and into the first several months of the following year. The summer months in the Northern Hemisphere meanwhile are typically a period of reduced activity from both investors and users. Investors often are not as actively managing their portfolios during this time, while many fabricators are reducing their output and inventories of silver-bearing products, making room for next season's products.

The monthly gold:silver price ratio ranged from 60:1 to 75:1 in 2009. Over the past several decades this ratio has ranged from 16:1 to 100:1, so this ratio should not be taken as seriously as some market participants appear to do in terms of it being an indicator of wise short and long term trading strategies. The ratio reflects the underlying trends

Monthly Silver Price Seasonality

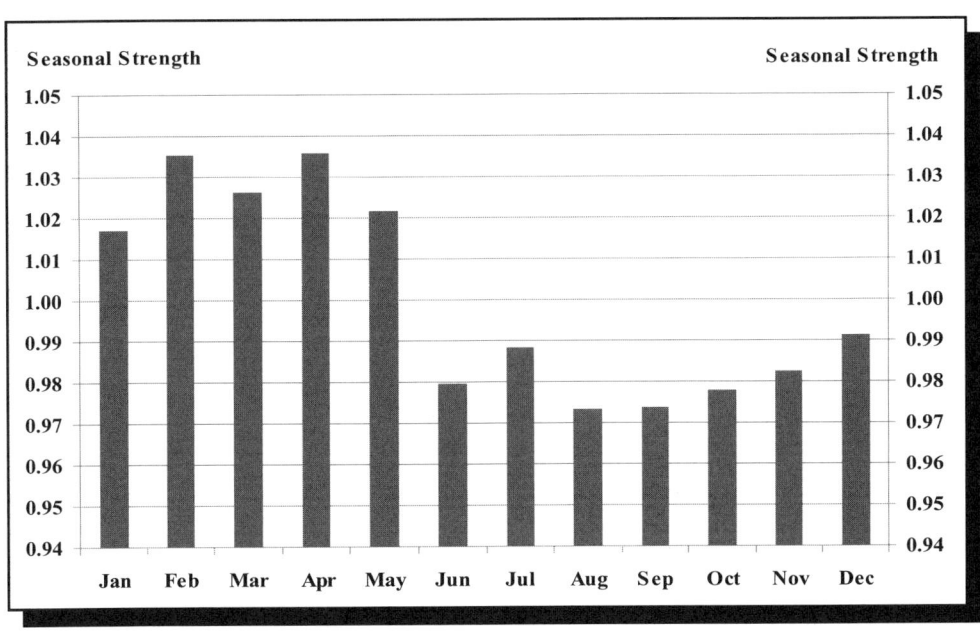

and the differences in the gold and silver markets. What would perhaps push prices higher or lower for gold may not necessarily do the same for silver and vice versa.

Price Review

Silver began 2009 trading around $11.00. Prices headed higher from late January into February. Prices peaked at $14.49 on 20 February. Over the next couple of months silver prices consolidated for the most part between $12 and $14. Prices began to break out of this range in May. Silver prices rallied from the middle of May into early June, touching $15.96 on 3 June before profit-taking set in. Prices fell toward $12.65, touched on 10 July, before recovering and moving back above $13. Over the next month silver moved mostly between $13 and $15. Prices then moved forcefully above $15, and then $16 in early September. In September and October silver managed to hold above $16 and tested resistance at $18. Prices eventually broke above $18 in November and head higher to peak at $19.33 on 2 December, the high settlement price for the year. Prices were $1.46 away from the 28-year high of $20.79 touched on 5 March 2008. Following the price peak in early December 2009, silver quickly sold off and tested $17.

Quarterly Real and Nominal Silver Prices
Through Fourth Quarter 2009.

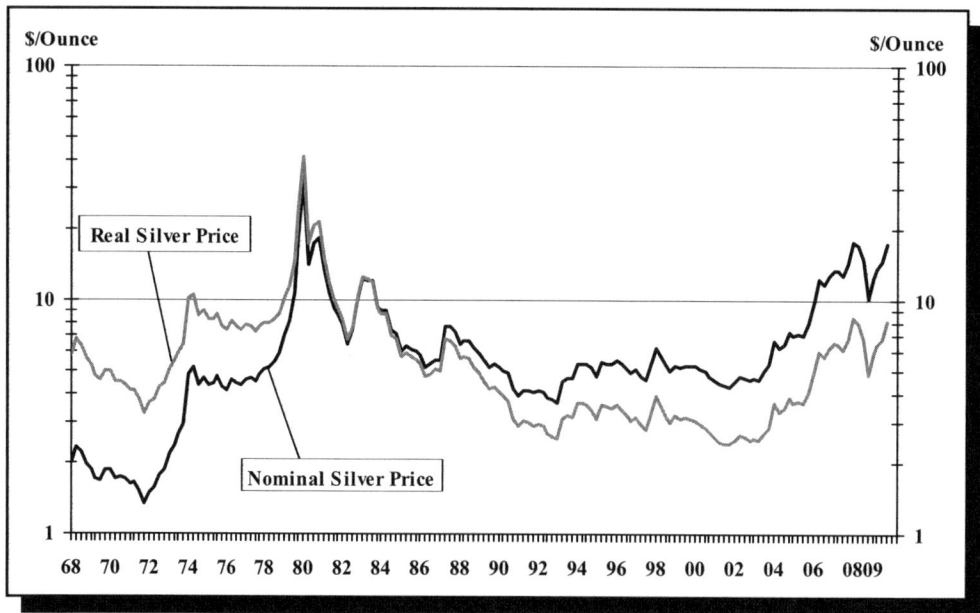

Daily Gold and Silver Prices

Through 11 March 2010.

The Gold/Silver Price Ratio

Monthly, Through February 2010.

Silver Yearbook 2010 - Prices

Prices picked up in early 2010, reaching $18.80 on 19 January before declining into the first half of February. Prices fell to $14.83 on 5 February, but strong investor interest and increased buying from fabricators helped push prices back above $15. Prices continued to head higher and had moved above $17 by March. On 12 March silver closed at $17.05.

Silver Prices in Rupees
Daily, Through March 11, 2010. Indexed to January 4, 1999 = 1.

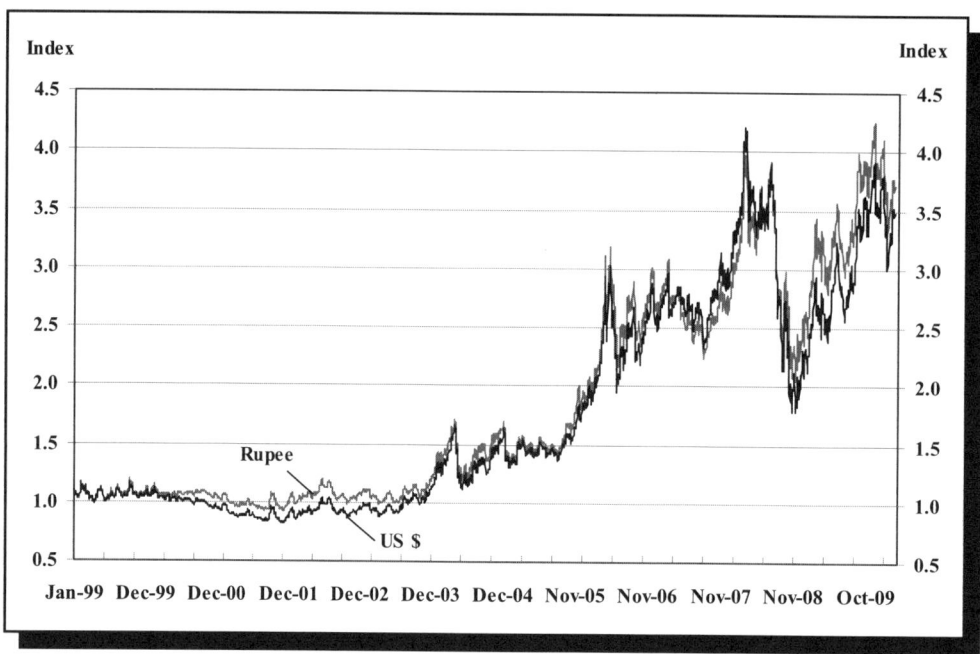

CPM Group — Silver Yearbook 2010 - Prices

Quarterly Silver Price Volatility
Through Fourth Quarter 2009.

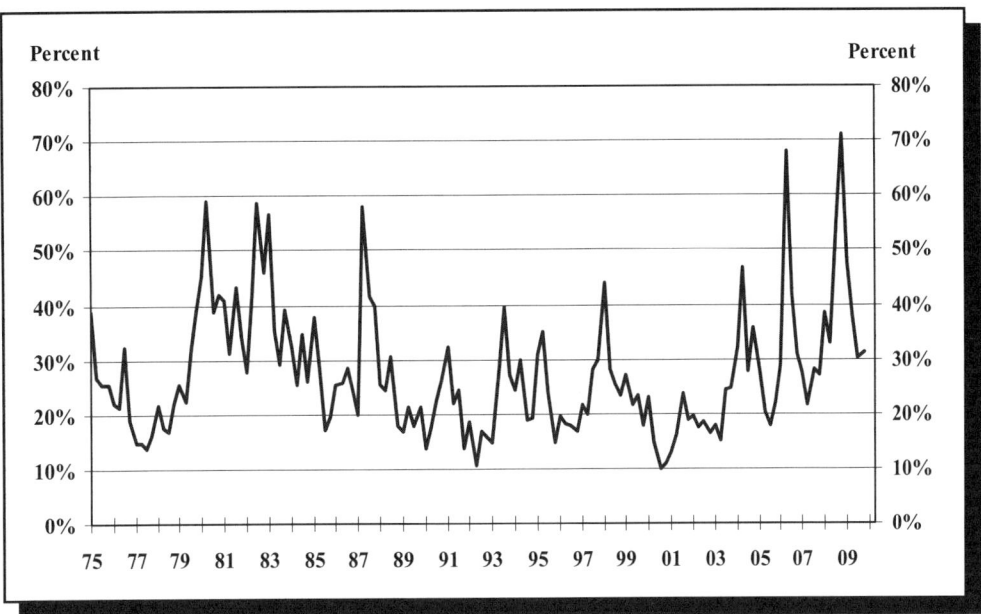

Annual Silver Price Volatility
Through 2009.

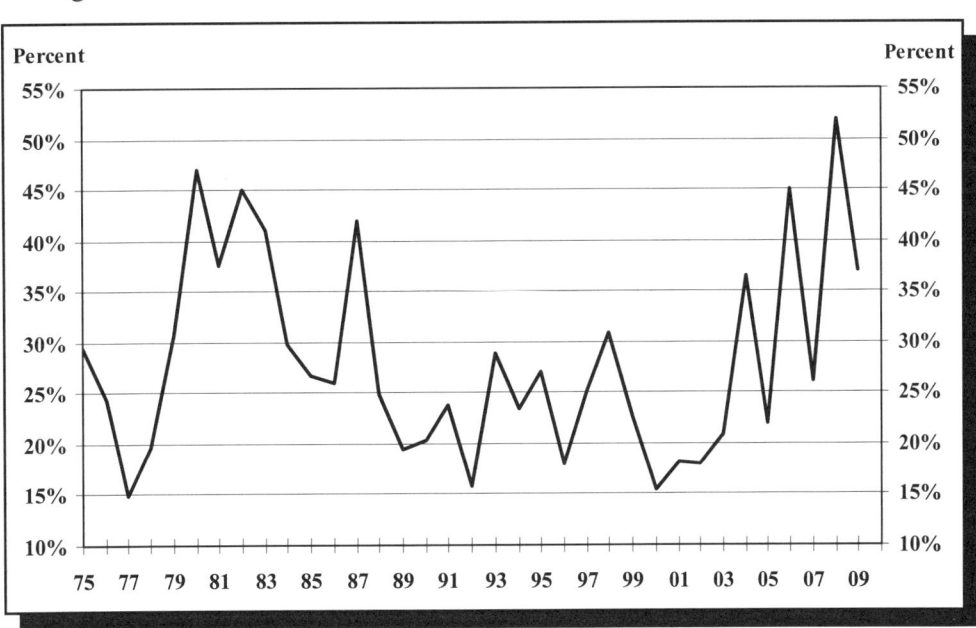

Silver Yearbook 2010 - Prices — CPM Group

Monthly Average Silver Prices
Comex Settlement Price

	1963	1964	1965	1966	1967	1968	1969	1970
January	—	$1.29	$1.30	$1.30	$1.29	$2.06	$1.98	$1.87
February	—	1.29	1.29	1.29	1.29	1.98	1.82	1.89
March	—	1.29	1.29	1.29	1.29	2.25	1.83	1.88
April	—	1.29	1.29	1.29	1.30	2.24	1.78	1.84
May	—	1.29	1.29	1.29	1.39	2.40	1.76	1.66
June	1.28	1.29	1.28	1.29	1.70	2.44	1.63	1.63
July	1.29	1.29	1.28	1.29	1.75	2.31	1.61	1.68
August	1.29	1.29	1.29	1.29	1.73	2.20	1.65	1.80
September	1.29	1.29	1.29	1.30	1.68	2.22	1.78	1.79
October	1.29	1.30	1.29	1.29	1.80	1.96	1.87	1.75
November	1.29	1.29	1.29	1.30	1.97	2.01	1.92	1.74
December	1.29	1.29	1.29	1.30	2.11	1.96	1.79	1.63
Annual	$1.29	$1.29	$1.29	$1.29	$1.82	$2.16	$1.78	$1.76
Percent Change	—	0.0%	0.0%	0.0%	41.1%	18.7%	-17.6%	-1.1%

	1971	1972	1973	1974	1975	1976	1977	1978
January	$1.64	$1.47	$2.01	$3.65	$4.19	$4.06	$4.41	$4.94
February	1.60	1.50	2.24	5.27	4.39	4.09	4.54	4.94
March	1.67	1.54	2.23	5.34	4.34	4.17	4.85	5.28
April	1.72	1.57	2.18	5.02	4.22	4.35	4.78	5.11
May	1.66	1.58	2.38	5.41	5.55	4.49	4.69	5.13
June	1.60	1.57	2.60	4.89	4.49	4.81	4.44	5.31
July	1.58	1.75	2.68	4.41	4.72	5.00	4.50	5.35
August	1.58	1.85	2.63	4.41	4.92	4.22	4.45	5.49
September	1.42	1.77	2.67	4.04	5.00	4.30	4.54	5.57
October	1.33	1.81	2.88	4.80	4.31	4.22	4.77	5.19
November	1.32	1.82	2.86	4.64	4.32	4.37	4.83	5.88
December	1.39	1.97	3.14	4.39	4.08	4.36	4.71	5.93
Annual	$1.54	$1.68	$2.54	$4.69	$4.54	$4.37	$4.63	$5.34
Percent Change	-12.5%	9.1%	51.2%	84.6%	-3.2%	-3.7%	5.9%	15.3%

	1979	1980	1981	1982	1983	1984	1985	1986
January	$6.25	$38.28	$14.78	$8.03	$12.51	$8.20	$6.11	$6.07
February	7.43	35.28	12.97	8.29	13.83	9.17	6.07	5.86
March	7.42	23.95	12.35	7.23	10.66	9.69	6.03	5.64
April	7.49	14.45	11.48	7.28	11.76	9.24	6.46	5.22
May	8.40	12.69	10.90	6.66	13.02	8.97	6.27	5.11
June	8.54	15.82	9.96	5.61	11.73	8.73	6.18	5.15
July	9.18	16.15	8.63	6.20	12.13	7.41	6.11	5.05
August	9.40	16.00	8.99	7.15	12.14	7.65	6.26	5.21
September	14.02	20.20	10.05	8.74	11.89	7.28	6.20	5.69
October	16.85	20.18	9.27	9.51	9.85	7.30	6.20	5.67
November	16.59	18.61	8.54	9.82	8.88	7.50	6.13	5.57
December	22.81	16.28	8.47	10.62	9.14	6.65	5.88	5.37
Annual	$11.20	$20.65	$10.53	$7.93	$11.46	$8.15	$6.15	$5.47
Percent Change	109.7%	84.4%	-49.0%	-24.7%	44.6%	-28.9%	-24.6%	-11.1%

Notes: Comex nearby active silver futures contract prices.
Source: New York Commodity Exchange, Metals Week.
March 6, 2010

CPM Group   **Silver Yearbook 2010 - Prices**

Monthly Average Silver Prices
Comex Settlement Price

	1987	1988	1989	1990	1991	1992	1993	1994
January	$5.54	$6.73	$5.98	$5.24	$4.03	$4.13	$3.67	$5.14
February	5.49	6.33	5.87	5.27	3.72	4.13	3.64	5.28
March	5.43	6.43	5.94	5.06	3.96	4.11	3.65	5.45
April	7.36	6.46	5.78	5.05	3.97	4.03	3.97	5.31
May	8.44	6.55	5.44	5.08	4.04	4.07	4.45	5.44
June	7.43	7.03	5.28	4.90	4.39	4.05	4.37	5.38
July	7.72	7.12	5.23	4.85	4.29	3.95	5.04	5.27
August	7.81	6.70	5.18	4.97	3.93	3.79	4.80	5.20
September	7.61	6.35	5.14	4.78	4.04	3.76	4.16	5.53
October	7.56	6.29	5.14	4.34	4.10	3.74	4.34	5.43
November	6.71	6.29	5.49	4.16	4.05	3.76	4.51	5.17
December	6.79	6.13	5.52	4.08	3.91	3.71	4.99	4.75
Annual	$6.99	$6.53	$5.50	$4.82	$4.03	$3.93	$4.30	$5.28
Percent Change	27.8%	-6.6%	-15.8%	-12.4%	-16.4%	-2.5%	9.4%	22.8%

	1995	1996	1997	1998	1999	2000	2001	2002
January	$4.75	$5.52	$4.79	$5.86	$5.17	$5.24	$4.71	$4.47
February	4.69	5.64	5.10	6.71	5.52	5.27	4.55	4.42
March	4.66	5.56	5.22	6.22	5.17	5.11	4.40	4.54
April	5.54	5.39	4.74	6.30	5.07	5.09	4.37	4.58
May	5.53	5.39	4.77	5.55	5.28	5.05	4.44	4.73
June	5.34	5.13	4.73	5.26	5.06	5.03	4.36	4.90
July	5.19	5.06	4.36	5.47	5.22	5.03	4.25	4.93
August	5.40	5.13	4.50	5.13	5.28	4.92	4.19	4.53
September	5.47	5.04	4.76	5.02	5.28	4.97	4.45	4.58
October	5.37	4.94	5.02	4.98	5.39	4.88	4.41	4.40
November	5.29	4.83	5.06	4.96	5.16	4.70	4.10	4.52
December	5.21	4.86	5.85	4.89	5.22	4.70	4.35	4.66
Annual	$5.20	$5.21	$4.91	$5.53	$5.23	$5.00	$4.38	$4.60
Percent Change	-1.4%	0.1%	-5.8%	12.7%	-5.3%	-4.5%	-12.4%	5.1%

	2003	2004	2005	2006	2007	2008	2009	2010
January	$4.84	$6.37	$6.65	$9.24	$12.91	$16.14	$11.39	$17.76
February	4.65	6.47	7.08	9.53	13.98	17.68	13.42	15.90
March	4.52	7.31	7.29	10.46	13.19	19.23	13.09	
April	4.52	7.06	7.13	12.65	13.76	17.50	12.50	
May	4.75	5.86	7.06	13.42	13.24	17.07	14.13	
June	4.53	5.85	7.32	10.72	13.11	17.03	14.63	
July	4.85	6.39	7.05	11.23	13.02	18.13	13.38	
August	5.01	6.70	7.02	12.24	12.31	14.49	14.41	
September	5.20	6.43	7.24	11.68	13.06	12.29	16.52	
October	5.02	7.17	7.72	11.67	13.79	10.37	17.23	
November	5.19	7.51	7.89	12.99	14.69	9.80	17.87	
December	5.67	7.14	8.29	13.38	14.52	10.36	17.63	
Annual	$4.90	$6.69	$7.26	$11.60	$13.47	$15.01	$14.68	$16.83
Percent Change	6.3%	36.6%	8.5%	59.8%	16.1%	11.5%	-2.2%	35.7%